Microsoft Windows XP Power Optimization

Microsoft® Windows® XP Power Optimization

John Paul Mueller

San Francisco   London

Associate Publisher: Joel Fugazzotto

Acquisitions and Developmental Editor: Tom Cirtin

Production Editor: Leslie E.H. Light

Technical Editor: Russ Mullen

Copyeditor: Cheryl Hauser

Compositor: Chris Gillespie, Happenstance Type-O-Rama

Graphic Illustrator: Happestance Type-O-Rama

Proofreaders: Nancy Riddiough, Amy McCarthy

Indexer: Lynnzee Elze

Cover Designer and Illustrator: Richard Miller, Calyx Design

Library of Congress Card Number: 2004113402

ISBN: 0-7821-4387-3

Manufactured in the United States of America

10 9 8 7 6 5 4 3 2 1

This book is dedicated to Russ Mullen, a gentleman in both word and deed, an expert worthy of respect, a fine technical editor, and my friend.

Acknowledgments

Thanks to my wife, Rebecca, for working with me to get this book completed. I really don't know what I would have done without her help in researching and compiling some of the information that appears in this book. She also did a fine job of proofreading my rough draft and page proofing the result. Rebecca also helps a great deal with the glossary, especially in this book, where I might have missed important words.

Russ Mullen deserves thanks for his technical edit of this book. He greatly added to the accuracy and depth of the material you see here. Russ is always providing me with great URLs for new products and ideas. Many of the utility descriptions found in this book started with his research.

A number of people read all or part of this book to help me refine the approach and to test the various procedures I provide. These unpaid volunteers helped in ways too numerous to mention here. I especially appreciate the efforts of Eva Beattie, who read the entire book and selflessly devoted herself to this project. Eva also provided a wealth of links and even ideas for some of the utilities. Maxine Mueller and my Aunt Barb provided insights into the optimization process and lent me a machine for research. Cheryl Hauser provided me with many Windows 9x insights that would not have appeared in this book otherwise. David Clark helped with accessibility, user interface, and PHP development issues. A number of other readers tested procedures and helped refine the book in other ways.

Matt Wagner, my agent, deserves credit for helping me get the contract in the first place and taking care of all the details that most authors don't really consider. I always appreciate his assistance. It's good to know that someone wants to help.

Finally, I would like to thank Tom Cirtin, Leslie Light, Cheryl Hauser, and the rest of the editorial and production staff at Sybex for their assistance in bringing this book to print. It's always nice to work with such a great group of professionals and I very much appreciate the friendship we have built over the last four books.

Contents at a Glance

Contents

Introduction

Are you optimized? It's a strange, yet important, question for anyone using Windows because Windows is notorious for eating memory like candy and hard drive space like a well-deserved meal. Fortunately, you have control. You can make Windows behave and it doesn't require a lot of work. All you need it a little information and some idea of how you want your computing environment optimized. Therefore, the question, "Are you optimized?" is more along the lines of whether you have control over Windows, or does Windows control you. This book is a doorway to knowledge—a key that unlocks the control that you need and want over Windows.

Optimizations both Subtle and Extreme

Many people confuse optimization and speed. Yes, speed is a part of optimization, but so are reliability, usability, stability, resource usage, and security. Optimization can encompass a variety of goals and needs. You might decide that your system is going to be the most secure system anywhere. Sure, performance and usability are going to suffer, but you've optimized your machine to meet the challenges presented by an increasingly hostile computer environment. No matter what your optimization goal, this book can help you achieve it. Whenever possible, you'll find not only a problem and one or more solutions, but also the trade-offs you'll make by implementing a particular solution. Optimization is more a balancing act than an ultimate destination where you achieve specific results.

It's also easy to think that optimization is a process where you beat your machine into submission using a gargantuan hammer. While this book does discuss a few extreme optimization techniques, many of the techniques are more subtle. Using subtle approaches to optimization ensures that you can adjust your machine a little at a time to maintain that balance between optimized and unworkable. For example, giving the user a great Windows experience is a fine productivity enhancer, but not when it comes at the cost of speed—a machine that's too slow to perform the required tasks isn't much use to anyone. The subtle approaches provided in many sections of this book help you improve the user experience without affecting system speed to the point that the user can't get anything done.

Optimization isn't a fad—it's something that you'll continue to do even after the current threats to your system cease to exist. The biggest threat that concerns most people is the invasion of viruses, adware, and spyware. Although this book does spend time discussing these issues and what you can do to solve them, it looks at invasions of all kinds and provides general advice on how to track your system's health. A healthy system can fend off many kinds of invasion and warn you about the intrusion of others. This book helps you become aware of the cues that your system provides when its health is in jeopardy—no matter what the source might be.

Speaking of system health, this book does discuss a number of maintenance issues, but from a new and interesting perspective. Instead of viewing maintenance as a boring task that you perform for some reason that might never occur (such as a system failure), this book views maintenance as part of the optimization process. By using maintenance as an optimization tool, you not only preserve data and reduce risk, you also assess how various components of the system work—whether you need to think about updates and repairs in the near future.

You'll find descriptions of, and instructions for using, many of the command line utilities that Windows stores in various locations, but doesn't really describe in any detail. In fact, this book is one of the best sources of information for many of the undocumented utilities that Windows provides. All of those utilities can help you perform system optimization tasks. You might be interested to know that some of those utilities do their job better and faster than the graphical counterparts that you've used to date. Whether command line utilities are better suited for your needs is something you'll need to judge for yourself. One special use for command line utilities is to automate many optimization tasks so you get the benefit of optimization with less work. This book shows you a number of automation tricks and techniques.

Goals for Writing this Book

I've always enjoyed reading the little tweaks and tips that I find in the various trade press magazines I read. Sometimes I'll find a book that provides me with some new productivity tips that really work. However, I haven't ever seen anything that considers the question of how to optimize a system. That's my reason for writing this book. It's important to find the balance in optimization—the point where the machine is precisely what you need it to be. The goal in writing this book is not to dictate a specific set of productivity guidelines for you, but to help you understand the optimization process where you create an environment that's optimized for your specific needs. In some cases, that means giving up a little productivity to enhance security or system reliability.

A second goal is to demonstrate that optimization is a process, not something you do once and forget about. Systems get dirty as they face the constant assault of nefarious entities online, so you have to clean them. As you work with computers, your needs will change too. The computer you work with has to change along with you to maintain an environment that's friendly and supportive, as well as productive. I wrote this book with the changing environment in mind, so you know how to modify your setup to meet needs that you haven't even considered yet.

My third goal in writing this book is to provide full access to everything Windows has to offer in the way of optimization tools. Many people are unaware of the vast array of tools that Windows provides simply because the GUI doesn't really emphasize them. These tools lurk in the background, ready to use, but only if you know about them. It's important to realize that the tool you need might appear as part of Windows today.

The final goal is to provide you with some alternatives to expensive utilities. This book discusses a wealth of third party utilities that you can use to perform specific tasks. Most of these utilities are a free download. Many of them are shareware, and you get to try the utility to see whether it really performs as advertised before you buy it. You might be surprised at just how well these utilities work and the features they provide.

Who Should Read This Book?

Everyone should read this book! Don't let some snobby geek tell you that you can't optimize your system because you haven't built it yourself out of spare electronic components found in a shed somewhere. Anyone can optimize their system, at least a little, by using the information in this book. However, some of the techniques in this book are a little on the advanced side. If you have any concerns about optimizing your system, read Chapter 1, "Cleaning for the Novice." You'll find directions on how to get around some of the complex areas in the book and get the best optimization possible. As your skills improve, you can move on to other areas of the book and try out advanced optimization techniques.

Anyone who has worked with their system for a while, but hasn't really optimized it before, should read Chapter 2. This chapter provides introductory material about the optimization process. It helps you understand why your system gets slower even though you haven't installed anything new. You'll begin considering an optimization path as you read this chapter and lay out a strategy—your personal strategy—for optimizing your system to meet your specific needs.

The remainder of the book is a reference. Each chapter discusses a different optimization issue. You'll find command line utilities, third party products, graphical Windows tools, and a wealth of information about various optimization tasks in each chapter. It's important to pay attention to the trade-offs that each chapter describes. Remember that there isn't any perfect optimization or even a complete optimization—only the optimization that works for you. Optimization is an ongoing process that meets specific goals to help you get the most out of your machine.

Conventions Used in This Book

It always helps to know what the special text means in a book. The following table provides a list of standard usage conventions. These conventions make it easier for you to understand what a particular text element means.

TABLE 1:   Book Typographical Conventions

CONVENTION	EXPLANATION
`Inline Code`	Some code will appear in the text of the book to help explain application functionality. The code appears in a special font that makes it easy to see. This monospaced font also makes the code easier to read.
`Inline Variable`	As with source code, variable source code information that appears inline will also appear in a special font that makes them stand out from the rest of the text. When you see monospaced text in an italic typeface, you can be sure it's a variable of some type. Replace this variable with a specific value. The text will always provide examples of specific values that you might use.
`User Input`	Sometimes I'll ask you to type something. For example, you might need to type a particular value into the field of a dialog box. This special font helps you see what you need to type.
Filename	A variable name is a value that you need to replace with something else. For example, you might need to provide the name of your server as part of a command line argument. Because I don't know the name of your server, I'll provide a variable name instead. The variable name you'll see usually provides a clue as to what kind of information you need to supply. In this case, you'll need to provide a filename. Although the book doesn't provide examples of every variable that you might encounter, it does provide enough so that you know how to use them with a particular command.

TABLE 1:   Book Typographical Conventions *(CONTINUED)*

CONVENTION	EXPLANATION
[`Filename`]	When you see square brackets around a value, switch, or command, it means that this is an optional component. You don't have to include it as part of the command line or dialog field unless you want the additional functionality that the value, switch, or command provides.
File ➢ Open	Menus and the selections on them appear with a special menu arrow symbol. "File ➢ Open" means "Access the File menu and choose Open."
italic	You'll normally see words in italic if they have special meaning or if this is the first use of the term and the text provides a definition for it. Always pay special attention to words in italic because they're unique in some way. When you see a term that you don't understand, make sure you check the glossary for the meaning of the term as well. The glossary also includes definitions for every acronym in the book.
`monospace`	Some words appear in a monospace font because they're easier to see or require emphasis of some type. For example, all filenames in the book appear in a monospace font to make them easier to read.
URLs	URLs will normally appear in a monospace font so that you can see them with greater ease. The URLs in this book provide sources of additional information designed to make your development experience better. URLs often provide sources of interesting information as well.

About the Author

John Mueller is a freelance author and technical editor. He has writing in his blood, having produced 65 books and over 300 articles to date. The topics range from networking to artificial intelligence and from database management to heads down programming. Some of his current books include several C# developer guides, an accessible programming guide, a book on .NET security, and books on Amazon Web Services, Google Web Services, and eBay Web Services. His technical editing skills have helped over 35 authors refine the content of their manuscripts. John has provided technical editing services to both *Data Based Advisor* and *Coast Compute* magazines. He's also contributed articles to magazines like *DevSource, InformIT, SQL Server Professional, Visual C++ Developer, Hard Core Visual Basic, asp.netPRO, Software Test and Performance*, and *Visual Basic Developer*. He's currently the editor of the .NET electronic newsletter for Pinnacle Publishing (`http://www.freenewsletters.com/`).

When John isn't working at the computer, you can find him in his workshop. He's an avid woodworker and candle maker. On any given afternoon, you can find him working at a lathe or putting the finishing touches on a bookcase. He also likes making glycerin soap and candles, which comes in handy for gift baskets. You can reach John on the Internet at `JMueller@mwt.net`. John is also setting up a Web site at: `http://www.mwt.net/~jmueller/`; feel free to look and make suggestions on how he can improve it. One of his current projects is creating book FAQ sheets that should help you find the book information you need much faster.

Chapter 1

Cleaning for the Novice

You unpack that great new computer you just bought, connect everything as shown in the diagram, and flick the switch. The monitor flickers on and you see all the lights flash for the first time. Nothing is more exciting! Your speed demon computer starts so fast that you don't even see the listing of hardware at the end of the tests. Suddenly, the Windows logo appears and things slow down—way down. In fact, the computer is so slow that you get a cup of coffee. Disappointment sets in and you wonder what all the hubbub is about—this computer isn't any faster than the dinosaur in your office and it might even be slower. Don't beat that computer or take out a hit on the salesperson. Your computer really is a speed demon. Windows, or should I say all the stuff installed on Windows, is simply consuming all of the computer resources.

NOTE A resource is something an application needs to run. The application is stored on the hard drive because the hard drive is the only permanent memory available to it. The Random Access Memory (RAM) used to run the application is temporary memory—it loses its content when you turn the machine off, but the hard drive doesn't. Windows loads the application into memory so it runs faster. Of course, any task the application performs requires the use of processing cycles. Applications also require access to the display and use of operating system services. All resources are consumable and finite. When one application uses a piece of memory, that memory is no longer available to any other application. When the system runs low on resources, it also begins to react slowly to your commands, so freeing resources to maintain good performance is essential. Chapter 2 describes these concepts in detail.

This chapter provides hints and tips for the novice (beginning) user. Many novices feel they can't work with their computer because they could damage it in some way. With careful setup, however, even novice users can help their computer use resources better. Don't let anyone tell you that the steps in this chapter are too complicated. All you really need to do is go slowly and make sure you understand a task completely before you begin.

The first section of the chapter helps you avoid basic problems that most novices encounter when cleaning their computer. For example, this section helps you understand that before you remove an application, you must make sure you save it and its settings. That way, when you discover you've made a mistake, you can restore the application to its former state. The second section describes some essential cleaning tasks you can perform once you set your system up properly. Always perform the steps in the first section before you do anything in the second section.

Novice computer users probably won't want to perform every possible computer-cleaning task. For example, it's very easy to make an incorrect registry setting change, so you'll want to avoid registry changes until you know a lot more about your computer. The third section describes a few cleaning aids that novices will want to avoid in this book. Even though these cleaning aids provide optimum performance, the cost is high when you perform the task incorrectly.

Everyone makes mistakes. The only way that I discovered many of the techniques described in this book was to make mistakes—lots of them. Every one of those mistakes cost me time. Don't feel bad about making a mistake, but the second you do, stop and check the fourth section of the chapter. I've included a number of tips on how to recover from mistakes or at least not make them worse.

Before You Begin Cleaning

Every cleaning task begins with some preparation. When you clean your home, you get out buckets, mops, dust cloths, and so forth. You make sure every one of these tools is ready for use before you begin cleaning. Likewise, when you clean Windows you need to check your equipment and make sure it's ready for use. The most important task is to ensure you protect your data, followed by your applications. Your data is irreplaceable, so concentrate on that part of the computer, followed by the application settings. The following sections discuss the preparation you should perform.

WARNING   Perform the steps in the sections that follow every time you clean Windows. These steps aren't a one-time process. In fact, you should consider performing these steps regularly, even when you aren't going to clean Windows. Everyone can benefit from a properly maintained system—one that has good recovery options.

Backing Up Your Hard Drive

Always create a backup of your hard drive. The backup process places the information on the hard drive onto a tape (a special tape recorder such as Digital Audio Tape or DAT for computer systems), recordable CD/DVD, or other backup media. The idea is to create a copy in case something happens to the original. Although a wealth of third party backup products exists, you can use the Backup application found in the Start ➤ Programs ➤ Accessories ➤ System Tools folder to create a backup of your system without spending exorbitant sums of cash. This application provides standardized backup options for all of your essential data and it's free. You can read more about this utility in the "Performing Backups" section of Chapter 8.

TIP   Most people cycle through several backups of their system. Using this technique ensures that even when one backup fails, you have other (albeit older) backups you can use. Even an old backup is better than no backup at all.

Knowing how to use the Backup application is only useful when you can easily choose the information to back up. Some novice users try to back up the entire hard drive. While this technique certainly protects your investment, it's also difficult to manage the amount of data that most people have on their hard drive today. In addition, making a backup of everything is overkill—you'll never use most of that data.

There's a practical reason for keeping backup sizes small. Large backups make it both difficult and time consuming to restore the data later. When you look through a large backup, you need to consider the age of the file and whether it's really the one you need. In addition, trying to sift through an entire hard drive's worth of data is time consuming when you only need one file. Creating a list of the items you want to restore is the best idea. Here's a list of common folders that you want to back up.

\Documents and Settings   Always perform a complete backup of this folder because it contains all of your user settings. This folder can also contain your email, browser data, and many of the documents you create. In fact, this folder affects everyone who uses your system, so this is potentially the most important folder on your hard drive.

Application-Specific Data and Settings   Some applications you install use a separate folder for data and settings. For example, older versions of Corel Draw store information in the **\Corel** folder. Many games, such as older ones produced by Microprose, also rely on a separate application folder. To ensure you can restore these older applications, make a backup of the application folder. The manual that comes with the application normally tells you where the application stores its data, but you can also use Windows Explorer to search for the application folder.

\Program Files   Some applications store settings and a few even store data with the application in the **\Program Files** folder. Generally, these are older applications, but many games and educational applications also store their data in the **\Program Files** folder. Use the Date feature of the Search Explorer Bar shown in Figure 1.1 as a means to locate recently modified files when you want to determine which applications in this folder to back up. Those folders that have files with recent modifications are good candidates for backup. Also, notice how I've set up the Advanced Options to help ensure Windows Explorer reports all of the recently modified files.

Custom Data Folders   Many users don't accept Microsoft's default folder scheme of placing everything in My Documents—they use custom folders to store data. In addition, anyone working in a group is likely to rely on some common folders that don't appear in My Documents. Always back up any custom folders you create. Make sure you include custom locations for email files and workgroup templates for applications such as Word.

FIGURE 1.1
Use the Date feature to locate the applications that store their settings locally.

Your hard drive might appear complex, and it is, but by limiting yourself to these four data folder types, you can greatly decrease the complexity of creating a good system backup. More importantly, by concentrating on just the items you need, you reduce backup time and make it easier to restore the data later. Fewer places to look for data translates into a system that's easier to maintain.

Creating a System Restore Point

A system restore point lets you take the system back to a previous stable state. It's as if you've taken a picture of your system so that you can see it as it was before you made a change. Use system restore points carefully because the picture is extremely accurate. For example, when you make a system restore point, it creates a picture of any installed application. When you roll your system back to that restore point, any new applications you installed become inaccessible. You can learn more about creating a system restore point in the "Defining a System Restore Point" section of Chapter 8.

Always create a system restore point after you back up your system, but before you make any changes to it. The restore point is a second option when fixing mistakes. It lets you remove all of the changes you make when cleaning Windows. When you make a significant mistake, one that can leave the system nearly unusable, this is the restoration option to choose.

Applying All Required Patches

Your system is stable and you have two forms of backup at your disposal: an actual backup and a system restore point. The next step is to apply all required patches to your system. Simply use the Start ➤ Windows Update command to get a list of patches from the Windows Update site. (Executing this command will connect you to the Internet, should you need to make the connection.) Make sure you also look for application updates. For example, visiting Windows Update doesn't update any Office products installed on your machine. To perform this update, select the Help ➤ Check for Updates command in an Office application such as Word. There are three reasons to patch your system before you do anything else.

◆ Patches can cause operating system problems that you want to know about before you begin cleaning Windows so that you don't accidentally confuse the source of an error.

◆ Sometimes patches make settings changes and start unnecessary services. Part of the cleanup process is to shut unnecessary services and background applications down, so installing a patch after you change the Windows settings is counterproductive.

◆ Installing patches not only fixes application errors and improves security, but can also correct known performance problems.

After you install the patches, wait a day or two to ensure the patches don't create problems. You might want to make another backup and create a second system restore point before you start cleaning Windows. The idea is to ensure your system is as stable and up-to-date as possible before you start making changes to it. A stable system with the most current patches and adequate backup is far less likely to cause problems and is easier to repair should you make a mistake.

TIP   Always allow plenty of time to perform tasks such as installing a patch or update. Depending on what the patch or update does, you might end up waiting anywhere from a few minutes to several hours for the patch or update to complete. A good rule of thumb is that larger patch or update files require more time to install, but this isn't always the case. Always assume that cleanup tasks will require several hours to complete. For example, a hard drive backup requires more time when you have a lot of data to backup and you use a slower device such as a tape drive. A typical 8GB backup on my system requires around 4 hours using a DAT drive. Once you perform these tasks several times, you'll develop a "feel" for the time they require on your system and you can plan the required time better.

An Overview of Tasks to Perform Immediately

Everyone can perform some tasks immediately after performing the proper setup (see the "Before You Begin Cleaning" section for details). The three tasks described in the following sections represent minimal risk as long as you stay within the guidelines. For example, removing old cookies and Web site data from your system is relatively painless and unlikely to cause problems, but removing old application settings can cause problems.

Cleaning Your Hard Drive

The first resource usage problem that many users experience is a lack of hard drive space. Most hard drives today are extremely large compared to those of days gone by because hard disk storage has become so inexpensive. However, there are several hidden costs of large hard drives.

- ◆ They require more system resources to manage.

- ◆ Cleaning a large drive requires more time because there are more data files to go through.

- ◆ Files are easily lost because the hard drive contains more folders.

It's better to locate problem files and remove them from your hard drive than to continually update it. The techniques described in Chapter 3 help you perform this task. Most novices will want to begin with the "Taking Out the Internet Explorer Trash," which tells how to optimize your Internet Explorer setup. You'll be amazed at how much space this one application can gobble up on your drive. It's also important to consider using the techniques in the "Scrapping Temporary Files" section to get rid of excess files created by other applications.

As your skills increase, you'll want to explore sections in Chapter 5. For example, it's helpful to know how to archive old email files, so you'll want to read about the techniques in the "Preventing Email Overload" section of the chapter. Keeping your application data organized is also important, so check out the archival techniques in the "Cataloging and Archiving Data" section. Of course, you won't want to archive group data unless the group is done using it, but archiving your personal data as you complete projects can save considerable space.

TIP   It helps to organize email and application data into projects or by type so that there's a definite starting and stopping point for adding new data. This technique ensures that you can find data to archive on your system. When you store data as one continuous store, it's hard to find information that you can easily place in permanent (or archived) storage.

Clearing the Cobwebs from Memory

Memory can be a lot harder than the hard drive to monitor and clean. For one thing, everything disappears from memory the second you shut the system down—it's not permanent. Before you begin to think that you can clear memory by shutting your system down often enough, however, you need to know that Windows fills part of memory the second you start the system and every time you start or use an application. Memory is a precious commodity to track. Fortunately, anyone can see how their system uses memory by relying on the Task Manager. Figure 1.2 shows an example of how the Task Manager lists the applications running on your machine. The "Using Task Manager" section of Chapter 7 describes how you can perform this task.

At some point, you'll know that some applications are using more than their fair share of memory and other applications shouldn't even be running. This information is invaluable because it gives you a starting point for clearing memory and making more available to the applications you do use. Memory starvation is the biggest reason applications run slowly and it can be a contributing factor in application crashes. The "Using MSCONFIG" section of Chapter 7 provides some of the best advice that a novice can use to clear enough memory to make their system run well again.

As your skills improve, you might want to tackle the "Clearing Unnecessary Services" and "Modifying Network Connections" sections as well. Microsoft usually creates a default Windows setup that includes a number of services that you won't need because they have the corporate environment in mind. For example, you don't necessarily need to have some network support features installed when you don't attach your machine to a network. Even when you access a network, you can often modify the connections or perform other optimizations to keep memory usage down. Remember that the whole idea is to make more memory available to applications that actually need it.

FIGURE 1.2

Check which applications are running on your system using Task Manager.

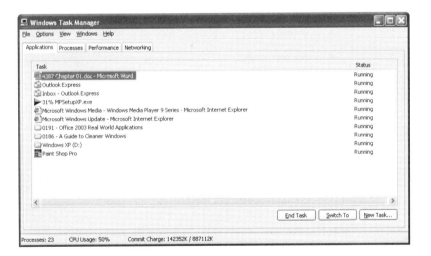

Tuning Your Applications

Applications use memory, hard disk, and processor resources as a minimum. A simple change in an application setup can make a big difference in system performance. As a minimum, you can remove applications you don't need to save hard drive space and, in some cases, prevent the application from executing automatically. Windows is one of the worst offenders when it comes to installing excess applications that you don't need or want. The "Controlling Microsoft Additions You Don't Want" section of Chapter 4 tells you how to remove excess Windows applications from your system, including a number of hidden applications that Microsoft doesn't necessarily want you to see.

The easiest application element to control is fonts. I'm often surprised at how many fonts an application installs on my system even though I haven't asked it to. In some cases, the application actually uses the font to create a special display, but in many cases, the setup program installs the fonts to support the samples that come with the application or simply because the vendor assumes you want them. The "Removing Fonts You Don't Need" section of Chapter 4 shows you how to view and optionally remove the fonts you don't need on your system. Even this seemingly small change can net a large return in hard drive space.

TIP   Many users will install the application with the samples, list the fonts the samples use, and then remove both the samples and their associated fonts once they've explored the samples sufficiently. Fonts are also one of the easiest files to restore to your system. Even if you accidentally remove one you need, the application will usually display an error message to tell you which one it does need. Consequently, optimizing your font setup is one of the best ways to get a little hard drive space back and potentially some memory too.

Part of the problem with today's application setup is that the vendor thinks their product is so good that you'll want to use every feature—most users don't need even half of the features provided by a typical application, so the extra features just consume memory and hard drive space. The "Tweaking Application Feature Sets" section of Chapter 4 helps you uncover application setup problems and correct them as needed.

Most people don't realize that applications have two other problems. First, the vendor assumes that you want to retain all of those setup files on your system even though you'll never need them again and they're readily available on the CD. The "Removing Application Installation Crumbs" section of Chapter 4 helps you start out on the right foot with an application by removing the excess files safely. Applications are even worse at removing files during an uninstallation. Fortunately, you can usually find these remains quickly and remove them. The "Discovering Application Uninstall Remains" section of Chapter 4 shows you how.

Potentially Hazardous Cleaning Aids

I don't like to place limits on what novices should do because I'm constantly surprised at what people can accomplish given a little time and assistance. However, some cleaning aids are so strong that you'll want to avoid them. The problem is complexity—most of these cleaning aids require an in-depth knowledge of Windows and offer a no-frills interface that's easy to misunderstand. Microsoft designed these tools for professionals, for the most part, so you'll want to leave them alone.

Getting Bit by the Registry

The registry is the most dangerous part of your system because it contains all the settings required for many applications and all the settings for Windows. When you make a mistake in the registry, it's often impossible to recover. A few settings are so important that the system won't start in any mode, not even Safe mode. Failure to follow the rules when working with the registry can mean starting from scratch by formatting the hard drive and reinstalling Windows.

Once you gain some experience with Windows, you might discover a need to make a change to the registry based on a Microsoft Knowledge Base article. Make sure you understand the change completely and read the "Using the Registry Editor" section of Chapter 6 before you do anything. I would highly recommend asking an experienced user to help you make several registry changes before going solo.

Avoiding the Pitfalls of Programming

A number of the resource optimization techniques described in this book depend on some programming. I'm not talking about the sort of programming you'd perform to write an application, but writing scripts to automate the task. You could possibly complete the task without programming, but doing so is often mind-numbingly difficult. In many cases, you'll want to avoid script writing until you understand how Windows works. The selection of the wrong object or technique could have unfortunate results. For example, it's relatively easy to erase a hard drive using the wrong scripting technique.

Zapping Important Application Settings

Some parts of the book describe how to get rid of nuisance applications. Some of these applications require a significant amount of effort to remove even if you're an intermediate to advanced Windows user because they wind themselves around the registry and other areas of Windows. Getting rid of a nuisance application always requires removal of the application settings. The only problem is that the application might include links to other applications. Accidentally removing the wrong settings can make these other applications unusable as well. In short, you generally want to avoid zapping an application until you understand both Windows and the application involved.

In a very few cases, a Microsoft Knowledge Base article will tell you to make an application setting adjustment to fix an error. Always try to make this change within the application to ensure the application makes the change for you. When you must make a change to the registry or an initialization (INI) file, make sure you make a copy of the settings first. Read the instructions for making the change carefully and ensure your backup is up-to-date before you make any changes.

Some application settings are a little easier to make than others are. Many novices can make changes to the Windows setup with relative ease. In addition, Windows provides a modicum of protection against errors in this area. You can read about these changes in the "Controlling Microsoft Additions You Don't Want" section of Chapter 4. As always, make these changes with care and create a backup so you don't lose any application settings you permanently need.

Dodging the Command Line

Microsoft buries the command prompt for good reason. The command prompt requires knowledge of commands, command line switches, and hard drive location to use correctly. Execute a command with the wrong switches or in the wrong location and you can cause major system damage. Most of this damage is permanent. For example, the simple act of erasing a file has no recovery option when working at the command prompt. That's right; your Recycle Bin remains empty when you erase files at the command prompt.

There's only one use of the command prompt that I recommend novice users even attempt—locating all those files that Windows Explorer tells you don't exist. Use the instructions in the "Windows Explorer Lies to You" section of Chapter 3 to perform this task. Generally, you'll find that the search features in Windows Explorer work well for data files in locations that Microsoft expects you to search, but doesn't work especially well for other kinds of searches.

Oops, I Made a Mistake

Everyone makes a mistake from time to time. Mistakes need not be fatal or even embarrassing. No matter what mistake you make, someone else has already made it at some point. The goal is to realize that you made a mistake as quickly as possible and to understand that many mistakes are relatively easy to fix when you catch them early enough. Many users run into problems when they fail to recognize a mistake and then try to avoid responsibility for it when someone else does see it. Therefore, the first step in fixing a mistake is to look for it in the first place. The earlier you catch a mistake, the faster you can fix it.

Chapter 12 helps you overcome mistakes. Some of the fixes in this chapter are difficult; others are quite easy. For example, most novice users can try the fixes listed in the "Fixing Operating System and Disk Problems" section of Chapter 12. After all, if you can save the data on your system to a tape or other media, you can probably retrieve it. The same goes for restore points—they're very easy to work with.

Depending on how well you know the applications you use, you can also try the techniques in the "Repairing Application Settings" section of Chapter 12. However, if you're also a novice with the application, you might want to get someone to assist you the first time you try to restore the application settings. Generally, applications give you two or three chances to fix the settings before strange things start to happen.

Novice users should avoid the "Restoring DLLs and Executables" section of Chapter 12. Restoring executable files isn't something that even advanced users take lightly because all sorts of odd things can happen. For example, even when you restore a DLL correctly, it could be the wrong version. The application might fail to work because the code in the DLL is too old. Because you've written over the damaged DLL, an advanced user won't be able to fix the problem very easily because the version information appears within the DLL. In short, it's normally best to leave executable file repairs to the professional.

NOTE When you notice an error that requires professional assistance, try to contact the professional before you do anything else. The professional will help you shut the system down, if necessary, and might be able to provide an estimated time of repair. The less you do after noticing an error, the better. When in doubt and you can't contact a professional, close all applications and shut the system down.

Other chapters in the book contain repair tips and hints as well. These tips and hints are specific to one situation, so you should avoid generalizing them. For example, just because you can recreate an INI file for one application doesn't mean you can recreate it for another application. In fact, recreating the INI file could damage the application further and make it difficult to fix. Only use the other repair tips and hints in the book when you understand the tip or hint completely and you can use it for the specific situation that it addresses.

Let's Start Cleaning

This chapter directs novice users to various locations in the book. It emphasizes the tasks that anyone can perform. However, it's important to realize that not everyone understands computers or even wants to understand them. A good rule of thumb for the novice is to perform the tasks that feel comfortable and stay away from those that don't. A failed optimization can create a machine that won't run at all.

The essential tasks to perform as you leave this chapter appear in the "Before You Begin Cleaning" section of the chapter. Before you do anything else, make a backup of your system, create a restore point, and apply any patches that your system might require. In fact, these three tasks are important even if you don't plan to optimize your system immediately because they help you recover from errors that occur during any activity.

Once you get the process for protecting your system down, try optimizing one part of your system at a time. Don't optimize everything in one day. Take time to discover the effects that one change can make. Now that you have the basics down, proceed to Chapter 2 to discover just how valuable various types of optimization can be to your system health and performance.

Chapter 2

A Gentle Introduction to Windows Washing

Slow machines abound in the world and it's not due to any lack of processing power or an overabundance of antiquated equipment. Someone didn't suddenly steal the thunder from these machines—a gremlin didn't replace the good components with bad. The problem is one of dirt—computer dirt. Few people bother to clean their machines. I'm not talking about the case (although you should clean it, too), but the hard drive and the odd accumulation of running applications that no one needs. This dirt gobbles up system resources up until there aren't any left to perform the work you need to do.

One common solution for the problem of computer dirt is to throw the machine out the window and start from scratch, but this option is becoming less palatable for most people because newer machines only offer incremental performance increases. (In addition, most people are concerned about the machine ending up in a landfill—recycling is becoming an essential part of owning a computer.) Most companies have placed spending limits on new equipment, so you need a good reason to get a new machine. However, you don't have to be stuck with a machine that lets you take a coffee break after every letter you type.

This chapter introduces you to the concepts of machine optimization, including a definition of precisely what optimization means. Many people equate optimization with speed, but this definitely isn't the case. You'll find that optimization means so much more. For example, an optimized machine is also more reliable—something that many people haven't considered.

Is Your GUI Gooey?

The first indication that most people have about a problem with their system is that the Graphical User Interface (GUI) slows to a crawl. Applications no longer start as fast as they once did and when they do, they don't process information very quickly. Every keystroke becomes a laborious act of a dying machine. Frustration builds and the user quickly blames aging machinery as the source of the problem.

Computers don't have joints that age as you and I do. They don't suddenly become slower as they age because there's nothing that aging can do to slow the computer's processing speed. I've seen more than a few people get perfectly acceptable performance from a machine that's five or six years old (well beyond the time needed to write the machine off as a tax deduction). Other factors contribute to the perception that the computer is getting slower. You can divide the problems with a slowing machine into the following categories:

◆ Too many running applications

◆ Newer applications that require more resources

◆ An accumulation of old data

◆ User experience increases

Considering the Effects of Too Many Running Applications

Some people look at the applications listed on the Taskbar and think that there's nothing else running on the machine. It's true that you started all the applications on the Taskbar, but the applications that appear in the Notification Area also count toward the resource usage on your system, as do services that run in the background. Every application that starts on the machine, including Windows itself, uses resources. An executing application is a process, and you can easily monitor them using the Task Manager. To access this information, right-click the Taskbar and choose Task Manager from the context menu. You'll see a listing of running processes such as the one shown in Figure 2.1 on the Processes tab. (The "Using Task Manager" section of Chapter 7 describes this utility in greater detail.)

Even though the machine only has four applications running on the Taskbar and another four in the Notification Area, Task Manager shows that 21 processes are running on the machine. When too many applications ask for the limited supply of system resources, you see a decrease in system performance. However, system performance is just the tip of the iceberg. Overextending resource use can also cause other problems such as:

◆ Lost data

◆ Overheating

◆ User inefficiency

FIGURE 2.1
Task Manager shows a list of the visible processes running on your machine.

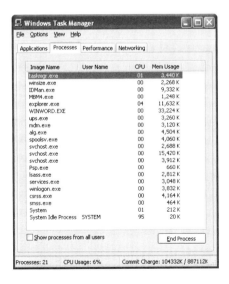

Whenever conditions starve an application for memory or other resources, it tends to experience errors. These errors can cause something as simple as slow performance or a serious crash. Application crashes often result in lost data. The data is in memory as you work with it. When this memory suddenly becomes unavailable due to the application crash, the data is lost—it isn't stored on the hard drive where you could easily access it again.

You might find it interesting that running too many applications can cause a system to overheat or at least experience the life-reducing effects of heat, but the problem is the result of a simple fact. As you ask the machine to perform more work, it draws more power. The system forces resting transistors into work mode, which ultimately increases the heat produced by these components. Some vendors skimp on the number of fans included with their systems because fans are noisy, attract dirt, and aren't a sales point on their brochure. Ultimately, as the fans age and become less efficient, the system overheats, causing damage to system components and eventual system failure.

It's possible to measure the heat effects of running applications when your system includes one or more heat sensors and you install an appropriate monitoring application, such as Motherboard Monitor (`http://mbm.livewiredev.com/`) shown in Figure 2.2. This application also monitors fan speed, power supply voltages, and other essentials. A motherboard that includes a temperature sensor also includes the software required to use it.

Distractions and a slow interface are the bane of user productivity. The more applications that run on a system, the slower the system responds and the more distractions the user encounters. Consequently, not only the system experiences a loss of speed, but the user as well.

FIGURE 2.2
Asking the machine to perform more work increases system heat.

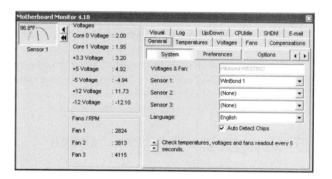

Working with Newer Applications

Product differentiation and the idea that the buyer is getting more for their purchasing dollar drive vendors to constantly add new features to applications. Whenever a feature is active, whether you use it or not, it consumes system resources. In some cases, application features provide an essential service, such as the spelling and grammar checking that most word processors provide in the background. However, some of these features consume so many resources that the application slows to a crawl. The feature might be a good idea, but the cost of running it is too high. Finally, some application features don't have any useful purpose for a particular user at all. For example, Microsoft Office provides Smart Tags—a useful feature for some office workers, but not necessarily important for the home user.

The problem with all of these new features is that the vendor simply assumes that you want to use them. After all, the vendor has devoted considerable time and resources to create the feature, so someone must need it. An application, such as a word processor, which works fine on your machine today, might not work well tomorrow because of the new features the vendor provides. When you don't need the feature, then the application is actually creating a dirty environment—one that doesn't use resources efficiently. Your old hardware would probably work with the new application if you remove the features you don't need. In short, applications require installation tuning to ensure they include just the features you need. For additional information on application tuning requirements, see the "Tuning Your Applications" section of Chapter 1.

Understanding the Need to Archive Old Data

Hard drives are like attics—they both collect a lot of junk that someone thinks they need, but never uses once the item is stored. Some users are worse than others when it comes to storing old data. It's not very hard to find files on someone's system that date from several years before. In fact, it's possible to find files that you can't open because the user no longer owns the required application. The "Cleaning Your Hard Drive" section of Chapter 1 describes other related hard drive problems. The bottom line is that you can often rid yourself of old files and clear up hard drive space as a result.

Sometimes people need to keep older files. A home user won't want to get rid of the pictures of mom and dad simply because the files have become old. Imagine the chaos if your doctor or lawyer purged old files that you really need for medical or legal reasons. Corporations have certain legal requirements for data storage. When a file isn't in use, but you do need to retain it, then it's time to archive the data. Archiving preserves the data, but still moves it out of the way.

Don't confuse archiving with the backup process described in the "Performing Backups" section of Chapter 8. A backup is a medium-term storage and recovery method for protecting your computing investment—it doesn't remove data from your system; backups create a copy of that data. An archive, as described in Chapter 5, moves data from your hard drive to a permanent storage media such as a Compact Disk (CD) or Digital Video Disk (DVD). The idea behind an archive is to preserve the data while making your system more efficient.

Tuning with User Experience in Mind

Nothing changes so much or so fast as the user experience. When someone begins using a computer or even a new application on the computer, everything seems to move too fast. Screens flash by at lightning speed and the user would love to have everything slow down just a little so they can actually understand what's going on.

Flash forward a few months and you'll see that the user has become a lot more proficient with the computer and its applications. Tasks that used to require days now take hours to complete. However, a new problem has surfaced—the computer is extremely slow. The user begs for an upgrade, any upgrade, to make the excessively slow computer perform its job quickly.

The problem is that nothing has changed except the user. The computer still runs at the same pace it always did—in fact, it often helps to time the computer to prove this fact. Experience makes a great deal of difference in the way the user perceives computer execution speed. In fact, the computer can slow down and speed up daily based solely on the user's mood at the time.

Optimization can help with this particular problem too. However, this is a case where optimization doesn't mean increased system speed. Helping the user become more efficient—tuning the user—is an important part of the optimization process. When a user gains enough experience, it's often possible to improve user efficiency and keep things moving fast by helping the user make better use of system resources. For example, an email download can take place in the background while the user types a document or performs some other task. Believe it or not, the computer often spends more time waiting for the user than the other way around.

There Is No Magic Bullet

Before you go any further, you need to understand that there's no magic optimization bullet. Nor can you wave a magic wand and say the correct words to optimize a system instantly. Optimization requires time and doesn't always result in higher system speed or better user productivity. Sometimes optimization means that you don't buy a new machine this year—that you can wait until next year or even the year after to make the purchase. Optimization could mean finding the data you need more quickly, not the ability to perform tasks with that data faster.

It's important to understand that optimization depends on goals and produces specific results that might incur a penalty in another area that doesn't matter as much. For example, you might decide to get rid of a background application, such as a search toolbar, to save memory and processing cycles. The system generally runs faster because it has more resources to perform tasks. However, one task is a lot slower as a result—the loss of the search toolbar means you can't find information as quickly. When you search for something just once or twice daily, the loss of the search toolbar probably isn't a big deal, but if searching is a main part of computing experience, the loss of the search toolbar can be significant.

Optimization takes many forms, and you always base optimization on need rather than perception. When you tell someone that the computer is slow, just how is it slow? Do you mean that applications run slowly or that you can't find a file as quickly as you should? Someone who works with documents all day needs to find files quickly, but speed is unlikely to cause problems because the computer is probably spending most of its time waiting for input. An analyst (perhaps someone in the insurance industry) needs great access to statistics, so a high-speed Internet connection and optimized network resources are important, but again, local machine processing speed probably isn't as important.

Part of the optimization process is considering your needs, not what you perceive as fast. Optimize the machine to meet your needs and it will seem fast even when it isn't from someone else's point of view. Optimization is a long-term and continuous process that makes the computer easier and faster for you to use based on specific needs and requirements.

Performance Isn't Just Speed

Performance is a measure of how well your computer accomplishes a given task, not how fast it accomplishes the task. Sure, it's always nice to get the job done quickly, but quickly doing it wrong doesn't accomplish much. A computer that performs well provides these elements:

- A usable interface
- Reliable operation and data handling
- Efficient resource usage

After a computer accomplishes all of these goals, then you concentrate on making it faster. Speed is part of the performance picture, but speed is actually the last element you consider. When a computer performs well, it's less likely that a user is going to notice speed and even when the user does notice speed, the effect is short-lived. Users tend to get used to speed, but notice these other elements whenever they're missing. No matter how fast the computer is, the user will notice a bad interface and applications that aren't reliable.

Considering Usability

Windows lets you perform a huge amount of customization. It's unlikely that two copies of Windows will look alike unless someone installed the copies recently or some draconian corporate policy mandates a particular configuration. Even so, you have to consider optimization from a usability perspective. You need to determine how well the user interface works for a particular user and what the user needs to accomplish a given task. For example, Microsoft installs theme support in Windows by default, yet themes aren't an essential part of the user interface and many users can get along just fine without them.

Themes provide an aesthetically pleasing appearance and work environment. Adding a theme can make some users more productive because the work environment is less boring. However, themes require the installation of the Themes service. To see whether you have this service installed, open the Services console found in the Administrative Tools folder of the Control Panel. (The consoles in the Administrative Tools folder are special applications that help you configure Windows, your applications, or your hardware in some way.) Figure 2.3 shows how the Themes service normally appears—Microsoft sets it to start automatically.

Unfortunately, starting a service consumes memory and processing cycles, not to mention hard drive space. Consequently, when optimizing your system you have to consider whether the user productivity gained by installing theme support is worth the resources used to support themes. In some cases, you may decide to rely on a plain interface to get a speed or other performance increase.

The Themes service provided with Windows XP is also unique. Because it doesn't contain any visual elements itself, it doesn't show up in Task Manager. Consequently, you don't know what the cost of using themes is unless you work with some of the specialized tools Windows provides such as System Monitor (see the "Using System Monitor" section of Chapter 7 for details). You'll find that the Themes service uses about 1MB of RAM when it isn't doing anything and a lot more when it is. The Themes service is always using processing cycles, but again, they don't show up in Task Manager.

Here's a way you can see what's happening. Try stopping the Themes service for a while by right-clicking its entry in the Services console shown in Figure 2.3 and select Stop from the context menu. Nothing bad will happen, but you'll notice your system is significantly faster. Compare the number of processes reported by Task Manager before you stopped the Themes service and again after you stop it. The number of processes will remain the name. To restart the Themes service, right-click its entry in the Services console and choose Start. After a few seconds, your system will regain its themes appearance and you'll notice it slows down.

The usability of the Windows interface is subjective—one user will find a particular feature essential, while another user works fine without it. That's why optimization is an individual task in many cases. For example, most users will agree that they can get along just fine without special effects such as zooming windows and fade effects. However, some users will find that they can't get along without smoothed screen fonts. Even though smoothing robs the system of processing cycles and a little memory, the loss in user productivity is far greater. What you need to remember, at this point, is that nothing is free. Whenever you see a special effect on screen, the system is expending resources to provide that special effect. Consequently, an optimized system uses special effects sparingly—only those special effects that actually make the user more productive, efficient, or simply feel better about the application environment are worthwhile. Chapter 7 discusses the effects of Windows setup decisions in more detail—pay special attention to the "Removing Gizmos from Your Systems" section of the chapter.

FIGURE 2.3

The Services console shows which services you have installed and started on your machine.

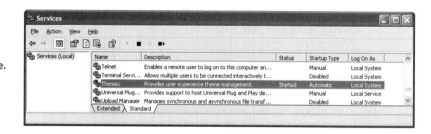

Adding Reliability

It might not seem obvious, but whenever your system is stressed—lacking resources to accomplish a given task—it also becomes less reliable. Just how unreliable your system becomes depends on the kind, duration, and intensity of the stress. For example, your system will freeze completely when you run out of memory and there's no recovery for the problem. Windows will usually try to warn you about the problem, but many users are so used to simply clicking OK for all message boxes that the system crash becomes inevitable.

Stress need not be as severe as complete loss of memory to cause problems, however. For example, try defragmenting your hard drive when the free hard drive space is less that 10 percent and you'll find it takes a long time to complete (if it ever does complete). The problem is a lack of hard disk resources. Even though your hard drive has 10 percent free memory, the disk defragmenter might not have enough space to move large data segments around and will spend its time thrashing (a condition where an application tries to find enough hard drive space to perform a task to no avail).

Sometimes reliability problems occur even when the system seems to have enough resources, but you haven't optimized it. For example, some applications begin to act oddly when they can't request large enough pieces of memory, even though enough memory is available to answer the request. Windows memory can fragment over time and running too many applications at once only makes the problem worse.

The bottom line is that optimizing your system can make applications more reliable. Of course, there are various kinds of reliability, and you'll want to ensure your optimized system provides them all:

- The application starts without displaying weird resource messages.

- The application runs without crashing (even gracefully).

- User settings are tracked properly and changes accepted as anticipated.

- All data remains accessible and intact.

- Data updates always occur as anticipated.

- None of the other running applications experience problems after starting a new application.

The problem of stress is so significant that many vendors provide a stress-testing tool as part of their development product packages. The stress-testing tool lets the developer set up memory, processor, and hard drive conditions that mimic various environments so the developer can see how the application reacts to the stress. Some of these tools even appear as part of the Windows Resource Kits. For example, the CPU Stress tool found in the Windows 2000 Resource Kit lets you create an application that uses a specific amount of processing power so you can see the effects on your application. Figure 2.4 shows how this application looks.

You can tell the application to perform multiple tasks (threads of execution), set the activity level of each thread, and give each thread a priority (Windows handles the needs of higher priority threads first). Although this tool might not look like much, it can help you judge just how stressed your system is now and how much additional stress it will suffer when running certain kinds of applications.

TIP   Microsoft has a habit of making tools obsolete when it no longer feels like supporting them. The tool works fine, but Microsoft removes it from its Web site. You can often find these tools on other Web sites. In most cases, the download should be safe, but always check the download to ensure it's the tool and not a virus in disguise. A number of Web sites keep track of the various Windows tools. One of the more interesting is the Information on NT Tools site at `http://www-rtsl` `.cs.uiuc.edu/tools/`. This site contains a complete list of the various tools in the Windows NT Resource Kit, including the stress testing tools. Some third party products, such as BCM Diagnostics Pro (`http://www.bcmdiagnostics.com/`) also provide stress testing, so you might want to use this alternative when you have a lot of stress testing to perform.

Chapter 8 discusses many of the tasks you can perform to keep your system running well, making it consistently reliable. For example, defragmenting your hard drive regularly will help maintain the reliability improvements you see after you initially optimize your system. Make sure you enhance your own reliability and efficiency by automating the process as much as possible using the tips and techniques found in Chapter 11.

FIGURE 2.4
Create a processor stressed environment for testing applications using the CPU Stress tool.

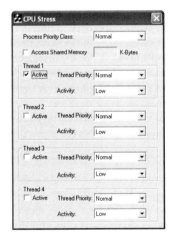

Using Resources Efficiently

Upgrades are expensive and buying a new computer every year is even worse. An upgrade or new computer doesn't just include hardware; it also includes software, training time, and support, among other cost factors. Simply looking at the cost of the hardware is shortsighted. To understand the full cost of an upgrade, you must include all other factors including the downtime to install the upgrade or new system. In short, inefficient resource use costs more than just user time; it also costs money for upgrades.

Part of the goal of optimizing your system is to save money on upgrades. For example, it's relatively easy to double or triple the life of a hard drive simply by maintaining it. Keeping it free of old data and unneeded applications helps the user locate information faster and improves overall performance. Optimization offers several cost savings when it comes to hard drives:

♦ Reduced wear because the heads don't move as much to find data.

♦ Reduced electrical needs.

♦ Faster data search times.

A successful optimization can often result in a larger increase in resources and performance than buying a new machine. New machines today offer incremental performance increases, so doubling the performance of a system through optimization is actually a better use of time and money.

The act of optimizing a system and maintaining it is more than just a cost-saving measure, however. Performing this task teaches good maintenance and management techniques. The common computer science wisdom holds that data will expand to fill any increase in hard drive space. The reason for this bit of wisdom is that people don't manage resources until they're almost gone. Increasing the size of the hard drive gives someone more space to use and reduces the need to manage the resource carefully.

Most of the chapters in this book contain some type of management element for the topic they discuss. However, Chapter 10 discusses an especially important need in today's computing environment. Not only are people filling up the hard drive and memory with excess, but outside sources are also too willing to help them do it. Chapter 10 contains the essential discussion for keeping outside sources of dirt at bay.

Making the Application Fast

Only after you make your system usable, reliable, and efficient, should you consider making it fast. In fact, when you make your system usable, reliable, and efficient, it's going to be faster by default, but not due to any actual increase in system speed. The increase in speed will come because you spend less time trying to accomplish a task and fixing system errors. You might be surprised if you monitor the time lost due to various inefficiencies today. However, the fact remains that you can usually speed your system up once you have all of the other problems under control.

The problem for many people is deciding what to first. There are many sources of application time wasters. The "Tuning Your Applications" section of Chapter 1 provides a good starting point. Optimizing Windows first and then moving on to individual applications is a good plan. By removing the waste from Windows, you gain an overall speed increase for all applications. In some cases, the speed increase might not be enough, so you also need to look at individual applications.

Optimizing applications isn't the ending point for the optimization process. When a user opens too many applications, the system will still slow down and have reliability problems. Part of the optimization process comes in the form of user training. It's usually not a good idea to keep five or six main applications open at once unless they're actually in use. Many users will open every application they plan to use for the day and keep them open all day long. The result is an overburdened system. Closing and opening applications as needed results in a system that's less confusing to use, performs faster, and makes better use of resources.

Consider the scenario of a simple download. The application in question can open several threads to perform multiple download tasks at once. This process uses network bandwidth more efficiently and to a fuller extent, which means the application completes the download more quickly. However, because the user has five or six other applications open—applications that aren't even in use—the download application doesn't have access to the required memory, so the download languishes. The user naturally blames the slow download application, rather than the true source of the problem: lack of memory to complete the task.

Sources of Grime

Having optimization goals and knowing what optimization will accomplish for you are good starting points, but it's also important to know where the sources of optimization problems lie. Sometimes, the source of a problem isn't apparent, or you might pass it by without really understanding that the resource is having problems. Part of the problem is that Windows is all too willing to gobble resources behind the scenes, making it impossible to know whether that hard drive problem is really your fault. For example, Windows will often grow the page file (the area on the hard drive that acts as virtual memory) to fulfill memory requirements. Because there isn't a big sign saying that Windows has performed this task, you might suddenly find yourself without the hard drive space required to store a download. The following sections discuss the three most common sources of grime in your system.

Locating Dirty Hard Drives

For some people, the hard drive is a black hole where data disappears and reappears as needed. In fact, it's quite possible that some users don't even realize their system has a hard drive and that it's a finite resource. All they know is that My Documents exists somewhere and it has all of their data. Unfortunately, this lack of knowledge is the source of many problems—most of which are quite easy to fix.

The fix begins by knowing how to check the hard drive. Windows provides this information in a number of ways, all of which it hides from the average user. For example, most users have no idea of what purpose the My Computer icon serves. All they know is that it's another icon on the desktop. Double-click this icon to open it and you see a list of drives that your system can access. Figure 2.5 shows a typical example of a machine with both removable storage and a network connection.

The entries of concern are the hard drives that appear at the top of the list. Right-click any of these entries and choose Properties from the context menu. You'll see a display similar to the one shown in Figure 2.6.

FIGURE 2.5
My Computer shows all of the drives you can access from your system.

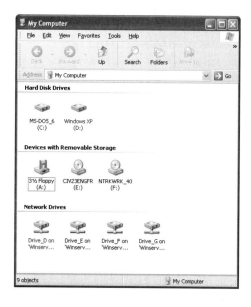

FIGURE 2.6
The pie chart shows how much disk space is left on your system.

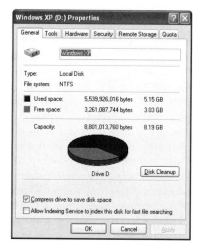

This figure shows a healthy hard drive—it has at least 25 percent of its space left. If this figure falls below 25 percent, it's time to start looking for old data to archive, temporary files to delete, and Internet files to remove. Chapters 3 and 5 tell you more about this process, but for now, consider any hard drive choked with files as a potential cleaning candidate. The less hard drive space remaining, the more critical it is that you begin cleaning immediately. Figure 2.6 also shows two potential fixes for your hard drive problem.

Click Disk Cleanup This utility helps you look for common areas of the hard drive that can contain excess files, such as temporary files. The "Using Disk Cleanup" section of Chapter 8 tells how to use this utility.

Check Compress Drive to Save Disk Space This option can take a little while to execute, but it's well worth the effort. When you check this option, the system asks whether you're sure that you want to compress the drive and asks which files to compress. Always compress everything that you can on the hard drive. Compressing your hard drive is akin to creating a giant ZIP file, but in this case, the support for reading the file is built into the operating system and the emphasis is on speed, rather than absolute compression.

TIP Depending on the kind of data stored on your hard drive, you can double the amount of available space by compressing it—executable files compress a lot less than most data files do. Compressing hard drives with graphics files can save a tremendous amount of space because graphics compress extremely well in many cases. Unfortunately, it's also possible that the graphics application has already compressed the graphics files, as is the case with some Tagged Image File Format (TIFF), which means you won't see much of a compression effect. Even so, disk compression is a very easy way to increase your disk space one time.

Detecting the Ever-growing Registry

The registry is a special set of files on your hard drive that contain all of the settings for applications, Windows, hardware, security, and you personally. It's really a kind of database. As such, the registry stores a lot of information and it can be very tough to make much sense out of the entries until you know what's going on. The Registry Editor, `RegEdit.EXE`, is a hidden file that can show you the content of the registry. Figure 2.7 shows a typical Registry Editor view. Generally, you don't want to work with the Registry Editor until you know how Windows works and then only in very specific ways. Chapter 6 shows how to work with the registry.

Fortunately, you don't have to open a copy of the Registry Editor to look for a dirty registry. To see how much space the registry currently consumes, right-click My Computer and choose Properties from the context menu. When you see the System Properties dialog box, select the Advanced tab. Click Settings in the Performance section. Click Change in the Virtual Memory section of the Performance options dialog box. The current registry size appears at the bottom of the Virtual Memory dialog box. A value of 40 to 55MB is normal for any registry. When the registry begins to exceed this value, you'll want to add it to your list of things to optimize.

You might also want to use a utility provided by Microsoft called `DuReg.EXE` (`http://www.microsoft.com/windows2000/techinfo/reskit/tools/existing/dureg-o.asp`). This command line utility displays registry statistics in an easy to understand manner. In addition, you can use it to check specific registry sections to determine when a particular section is causing problems. For example, on a particular machine a user might have installed a number of applications and now that user's settings are filling the registry with data. If the settings remain behind after the user uninstalls the application, you can remove them using any of a number of registry tools. Figure 2.8 shows typical output from the DuReg utility.

FIGURE 2.7
Careful use of the Registry Editor can help keep your system in shape.

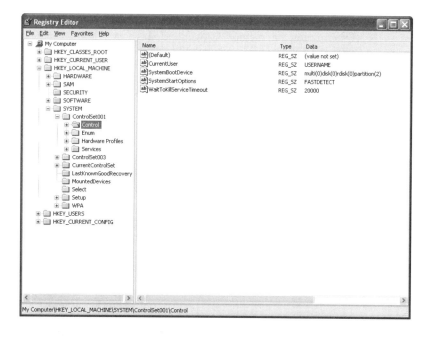

FIGURE 2.8
Microsoft provides the DuReg utility to obtain a precise registry size.

To obtain the complete registry statistics shown in Figure 2.8, type **DuReg /A** at the command prompt and press Enter. The check takes a while—up to 5 minutes, so don't worry if you don't see something immediately. The output is in bytes, so this registry has 45MB of data in it. You can also use this utility to check for a specific user or even a specific string in the registry. For example, you might want to know how much memory entries with the word Microsoft consume, so you could type **DuReg /S "Microsoft"** and DuReg would find them for you.

Assessing Overloaded Memory

Determining that memory is overloaded is easy. Right-click the Taskbar and choose Task Manager from the context menu. Select the Performance tab and you'll see a display similar to the one shown in Figure 2.9. This display shows current processor and memory usage in general terms. The processor usage should decrease to nearly 0 percent when you're not doing anything with the system. When this value remains high, it means that something is going on with your system that you need to check, including various kinds of hard drive or memory thrashing. A high memory usage percentage tells you that you need to clear some memory.

FIGURE 2.9
Task Manager provides
an overview of both
processor and memory
usage.

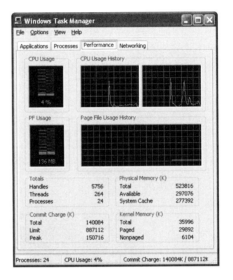

NOTE Sometimes an application that runs in the background will try to use 100 percent of the system resources when you aren't doing anything. For example, United Devices peer network runs in the background and performs tasks when you aren't using the system. If you see an application using 100 percent of the system resources, try to place it in a snooze mode so that it's resting and you can make the appropriate measurements. When this fails, exit the application, make your measurements, and restart the application whenever possible (make sure nothing terrible will happen before you stop the application).

Below the graphs showing overall memory and processor usage are statistics such as the number of processes (applications) and threads (application tasks) running. Look at the Physical Memory (K) statistics as a good indicator of the memory health of your system. This value isn't a true indicator of the memory that Windows is using—it merely shows how much physical memory is in use. Windows pages physical memory to the hard drive to create virtual memory. However, for the purposes of determining health, you want at least 25 percent of physical memory free. Lower values mean that Windows is having a hard time finding memory to place on disk. When the physical memory approaches 0 percent, the system will crash. In this case, the available memory is 297,076 KB or 56 percent of the physical memory is free.

Let's Start Cleaning

This chapter provides an introduction to cleaning Windows—to making it work efficiently. Optimization doesn't necessarily mean faster. Sometimes optimization means making the operating system more reliable or easier to access. All users require a certain level of support before they become productive and work efficiently. Creating a plan that helps you maintain balance as you optimize the system is important. In addition, a good plan helps you keep on track and not optimize areas that don't provide some kind of payback.

You already know at least one optimizing tactic from this chapter (and perhaps more). Try turning off the Themes services for a while to see if you can live without it. Many people find that they don't miss themes support at all—that the standard interface elements work just fine. For example, you can still use wallpaper, but you don't necessarily have access to every kind of wallpaper and Windows won't resize it for you. The idea is to find areas that have a minimal impact on the way you work and a maximum impact on how well your system performs.

Chapter 3 is the first serious hands on look at optimization. In Chapter 3, you begin cleaning the hard drive, which can be a lot more work than you imagined. The hard drive can hide all kinds of useless data, temporary files, and data that you should have archived long ago. The important aspect of cleaning the hard drive is to provide space for other needs such as a larger swap file, fresh data, or the latest download from the Internet.

Chapter 3

Cleaning the Hard Drive

I'm constantly amazed at how fast hard drive prices are falling. Even a few years ago, a terabyte drive would have been considered the stuff of future computers. Not long ago, someone started work on such a drive. Even low-end systems have 80GB or larger drives now, so it's hard to imagine why someone would want to waste time optimizing a hard drive. After all, when the space on your current drive is consumed, you can simply add a new one. The problem is that there's a danger associated with the endless resource line of thought.

Creating more space for data isn't a problem. You can keep adding space as needed using a variety of technologies. The problem is managing all that data. When you lose track of the data stored on your system, it's easy for someone to add a few files or two that you'll never see. The files could contain anything, but it's unlikely to be something nice (a virus comes to mind).

Unfortunately, the problem is worse than you might think. It's not limited to outside interference. When data becomes disorganized, you have to consider problems such as locating the information you want and ensuring your backup applications backs everything up properly. Search times become progressively longer and Windows can become starved for disk space to use for virtual memory. Because the hard drive is the only permanent memory that your system contains, using it carefully and efficiently is important.

Hard drive optimization requires several phases. You don't have to perform them all every time you optimize your system, but it helps when you do. First, you must identify the files you can archive or remove. Second, you need to ensure the files aren't in use. Third, you must archive the files you can use later. Fourth, you can delete the files you no longer need. This chapter discusses the basics of this task for files you can definitely remove from the system once you identify them. Chapter 5 discusses the complex task of archiving data you need and Chapter 8 shows maintenance tasks you should perform as part of optimization.

Finding Where Excess Files Hide

Windows is great at hiding files. In fact, Windows will go out of its way to lie to you about the location of some files you need to locate. Microsoft's philosophy is that users as are whole aren't prepared to work with their computer, so Microsoft tries to create a safe default environment where the user is kept completely in the dark. Consequently, Windows tells you that many files don't exist, when in reality, they do.

Windows Explorer Lies to You

Windows provides a number of utility applications that help you manage the environment in which your applications run. One of the most important utility programs is Windows Explorer—an application designed to help you manage the hard drive. Yes, you can use Windows Explorer to start applications, apply settings to files, and perform a range of other tasks—many of which appear in this chapter. However, the essential goal of all these features is management.

Consequently, it's a little odd that Microsoft configures Windows Explorer to hide a number of important files from sight as part of the default setup. Theoretically, this intentional data hiding prevents novice users from making incorrect choices, but the result is often frustrating to advanced users who do need to locate and modify files. Even when you change the Windows Explorer configuration to allow display of "all" files, you'll find that some files remain hidden. In addition, locating files can become difficult because the search mechanism provided by Windows Explorer is feeble at best and nonfunctional at worst.

NOTE Windows XP offers the most flexibility when it comes to working with Windows Explorer of any version of Windows. Although some of these sections apply to Windows 9x and a few more application to Windows 2000, they don't all apply. When you see a section that references a feature you don't see in an older version of Windows, ignore it.

WORKING WITH STANDARD HIDDEN FILES

Anyone who seriously wants to work with files in Windows must make three changes to the Windows Explorer settings. Fortunately, all of these changes appear in one place. Choose the Tools ➤ Folder Options menu selection in Windows Explorer. You'll see the Folder Options dialog box. Select the View tab and locate the Hidden Files and Folders option shown in Figure 3.1. Change this setting to Show Hidden Files and Folders as shown in the figure. You'll also want to clear the Hide Extensions for Known File Types and Hide Protected Operating System Files (Recommended) options. Check the Display the Content of System Folders option to ensure you can see all of the system folder files. Click OK. Windows Explorer will complain a few times—simply let it know that you really do want to view the selected files.

NOTE The screenshots in this book show the Windows XP version of Windows and the applications it supports. Your dialog boxes will very likely differ from the ones shown when you use an older version of Windows. In many cases, Microsoft will also provide slightly different wording for the dialog boxes and the options they contain. You might even see some options not included in the screenshots shown. Generally, you can assume your option is similar to mine when the wording is similar.

At this point, Windows Explorer will show you all of the files that it can show you, but not all of the files on your hard drive (see the "Locating the Truly Hidden Files" section for details). At least you can see the essential files and locate most of the excess files on your system. This little change is enough to make finding nuisance files possible. While you're changing the Windows Explorer settings, you might consider these other optional settings changes.

FIGURE 3.1

Change the Windows
Explorer settings to
match those required
to manage files better.

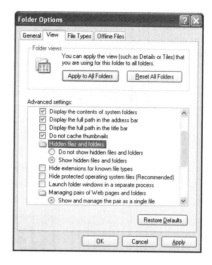

Automatically Search for Network Folders and Printers   Clear this setting. Otherwise, Windows Explorer can spend an inordinate amount of time searching for information you might not use during a particular computing session. The trade-off is that a click on a network drive will result in a short delay as Windows Explorer reads the data. Depending on the network drive and your connection to the system, you might not even notice the delay.

Display File Size Information in Folder Tips   Check this setting to make it easier to assess the size of a given folder. Large folders often offer better opportunities for optimization, so locating them is important. Because Windows Explorer doesn't actually assess the size of the folder until you hover the mouse over it, using this option doesn't cause a performance penalty. Determining the hard drive space used by a folder does take a few moments, however, so the folder tip might not appear immediately.

Do Not Cache Thumbnails   Check this option to save the hard drive space used for thumbnail images. A thumbnail image is a small, standard sized (normally 96 × 96 pixels), version of a standard image file. Windows creates thumbnails so you can see a list of pictures as shown in Figure 3.2 (notice that only the image files have thumbnails). The thumbnails can begin consuming a lot of hard drive space, so you shouldn't use them unless you mainly use your computer for image management and require the performance benefit that caching can provide.

Remember Each Folder's View Settings   Clear this setting to save some memory and hard drive space, as well as make your computer work more reliably. That's right, checking this setting tends to create reliability problems in the way Windows Explorer works. It seems that Windows stores a limited number of folders, so when you regularly use the entire hard drive (as I do), the setting is useless. The intent of this setting is to let you save the settings for each folder you visit and it does work as long as you only visit a few folders and really do need the unique settings storage. To see a more complete discussion of the problems encountered getting Windows to remember folder view settings, check out the article entitled, "A Solution for Windows XP Folder Amnesia?" at http://www.pcmag.com/article2/0%2C1759%2C1420796%2C00.asp.

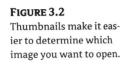

FIGURE 3.2
Thumbnails make it easier to determine which image you want to open.

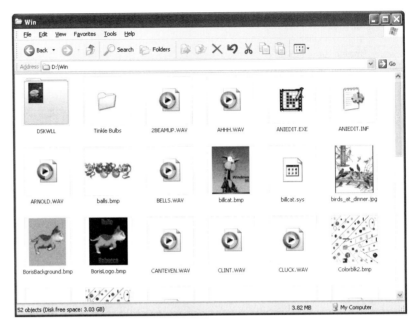

Restore Previous Folder Windows at Logon   Clear this setting to save a little memory and hard drive space, as well as reduce shutdown time a little. This setting ensures that the folders you were using yesterday are the same ones that Windows opens automatically for you today. In some cases, this setting is worthwhile—you might work on the same project for a long time, so it saves effort to have the folders for that project open automatically. However, most people don't work on the same project every day, so this setting isn't as useful as it could be and it does consume your time along with a modicum of system resources.

Show Encrypted or Compressed NTFS Files in Color   Check this option to gain a clear understanding of which files aren't compressed on your system and why. Windows won't compress an encrypted file, so you have to choose between the two features. In addition, Windows won't compress certain types of executable and information storage files. However, unless you check this option, it's very difficult to determine which files aren't compressed. In some cases, a simple file compression can save you a considerable amount of hard drive space. See the "Compressing Data Files" section of Chapter 5 for additional information on compressing data files.

UNDERSTANDING THAT SEARCHES DON'T WORK CONSISTENTLY

Windows Explorer includes a Search Explorer Bar that you can access by clicking Search on the Standard Buttons toolbar. The Search Explorer Bar includes options for locating particular files using the filename or the content of the file as a basis for the search as shown in Figure 3.3. Generally, the search feature works poorly or not at all, making it difficult for anyone to locate needed information. From an optimization perspective, the lack of good file search capability means your cleaning efforts are less effective and you might find some files hanging around that you thought were gone.

FIGURE 3.3

Use the Search Explorer Bar to locate files on your system.

TIP Don't confuse the Search Explorer Bar with Search Companion. Windows XP defaults to using Search Companion, which makes searching for files friendlier, but less flexible. The article entitled, "Windows Tips: Give XP's Search Tool a Good Going Over" at `http://yahoo.pcworld.com/yahoo/article/0,aid,78055,00.asp` explains a number of the differences between the two features and tells how you can switch your system to the Search Explorer Bar.

To demonstrate the problem, create a new folder on your hard drive—call it something like `MyTemporaryFolder`—the actual name doesn't matter. Right-click anywhere within this folder and choose New ➤ Text Document from the context menu. Rename the file to anything simple—I chose `Test1.TXT`. Open the new file using an editor such as Notepad and type several lines of text and numbers. Make sure you include some search words in the list. My test document included four lines of text and was 57 bytes in size—not too large to search. Copy this file by right-clicking it and dragging it to a new location. Choose Copy Here when you see the context menu. Give all the files the same name, but different extensions. I created two copies: `Test1.123` and `Test1.XYZ`.

Now that you have three files with precisely the same content, click Search on the Windows Explorer Standard Buttons toolbar. You'll see the Search Explorer Bar shown in Figure 3.3. Type any of the common keywords found in the three files. Generally, Windows Explorer will find the TXT extension file, but not either of the other two files, even though it's set to check for all files.

OK, so the use of odd file extensions probably wasn't fair. Try using file extensions that include TXT, INI, and HLP for the same three files. You'll find that search still doesn't find all of the files that contain the keyword. In short, if you're depending on the Search Explorer Bar to help you find the files you need to get rid of on your system, you're going to be disappointed. Interestingly enough, the command line utilities described in the "Command Line Utilities You Should Know About" section of the chapter work, but they're a little less convenient to use. Pay special attention to the FindStr utility because it helps you locate just about any string in any file.

LOCATING THE TRULY HIDDEN FILES

Even when you reconfigure Windows Explorer to show you the maximum number of files, it doesn't. Microsoft has a few files that they don't trust anyone to see, so Windows Explorer hides them. These files appear many levels deep in the drive hierarchy—so deep that you must often know precisely where to look to find them. For example, when you install Office 2003 with .NET Extensions support, the installation program creates files that you can't see using Windows Explorer. You can check this Windows Explorer feature out for yourself when you have Office 2003 installed. Look in the \WINDOWS\assembly folder. At most, you'll see a list of files and a \Download folder as shown in Figure 3.4.

Open a command prompt, type **CD \WINDOWS\assembly\GAC\Office\11.0.0.0__71e9bce111 e9429c**, and press Enter. Suddenly, you'll see a folder well below the \WINDOWS\assembly folder that Windows Explorer tells you is the final stop. Type **DIR** and press Enter. You'll find two files in this folder, as shown in Figure 3.5. The interesting thing is that these files aren't hidden from the command prompt—only from Windows Explorer.

I chose this particular entry because many people own Office, so your chance of seeing it live are good. Microsoft could almost make a case for hiding this directory, but you'll find a number of others that aren't so easy to defend. It's true that most users will never need to look in this folder and many problems could occur if the user accidentally erased the DLL it contains. However, Microsoft also makes it a practice to hide other installation, temporary, and other files on your drive. (You'll see other examples as the book progresses.)

FIGURE 3.4
Even with Windows Explorer properly configured, you can't see everything.

FIGURE 3.5
The command prompt demonstrates your ability to locate files Windows Explorer won't tell you about.

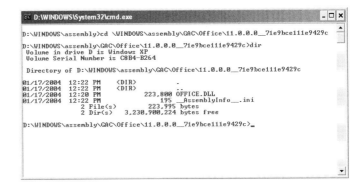

Indexing the Drive

The search feature of Windows XP is definitely broken. However, it works well enough for some uses, especially when you need to search for common files—those with a TXT, DOC, or other common extensions. Unfortunately, you still have a decision to make about how best to use the Windows XP search feature and it depends on how you use it. When you use the search feature occasionally, it's best to let search look for the file each time. However, when you search for files several times daily, you can gain a performance advantage by indexing all or part of the drive.

NOTE Never index a drive when you plan to use command line utilities to search it. Command line utilities don't gain any benefit from drive indexing, so the resources used to index the drive are wasted.

You pay for indexing the drive in two ways. First, there's the cost of running the Indexing Service. As a minimum, the Indexing Service uses about 1.5MB of RAM, along with the memory, processing cycles, and hard drive space to maintain the indexing catalog. Even a small catalog can consume 1MB or more of hard drive space.

INDEXING ONLY WHAT YOU NEED

Some people index all of the drives on their system. The only time you should index an entire drive is when the drive contains only data. Otherwise, it's far more efficient to index just the parts of the drive you need. Fortunately, you can index a folder or even an individual file—Microsoft simply hid the required resources. To index a file or folder, right-click it and choose Properties from the context menu. On the General tab of the file or folder Properties dialog box, click Advanced. You'll see the Advanced Attributes dialog box shown in Figure 3.6. Check the For Fast Indexing, Allow Indexing Service to Index this Folder (or File) option and click OK twice to close both the Advanced Attributes and the file or folder Properties dialog box.

CHANGING THE INDEXING SETTINGS

Part of the problem with the Indexing Service is that some of the settings are less than optimal for someone who really wants to look for files on their system. To fix this problem, begin by opening the Computer Management console found in the Administrative Tools folder of the Control Panel. Locate the `Services and Applications\Indexing Service` folder. Right-click the `Indexing Service` folder and select Properties from the context menu. You'll see the Indexing Service Properties dialog box shown in Figure 3.7.

FIGURE 3.6
The Advanced Attributes dialog box hides more than attributes in the conventional sense.

FIGURE 3.7
Set the Indexing Service
to provide maximum
functionality.

Checking Index Files with Unknown Extensions might be one of the most important changes you make. Normally, the Indexing Service, like Windows search looks only at file extensions that it knows about. Unfortunately, many of your searches for files to remove from the system will require looking at the unknown extensions too.

Abstracts can be helpful when optimizing your system, but generally, they use up a lot of disk space for dubious results. Consequently, you'll want to check the Generate Abstracts option with care and keep the size of the abstract as small as possible to save disk space.

TIP You can modify these settings on a catalog level as well. Simply right-click the catalog in question and choose Properties from the context menu. The settings described in this section appear on the Generation tab.

After you change the Indexing Service properties and close the Indexing Service Properties dialog box, right-click the Indexing Service again and choose All Tasks ➤ Tune Performance from the context menu. You'll see the Indexing Service Usage dialog box shown in Figure 3.8.

FIGURE 3.8
Adjust the Indexing
Service performance
to meet specific needs.

The four settings in this dialog box help you select the level of performance the Indexing Service provides. Microsoft assumes that you'll index everything on your system, so the Indexing Service uses the slowest method possible. It can literally take days to create an index you needed five minutes ago. A better solution is to select Customize and then click Customize. You'll see a Desired Performance dialog box that contains two sliders. To generate an index quickly, yet keep performance at acceptable levels, you can set the Indexing slider to Instant and the Querying slider to Low Load. In most cases, these settings create the index quickly, yet allow you to query the Indexing Service without burdening the system.

Using Indexing Successfully

You can create a situation where indexing does work to your advantage and it works pretty well—you just can't use it with Windows Explorer. The first task is to create a special search catalog that meets your needs. The following steps get you started.

1. Open the Computer Management console found in the Administrative Tools folder of the Control Panel.

2. Open the `Services and Applications\Indexing Service` folder. You'll see a list of current catalogs in the right pane.

3. Stop the Indexing Service by right-clicking its entry and choosing Stop from the context menu. All of the entries for the current catalogs will disappear when the service has stopped (be patient).

4. Right-click the Indexing Service and choose New ➤ Catalog from the context menu. You'll see an Add Catalog dialog box where you type the name and location of the new catalog. Use the Browse button to find the location without typing it manually. For the purposes of this procedure, I'm using the same folder described in the "Understanding that Searches Don't Work Consistently" section of the chapter. The biggest reason for making this selection is to allow you to see the differences between using Windows Explorer and the Indexing Service.

5. Type the name (the example uses MySpecialCatalog) and location (the example uses `D:\MyTempFolder`) of the new catalog. Click OK. The Indexing Service displays a message telling you the catalog will remain offline until you restart the service.

6. Click OK. The Indexing Service adds the new catalog to the list. Before the new catalog will work, you need to provide one or more directories for it to index.

7. Open the new catalog and select the Directories folder.

8. Right-click the Directories folder and choose New ➤ Directory from the context menu. You'll see an Add Directory dialog box. This dialog box lets you add a local or remote directory.

9. Click Browse and choose the directory you want to index. Click OK. The Indexing Service adds the new directory to the list.

At this point, you're ready to go. All you need to do is restart the Indexing Service by right-clicking its entry and choosing Start from the context menu. Here's where things can get interesting. The Indexing Service doesn't necessarily create the index right away because it normally works in the background. Before you attempt to use the indexing service, look at the Docs to Index column of the display shown in Figure 3.9 to ensure it's at 0. Now you can make queries on the index—otherwise, you need to wait until indexing is complete.

The catalog is finally ready for use. Click the Query the Catalog entry shown in Figure 3.9 and you'll see an Indexing Service Query Form. Type your query in the field provided and click Search. The Indexing Service locates all three files in the folder as shown in Figure 3.10. Compare these results with those in the "Understanding that Searches Don't Work Consistently" section.

FIGURE 3.9
Set the Indexing Service to provide maximum functionality.

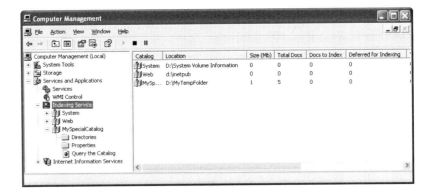

FIGURE 3.10
Using the Indexing Service directly will produce better results than Windows Explorer can.

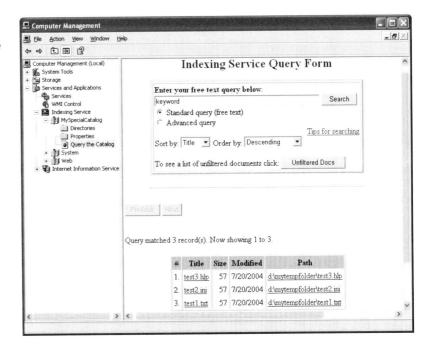

Notice that you aren't limited to a simple search. By using an advanced search, you can define specific circumstances for matches. However, it's important to look at the real cost of implementing this solution. You do get a nice GUI to use to search for files on your system, but it's inconveniently located in the Computer Management console. This solution requires that you turn on the Indexing Service and create a catalog to search for your data. The real cost of that catalog is around 9MB, even though the Computer Management console tells you that only 1MB is in use. To verify this requirement for yourself, look at the `catalog.wci` folder that the Indexing Service creates as part of setting up your custom catalog (it appears as a subdirectory in the target folder). Using the Indexing Service is better than relying on the Windows search feature because you do get good results, but the results are expensive in terms of resources.

Using the Command Prompt to Your Advantage

Many people associate the command prompt with antiquated DOS applications. When it comes to optimization, however, the command prompt can be your best friend. For example, you can achieve very fast results in a search using the FindStr utility. However, FindStr provides more than just speed—you also get everything it has to offer for an extremely low cost in processor cycles, memory, and hard drive space.

Command line utilities can often accomplish things that GUI utilities can't—at least not without a lot of extra effort. For example, it's possible to compare the content of two files using a GUI utility, but the Comp command performs that task faster. In addition, a GUI utility might prove hard to script, schedule, or place in a batch file so you can perform multiple tasks at once, yet command line utilities excel in these areas.

The biggest problem with using command line utilities is that they don't have a friendly interface. You have to know how to use the utility, which means delving into the purpose behind command line switches and other arcane facts that many users abhor. GUI utilities are still best when the interface is the most important feature of a utility, but don't count command line utilities out when you need speed, flexibility, and reliability at a low resource cost.

Because the file system has become so large and complex, many people now create a special means for displaying a command prompt wherever they need it. Use the following steps to add this feature to your system.

1. Open a copy of Windows Explorer.

2. Use the Tools ➢ Folder Options command to display the Folder Options dialog box.

3. Select the File Types tab and locate the Folder (not the File Folder) entry.

4. Click Advanced. You'll see the Edit File Type dialog box. This dialog box helps you add new commands to a particular file type, including system types such as folders.

5. Click New. You'll see the New Action dialog box. This is where you define a name for an action, along with the command required to execute it.

6. Type **Command Prompt Here** in the Action field.

7. Type `cmd.exe /k \"cd %1\"` in the Application Used to Perform Action field. This command tells Windows to open a command prompt using `CMD.EXE`. The /k argument tells `CMD.EXE` to execute a command, and then remain open. The command, in this case, is Change Directory (CD) to the current folder (%1).

8. Click OK three times to close the New Action, Edit File Type, and Folder Options dialog boxes.

Whenever you right-click a folder in Windows Explorer now, you'll see a new command called Command Prompt Here. Select this command and you'll see a command prompt in the folder that you selected. Using this technique means you don't have to worry about executing a lot of commands just to get to a specific location on the hard drive—you can go directly there and begin working.

Command Line Utilities You Should Know About

Windows has a number of command line utilities that can make optimizing the hard drive a lot easier—more than most people realize. Many of these utilities saw their first use with the Disk Operating System (DOS) that preceded Windows. Of course, Microsoft updated these utilities for use with Windows, but it's important to know where the utilities originated when you begin working with them. Although DOS was a great operating system for its time, Windows is much easier to use and more capable as well.

The following sections describe the more important features of utilities you'll want to discover to get the most out of your optimization experience. However, you don't have to work with these utilities at all—it's possible to skip this section and still do a relatively good job of optimizing your hard drive. These utilities simply make the task a little faster.

USING ATTRIB

The Attrib (attribute) utility lets you discover the attributes attached to a given file in an unambiguous way. Attributes are special notations that the file system makes about the folder or file. For example, when you modify a file, the file system sets the archive attribute, which tells your backup program that the file has changed. When the backup program makes a copy of the file, it resets the archive attribute. Here are the three other attributes the Attrib utility can control.

System   A system file is one that the operating system relies on. You shouldn't change operating system files except in very special situations because modifications could cause a system failure or make the system unbootable.

Hidden   A user can't see hidden files normally. Of course, you can change the Windows Explorer settings as described in the "Working with Standard Hidden Files" section to see hidden files, but they remain hidden at the command prompt.

Read-only   Setting a file to read-only means that the user can't erase it. A read-only file is one that you can look at, but can't modify in any way. (Although you can copy and move read-only files, Windows will normally ask whether you're sure that you want to do so.)

You can also use Attrib to locate files with a specific attribute. It works much the same as the `Dir` (directory) command at the command prompt, but the focus is on the attributes, rather than other file or folder information. To test this command, open a command prompt in the root directory (the uppermost directory) of your C drive and type `Attrib *.*` at the command prompt. You'll see a list of all of the files in the root directory, along with their associated attributes. For example, many of the files will have an A for archive next to them. Some files, such as ntldr will have the S (system), H (hidden), and R (read-only) attributes.

It's possible to view and change the attributes (except system) for a file using Windows Explorer. To change an attribute, right-click the file and choose properties from the context menu. You'll see the file Properties dialog box. The Read-only and Hidden options on the General tab modify these attributes on the file. Click Advanced and you'll see the Advanced Attributes dialog box that contains the File is Ready for Archiving option that controls the archive attribute. Although this method is aesthetically pleasing, you have to change the files one at a time. Using Attrib, you can change a number of files using a single command. For example, if you want to remove the system, hidden, and read-only attributes from every executable in a particular folder, you would type:

```
Attrib -h -r -s *.EXE
```

USING *COMP* AND *FC*

The Comp and FC commands perform the same task—they compare two files. In some cases, you need to know whether two files are the same. Someone might give a file a slightly different name, so knowing how two versions differ is very important when you plan to get rid of one of the two copies.

TIP The Comp command has the advantage of providing a user interface of sorts. When you don't provide any files or command line switches as part of issuing the command, Comp asks you questions that prompt you to provide the required information.

The Comp and FC commands can perform a strict comparison of two files where the case of the letters matter or you can choose to perform a soft comparison where case doesn't matter. In addition, the FC command can perform a binary comparison, where the command compares the actual bits of the characters. A binary comparison is most useful for files that contain special characters or for comparing non-text files such as images.

To use either of the commands, type the command name followed by two filenames and the command line switches you want to use. For example, if you wanted to perform a binary comparison of Test1.TXT and Test2.INI using the FC command, you would type **FC Test1.TXT Test2.INI /B**. Table 3.1 shows a list of the commonly used command line switches for the Comp and FC commands.

TABLE 3.1:   *Comp* and *FC* Command Line Switches

COMP	FC	DESCRIPTION
	/A	Display only the first and last lines for a set of differences, rather than every line. This option makes the output easier to read for two files with many differences.
	/B	Perform a binary comparison of the two files.
/C	/C	Disregard the case of the letters when performing a comparison.

TABLE 3.1: *Comp* and *FC* Command Line Switches *(CONTINUED)*

COMP	FC	DESCRIPTION
	/L	Compare the two files as ASCII text.
/L	/N	Display line numbers for an ASCII text comparison.
	/T	Don't expand tabs into white space for comparison. This ensures both files have tabs as needed.
	/U	Compare two files as UNICODE text.
	/W	Compress all white space during the comparison to reduce the number of mismatches.
/A		Display differences as ASCII characters. The default setting is to display the character values in hexadecimal format. So, if one file had an A and another an a, the default output would show that one value is 41 and the other 61, but you would see the actual characters when using this option.
/D		Display differences in decimal format. When you select this option, you see the decimal value of the characters, rather than the ASCII character itself.

USING COMPACT

Sometimes you need to compact files so that you can save space on the drive. You can perform this task by creating a file with a Zip extension and stuffing files into it because Windows XP comes with this functionality built in. As far as Windows XP is concerned, the Zip file is just another folder on the system. A number of third party products such as WinZip (http://www.winzip.com/) and WinRAR (http://www.rarlab.com/) also help you compress data into a smaller area. All of these methods place the files you want to compress into a special file. Windows XP also provides the means to compress files in place. The Compact utility lets you perform this task from the command line.

To use the Compact utility to compress files, type **Compact /C** followed by the name of the file. For example, when you want to compress Text1.TXT, you type **Compact /C Test1.TXT**. Uncompressing the file is similar. All you need to do is type **Compact /U Test1.TXT**.

An interesting feature of the Compact utility is that you can use it to detect how much Windows has compressed the files in a folder you have marked for compression using either Compact or Windows Explorer. The display tells you the actual file size, the compressed file size, the compression ratio, the compression state (either C for compressed or U for uncompressed), and the name of the file, as shown in Figure 3.11. To use this option, simply type **Compact** in the directory that you want to see.

USING DIR

The directory (Dir) command is one that many users forget about and yet it's an incredibly simple means of getting predictable and reliable results when looking for a file. The Microsoft search engine doesn't encumber the Dir command and the Dir command doesn't observe any of the restrictions placed on Windows Explorer. Although Dir lacks some of the display features of Windows Explorer, it's possible to locate the files you need and then use Windows Explorer if necessary to perform any required cleanup.

FIGURE 3.11

The Compact utility tells you the compression status of files on your system.

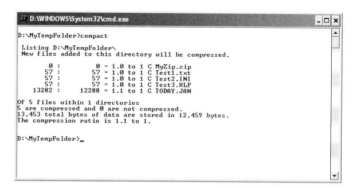

```
  D:\WINDOWS\System32\cmd.exe                                  _ □ ×

D:\MyTempFolder>compact

 Listing D:\MyTempFolder\
 New files added to this directory will be compressed.

         0 :           0 = 1.0 to 1 C MyZip.zip
        57 :          57 = 1.0 to 1 C Test1.txt
        57 :          57 = 1.0 to 1 C Test2.INI
        57 :          57 = 1.0 to 1 C Test3.HLP
     13282 :       12288 = 1.1 to 1 C TODAY.JAN

Of 5 files within 1 directories
5 are compressed and 0 are not compressed.
13,453 total bytes of data are stored in 12,459 bytes.
The compression ratio is 1.1 to 1.

D:\MyTempFolder>_
```

The default Dir command displays only visible files in the current folder. By adding wildcard search strings and command line switches, however, you can request almost any kind of file using Dir. For example, if you want to locate all executable files on a certain hard drive, open a command prompt in the root directory and type **Dir *.EXE /S**. The *.EXE portion tells Dir to look for all files with an EXE extension and the /S switch tells Dir to look in all subdirectories as well as the current directory. Here's a list of common Dir switches.

/A   Display entries with a specific attribute. Add a second letter to define the attribute type including A (archive), D (directory), H (hidden), R (read-only), and S (system). The attribute can also include a – (minus sign) to show you don't want files with a particular attribute. For example, to look for read-only files without the system attribute, you would include both the /AR and /A-S attributes.

/O   Sorts the data using a specific criterion including D (date—oldest first), E (extension), G (group directories first), N (name), and S (size—smallest first). You can add a – minus sign to reverse the sort order. For example, if you wanted to see the newest files first, you'd use the /O-D switch.

/P   Tells Dir to pause the display after each screen so you can see the results.

/Q   Displays the owner of the file, in addition to all of the other information that Dir provides.

/S   Displays the current directory and all subdirectories.

/T   Controls the source of the time information provided with the file including C (creation), L (last access), and W (written). For example, if you want to display the date the files were created, you'd use the /TC switch.

/W, /D, and /B   Controls how Dir displays the filenames. All three options remove any ancillary information and display just the filenames. The /W switch displays the filenames in as many columns as will fit across the screen with the files sorted in row order. The /D switch creates the same display as the /W switch, but the files are sorted in column order. The /B switch displays just the filenames in a single row—this format is especially useful when you want to send the output of the Dir command to a file for later analysis.

SAVING COMMAND OUTPUT

You can save the output of any command line utility to a text file for later processing using redirection. For example, you can save the output of the Dir command to a file for use in another application or as part of a script.

To redirect the output, you using the > and >> output symbols. The > symbol always creates a new file. The >> symbol adds the current output to an existing file when one exists or creates a new file when one doesn't.

Saving the results of a command line utility to the file means adding the correct symbol and a filename to the end of the command. For example, when you type `Dir *.* /B >> DirOut.TXT` and press Enter, the `DirOut`.TXT file receives the information from the `Dir` command.

USING FIND AND FINDSTR

The Find and FindStr utilities both locate files based on their content. The Find utility is less capable than FindStr, in most cases, so this section describes the FindStr utility in detail. However, there's one use for Find that isn't found in FindStr—you can use Find to determine just the number of occurrences of the search string in the target file using the /C switch. This particular feature and the smaller size of Find make it useful for scripting tasks where FindStr is overkill.

The easiest way to use FindStr is to define a simple string and make the call. FindStr will look in all of the files in the current folder for any words in the string. For example, `FindStr "Hello World" *.*` will look for the individual words Hello and World in all files in the current folder.

The true power of FindStr is that you can create specialized strings using a concept called regular expressions. A regular expression defines how to look for a string, rather than precisely which string to find. Regular expressions can contain the special characters described in Table 3.2.

TABLE 3.2:   Regular Expression Special Characters

SPECIAL CHARACTER	DESCRIPTION
. (Period)	Provides a placeholder for any single character. For example, "w.ll" could represent the words wall, well, or will.
* (Asterisk)	Represents 0 or more occurrences of the previous character or class. For example, "to*" could represent the words to or too, or simply the letter t.
^ (Circumflex)	Represents a character or class at the beginning of a line. For example, "^Hello" would find the word in the line, "Hello World", but not in the line, "George said, Hello."
$ (Dollar sign)	Represents a character or class the end of the line. For example, "World$" would find the word in the line, "Hello World", but not in the line, "World Peace."
[Characters]	Contains a character class (set of characters) from which FindStr selects. For example, "w[ai]ll" will match the words wall and will, but won't match well.

TABLE 3.2:   Regular Expression Special Characters *(CONTINUED)*

SPECIAL CHARACTER	DESCRIPTION
[^*Characters*]	Contains a character class (set of characters) that FindStr won't select. For example, "w[^ai]ll will match the word well, but won't match the words wall or will.
[*Character-Character*]	Specifies a range of characters that FindStr will use for selection. For example, "[a-z]" selects all characters a through z, but not numbers or special symbols.
Character	Tells FindStr to use the character literally, rather than as a special character. Programmers call this process escaping the character. For example, "z**" locates terms that begin with z followed by 0 or more asterisks within the file.
\\<*Characters*	Locates the characters when they appear at the beginning of a word. For example, "\\<we" locates the words welcome and well, but not the word owe.
Characters\\>	Locates the characters when they appear at the end of a word. For example, "we\\>" locates the word owe, but not the words welcome and well.

Using regular expressions lets you create complex search patterns that reduce search time and ensure good results. For example, you could create a telephone number search pattern using the search string "(...)...-...." assuming that your telephone numbers always include an area code and are formatted using the method shown. I've actually used this search pattern to locate telephone numbers hidden in DLLs.

NOTE   Some of the FindStr features are line related. A line of text or other data ends when FindStr encounters a special carriage return (character number 13) and line feed (character number 10) combination. When looking at a text file, you see one line of text separated from another by white space. The carriage return and line feed combination causes the white space. In DLLs and other unreadable files, there's no need for lines of text, so the carriage return and line feed combination appear irregularly, if at all, which means the lines are much larger and could include the entire file.

FindStr also has a number of useful command line switches. These switches affect FindStr operation or changes the way it interprets the search string. The following list describes the various command line switches.

/A:*ColorAttribute*   Tells FindStr to display the filenames using colors. You must provide two hexadecimal (base 16) values from 0 through F (these values are the same as 0 through 15 decimal). The first value is the background color and the second is the text color. This switch doesn't affect display of the matching text color, which relies on the current background and foreground colors of the command prompt.

/B   Matches the search string against the beginning of the line.

/C:*String*   Performs a literal search with the search string. For example, normally when you type "Hello World" as the search string, FindStr looks for the words separately—lines containing either Hello or World will match. However, when you specify this option, FindStr only matches lines that contain the whole term, Hello World.

/D:*Directories*   Defines a list of directories to search. You must separate each directory entry with a semicolon.

/E   Matches the search string against the end of the line.

/F:*File*   Reads the list of files to process from a file. You can also supply a value of "/" to type the names of the files to check at the command line.

/G:*File*   Reads the list of search strings to look for from a file. You can also supply a value of "/" to type the search strings at the command line.

/I   Performs a case-insensitive search. Normally, FindStr differentiates between "Hello" and "hello"—using this command line switch changes that behavior so the two capitalizations are treated the same.

/L   Interprets the search strings literally. This means you no longer have access to regular expressions, and you also don't have to escape the special characters.

/M   Prints only the filenames of files that contain a match. You can redirect the output from Find-Str to a file to use an input for a script or other additional processing.

/N   Prints the line number before each line that matches. This option helps you find the line faster in a text editor that supports line numbering.

/O   Prints the character offset of the matching text in each line. This option helps you find the text faster in text editors that provide column number support.

/P   Tells FindStr to skip files that contain non-printable characters, such as executable files. Given that most data files now contain non-printable characters, you should probably avoid using this option unless you know the data appears in pure text files.

/S   Looks for the search string in the specified files in the current directory and all subdirectories. When you use this command line switch in the root directory of a hard drive, you can search the entire hard drive for a search string. Because FindStr actually looks in every file, you'll find this process can take a long time.

/V   Prints only the lines that don't contain an exact match.

/X   Prints only the lines that match the search string exactly.

Using *Tree*

One of the interesting commands that Microsoft provides with Windows is Tree. This command shows the structure of a directory tree and can help you locate hidden folders on your system. In addition, by using the /F command line switch, you can display the files contained within the folder. However, it's usually better to use the Dir command when you can to locate files. The Tree command helps you discover hard drive structure. For example, you might want to learn how Microsoft Office stores files. Figure 3.12 shows Tree output for the \Program Files\Microsoft Office folder.

FIGURE 3.12
Use the Tree command to discover the directory structure of any application.

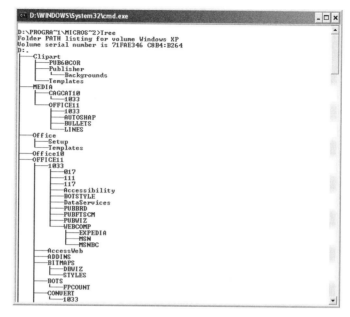

Figure 3.12 shows that the output uses special characters. You can redirect it to a file and print the result out for use in working with an application. If you decide that the special characters could cause problems in storing the data, you can tell Tree to use simple ASCII characters with the /A command line switch.

USING *XCOPY*

The XCopy command is one of the older and more useful commands for moving data around. The purpose of this command is to move entire directories and associated subdirectories from one place to another. However, Windows Explorer has largely replaced it and I would recommend you use Windows Explorer whenever possible. There are several situations where XCopy is especially important:

◆ Script for manipulating files

◆ Only some files in a complex structure are moved from one place to another

◆ Copying all available files, even when some files can't be moved

◆ Archiving data from one system to another

◆ Moving files with specific attributes

Many people use XCopy as a very inexpensive backup application because it does its job so well. You can simply copy the data files from a folder to a backup media such as another hard drive, floppy disk, Zip drive, or network location. Unfortunately, XCopy doesn't work with traditional media such as tapes and you must use initialized media so you can't use it for copying to CDs.

You use XCopy as you would the standard Copy command—by specifying the source files and destination. For example, when you want to copy all of the files in MyDir from the C drive to the D drive type **XCopy C:\MyDir*.* D:\MyDir*.*** and press Enter. However, it's the command line switches that set XCopy that appear. Here's a list of the most important options.

/A and /M   Both of these command line switches copy only files that have the archive attribute set. This feature makes either command line switch useful for backup purposes. However, the /M switch also resets the archive attribute to show the file is backed up, so this is the switch you should use when working with XCopy as your only backup solution.

/C   Continues copying even when data errors occur. Use this feature to copy everything you can from a damaged directory to a new location. Windows Explorer doesn't have this feature—it always stops after encountering the first data error.

/G   Allows copying of encrypted files to a location that doesn't support encryption. This feature removes the encryption from the file, assuming you have the rights to make such a change.

/H   Copies hidden and system files.

/K   Copy the file attributes as well as the file. Normal XCopy behavior resets the read-only attribute as part of the copying process.

/O and /X   These two command line switches help you maintain file security in the copied files. The /O switch copies the file ownership and Access Control List (ACL) information with the file. The ACL is especially important because it defines who can access the file and what they can do with it. The /X switch also copies the auditing information for the file. This feature is important when you want to track file access.

/R   Overwrites read-only files in the destination folder during the copy process. Use this option when making backups to ensure updated versions of read-only files appear in the backup folder.

/S and /E   Both of these command line switches copy the selected files in the current directory as well as those in subdirectories. However, the /E switch also copies empty subdirectories. You use this command line switch to retain the directory structure as well as copy the files.

/T   Creates only the source directory structure to the destination. This option prevents XCopy from copying any files. Use this feature to setup new projects or users. Sometimes you want to create just the directory structure without copying any private information in the source directory.

/U   Copies only the source files that already appear in the destination folder. This feature helps you update some files in the destination, but not others, without having to specify the files individually.

/V   Verifies all of the copied files by comparing them with the source files. This command line switch increases copy time. However, you should always use this option when using XCopy for backup purposes. Otherwise, your backup could contain corrupted data and you wouldn't know it.

Taking Out the Internet Explorer Trash

Internet Explorer is one of the worst offenders for accumulating garbage. In fact, you might be amazed at just how much data Internet Explorer collects. A single session with a graphics-filled Web site can chew up a significant portion of your hard drive because Internet Explorer downloads all those files. In many cases, it holds on to those files just in case you need them later. You can see some of these files in the \Documents and Settings\User Name\Local Settings\Temporary Internet Files folder of each user who accesses the machine. Other file stores appear in the \Documents and Settings\User Name\Local Settings\History, \Documents and Settings\User Name\Cookies, and \WINDOWS\Downloaded Program Files. Fortunately, you won't have to spend your time looking for trash because the following sections show how to clean it up.

Getting Rid of Cached Data

Of all the information that Internet Explorer collects, the least useful is cached data. The theory is that by caching all of the data for a Web site locally, Internet Explorer can improve performance when you visit that site again. It really is a good theory, it just doesn't seem to work very well in practice and you end up losing a lot of hard drive space as a result for almost no performance gain. The common reasons this strategy fails include:

◆ You don't visit the Web site often enough to make the cache effective.

◆ The cache size is too small.

◆ The Web site includes any number of tags that forces a refresh of the content so you end up downloading it anyway.

◆ You visit so many Web sites that Internet Explorer removes the cached data before you visit it again.

No matter what reason the cache doesn't work, the storage problem can become significant. Fortunately, you can clean out the data cache and restore the space to your system. (Depending how much time you spend on the Internet, you should clean the cache at least once a month and preferably once a week.) To begin, open the Internet Options applet located in the Control Panel. You can also access this applet using the Tools ➢ Internet Options command of Internet Explorer. Select the General tab and you'll see the Temporary Internet Files group shown in Figure 3.13.

FIGURE 3.13
Clear temporary Internet files as needed to keep your system clean.

Normally, you can simply click Delete Files to clear the cache. However, sometimes you want to be a little more selective in what you delete. Perhaps you do visit a particular Web site every day. The "Controlling a Voracious Drive Space Appetite" section of the chapter discusses how you can perform selective removal of files.

Killing the Cookie Monster

You have probably read any number of privacy statements and online notices that cookies are little text files that contain some information a Web site wants to store about you. At first, it sounds like a good idea—you can personalize your computing experience and ensure the Web site is just the way you like it for every visit. Cookies are even necessary in some cases—you must use them to perform certain tasks such as online shopping because the shopping cart data is stored in a cookie.

Unfortunately, cookies also present a good deal of room for misuse and they consume a lot of space on your hard drive. One of the most common misuses for cookies is that various banner ad companies use them to track your movements. Every time you visit another Web site with the banner ad, the vendor grabs the information it maintains about you from the cookie. At some point, the vendor has enough information to create a profile about you—perhaps as a means of customizing advertisements, but other uses come to mind such as figuring out enough about you to steal your identification. The hard drive space these cookies use seems paltry by comparison, but both issues are important reasons to keep cookies under control.

The first control measure is to kill your cookies regularly. Simply click Delete Cookies on the General tab of the Internet Properties dialog box shown in Figure 3.13. When you keep your cookies wide open, perhaps because you visit enough sites that require them that turning them off is difficult, you should delete the cookies daily or once a week at most.

Another way to keep cookies under control is to increase the requirements for using them. Select the Privacy tab of the Internet Properties dialog box and you'll see a slider that controls cookie usage as shown in Figure 3.14. Notice that the slider is set to High, which is the lowest setting I recommend anyone should use when they want firm control over cookie usage. This setting ensures the Web site storing a cookie on your hard drive has a privacy policy in place (one with vendor information) and doesn't use your personal information without alerting you first.

Some people complain that this setting is so high that few vendors meet the challenge and some of the bad guys still seem to get through. It's possible to control both problems by clicking Edit in the Web Sites area of the Privacy tab. You'll see a Per Site Privacy Actions dialog box. Simply type the URL for the Web site in the Address of Web Site field and click either Allow or Block. Even when a Web site meets all of the requirements, it can't place a cookie on your machine when you block it. Likewise, you can allow trusted Web sites that haven't gotten their act together to place cookies on your machine by using the allow option. The idea is to set a policy that generally protects your machine.

TIP   I generally look through my cookies before I delete them. Every cookie will have the URL of the Web site that created them. When you see a cookie from someone you don't know, it's likely a banner ad vendor who slipped through. Simply type the URL and add it to your blocked list. The "Controlling a Voracious Drive Space Appetite" section of the chapter shows how to view temporary Internet files or you can look through the files in your \Documents and Settings\User Name\Cookies folder.

FIGURE 3.14
Control cookie usage
by keeping nefarious
vendors at bay.

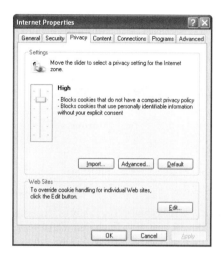

Forgetting History

Internet Explorer tracks all of the Web sites you visit and places the information in a history that you can access using the History Explorer Bar. The historical information can be quite useful because you don't have to remember a Web site that you visited yesterday or last week that contains useful information. However, the historical entries also consume hard drive space. The amount of space depends on how much time you spend surfing the Internet. The history display also consumes processing cycles and memory to display the history. You have to tune this feature to your particular needs. The default setting is high enough that you'll normally want to reduce it unless you perform extensive online research and the history is a requirement of your job.

The history settings appear on the General tab of the Internet Properties dialog box shown in Figure 3.13. You can set the number of days to retain the history to any value that meets your needs. Many people use 7 days because that seems to work well and doesn't clutter the hard drive. Because I never use this setting and prefer to maintain lists of useful Web sites in my Favorites folder, I set this value to 0. Even the 0 setting retains the Web sites you visit on a given day.

Whenever you change the history setting, make sure you also click Clear History to reset the history files. You can also click Clear History at the end of the day before you perform a backup to reduce the backup size. It's also a good idea to click Clear History before you leave a public computer to ensure no one else gains access to your history.

Controlling a Voracious Drive Space Appetite

Internet Explorer does provide methods for controlling its seemingly endless drive space appetite. To modify the settings that control Internet Explorer's use of drive space, click Settings on the General tab of the Internet Properties dialog box shown in Figure 3.13. You'll see the Settings dialog box shown in Figure 3.15.

FIGURE 3.15
Modify Internet Explorer
disk use with the options
in this dialog box.

The first setting doesn't actually affect hard drive usage. You set the Check for Newer Versions of Stored Pages option to match your history and cached data policy. Use the Never option to get the most out of both the history and cached data on your machine. Select the Every Visit to the Page option if you don't maintain either a history or a data cache. The Every Time You Start Internet Explorer option is best if you maintain enough data cache and history data for one day. The Automatically option is useful when none of the other options works well—this is probably a good setting for someone who doesn't use the Internet every day.

The Temporary Internet Files Folder group contains the settings of interest. The slider is the most important feature. You use it to set the amount of space that Internet Explorer sets aside for temporary storage. The amount of data you cache depends on how much time you spend on the Internet and how long you maintain a history for your system. The longer you spend on the Internet each day, the larger you should make the data cache when you want to cache information for performance reasons.

TIP   Internet Explorer generally selects your main Windows drive to store the temporary files. This option might not work well when your main drive is older and slower than a new drive you recently installed. In this case, click Move Folder and choose a new location for the temporary Internet files on the new drive.

Sometimes, you don't want to kill every temporary Internet file. You might visit a Web site daily and want to keep the files it provides. In addition, you might decide to remove some cookies, but keep others when you visit some sites that require setup or personal information. You can solve both problems by clicking View Files. You'll see the cached data and cookies that Internet Explorer has stored. Remove just the files you don't need any longer.

It might surprise you to know that Internet Explorer also stores objects on your system—usually ActiveX controls contained within DLLs located in the \WINDOWS\Downloaded Program Files folder on your machine. Generally, you can remove these files without causing any problems. To remove the ActiveX controls that Internet Explorer has downloaded, click View Objects. You'll see a list of these files. Don't press Delete to remove the file because most of these files are registered and deleting them will leave the registry full of entries you don't want. Right-click the file and choose Remove from the context menu to remove it.

Taking Back Your Identity

Internet Explorer stores even more information about you. For example, every time you fill out a form, Internet Explorer records the response. Later, when you fill out a form with a similar value, Internet Explorer displays a list of responses you provided earlier. All of this watching, storing, and presenting of information consumes hard drive space, memory, and processing cycles. This feature can also present security and identity theft problems as well.

To keep Internet Explorer from spying on you, select the Content tab of the Internet Properties dialog box. Click AutoComplete in the Personal Information group and you'll see the AutoComplete Settings dialog box shown in Figure 3.16.

Turning off all the Use AutoComplete For options is probably a good idea, but the Web Addresses presents minimal risk and can make you more productive. Even so, Internet Explorer often stores Web addresses longer than your history settings might allow and anyone who hits the correct address can see where you've been in the past. A little more problematic is the Forms setting because form data can consume a lot of space and someone could see the responses you've provided for that type of form field in the past. Never enable the User Names and Passwords on Forms option because it represents a significant security risk. It requires seconds to type your name and password, so this option isn't even much of a productivity enhancement. Whenever you change the AutoComplete settings, make sure you clear old AutoComplete data by clicking Clear Forms and Clear Passwords.

There's one other piece of personal information you need to control. Click the Security tab. At the top, you'll see the security zones. Select the Internet zone and click Custom Level. You'll see the Security Settings dialog box. Near the bottom of the Settings list, you'll see Userdata Persistence. Disable this feature to keep Internet Explorer from storing personal data.

Controlling Multimedia

Multimedia adds pizzazz to Web pages and many Web sites use multimedia in some way. However, multimedia also consumes a great deal of memory, processing cycles, and hard drive space. The problem is that the multimedia links are part of the Web page, so many people think there isn't much you can do about it. Fortunately, the Advanced tab of the Internet Properties dialog box shown in Figure 3.17 contains options for adjusting multimedia use with Internet Explorer.

FIGURE 3.16
Add or remove Auto-Complete options to make data entry fast without impairing security.

FIGURE 3.17
Tame multimedia use to
meet your needs using
these options.

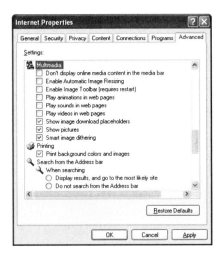

Most of the options can save precious resources on your system. However, the three options that matter most are: Play Animations in Web Pages, Play Sounds in Web Pages, and Play Videos in Web Pages. Disable these three options and you've gone a long way toward removing problems that multimedia can cause. Clear the Show Pictures option as well when you really want to save resources. However, removing all graphics from a Web site could mean losing access to content as well.

NOTE   Even if you decide not to display pictures as a default, you can right-click the picture place-holder and choose Show Picture from the context menu. Internet Explorer will download and display only the picture you select. Although this technique means more time clicking the Web page, it does mean you won't spend as much time downloading images you don't want.

Some of the features are more helpful than others are. For example, Smart Image Dithering makes the image appear smoother. The effect really works and will save your eyes when you spend a lot of time surfing the Internet. On the other hand, the Enable Automatic Image Resizing feature is less useful. Yes, it does make large images small enough to fit in your browser window, but most Web sites don't have images that are so large that you really need this feature. The feature also seems to affect other images and the Web page ends up reconfiguring itself needlessly until every image downloads. You can save time by disabling the Enable Automatic Image Resizing feature.

Scrapping Temporary Files

Windows and many applications create temporary files. A temporary file holds data that the application doesn't want to store in memory because memory isn't permanent enough, but also doesn't want to hold onto forever, as it would for a document you're typing. Temporary data falls into a kind of void—it's necessary, but only for a short time. The only problem is that some temporary data ends up staying around longer than anticipated. Often, the application that generated it doesn't clean up after itself.

WARNING   Always close as many applications as you can before you begin looking for temporary files to delete. The applications you run could rely on temporary files for short-term data storage or other needs. Deleting the temporary file while the application is still using it could result in data loss or other unfortunate results.

Choosing the *Del* Command over Windows Explorer

This chapter has already helped you discover just how broken the Windows Explorer search is and has shown you a number of alternatives. Windows Explorer does provide a great interface and it will locate most, but not all, of the temporary files on your system. Although this isn't perfect, the fact that you see all of the files you'll delete before you delete them provides a certain level of safety that you don't get with command line utilities. All you need to do after you locate the temporary files is highlight them and then press Shift+Del to remove them permanently from your system.

Fortunately, there's an alternative to Windows Explorer in the form of the Del and Erase commands. I recommend that you use this approach carefully. Make sure you have a complete backup of your system and have closed every application you can (everything but the command prompt if possible). The Del and Erase commands are the same, so I've used the Del form of the command in this section. To erase files using the Del command, simply type **Del *Filename*** and press Enter. This form of deletion is permanent, so the files won't appear in your Recycle Bin. The Del command includes the following command line switches.

/A   Delete files with a specific attribute. Add a second letter to define the attribute type including A (archive), H (hidden), R (read-only), and S (system). The attribute can also include a – (minus sign) to show you don't want to delete files with a particular attribute. For example, to delete read-only files without the system attribute you would include both the /AR and /A-S attributes.

/F   Force read-only file deletion. Normally, the Del command will ignore read-only files because deleting them would represent a change to the file status. You should never have to use this option with a temporary file. When you find a temporary file that has the read-only attribute set, make sure you check for the reason the file is set to read-only (it might have been a glitch with the application that created it).

/P   Tells Del to prompt you before it deletes a file. Use this command line switch if you have any doubts about deleting every file that matches a certain pattern. Although this method requires a little time, it's a lot better than deleting by mistake something you wanted.

/Q   This is the most dangerous command line switch because it tells Del not to display the files it's deleting. A better option is to redirect the screen output to a file when you don't want to see the files. For example, you could type **Del ~*.* /S > MyDeletions.TXT** to delete all of the temporary files beginning with a tilde from the hard drive and redirect the output to MyDeletions.TXT. This alternative keeps the list of files from appearing on screen, yet saves the list of deleted files for later analysis.

/S   Deletes all files matching the search criteria in the current directory and all subdirectories. When you use this option at the root directory of a drive, you can clean a specific kind of file from the entire drive. As always, use this option with care. Some subdirectories could contain files that match the search criteria that you really want to keep.

The advantages of using the `Del` command are that it's extremely fast and thorough. Unlike Windows Explorer, you won't miss any files and the process is much faster than Windows Explorer. It's possible to search and clean a hard drive in seconds, rather than the minutes required for Windows Explorer.

Eliminating Files Beginning with ~

Perhaps the most temporary of all files are those that begin with the ~ (tilde). Windows and many applications use files beginning with ~ and having no file extension in most cases as scrap files that contain bits and pieces of information. Neither Word nor other applications are very good at cleaning up these files.

When a file does have an extension, as in the case of a temporary file created by Word, the file is a temporary form of the document you're working on. However, if Word isn't open and you still see such a file, it usually means that Word didn't close correctly—the temporary file becomes a means of recovering any lost data from the document. Unfortunately, the document will remain behind even after you perform any required recovery, so you might find reason to remove these files manually. The point is that a file extension normally points to a temporary save of document you're working on and you don't want to delete them without thinking about it first.

No matter how many applications you close, Windows will usually have a few files that begin with a ~ in the filename open when you begin to delete the temporary files from the hard drive. Leave these files alone. Both Windows Explorer and `Del` will tell you that the files are in use and Windows Explorer will refuse to delete them under any condition.

Don't be surprised to find a number of these files appear to contain 0 bytes (no information). Some of them are indeed completely blank (others hide their data using a technique known as data streams), but you should still remove them from the system to free directory entries for other applications to use. In some cases, you can run out of directory entries, which makes the system unstable.

Zapping TMP and BAK Files

You can normally delete every TMP (temporary) file on a hard drive once you close all applications. Windows might have one or two of these files open, but the TMP file never contains application data you'll need later. The TMP file is one of the safest deletions you can make.

Likewise, BAK (backup) files contain an old copy of any documents you work with. When the application is closed, the BAK file is not in use and you can delete it. I normally retain the BAK files until I make a backup of the hard drive, and then delete them during the maintenance that follows. The BAK is a temporary backup of your data and you can usually use it to recover a lost document, should the document get lost due to an application error.

Some applications don't use the BAK extension. For example, Microsoft Word uses the WBK (Word backup) extension. The purpose of these files is the same as the BAK files, the vendor simply chose to use a different extension to make things as confusing as possible. The manual that comes with the application should tell you the extension for any backup files, but sometimes you have to discover the extension by creating a file and making several saves. Be sure you make small changes to the file between saves. You should see the backup file in the same folder as the original—it has the same filename, but uses the application's backup extension.

Looking for LOG Files

LOG files are text documents that generally tell you the result of an activity such as installing an application. When errors occur, the LOG file tells you about the error and sometimes provides clues as to how to fix the problem. Windows creates LOG files during an update to tell you which of the files it updated and any other actions taken by the update application. In short, LOG files are useful descriptions of system activity.

Unfortunately, neither Windows nor applications ever remove LOG files. In this case, the vendor or programmer who created the application isn't the problem. The assumption is that you'll read the LOG file and either archive it or erase it as dictated by company policy. In some cases, the application even tells you about the LOG file and provides some information on what you should do; but, in most cases, the application doesn't even make you aware of the LOG file—you need to know the file is generated and where to find it.

To make things more interesting, you could conceivably find LOG files that an application uses on a continuing basis, so you really don't want to remove it. For example, the UPS application I use relies on a LOG file to tell me about power events such as power surges. The log also indicates the last time I ran diagnostics and performed other tasks. However, even if I erased this file, nothing terrible would happen to the UPS application—it simply wouldn't have any memory of past events.

The LOG files you can safely delete appear either in the application directory or within the `\Windows` directory. It's usually a bad idea to remove LOG files from the `\Windows\System 32` folder or other locations on the hard drive. Knowing this information, you can begin by deleting all of the LOG files that appear in the `\Windows` folder after you read or archive them as needed. After you perform this task, search for other LOG files on the system. Any LOG file in an application folder is suspect—read the vendor manual to learn whether the application uses the LOG file. If not, you can delete the LOG file without harm to the application.

Discovering Who Created a File

You can't assume that every file on a shared system is yours, but you might have the task of cleaning up the hard drive. At some point, you'll run into files that you didn't create and will need to do something about them. Even when you know the file is complete garbage and no one will ever use it again, you need to check with the person who created the file. Otherwise, you could destroy a file the person needs for historical reasons or one that they might still use. This requirement means discovering the name of the person who created the file.

Unfortunately, it's not possible to obtain owner information using Windows Explorer without many mouse clicks. To obtain the information you need quickly, open a command prompt, type **Dir \Q *Filename***, and press Enter. The `Dir` command shows who owns the file as shown in Figure 3.18, which is usually the same person that created it and is responsible for it. At the very least, this person can direct you to someone who can determine what you need to do. The advantage of this technique is that you can check multiple files quickly, especially when these files have a common file extension.

If you feel that you must spend hours performing this task, then you can use Windows Explorer to do it. Begin by right-clicking the file and choosing Properties from the context menu. Select the Security tab of the file Properties dialog box. Click Advanced. Choose the Owner tab of the Advanced Security Settings dialog box to see the Current Owner of this Item field displayed in Figure 3.19. The only good reason to use this second technique is to change the file owner—a task you can't perform as easily at the command line.

FIGURE 3.18
The fastest way to determine who owns a file is to use the Dir command.

FIGURE 3.19
Windows Explorer lets you view the owner of a file one file at a time.

Choosing a Paging File Size

The paging file is a location on the hard drive where Windows stores items from memory. It makes the system think that you have more memory than you actually do and allows you to perform more tasks at once. Windows uses a number of techniques to determine what data goes into the paging file and which data uses physical memory. The important concept for this section is to understand how to set the paging file for optimal use.

You'll read any number of articles about the Windows paging file, many of which seem contradictory because they're trying to achieve different goals. There isn't a single right strategy for working with the paging file and you might even find that you have to use different strategies depending on how you set up a machine and what purpose you plan for it. This section emphasizes optimizing the paging file to reduce a number of problems with hard drive usage and overall system performance.

The default Windows XP setup deletes the paging file after every Windows session and creates a new one when Windows starts up. The size of the file changes continuously as Windows executes applications because the size is under Windows control. In addition, Windows normally uses a single paging file on the same hard drive as Windows executes. This approach to managing the paging file works from a generic perspective—it's equally bad for everyone. Here are some problems with this approach:

◆ You can suddenly run out of memory because an application creates a large file on the hard drive or because Windows keeps allocating more paging file space without telling you.

◆ The paging file ends up in small pieces all over the hard drive. Not only is reading from the hard drive slow, but the additional drive head movement (to locate those small pieces) also increases the performance burden.

◆ The paging file itself is quickly fragmented (a single piece of memory ends up in several locations on the hard drive). This also increases the performance burden because even a single application can't gain access to memory without several hard drive reads.

◆ Performance suffers when the drive Windows is on isn't the fastest drive on your system. This problem occurs when you add a new drive to your system that's faster—always use the fastest drive for your paging file.

The best way to approach the paging file is as temporary memory that you let Windows use as necessary. Having two disk drives can be a significant advantage when setting the paging file, but it isn't always necessary. To ensure you get the maximum benefit from the paging file, however, you need to set it up in such a way that it resides in contiguous blocks on the hard drive to minimize head movement (a significant performance inhibitor). You also need to clear the page file regularly to ensure it doesn't become fragmented.

To begin the optimization process, right-click My Computer and choose Properties from the context menu. You'll see a System Properties dialog box. Select the Advanced tab and click Settings in the Performance group. You'll see the Performance Options dialog box. Select the Advanced tab. Click Change in the Virtual Memory group so you see the Virtual Memory dialog box shown in Figure 3.20. This dialog box shows the drives that can hold the paging file and how the paging file is set up.

FIGURE 3.20

Use the Virtual Memory dialog box to modify the paging file setup for your system.

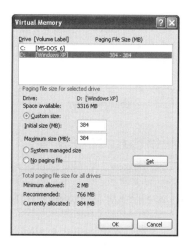

Notice that the system shown in Figure 3.20 has both a File Allocation Table (FAT) formatted drive and a NT File System (NTFS) formatted drive. Normally you want to choose the NTFS drive when possible because NTFS has performance benefits over DOS. However, when your fastest drive is FAT formatted, it's probably better to use it to gain the performance benefits of the drive.

Look at the Paging File Size setup at the top of the dialog box in Figure 3.20. The D drive has a 384MB paging file. The minimum and maximum values are the same, which prevents this file from growing and shrinking. The reason I used this approach is to keep the file in one place on the hard drive and reduce disk head movement. No matter what size paging file you create, the optimum approach is to make the minimum and maximum file sizes the same.

Choosing the paging file size is something that many people debate. The optimum approach is to size the file to take physical memory and the applications you run into account. A system with 128MB of RAM generally benefits from a larger paging file; although there are limits to how much a paging file can help overcome limits in physical memory. Because the target system has 512MB of RAM, it could probably use a smaller paging file than shown. In fact, it's possible to disable the paging file using a registry tweak discussed in the "Disabling the Paging File" section of Chapter 6. The only problem is that you must have enough RAM to support Windows when you use this approach and few people do.

To change the size of the paging file, select the drive you want to use. Select the Custom Size option. Type the same value in the Initial Size and Maximum Size fields. Click Set and verify that the drive is set to the new size. Click OK. Windows XP will tell you that this change requires a system reboot. Click OK twice to clear the System Properties dialog box and reboot the system.

When you initially want to create a paging file, the hard drive usually isn't set up right to accept it. Yes, you can set it and the paging file will work, but it won't work as optimally as it could. The problem is that the hard drive is fragmented, so you want to defragment it using the process described in the "Defragmenting the Drive" section of Chapter 8 and then create the paging file so that it resides in one location. You can take two approaches to begin.

◆ Set the paging file to the smallest possible size of 2MB on the target drive when there isn't a second drive.

◆ Move the paging file to the second (slower) drive during the defragmenting process.

After you resize or move the paging file, defragment the drive. Once the drive is completely defragmented (this usually requires several passes), change the size of the paging file again so it matches the final value you want to use. This technique results in an optimized paging file that runs as quickly as possible and uses both processing cycles and hard drive space efficiently. It might not be the fastest possible configuration and you might have to experiment with the paging file size before you find one that performs well for your needs.

Understanding NTFS

At one time, there was just one file system for DOS and Windows users, FAT. Unfortunately, FAT has problems, not the least of which is how it allocates hard drive space. Therefore, Microsoft tried patching FAT and we ended up with a number of versions of it, all of which finally had the same problems. In the end, Microsoft finally decided that it might be better to start from scratch, so they created NTFS.

I don't want you to be mystified about FAT and NTFS—they both accomplish the same task—saving your data in a permanent form on a hard drive. The essential difference between the two file systems is that NTFS is newer and contains a wealth of features that FAT doesn't. For example, NTFS includes security features that FAT doesn't provide so that you can do things like encrypt your data files so no one else can read them. From a performance perspective, NTFS is generally the best choice for the following reasons:

◆ Supports file compression

◆ Allows better management of drive space

◆ Uses smaller clusters (storage units) for more efficient data storage

◆ Provides a better directory system for faster data access

The "Using Compact" discusses the file compression feature, so I won't discuss it again here. You'll find discussions of various file management features in the "Performing Regular Maintenance" section of Chapter 8.

The most important feature from an optimization perspective, however, is the smaller cluster size. Think of a hard drive as being a series of storage bins. One piece of data can fit in each storage bin. Even if the data is only one byte, it consumes the entire storage bin. When the data is larger than the storage bin, Windows uses as many storage bins as needed to hold it. Using FAT means that most people will have a 256KB cluster size—even a small 1 byte file uses 256KB on such a drive. Contrast this with NTFS, which has a 4KB cluster size in most cases. Sure, you're still using 4KB for that 1 byte file, but that's a lot better than the 256KB used by FAT.

The directory system is also important. I don't plan to discuss this feature in the book because there isn't any simple way to describe it and the benefits of knowing how it works are small. This feature is automatic and you don't have to do anything to gain the benefits it provides except use NTFS rather than FAT. The bottom line is that you'll notice the performance difference of using one file system over the other.

Let's Start Cleaning

This chapter has shown you a lot of commands and techniques for working with your hard drive. It's a lot to take in and there isn't any reason to commit all of this material to memory. Simply rely on this chapter as your quick reference to all of the commands discussed.

It's time to start cleaning your system. The hard drive is important because it's the only permanent memory your computer has. Consequently, the hard drive is the one resource that gets clogged with old files and remains that way until you clean it up. Before you clean anything up, make sure you perform a backup of your system. Try the search commands so you can see just how clogged your system is before you begin deleting files. Finally, locate and destroy the temporary files on your system as a minimum. Make sure you clean Internet Explorer up as well and change the settings to ensure Internet Explorer behaves itself.

Chapter 4 is an extension of this chapter in some respects because it tells you how to clean applications you don't want from your system—freeing the hard drive space the applications use for other purposes. However, Chapter 4 goes further because it helps you refine your application setup. Consequently, the changes that you make in Chapter 4 can also affect processor and memory use, which means you'll start to see a definite change in system performance and usability by the time you complete this chapter.

Chapter 4

Performance Tuning Applications

Applications are the part of the computer that you see most, so when they aren't working efficiently, it's very noticeable. In fact, applications are the most common reason people have for updating their hardware—sometimes replacing an entire system to run the latest version of a new application. Consequently, tuning an application can have some very noticeable results—at least for that application.

Most people use two kinds of Windows applications: those that Microsoft forces on you and everything else. However, sometimes you really don't want the Microsoft applications and leaving them hanging around only uses up resources you could employ somewhere else. Because Microsoft thinks they're the center of the universe (figuratively speaking), they often make it difficult to remove old applications, so this chapter discusses controlling Windows applications first.

Other applications have problems, too. You can categorize these problems in several ways: installation leftovers, feature bloat, uninstall leftovers, and misbehaved applications. The chapter discusses all four issues and helps you make the most out of your applications. A lot of this information affects Windows as well, but it's focused on your other applications—the ones you chose to install.

Controlling Microsoft Additions You Don't Want

Microsoft has a habit of assuming that their product is the only one that you'll ever need, whether you want it or not. This practice has led to a number of problems, some of them legal. Entire countries are engaged in legal battles or other efforts to ensure that Microsoft knows that their way isn't the only way. For example, many countries now actively promote open source as the preferred software (see the internetnews.com article at `http://www.internetnews.com/bus-news/article.php/6_408271` and the C/NET article at `http://news.com.com/Munich+to+stick+with+open+source/2100-7344_3-5237356.html` for just two of many examples). The European Union's hefty fine on Microsoft is an example of the legal battles taking place (see the eWeek article at `http://www.eweek.com/article2/0,1759,1553423,00.asp` for details). However, until someone actually declares war on Microsoft and assails the Microsoft campus with tanks, you'll have to live with a few Windows applications you don't want. For example, you can tell Windows to get rid of Internet Explorer, but it doesn't really go away—Windows simply hides the files from view.

NOTE   Theoretically, it's possible to get rid of Internet Explorer. People have come up with techniques that get rid of most, if not all, of Internet Explorer. In fact, this issue is an old one dating back to at least 1999 and quite probably earlier (see the CNN article at http://www.cnn.com/TECH/computing/9903/09/removeie.idg/.) Don't believe Microsoft when they tell you that removing Internet Explorer is impossible or that Windows will stop working completely. However, the result of removing Internet Explorer is that some other applications break because they rely on it and you can't use some Windows features such as Windows Update. Consequently, even though you don't like some Windows features, you should retain them to receive maximum benefit from Windows.

Fortunately, you can remove other Windows utilities. For example, some people prefer not to use Windows Messenger. Unfortunately, Windows hides the entries for removing this application from sight unless you know how to expose them. That's what this section discusses—techniques you can use to expose the application uninstall so that you can remove them.

TIP   Sometimes the techniques in this chapter don't work. When you run into a Windows application that you can't remove, but don't want to use, you can usually disable it. The "Using MSCONFIG" and "Clearing Unnecessary Services" sections of Chapter 7 discuss disabling applications you don't need in detail.

TIP   Windows XP comes with built-in ZIP support. This feature is welcome in some ways because it lets you access a ZIP file without using a third party product such as WinZIP. However, the built-in support also has a number of flaws, including the fact that is slows searches to a crawl because the Windows search engine insists on searching within ZIP files. The problems get worse when you want to create an archive and discover you can't because Windows XP doesn't provide full ZIP support. To disable the Windows XP built-in ZIP feature, type `RegSvr32 /U %windir%\system32\ZIPFldr.DLL` at the command prompt and press Enter. You'll see a success message from RegSvr32. If you decide later that you want to re-enable the built-in ZIP file support, type `RegSvr32 %windir%\system32\ZIPFldr.DLL` at the command prompt and press Enter.

Modifying the *Sysoc.INF* File

The \WINDOWS\inf folder on your machine contains a number of information or INF files. The INF file has a special purpose in Windows because it provides configuration details. Whenever you install a new piece of hardware, Windows relies on an INF file to tell it the settings and other information for that hardware. Even though Plug and Play detects the hardware, you'd never get it installed correctly without a well-designed INF file.

The Sysoc.INF file is a special kind of information file in that it tells Windows how to treat installed features. This file doesn't affect third party applications you install, just the Windows features. Some of these features it hides, while others remain in full view for you to remove. By modifying this file, you can change a hidden option to a visible state. Figure 4.1 shows how the Sysoc.INF file might look on your system.

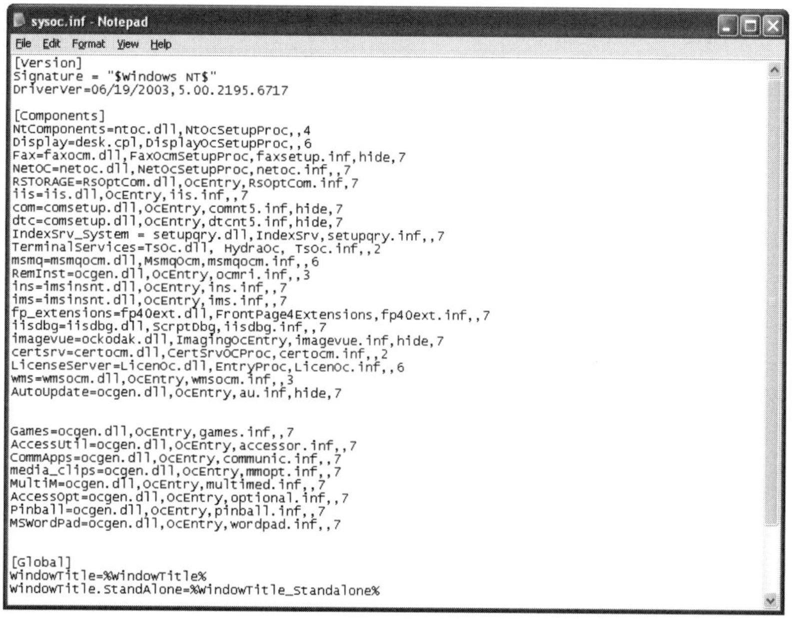

```
[Version]
Signature = "$Windows NT$"
DriverVer=06/19/2003,5.00.2195.6717

[Components]
NtComponents=ntoc.dll,NtOcSetupProc,,4
Display=desk.cpl,DisplayOcSetupProc,,6
Fax=faxocm.dll,FaxOcmSetupProc,faxsetup.inf,hide,7
NetOC=netoc.dll,NetOcSetupProc,netoc.inf,,7
RSTORAGE=RsOptCom.dll,OcEntry,RsOptCom.inf,7
iis=iis.dll,OcEntry,iis.inf,,7
com=comsetup.dll,OcEntry,comnt5.inf,hide,7
dtc=comsetup.dll,OcEntry,dtcnt5.inf,hide,7
IndexSrv_System = setupqry.dll,IndexSrv,setupqry.inf,,7
TerminalServices=TsOc.dll, HydraOc, TsOc.inf,,2
msmq=msmqocm.dll,MsmqOcm,msmqocm.inf,,6
RemInst=ocgen.dll,OcEntry,ocmri.inf,,3
ins=imsinsnt.dll,OcEntry,ins.inf,,7
ims=imsinsnt.dll,OcEntry,ims.inf,,7
fp_extensions=fp40ext.dll,FrontPage4Extensions,fp40ext.inf,,7
iisdbg=iisdbg.dll,ScrptDbg,iisdbg.inf,,7
imagevue=ockodak.dll,ImagingOcEntry,imagevue.inf,hide,7
certsrv=certocm.dll,CertSrvOCProc,certocm.inf,,2
LicenseServer=LicenOc.dll,EntryProc,LicenOc.inf,,6
wms=wmsocm.dll,OcEntry,wmsocm.inf,,3
AutoUpdate=ocgen.dll,OcEntry,au.inf,hide,7


Games=ocgen.dll,OcEntry,games.inf,,7
AccessUtil=ocgen.dll,OcEntry,accessor.inf,,7
CommApps=ocgen.dll,OcEntry,communic.inf,,7
media_clips=ocgen.dll,OcEntry,mmopt.inf,,7
MultiM=ocgen.dll,OcEntry,multimed.inf,,7
AccessOpt=ocgen.dll,OcEntry,optional.inf,,7
Pinball=ocgen.dll,OcEntry,pinball.inf,,7
MSWordPad=ocgen.dll,OcEntry,wordpad.inf,,7


[Global]
WindowTitle=%WindowTitle%
WindowTitle.StandAlone=%WindowTitle_Standalone%
```

FIGURE 4.1
Use the `Sysoc.INF` file to change how Windows treats installation options.

The entries under the `[Components]` heading are the ones you want to change. A typical entry looks like this:

```
Fax=faxocm.dll,FaxOcmSetupProc,faxsetup.inf,hide,7
```

The five entries tell you about that system component. For example, the first entry defines the Dynamic Link Library (DLL) responsible for this particular feature. You don't want to modify any of the entries in this list except the one that says "hide." This special entry tells Windows to hide the entry so the user can't see it in the Windows Component Wizard. In this case, the entry tells Windows that the user can't remove Fax support, even if the user doesn't have a fax installed in the machine. To make the Fax entry visible, simply remove the word hide, so the entry appears like this (don't remove the extra comma):

```
Fax=faxocm.dll,FaxOcmSetupProc,faxsetup.inf,,7
```

After you make the change and save the `Sysoc.INF` file, open the Windows Component Wizard. You'll find this feature in the Add/Remove Programs Applet—just click Add/Remove Windows Components in the Add or Remove Programs dialog box. As shown in Figure 4.2, you can now see the Fax Services entry so you can remove the support when you don't need it. (Depending on the version of Windows you used and the features you installed, you might not see the Fax Services entry even if you unhide it.)

FIGURE 4.2
The new entries in the Windows Component Wizard let you tune Windows better.

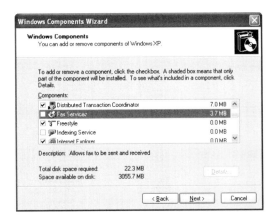

Removing Unneeded Applications

As previously mentioned, Microsoft assumes you need quite a few more applications than you really want. The argument is that hard drive space is cheap and you should at least try the applications before removing them from your hard drive (when you can at all). The problem is that many of these applications get installed and are never used, not even once. They simply sit there consuming resources and never provide the user with one iota of benefit.

The following sections discuss two kinds of application removal. The first type is third party applications that you actually install on your system (or someone installs for you as part of a new computer setup). This group includes Microsoft applications such as Microsoft Office that aren't part of the Windows operating system. The second type is Windows components that you didn't have any choice about installing, even when you install Windows on your machine. Microsoft has removed many of the optional installation features, which means your copy of Windows is full of all kinds of extra features that you'll never use.

CLEANING UP THIRD PARTY APPLICATIONS

Once you expose all of the application groups you can by editing the Sysoc.INF file (see the "Modifying the *Sysoc.INF* File" section for details), you can begin removing applications from your system. Open the Add or Remove Programs applet located in the Control Panel. You'll see an Add or Remove Programs dialog box like the one shown in Figure 4.3.

This dialog box contains third party applications and Microsoft applications that aren't actually part of Windows. Normally, you have to perform an installation process to place these applications on your system. These application entries provide several important pieces of information—some you can believe and some you can't. The application name is always correct, but Windows sometimes loses the application icon, so it's important to know the full application name to ensure you remove the correct application.

FIGURE 4.3

Use the Add or Remove Programs dialog box to work with third party applications.

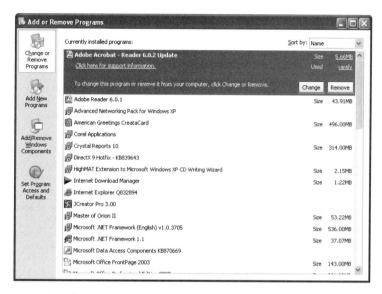

The Size field is also correct. It tells you the uncompressed size of the application. Generally, when you remove the application from your hard drive, you free up that much hard drive space for another use.

NOTE Windows Explorer doesn't always report an increase in hard drive space when you uninstall an application. Sometimes it won't even report the increase when you close the existing copy of Windows Explorer and open a new one. Windows Explorer always reports the value correctly after a reboot.

The Used field is frequently incorrect. The problem appears to happen when you open an application as the result of double-clicking on a data file, rather than opening the application directly. In short, while you could use this field as a sort of guide, don't depend on it to make decisions on which applications to remove.

TIP Notice the Click Here for Support Information link in Figure 4.3. Click this link to display a dialog box containing support information, including where to obtain updates for your application. In some cases, the application update information appears here, rather than as part of the application. Keeping your applications up-to-date reduces data-destroying bugs as well as helping to keep viruses at bay.

All of the entries will include a Remove button. Click Remove to uninstall the application. Some entries will also include a Change button you can use to remove application features or perform update tasks. Some entries will also include a Repair button you can use to correct application errors.

Each time you click Remove, the application will display the uninstall application. Sometimes you'll need to provide additional information. For example, sometimes the uninstall program wants to know whether it should remove a shared DLL from the system. Generally, when the application asks about this DLL, it means that no other application is actually using it so you can click Yes. However, you can record the name of the DLL on paper so you can reinstall it later if necessary (see the "Restoring DLLs and Other Executables" section of Chapter 12 for details on this process). In addition, some applications will ask that you restart the system so they can remove application-specific files that the system loads when it starts. When the uninstall is complete, the application will display a completion dialog box.

Sometimes an uninstall program will encounter a problem removing all of the files for an application. Generally, this problem occurs when you've made changes to the application or have application data stored in the application folder. Make sure you create a list of additional files to remove based on the uninstall report. This could mean archiving data files or performing other tasks. See the "Discovering Application Uninstall Remains" section of the chapter for details.

CLEANING UP WINDOWS COMPONENTS

To display the list of Windows features on your machine, click Add/Remove Windows Components (on the lower left side of the Add or Remove Programs dialog box). You'll see the Windows Components Wizard dialog box shown in Figure 4.4.

Notice that some of the entries in Figure 4.4 have no name. I purposely removed the Hide entry from all of the components in the Sysoc.INF file to show how the Windows Component Wizard would appear. These two mystery entries are features that Windows needs to run. You can try to clear the check in order to uninstall them, but you can't. In some cases, you also can't remove named entries. For example, your system uses COM+ for a number of purposes, including the event log, so you can't remove the check from it.

Next to each of the Component entries, you'll see an entry that describes the amount of hard drive space the component requires. This number is the uncompressed size of the component. However, the entry usually tells you about just the component, not any subcomponents that the Windows Component Wizard removes, so the size savings can be larger than shown. To remove a component from your system, simply clear the check next to its entry.

FIGURE 4.4
Remove Windows features, at least from view, using the Windows Components Wizard.

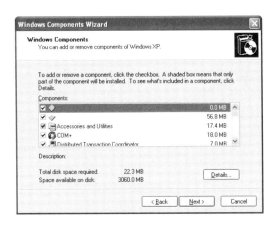

Sometimes a component will include a number of subcomponents. For example, the Accessories and Utilities component has a wealth of subcomponents. To see these subcomponents, select the component and click Details. You'll see a list of subcomponents such as the one for Accessories and Utilities shown in Figure 4.5.

In some cases, subcomponents have additional subcomponents you can remove. Again, just click Details when enabled, as shown in Figure 4.5. When you select just part of a component, Windows Component Wizard grays its check box instead of displaying it as cleared or having a standard checkmark. For example, I've selected only some of the Games component, so its entry appears grayed, as shown in Figure 4.5. When you finish removing features from Windows, click Next. The Windows Component Wizard will display a progress bar and finally a completion dialog box. Click Finish to complete the process.

Unfortunately, unlike third party applications, removing a Windows component doesn't mean it's actually gone. When you remove a game, Windows Component Wizard actually does remove it. However, when you remove a feature such as Internet Explorer, Windows Component Wizard only hides the application from view. Microsoft claims that some of these components aren't removable because Windows needs them to perform tasks.

FIGURE 4.5
Subcomponents let you remove part of a Windows component.

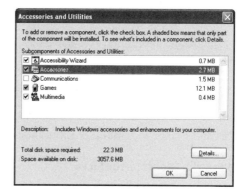

Removing Application Installation Crumbs

Installing an application means decompressing files, saving configuration settings, and performing a number of other tasks to prepare the application for use. All of this work generates extra files on your hard drive and consumes other resources such as memory and processing cycles. The memory and processing cycle use are temporary, but the hard drive additions can be long term. Some applications are good citizens and remove all of the extra installation files they create, including temporary files that you probably won't need for any other purpose. However, other applications simply assume that you have an unending supply of hard drive space and retain all kinds of files that you'll never need.

The following sections describe two kinds of installation leftovers. The first type is the setup files that some applications leave behind. Finding these files is usually easy, but some vendors hide them deep in the application hierarchy. The second type is temporary files. Generally, vendors know to place these files in your Windows temporary folder, but again, the files can end up anywhere. Sometimes the vendor even makes it hard to locate the temporary files for reasons that only the vendor knows.

TIP   All setup (installation) programs have two things in common—the vendor generally defaults setup options in the vendor's favor and every setup program is generic. You can always do better than the setup program can at optimizing an application installation to meet your particular needs. Remember, you don't need to meet someone else's needs; you need to meet your needs. Someone else might view your installation as the worst conglomeration of application features they've ever seen, but that doesn't matter. An optimized setup works best for the person who's using the application.

Discovering Setup Files

Almost every application you use requires some type of setup because you need to provide an executable file storage location, data file information, and other configuration settings to use the application. Setup files include a number of elements including:

◆ Setup application executable files

◆ Setup application configuration files

◆ Registration and other optional setup features

◆ Extra setup files, most of which are compressed

◆ Compressed application executable files

◆ Compressed application data files (including help files)

◆ Demonstration and sample files, most of which are compressed

◆ Slideshow and other training files

◆ Demonstration files for other applications sold by the vendor

REMOVING THE EXCESS SETUP FILES

Many vendors are beginning to leave setup files behind because they feel this addition makes it easy for you to change your configuration later. It's true that keeping the files can make updates faster and even speed some types of repairs. The only problem with this strategy is that you generally need the installation CD anyway, so the files are always available on the CD. Storing the files on the hard drive represents a waste of resources you can use for other tasks. In addition, because many of these files are compressed, placing them on the hard drive thwarts any hard drive compression you have in place—those files use up all of the space they normally need on any drive. An 80MB setup file isn't compressed—it really does require 80MB of hard drive space.

WARNING   Some vendors have engaged in a dubious practice of preloading your machine with software and not offering you a copy of Windows or the applications on a CD. This means that you can't easily add and remove applications as desired. The actual copy of Windows resides in CAB (cabinet) files somewhere on the hard drive along with any applications the vendor provides. This practice will cost you money at some point because you'll eventually end up buying a copy of Windows on CD anyway (your hard drive fails or the CAB file is accidentally erased). Always make sure that you get a bona fide copy of Windows and all supplied applications on a CD so you can optimize and repair your system as needed.

Most of these setup files appear in an easy-to-see location on your hard drive. For example, Microsoft Office 2003 users will find an MSOCache folder on their systems that contain these setup files. The Microsoft Office 2003 setup program will read from this folder, but it can just as easily read the data from the CD, so there is no reason to keep the folder. This folder is a minimum of 7.8MB of wasted space. It keeps growing as you work with Office until the MSOCache folder can actually exceed the size of your installation, depending on how you set up the application. To get rid of this file, simply highlight it in Windows Explorer and press Shift+Del.

A few vendors hide the setup files within the application folder. Because the developers that work for the vendor want to make life easy for themselves, you'll normally find these setup files in a Setup or other appropriately named folder. In this case, I usually move the folder to some other location on my hard drive, such as my Temp folder, and use the application for a few days. When the application continues to work as expected, I delete the Setup folder.

In a few select cases, the vendor mixes in Setup files with the other application files, making it difficult to determine which files the application uses for a particular purpose. Unless you're adept at ferreting this kind of information out, I'd suggest leaving the Setup files in place and letting the vendor know your opinion of using this option.

DELETING REGISTRATION AND OTHER SHORT-TERM FILES

Sometimes an application has a legitimate short-term use for a particular file. For example, most applications include a separate registration program. You use the registration to tell the vendor about your use of the application. Generally, filling out the form means that you discover program updates faster and learn about patches directly from the vendor. Of course, the vendor will also swamp you with offers from any of a number of sources for additional products. The point is that once you complete the registration (if you do), the application is useless and you can easily get rid of it without causing problems. One point to think about here is to try to remove the excess files using the Setup program before you try the manual approach discussed in this section.

WARNING   Don't confuse registration applications with authentication application. Products such as Windows XP and Microsoft Office 2003 come with an authentication application that unlocks the application by sending information about the application to the vendor. It's risky to tamper with the authentication feature of an application—you could end up with an unusable application.

The easiest way to locate the registration application is to right-click its entry in the Start menu and choose Properties from the context menu. You'll see a list of application specifications, such as those shown in Figure 4.6 for an American Power Conversion (APC) registration program.

The Target field of the Properties dialog box tells you the name of the application and shows where it appears on your hard drive. Make sure that the registration program isn't tied in with any of the application programs (normally it isn't). In this case, it turned out that the registration program also included a number of ancillary files, so the cost savings was 2.4MB on my hard drive. Make sure you remember to right-click the icon in the Start menu and select Delete from the context menu after you remove the registration program so you don't try to click that entry later.

FIGURE 4.6
Location registration
programs through the
shortcut provided in
the Start menu.

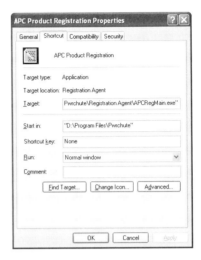

Unfortunately, sometimes you'll open the Properties dialog and find the Target field grayed out with some text in it. This means the vendor is using a special setup to create the entries in the folder. The time required to locate and kill this registration file sometimes exceeds the benefit, even in long-term disk storage. The best approach, in this case, is to look in the application folder. If you find a registration application, double-click it to verify it. Exit the registration application and delete only this file. After you remove the registration application, you can also delete the shortcut that starts it.

This technique works with other kinds of application add-ons as well. For example, you might find that the vendor has included quirky links to a Web site that won't serve any purpose in your case. The Setup program normally doesn't include any means of removing these excess files, so removing them manually is perfectly acceptable.

GETTING RID OF OTHER PRODUCT DEMONSTRATION FILES

A final category of setup file that you should delete immediately is the demonstrations of other products the vendor provides. I have to admit that this particular category used to cost me a big chunk of my hard drive. The vendor places these files on your hard drive and includes links to them in the Start menu with the idea of increasing sales. What really happens is that most people are so busy that they keep thinking about running the demo, but never do it, so the files remain on disk consuming resources and not really accomplishing much. It's nothing to find 20 or 30 such files on a user's hard drive—all of which demonstrate cool looking products that most users are never going to try because there simply isn't time to do it.

You might not think that demonstration programs, even 20 or 30 of them, are such a big deal. However, vendor demonstration programs have become increasingly larger over the years. At one time, it was odd to find a demonstration program that exceeded 1MB, now it's odd to find one that's less. Recently, I downloaded a 17MB demonstration program for a quick check of an application that looked useful and I understand that some demonstration programs are far larger. Can you really afford to lose the disk space taken by 20 or 30 demonstration programs that exceed 1MB?

Normally, I try to set aside enough installation time for an application now that I can try out the demonstration programs when they look interesting. Immediately after I run the demonstration, I make notes (when appropriate) and delete the demonstration program using the same technique found in the "Deleting Registration and Other Short-Term Files" section of the chapter. If the installation day ends and I still haven't run those demonstration programs, I realize that I probably won't ever run them, so I delete them and recover the space.

Removing Temporary Data

Once you install an application and configure it, you might think the work is done, but it's really just beginning. Very few installations are clean—most leave some kind of temporary data for you to delete. It's important to get rid of this temporary data as soon as possible to ensure you get the cleanest possible application environment.

STANDARD WAYS TO LOOK FOR TEMPORARY DATA

The first place to look is in the root directory of your hard drive. Microsoft and other vendors often create temporary directories for the installation and fail to remove it afterward. In some cases, the temporary directory is hidden, so it's important to use a copy of Windows Explorer with all of the features enabled or use the Dir command with the /ah command line switch. Once you find the temporary folder, highlight it in Windows Explorer, verify that it doesn't contain anything useful, and use Shift+Del to remove it.

Sometimes the vendor places the temporary data in the Windows temporary folder or another folder that you designate to hold temporary data. You can remove these files as part of your normal disk maintenance. The "Using Disk Cleanup" section of Chapter 8 describes how to automate this task in more detail.

Another place to look for temporary setup data is in the application folder. Sometimes a vendor will place the data there so all of the mess is in one location. The "Scrapping Temporary Files" section of Chapter 3 tells you what to do in this case.

No matter what kind of temporary files the Setup application creates, it's likely that Setup will also create LOG files. These files tell you how the installation proceeded and help you understand any problems Setup might have encountered. Unfortunately, these files remain behind until you manually delete them because the vendor is hoping that you'll verify any problems by reading them. The "Looking for LOG Files" section of Chapter 3 tells you how to recognize and remove LOG files.

NOTE   Some applications, such as SQL Server and Internet Information Server (IIS) produce large quantities of log files. The application will use a log file for a specific timeframe, such as a day, close that log file, and create a new one for the next day. After you review the old log files, you can normally archive them or simply delete them from the system. You won't be able to delete the current log file because the application keeps this file locked—Windows displays an error message telling you that the file is in use. Review the vendor documentation and the application settings to determine how often the application changes log files. When you find the log files are getting too large, you can change the update interval to something that works better, such as from once a week to once a day.

USING THE EMPTY TEMP FOLDERS UTILITY

Another way to look for temporary data is to use a third party application designed for the task. One such product is Empty Temp Folders. You can download this freeware product from http://www.danish-shareware.dk/soft/emptemp/. The download is about 650KB, so it doesn't take long even with a dial-up connection. Don't assume that because this application is freeware that it isn't feature packed. Empty Temp Folders provides a great way to snoop around your hard drive looking for data that shouldn't be there.

When you first open Empty Temp Folders, you won't see much. You have to configure the application to match your system. Fortunately, the configuration process doesn't take long. Simply select the Options ➤ Add Predefined Folders command to display the Add Predefined Folders dialog box. Click Select All and then Apply to add these predefined folders to your list of places to check for files. Click Close to close the dialog box. Figure 4.7 shows typical results.

Simply clearing the `D:\Documents and Settings\John.DataCon\Local Settings\Temp` folder on this system would clear up 17MB of hard drive space. When you want to view the files before deleting them (normally a good idea), select the File ➤ Open Folder in Explorer command to see it. The resulting window lets you delete files individually when desired.

You can also use this utility to perform tasks such as clearing the cookies from your system and looking for temporary files that reside outside the normal temporary folders. In short, using this utility lets you find the files that a Setup application leaves behind quite quickly.

However, one of the most interesting uses for Empty Temp Folders is locating broken links (LNK files) on your system. Each broken link represents a potential resource waster and performance inhibitor. Every time Windows tries to locate a broken link, it searches the drive for a related link and suggests that link to you in place of the one that is broken. When Windows turns up empty (after searching the whole drive), it asks whether you want to browse for the resource pointed to by the link. The problem is that this search takes time and sometimes takes place in the background. Other Windows elements also rely on links and you won't even see this time wasting activity taking place.

To use this feature of Empty Temp Folders, select the Clipboard and Shortcuts tab. Click Check All Drives (the drive icon with the magnifying glass). The check does take about 5 minutes, so be patient. After searching the drive and validating the links it contains, Empty Temp Folders displays the results. The text system had an astounding 438 broken links, as shown in Figure 4.8.

FIGURE 4.7

The Empty Temp Folders utility shows you the status of all the temporary folders and files on your machine.

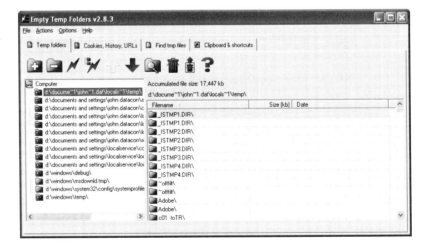

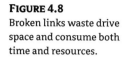

FIGURE 4.8
Broken links waste drive space and consume both time and resources.

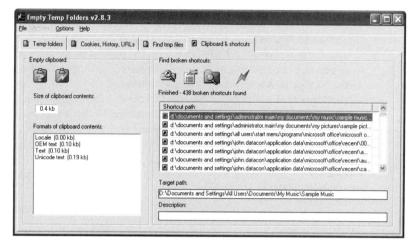

Cleaning up these LNK files only frees around 1.7MB of disk space. However, the biggest benefit of cleaning up the broken links is the perceptible performance increase in many activities. For example, you'll find that Windows Explorer works better after and that it's faster to do things such as open files with an application.

Removing Sticky Applications

Sometimes an application is sticky—you can't seem to get rid of it. Like double-sided tape, as soon as you've pulled the application off, it seems to be stuck somewhere else in your system. After you look through the list of applications in Figure 4.4, you discover there's apparently no uninstall program for this application either. In short, you're stumped about what to do with this application, but you do know that you don't want it around any more.

You feel like your machine requires an exorcism. Before you hire someone to perform the rites, try approaching it from a fresh perspective. For one thing, when the application runs every time your start your system, you need to stop it before you try to uninstall it. Once you do stop the application, you need to discover where it lives on your hard drive and remove it. This task usually requires a little more than just deleting the application—you have to ensure that you get all of it, including registry entries when required.

Stopping the Errant Application

Before you can remove a sticky application, you have to be sure it isn't running on your system. Some applications include features that make them even stickier by reinstalling themselves after you remove them—all they need is a running copy and sometimes an Internet connection to perform the task. Fortunately, it's easy to locate and stop errant applications.

WARNING   Stopping a running application using this technique doesn't provide any opportunity for the application to save data—Windows ends the application immediately. Make certain that you select only the application you want to end. Close any open applications with data files loaded before you attempt to perform this task.

To begin, you must know the name of the errant application. In some cases, you'll need to search the \Program Files folder to locate the executable filename. However, in many cases, just knowing the application name is enough. Once you know the application or executable filename, right-click the Taskbar and choose Task Manager from the context menu. Select the Processes tab and you'll see a list of running applications, as shown in Figure 4.9. Although this list isn't complete, it does contain all of the applications with any sort of user interface.

Notice that most executables use descriptive names, so even knowing the application name is often enough to find an errant application. Highlight the application you no longer want running and click End Process. Windows will display a warning dialog box. When you click Yes, Windows ends the application. Windows removes the application entry from Task Manager.

FIGURE 4.9
Locate the application you don't want by reading the executable names in this list.

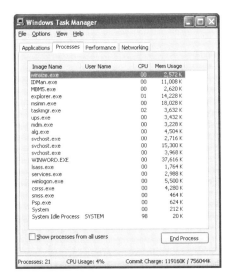

Removing the Application from Your Drive

Removing a sticky application from your drive might not be as easy as you think. In a few cases, you'll see an entry for the application in the Add or Remove Programs applet described in the "Cleaning Up Third Party Applications" section of the chapter. When this is the case, you should be able to remove the application using the techniques in that section. Unfortunately, you'll find that correctly installed sticky applications are the exception, rather than the rule. More often than not, you must remove them manually, which means performing the following three tasks:

◆ Remove the application files from the hard drive

◆ Delete any entries in the Startup folder

◆ Locate and delete any other application files

SEARCHING FOR THE APPLICATION

The best way to locate the application directory for a sticky application is to use the Dir command to search the entire hard drive for the executable. Don't be surprised if you locate three or four copies of the executable—sticky applications often create multiple copies of themselves, making the application even harder to remove. Record all of these locations to ensure you get them all.

TIP I normally place the Dir command output in a text file so I can display the information on screen as I work. To create such a text file type **Dir BadExe.EXE /S /B >> SearchBadExe.TXT** and press Enter. You won't see any output on screen, but you can open SearchBadExe.TXT and see the list of locations where the executable appears. See the "Using Dir" section of Chapter 3 for details on using the Dir command.

REMOVING FILES RELATED TO THE APPLICATION

Before you begin removing the application folder, you need to locate and delete any related files. An application can include data files and DLLs. The data files are relatively easy to find. Most applications rely on either generic file extensions (in which case, the presence of the application used to open the data file might not matter) or special file extensions. When working with special file extensions, simply use the Dir command to search for them on your system and make a list of locations. In most cases, deleting the special files requires only a few minutes.

The DLLs can pose a bigger problem. Applications can store DLLs in the local folder or within the \Windows\System32 folder. The DLLs can serve a single application or multiple applications. In addition to the problem of determining whether multiple applications use a DLL, there's also the problem of creating settings for it in the registry. Certain DLLs (most notably those used with the Component Object Model or COM) require registry entries. These entries can clog the registry and make working with Windows cumbersome.

The best course of action for sticky applications is to begin by ensuring it hasn't registered any of the DLLs in the application folder. Windows includes a special utility application that unregisters DLLs for you. Open a command prompt in the application folder. Type **RegSvr32 -u NameOfDll.DLL** and press Enter. When the DLL is registered, you'll see a success message. Otherwise, you'll see an error message that you can ignore, but at least you'll know that the DLL isn't creating a headache for later. Only after you unregister all of the DLLs, can you consider deleting them from the hard drive.

There's only one safe way to remove DLLs from the \Windows\System32 folder for a sticky application, and you have to observe a number of rules. First, you need to know the vendor's name. Second, you must know that this is the only application that uses DLLs from that vendor. Therefore, you couldn't use this technique with Microsoft DLLs.

Once you know whether the DLLs are safe to search, you can use the FindStr utility to help you locate the DLLs. Open a command prompt in the \Windows\System32 folder. Type **FindStr /M / C:"Name of Vendor" *.DLL** and press Enter. The FindStr utility will display a list of DLLs containing that vendor's name. You can delete these DLLs from the \Windows\System32 folder after you ensure you unregister them. If you want to be very sure that the DLLs you delete are from the correct source, right-click the DLL in Windows Explorer and choose Properties from the context menu. Choose the Version tab and you'll see entries like those shown in Figure 4.10. Notice that the name of the DLL appears at the top of the dialog box. Select the Company entry and you'll see the name of the company.

FIGURE 4.10
Use FindStr to help
locate potential applica-
tion files and then verify
them using this proper-
ties dialog box.

TIP It's possible to dig into an application program and learn about the DLLs that it uses with applications such as Depends (download from http://www.dependencywalker.com/). The Depends
utility comes with products such as Visual Studio. This utility is designed for use by professional
developers and those who know about Windows DLLs. Even though this utility is so complex, it does
help you locate even more DLLs from sticky applications. For example, you could use it to determine which DLLs to remove from the \Windows\System32 folder.

DELETING THE APPLICATION

Once you locate all of the places the application is hiding, you need to consider how best to get rid of
it. In many cases, you can delete the whole folder. For example, when the folder includes all or part
of the application name or the vendor name, you can feel safe deleting the entire folder from the hard
drive and saving the additional space. However, sometimes an application will hide itself in a folder
used by a number of other applications. For example, when the application resides in the \Windows\
System32 folder, you know that you can't delete the folder because many other applications rely on
it (not to mention Windows itself). In this case, you have to carefully remove only the application and
any DLLs you can verify.

CLEANING THE STARTUP FOLDER

Some sticky applications place their application link in the Start/Programs/Startup folder, so this
is the first place you should look for links left by the application. When you see a link to the application that you just deleted, right-click it and choose Delete from the context menu. This act places the
link in the Recycle Bin, so you should clean up the Recycle Bin immediately afterward.

Searching the Registry for Remains

The registry is essentially a database for holding settings of all types. For example, when you configure a new piece of hardware, the registry stores the settings you provide so it can access the hardware during each startup. Whenever you open an application and make changes to the settings, it's a good bet those settings will appear in the registry (sometimes they appear in other places, such as an INI or XML file on your hard drive).

WARNING The registry isn't just a repository of interesting settings, Windows relies on the registry to start your machine, interact with devices, and help you perform tasks. Consequently, you don't want to damage the registry by editing the contents carelessly. Always know precisely what a change will do before you make it. Make sure you backup your system and keep copies of any registry settings you change. Although the registry is sensitive to change, you can edit it without mishap as long as you exercise caution.

The registry also contains Windows settings, such as those used to determine which applications to start when you start Windows. This final use causes problems when removing sticky applications—the registry entries can restart the application seemingly without user permission. In fact, to remove a sticky application, you must consider the following types of registry entry:

♦ Startup

♦ Application configuration

♦ Component

Removing the startup registry entries should be your first task. Fortunately, the number of registry locations that Windows uses for startup information is limited, so you don't have to spend hours ensuring the application can't start again, even by mistake. The "Removing Application Tidbits" section of Chapter 6 describes the process of removing these entries in detail.

Once you remove the startup entries, you can concentrate on the application settings. In most cases, you'll want to export these settings first, just in case you need to restore them later or if you need to send them to someone for analysis. The "Using the Registry Editor" section of Chapter 6 tells you how to work with the registry editor so that you can preserve any data you need for later.

The final step is to remove any component entries. The "Removing Files Related to the Application" section gets you started on this task. Unregistering any DLLs that the application uses is a good first step. However, some sticky applications infiltrate the registry with a wealth of component entries that you can't easily locate. To ensure you really have gotten rid of every identifiable piece of that application, you need to open the Registry Editor and perform a search. Use the Start ➢ Run command to display the Run dialog box. Type **RegEdit** and click OK. You'll see the Registry Editor.

To search for any component entries, select the Edit ➢ Find command to display the Find dialog box. Begin by typing the vendor name and clicking Find Next. If the Registry Editor doesn't display anything (the search comes up empty) try the application name and any acronyms that you can think of that are associated with the vendor. Use acronyms carefully because some of them can result in false hits. When you do get a hit, check the registry entries using the techniques described in the "Using the Registry Editor" section of Chapter 6. When you find an entry that matches the sticky application, export the entry and then delete it from the registry.

AVOIDING THE UTILITY CRAZE

You might have noticed the number of utilities used in this chapter so far and you'll see even more in the sections that come. This book contains a number of utilities and sometimes several of each type. The question of which utility to use often comes down to personal preference—it's the same question that many people answer when buying any cleaning product. All of them do more or less the same thing, but there are personal preference issues to address in the selection of a cleaning product.

All of these utilities are humble servants ready to do your bidding. The problem with these utilities is that they all look so useful and appealing that you might find it difficult to decide on a particular utility. In fact, you might accumulate a number of these useful utilities and, like an attic overloaded with treasures of the past, your hard drive will slowly fill with helpful utilities.

The bottom line is that you need to look at the available utilities and then keep only the one utility that best suits your needs. There's no need to keep four or five font management applications on your hard drive when one will do the job. Likewise, you don't need four registry cleaners to fix your registry—you need only one to perform the task.

Sometimes you can go even further to reduce the utility load on your system. One of the best methods is to collect all of the utilities you like and place them on a CD. Label the CD as your utility CD and bring it out whenever you perform maintenance. Even if you have to temporarily place the utility on the hard drive when you perform maintenance, you can still save the hard drive space when you're working on a project.

Discovering Application Uninstall Remains

Even after you ask Windows to uninstall an application using the Add or Remove Programs applet, you haven't completed the task. The problem is that applications leave bits of themselves behind. Sometimes the files and folders are pieces the vendor simply didn't remove. In other cases, though, they include data you'll want to retain for later. In short, the vendor isn't completely to blame for this situation, but it would be nice if the uninstall programs were a little more complete and took care of some of these issues for you.

Archiving Your Personal Settings

Modern versions of Windows encourage you to place your documents in the My Documents folder. In fact, many applications open to this folder when you want to save a document. Therefore, many people wrongly assume that their data is safe when they uninstall an application and are concerned when they see the leftover folders that an application leaves behind. However, there are a number of good explanations for these remnants and an equally number of good reasons why you should archive the files before you delete them from your hard drive.

The fact is that not every application stores your data in My Documents—older applications that don't know about this folder are very likely to store your data in a folder that appears as part of the originally application installation. Consequently, you should never assume that the application folder is empty. Check the installation folder for your data files and archive them as needed.

NOTE Sometimes you'll find a data file that looks like it might contain your data, but you discover that it really doesn't. Such files are usually tutorial or sample files the vendor includes with the product to help you understand how to use it. Before you delete these files, however, check with everyone who might have used your machine to ensure that it doesn't contain someone else's data.

As you traverse the endless folders your application left behind, you might notice a few other files lying around and wonder where they came from. Some applications use special files with an XML or INI extension to hold the application settings. For a long time developers insisted that the registry was the only correct place to put settings, but the recent trend has been back to separate settings folders because the registry has become so packed with information. It's important to archive these settings files because you can restore them later when you reinstall the application. Saving the settings files can reduce the time and effort required to reinstall the application later.

TIP Record the location of any application-specific files that you archive. In some cases, it's simply easier to create a ZIP file with an application that saves the directory structure with the file. The main reason to record the file location within the application hierarchy is to ensure you restore the file to the proper location so it works as anticipated when you reinstall the application. In some cases, knowing the directory structure can also help you diagnose problems with the application (after the fact) or discover more about how the application works.

You might occasionally see a file with the same name as a help file, but with a different extension. For that matter, the application might simply save the help file. When an application allows you to add notes to a help file, it often fails to remove the help file and associated settings during an uninstall. Like the application settings files, you want to save these files for future use. Doing so ensures that you get your notes and other application comments back after you reinstall the application, which reduces the time required to get back up to speed on the application. In fact, you might want to archive additional application comments so that you don't forget things that you take for granted while using the application. For example, note any application quirks that you've successfully overcome.

As you become proficient in using an application, you might develop macros and other add-ins for it. The add-ins will normally reside in separate files within the application folder when they affect the application as a whole, rather than a single document. Like many other files, the application will leave the macros behind after an uninstall, so you can archive them. When you aren't sure whether a file contains macros, open it with a text editor such as Notepad and view the contents. In many cases, you'll see your macro code in plain text, even when the macro file doesn't have a TXT extension.

Removing Unneeded Folders and Files

Many applications leave folders behind after you uninstall them. Generally, you'll find these folders in the \Program Files folder of your machine, but some older applications use a special application-specific folder that you'll find in the root directory of the hard drive. Sometimes all you find after the uninstall program finishes uninstalling is the application directory structure—all of the folders are empty. When you find a folder hierarchy that's empty, you should delete the entire hierarchy by removing the topmost folder in Windows Explorer (this is one case where Windows Explorer is faster and better because you'd have to delete the folders one at a time at the command prompt).

Folders don't consume a large amount of hard drive resources. They do consume a little space within the directory structure, but nothing at all in the data area. You might wonder why you would even remove them. The problem is that folders create visual litter. The empty folders eventually clutter the hard drive so much, that you can't find the files that you need. In short, removing extra folders helps you keep the directory structure trim so that unwanted additions become evident.

Before you delete any folders, make sure they don't contain files. Check every folder in the hierarchy—don't assume anything about the folder. In fact, I usually open a command prompt (because Windows Explorer tends to hide things) and use the Dir *.* /S command to look for files. I then make a second sweep using the `Dir *.* /S /AH` command. The reason you need to use two sweeps is that the first looks for files that are visible and the second looks for files that the application has hidden.

At some point, you'll run into a folder that has files that you don't know anything about and I haven't mentioned them in the "Archiving Your Personal Settings" section of the chapter. Just as there are files you should archive before removing them from your system, there are also files that you should remove without archiving. One such file type is DLLs. An application will sometimes keep updated versions of DLLs in the application folder after an uninstall. The most common cause is that you applied a patch or other fix to the application and the application didn't record the new DLL for removal. Because a patch can do more than simply update files, you should install the application and then the patch when you perform a reinstallation. Otherwise, you can't be certain that the application will work as expected.

Windows also places some files in the application folders that have nothing to do with the applications. In fact, the applications don't even know these files exist. For example, when you see an `MSCREATE.DIR` file in the folder, you know it isn't part of the application, so you can delete it. Windows also has a tendency to place thumbnail files in any folder that includes graphics files, even when the user will never need thumbnails in the folder. Thumbnail files are essentially small versions of the images in a folder so you can see them all at a glance. Finally, depending on how you have Windows setup, you might see a `DESKTOP.INI` file. This particular file contains the Windows Explorer view settings for the folder. If you want to save your view settings in case you reinstall the application, make sure you archive this file. However, given that most people don't spend a lot of time looking through application folders, it's probably best to delete this file. Windows can (and does) create myriad other files, but these are the most common.

DISCOVERING THE UNKNOWN FILE

It's possible that you could run into a file that I haven't discussed in this chapter so far. You might not have any idea of what the file does or whether you need to archive it. Of course, you don't want to delete a file unless you know you won't need it (because Murphy's Law says you'll most assuredly need the file when you do delete it without knowing). You still have a few options for figuring the file out.

First, you can right-click it and choose Properties from the context menu. Select the Version tab (when available) and you'll see a display similar to the one in Figure 4.10. This display usually tells you enough about the file that you know whether you can delete it without harm.

Second, you can look for the file on the Internet—that's right, simply search for it with Google. I normally use the Advanced search page (`http://www.google.com/advanced_search`) and look for the filename using the With the Exact Phrase field. In some cases, when the file turns up too many hits, I'll add Windows XP to the With All of the Words field. If the file proves too popular for even the Windows XP addition, I'll continue to narrow it down by adding an application name or looking for it in a specific domain. The idea is to narrow the search enough so you can determine whether you need to delete or save the file.

Third, you can look for the file in the Microsoft Knowledge Base (`http://support.microsoft.com/default.aspx?scid=fh;EN-US;KBHOWTO`). When you don't find the file here, at least you know that it probably isn't a Microsoft-specific file, but you still aren't completely certain that the application doesn't need the file when you reinstall it.

At this point, you've considered all of the reasonable possibilities. You can probably delete the file safely, but those who are especially paranoid (like me) will probably archive it just to be safe.

Tweaking Application Feature Sets

Installing applications is a time-consuming process that many people hate to perform. After all, there isn't much you can do while waiting for the application to finish installing itself. In addition, the documentation provided with most applications today is terrible. It doesn't tell you about the application features or how to optimize them. The vendor is hoping that you'll just roll over and accept whatever features the vendor thinks are best for you, rather than delve into the application at the outset. However, you need to express an interest in the application from the outset to ensure you get the most out of it when you need it.

One of the worst things you can do is choose either a typical or a full installation of an application unless you really know what those options means. Generally, these automated options give you no choice on which application features the setup will install—leaving you at the vendor's mercy. The vendor is interested in promoting additional purchases from you and making it easy to provide product support when needed. In most cases, the vendor also wants you to create a generic setup that meets the majority of people's needs, rather than a specific setup designed to meet your needs. In short, the vendor has your money and wants to create an environment that reduces potential future contact. (If this viewpoint sounds a tad paranoid, think about it for a moment from the vendor's perspective and you'll see that it makes perfect sense.)

TIP   This section of the chapter describes generic tweaks you can use with Windows and any application that Windows runs. However, most applications also have specific tweaks you could perform. The best place to locate tweaks of this kind is newsgroup or list servers online. Most popular applications, including Windows, have a contingent of dedicated followers who are all too happy to point out interesting tweaks you can perform on your application.

The sections that follow describe some of the issues you should consider when tweaking your application. Generally, when you perform a tweak, you give something up to buy something else. For example, when you remove the demonstration programs from your system, you give up information on add-on products that could solve problems with your current application scenario. Consequently, it's important to consider whether the cost of tweaking a feature is worth the gain you'll receive.

Removing Demonstration Programs

Many vendors assume that if you buy one product from them, you'll likely buy other products as well. That's why many products include demonstration programs of dubious functionality.

Some demonstration programs tell you about the product in slideshow fashion and that's it. If you think that you might have any interest in the product at all, watch the slideshow immediately after you install the product, make notes, and then delete the demonstration program. These slide show demonstrations normally appear in a subdirectory of the application directory. Simply delete the subdirectory and any associated application shortcuts in the Start menu. However, when the demonstration program appears in the main application folder, delete just the demonstration program executable, not the entire directory.

TIP   There's an easy way to locate demonstration program folders on your machine. Right-click the demonstration program shortcut in the Start menu and choose Properties from the context menu. You'll see a Properties dialog box. Select the Shortcut tab and highlight just the directory portion of the Target field. Don't include the application name or the double quotes that surround the entry. Press Ctrl+C to copy this information to the clipboard. Click Cancel to close the Properties dialog box. Select Windows Explorer. Highlight the entry in the Address field and press Ctrl+V to paste the directory information from the clipboard. Press Enter and Windows Explorer will take you directly to the demonstration application folder.

Another type of demonstration program is actually useful, and you'll need to think about removing it. A vendor might include a limited use or reduced functionality version of a program to entice you to buy the full-fledged product. Sometimes the demonstration program provides enough functionality that you can perform useful work with it. For example, a graphics application could come with a special printing program that lets you create color separations. The feature works, but it doesn't provide quite all the widgets the vendor thinks you need. You might find that such a demonstration program provides all you need and will find it useful to retain on your hard drive. However, even a partially useful demonstration that you never use is something to erase from the hard drive. Make sure you don't let receiving free software blind you—remove any partially functional demonstration program that you don't need.

Deleting Training Programs and Sample Files

Vendors include training programs and sample files as a means to reduce support costs and to enhance the illusion that you're getting something of significant value for nothing. Few people ever take the time to complete training programs or work with sample files. However, of the two, it's more common for people to complete a training program because there's less to figure out. The most common use of sample files is as part of working through the examples in a third party book. Authors commonly rely on sample files provided by the vendor so that you don't spend time creating sample files when you should be learning to use the product. The first question you need to ask about installing a training program or series of sample files for an application is whether you'll use them at all. If not, don't install them—both features tend to consume a lot of hard drive space.

When you do decide to work through the vendor training program or tutorial that relies on sample files, you should do it immediately after installing the application. The reason is that you're more likely to complete the training if you set up a scheduled time to do it. When you wait to use the training materials until later, it's likely that you won't get started with them at all or that you will only complete part of the training before you stop due to workload or other influences. Make sure you remove the training program or sample files immediately when you finish working with them—don't wait until later.

TIP   Some people actually use the training programs and sample files as a means for learning a product. In some cases, it's helpful to return to the training program or sample file when you need to remember how to perform a task that you perform infrequently. When this is the case, make sure you archive the training program or sample files before you remove them from the hard drive.

Many applications now provide a means of removing these files as part of the setup program. Make sure you run the setup program first to remove the training program or sample files. However, if you modify the files in any way, the setup program will often tell you it has removed the files, when they really aren't. Consequently, check the required folders on your system to ensure the files are gone when you complete the setup. (Don't assume the setup program will fail—always use the setup program first, and then remove the files to ensure the setup program isn't confused later.)

Sometimes an application won't include the training programs or sample files as part of the setup program. Make sure the application didn't install them as a separate item by looking in the Add or Remove Programs applet on your machine. If you find a separate entry for the training programs or sample files, use the Add or Remove Programs applet to get rid of them. Otherwise, you can simply delete the requisite subdirectory or files in the application directory.

Considering the Features that You Really Use

Everyone is a kid in the candy store when it comes to a new application. You start the setup program and imagine all of the tasks that this new application will perform. When you perform a custom installation (the type you should always perform), the problem becomes worse because you see a list of all of the new features the vendor has provided laid out before your very eyes. It's really too much for the average person to resist, but it's better when you do.

One of the problems that people have with application features is that the setup program doesn't explain them very well. However, the features are explained in other places, and you should take time to learn about them even if you have to do it as part of the installation. One technique to try is to keep the vendor's Web site open so that you can see the feature list and the marketing information the vendor provides about it. Some vendors also include online help files that you can use for reference as you install the product. However, these two sources might not be enough.

Another good place to look is a search engine such as Google. When you can locate product reviews, list server messages, or other sources of hands-on information, you can learn about product features and discover which features you need most. It isn't a matter of saying the feature is good or bad, but whether you need it or not. Certainly, someone will need it, but you might not. For example, if you're an independent developer, you probably don't need the workgroup features provided by a programming language product. However, someone who is working in the corporate environment will very likely need this feature to manage large projects.

TIP Sometimes an application will include features that you can't remove, but don't want to use. You can't recover the hard drive space these features use, in most cases, but you can at least reduce their impact on memory and processing cycles. For example, many users notice the slow speed at which Adobe Acrobat operates across an Internet connection—even a fast connection. The problem is one of too many unnecessary widgets. The PDF SpeedUp for Adobe Reader at http://www.majorgeeks.com/download4294.html is an example of a class of utilities that help you remove unwanted features and speed up an application. You do pay a price in the added hard drive space the utility requires, but this cost is small in comparison to the performance boost such a utility can provide.

Once you know what task a feature actually performs, you can determine whether you'll use it. This might seem like an unnecessary or obvious step, but it's easy to think you'll use a feature until you actually try to accomplish a task with it. When you can't decide how you'll use a feature to accomplish a specific task, it's time to take it off the list of installed features. If you ever find that you have some extra time on your hands for experimentation, you can try installing the feature and testing it out. In the meantime, the feature will only consume hard drive space and potentially other resources that you could use for other tasks.

In a few cases, a feature is useful, but it carries a heavy burden. This is the most difficult kind of feature to decide on because you don't know whether the cost of the feature is worth the investment it requires. Think about it this way: Every feature is going to consume system resources, but you're allowing it to consume those resources because it provides a tangible benefit.

Some features are simply nice to have, but they don't pull their weight when it comes to resources. For example, you might use a word processor that enables you to embed graphics as part of the document. One feature lets you view the graphics rather than a simple placeholder. Because you don't work in the production department (the group that will actually produce the final document), the feature is nice to have, rather than a requirement. The benefit of seeing the graphics in place isn't worth the heavy processing and memory burden the feature places on your system. Using placeholders works fine because you still see the placement of the image on screen.

Discovering When You Get Too Much Help

It's easy to get too many bulky help files installed on your system. I'm a real promoter of using help files, but sometimes an application installs help files you'll never use, especially when you perform a full application installation, rather than a custom application installation. For example, many applications come with supplementary help files that you might need. A common example of this problem is the Word for WordPerfect Users help file that comes with Microsoft Word. Some people install this file even though they have never used WordPerfect.

Another example of a common useless help scenario is installing help in a language you don't understand. Many applications today offer help in a number of languages—each of which is a copy of the information found in the single help file you do need in your language. When you perform a full product installation (or even a typical installation in some cases), Setup places all of these help files on your system even if you don't understand the language the help file is written in.

Newer applications are relatively easy to configure for optimum help support in most cases. Generally, the application setup program will let you remove excess help or your can reconfigure help as part of an application option. Don't assume that you'll see all of the help setup features during the initial installation. Some applications use a separate setup program for the help files that you can access through the Add or Remove Program Files applet in the Control Panel. Start the help setup application to remove the excess help.

Older applications commonly require you to remove the help files manually. The help files reside in the main application directory or within a separate (clearly marked) help file folder. Exercise care in removing a help file, in this case, because a wrong move could delete the entire help file, rather than the excess. Open each of the help files in turn by double-clicking the icon to ensure the help file doesn't contain information you need.

Removing Fonts You Don't Need

One of the least understood problems with most installations is that every application seems to want to install custom fonts. In fact, some applications aren't happy installing just one or two fonts required for a special task, some want to install hundreds of fonts—most of which you'll never use. The problem is significant. Not only do these fonts require hard drive space, but they also use memory and processing cycles when you work with certain classes of applications, such as word processors. It wouldn't be so bad if these applications simply told you the font is available, but the hidden secret is that some applications actually load all of these fonts into memory whether you use them or not.

Unless you're a graphic artist or have some special need such as making greeting cards, you can probably get by with four or five fonts on your system. You don't need hundreds of fonts. The application that tells you that it must have a certain font to work is lying to you. When an application requests a font that Windows doesn't have installed, Windows will automatically substitute the closest possible font. The application is completely unaware that the substitution has taken place, so removing the excess fonts will only help performance and not create a problem for the application.

You do lose two features by removing excess fonts. First, an application designer might use an especially narrow font in order to display a lot of text in a small space. When you remove this custom font, the text consumes the standard amount of space, so you might not be able to see all of the application text with ease. However, this is rarely a problem. Second, you do lose some flexibility from an aesthetic perspective. The fewer fonts installed on your machine, the greater the chance that you won't have the specific font you need to convey a particular message to a business partner. Again, this is an issue that you'll have to consider and perhaps tune your font usage for specific needs.

Using the Fonts Folder

The Fonts Folder provides limited font support. It lets you view fonts, install new fonts, remove old fonts, and perform a few font comparisons. You can find this folder in the Control Panel. Figure 4.11 shows a typical view of the Fonts Folder.

This view shows every font file in the folder. The Large and List views show you just the filenames and aren't particularly useful when locating files you want to delete. The Details view shown in Figure 4.11 is the option of choice when you want to locate large files to delete. Notice that the figure shows the files organized by size. In this case, the largest font file is 479KB.

FIGURE 4.11

Perform simple font management using the features of the Fonts folder.

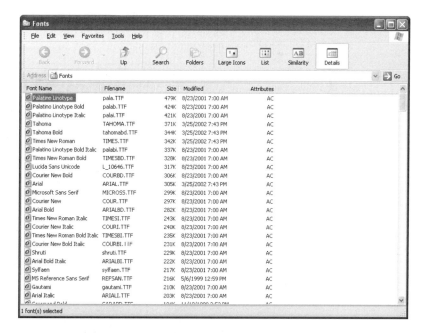

Unfortunately, deleting a font isn't as simple as looking for the biggest files. For one thing, Windows requires multiple files to create a single font in most cases. A font that includes bold and italics versions requires four font files: normal, bold, italics, and bold/italics (combined). The Palatino font shown in Figure 4.11 actually requires four files and the total savings of removing this font is 1.6MB.

It might sound as if removing the Palatino font would be a good idea. However, there's another question to answer. You need to consider whether there's a good replacement for that font on the system when you use the font for decorative or other reasons. The Similarity view shown in Figure 4.12 helps you determine which fonts are closest to Palatino. The Book Antiqua font is very similar to Palatino according to Windows and it only requires 593KB or about a third of the space that Palatino requires.

You don't know that Book Antiqua is a good match though. To see how the Book Antiqua font looks, double-click the icon. Figure 4.13 shows how the Book Antiqua font looks.

Once you determine that you have found a good replacement for the font, you can delete the large font from your system. Make sure you highlight all of the font file entries, right-click the selection, and choose Delete. Windows will ask whether you're sure that you want to delete the fonts. Click Yes. Unfortunately, Windows hasn't deleted the fonts yet—they're stored in your Recycle Bin.

NOTE You can't delete some fonts even though they're immense and you don't see any need to keep them around. For example, the Tahoma font normally registers an error when you try to remove it from the system. It's also important to keep some standard fonts such as Courier and the various symbol fonts handy for use within applications designed to use them.

As it turns out, storing the fonts in the Recycle Bin isn't a bad idea when you know which application installed the font. You can try the application with the replacement font to determine whether it works as well as you had hoped. If so, simply empty the Recycle Bin—if not, you can restore the font to its former location. Just open the Recycle Bin, highlight the font files, right-click the selected entries, and choose Restore from the context menu.

FIGURE 4.12
Look for a similar font before you perform any font deletions.

FIGURE 4.13
Sight verify that the replacement font will work as a replacement for a font you want to delete.

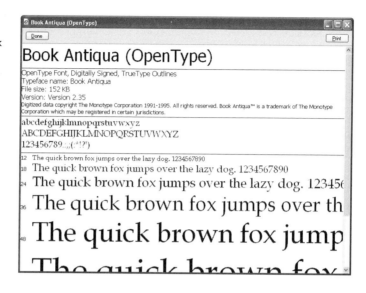

Using FontView

The FontView utility you download at http://meesoft.logicnet.dk/FontView/index2.php isn't so much a font management utility as a font viewing utility. One of the problems with the Fonts folder is that you have to open each file individually to see what it looks like. Using FontView, you can see all of the fonts at once, as shown in Figure 4.14.

FIGURE 4.14
Use FontView when you want to get a good look at the fonts on your system.

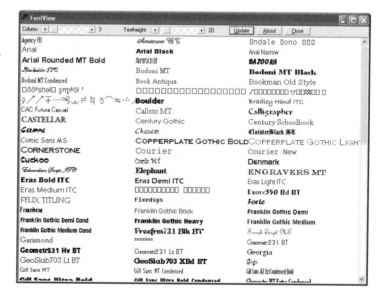

You can combine FontView with the Fonts folder to create a good management tool for fonts. Neither product is complete, but the FontView price is right and its addition to the Fonts folder makes managing fonts a lot easier. This combination works best when you use fonts occasionally and only need to check your font list after a new application installation.

Using Font Runner

Using Font Runner makes managing fonts considerably easier than using the Fonts folder because you can work with the entire font, rather than individual font folders. In addition, you can create various test scenarios to see how the font will work in a standard environment.

This is a good utility for someone who works with fonts occasionally or has more than one machine to manage. You download Font Runner at `http://www.fontrunner.com/fontrunner/`.

When you start Font Runner, it displays a window with a test phrase, but without any fonts loaded. Fonts can actually appear anywhere on your system, not just the Fonts folder, so this feature makes the application more flexible. To see the installed fonts, those that do appear in the Fonts folder, click View Installed Fonts. Figure 4.15 shows a typical view of the Font Runner window.

The left side of the display lets you select other folders on the machine. You can even choose folders on networked drives and view their content, making it possible for network administrators to manage fonts on all of the machines accessible from the network without leaving their desk.

The upper right pane contains a list of fonts in the current folder. Notice that the list shows the font name using the font, so you can make a quick determination of which fonts you want to test. The list shows just the font name, not the list of font files. To see the standard Windows font display shown in Figure 4.13, right-click the font entry and choose Open from the context menu. This context menu also contains options to install the font and to view the font information. You can't use this utility to remove fonts—use the Fonts folder to remove fonts that you don't want.

FIGURE 4.15
Use Font Runner when you need complete system management of fonts.

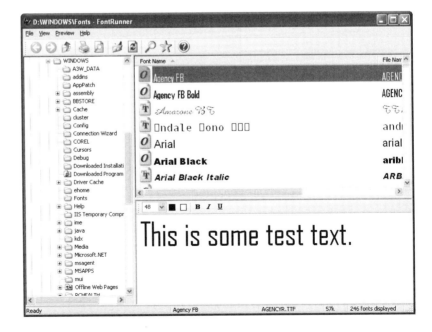

The lower right pane contains a test phrase that you want to use. You can right-click this pane to adjust the font display. This display includes setting italics and bold, as well as changing the font color and background. The display makes it easier to see the font as it will appear in the environment in which you'll use it. Consequently, you can make better decisions on which fonts to remove or keep.

Using FontFrenzy

FontFrenzy is the complete replacement for the Fonts folder in this section. You can download it at `http://www.fontfrenzy.org/`. This utility is one of the best offerings there is for several reasons. First, you can restore a previous font configuration with a touch of a button—none of the other font management strategies comes close to this level of convenience. Second, you can use this single utility to test, check, view, install, and delete fonts on your system. Figure 4.16 shows a typical view of this utility.

To begin using this utility on the local machine, select the View ≻ Installed Fonts command. FontFrenzy will display all of the installed fonts on the current machine. You can select fonts on other machines by clicking FrenzyMan on the toolbar, selecting the View Fonts in a Folder option in the left pane, and clicking Select. The font folder you select appears in the right pane. To see a particular font, select FrenzyInfo on the toolbar and double-click the font entry. FontFrenzy will display a new window with the list of characters for that font.

Before you begin modifying the current font list, click FrenzySnap. This feature lets you save a snapshot of the current font setup so you can restore it later using the Refrenzy option. When you want to restore the font list to those originally shipped with Windows, select the Defrenzy option. FontFrenzy will save the files you remove and you can delete them from the hard drive later. The idea is to ensure your applications will work with just the original Windows fonts (business applications normally will).

FIGURE 4.16
Select FontFrenzy when you need a complete font management utility.

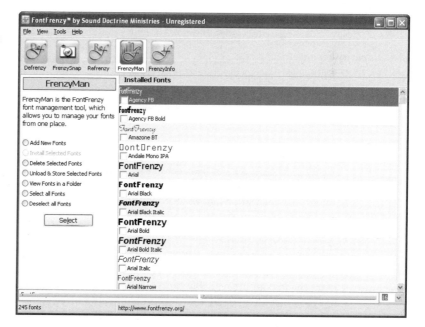

As you can see from Figure 4.16, you can also work with individual fonts. You can remove them or add new fonts as needed. In short, FontFrenzy is a great utility for someone who needs to manage many machines and perform font management quickly. It also provides a complete environment for people who use fonts as part of their work.

Controlling Processing Cycle Usage

An essential part of any optimization process is controlling the processor. The processor should be available for your applications to use. When it isn't, you have to question just how the system is using the processor. In fact, non-user-application processor usage is a significant problem on most systems today. You might find that other processes are stealing the processor cycles you need for the following activities:

◆ Background tasks such as downloads

◆ System monitoring tasks such as those performed by agents

◆ Virus activity

◆ Other monitoring tasks such as those performed by spyware and adware

◆ Configuration problems such as a failure to install the correct drivers

◆ Hardware problems such as motherboard setup problems

Before you go much further, it's important to determine whether you actually have a processor cycle usage problem. The best way to perform this task without breaking out a host of monitoring applications is to right-click the Taskbar and choose Task Manager from the context menu. Select the Performance tab and you'll see a display similar to the one shown in Figure 4.17. This particular display shows two processors, but it works the same for single processor machines.

NOTE   Windows 9x users will notice that they don't have Task Manager directly available the way Windows NT and above users do. To display the Task Manager in Windows 9x, press Ctrl+Alt+Del. The resulting dialog box shows which applications are running on your system. Unfortunately, Windows 9x does lack some features found on newer Windows versions. For example, you can't track the amount of memory each application uses or overall system performance using Task Manager.

NOTE   Windows 2000 users will notice that they don't have a Networking tab like the one shown in Figure 4.17. Although this book doesn't use that tab very often, it does come in handy when you need to optimize remote applications or those that use resources on other machines. To gain the same functionality in Windows 2000, you need to rely on the System Monitor snap-in of the Performance console located in the Administrative Tools folder of the Control Panel.

Let your system become idle—don't touch the mouse or keyboard. After a few seconds, the CPU Usage indicator in the upper left corner should read somewhere between 0 percent and 5 percent. When your system idles at this level, your system doesn't have a processor usage problem. Your system has the maximum available processing cycles for the foreground application. However, when your system won't zero out, there's a problem, but it need not be a concern.

FIGURE 4.17
Determine whether your machine has a processor usage problem before you begin troubleshooting it.

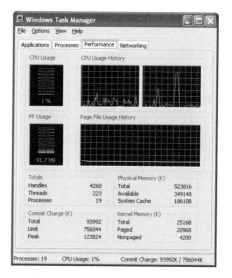

The first issue to consider is whether you have other tasks running. For example, your system won't zero out when you have a download occurring in the background. Wait until the download completes and try checking processor cycle usage again. Background tasks always require processing cycles. However, this is a good time to determine how much processor that background task is consuming. You might find that you want to run it at a different time (such as during lunch when your system isn't otherwise engaged).

Another problem that you might encounter is a hardware or driver problem. For example, some motherboards in the past didn't implement some advanced features correctly, resulting in a 50 percent processor usage indication at all times, even though the processor wasn't actually working that much. (See the Microsoft Knowledge Base article at http://support.microsoft.com/?kbid=241532 for one example of this problem.)

Drivers can also cause problems. An incorrect driver can increase system processor usage significantly and in this case, the processor is actually working at that pace. One such example of this problem is the Microsoft Knowledge Base article at http://support.microsoft.com/?kbid=822603.

A high processor usage indication can even occur as the result of outside sources such as Denial of Service (DOS) attack. Learn more from the Microsoft Knowledge Base article at http://support.microsoft.com/?kbid=273854.

When you're part of a corporate environment, the administrator could install agents on your system to perform special tasks. One of the most common tasks is background backup—this feature helps protect your data from harm, but the cost is the use of some system resources. Check with your administrator when you're not sure whether your system has an agent installed.

Sometimes, high background processor usage is an indication of something far more nefarious. Viruses are the worst offender, but you also need to consider how much the spyware that you might have accidentally downloaded is costing you. Even though adware downloads and installs with your knowledge, it also works continuously in the background, burning up processing cycles and other resources that you could use for other purposes. Chapter 10 discusses these problems in detail and provides you with information you can use to rid yourself of these system resource leaches.

Let's Start Cleaning

This chapter has outlined a number of application optimization techniques. Not all of these techniques result in faster computer operation—many simply return resources that you would have otherwise gotten had the application install or uninstall utility worked properly. Some techniques do result in a performance gain, but usually at a loss of something else. In fact, a major consideration of any optimization technique is that you don't get something for nothing—a gain in one place usually costs something else, well, except for getting rid of those excess uninstall files on your system. The one piece of information that you should take away from this chapter is that you can usually do better than the automation provided with an application can at optimizing a setup for your specific needs.

Your goal, once you complete this chapter, is to optimize the applications on your machine and to optimize the future installations that you perform. Sometimes, optimization means removing an application that you really don't need, but in many other cases it means defining which application features you really use and getting rid of everything else. An application optimized for your needs might not make sense to someone else—their needs are different from yours. Consequently, knowing what you need to perform your tasks is essential. Keeping track of what you use can help in achieving the goal of an optimized machine.

Chapter 5 discusses various kinds of data archiving. Don't assume that data archiving is simply storing documents away for later. Sometimes you have to store the document context, the application settings, templates, or other tools used to create the document as well. Archiving can also mean saving the conversations used to create a document or the note you took while creating the document. The form of archiving you perform is also important. Chapter 5 discusses all of these issues and arms you with the information you need to make good archiving decisions.

Chapter 5

Saving Data for Later

Some people wrongly equate the term *data* with something they have created such as a document. Data can mean any assembly of computer information bits that you want it to be. You can use the term *data* to refer to materials you download from the Internet or the settings files created by an application. For that matter, applications are a form of data—they're simply a binary (or computer formatted) kind of data. Data does include the documents and other files you create, but don't limit the suggestions in this chapter to that small subset. It's possible to save any kind of data you want for later use.

I was watching television the other day and a guy came on screen with a miracle system for compressing bulky items like sweaters and comforters using a special plastic bag and a vacuum. He showed a closet in a shocking state of disarray. The goal was to store more stuff in a smaller space. The commercial ended by showing a neat version of the same closet—all made possible by this miracle device. Computer hard drives are a lot like closets and most of them are in a shocking state of disarray. Compression utilities can serve the same purpose as this miracle device on television—they can help you make better use of the space and enhance the appearance of your hard drive.

Eventually, no matter how many gizmos you use, the closet in your home is filled and you need a storage shed to store more stuff. Offline computer storage serves the same purpose. You move the compressed data files from your hard drive to a Compact Disk (CD), Digital Video Disk (DVD), tape, or other storage device for later use. Of course, not all storage media is equal. Just as any storage shed can have leaks and can cause damage to your household goods, offline computer storage eventually loses contact with your data and damages it. Unfortunately, just as these storage sheds don't advertise the fact that they're leaky, computer storage media tends to make claims that the facts don't support.

Email presents a special problem for archiving because you use it daily and it accumulates fast. Making things even more interesting—it's hard to find a cutoff point for some types of email so you can archive it easily. Often the result of filing email for too long is chaos that you can't quickly clean up. Email is a data store that requires constant vigilance and maintenance if you want to make it useful.

TIP The most important principle of organizing anything—small kitchen appliances, bank records, a mechanic's tools, whatever—is that items you use frequently need to be easily at hand, while items you use infrequently should be out of the way, but secure. The same rule applies to electronic files.

Compressing Data Files

Unlike the vacuum-pack metaphor I used earlier, applications don't fill data files with air—you can't press them down to remove extra content because normally there isn't any extra content. Data compression often involves a more subtle approach. For example, when you have five spaces in a row, you could simply come up with a code that says there are five spaces. The code might require two bytes versus the five bytes used by the spaces. This is just one of many compression techniques.

WARNING   Never attempt to compress files on your system using the Windows built-in support with any applications open (except Windows Explorer). Always close every application to ensure the compression feature works as intended. This warning is especially important when you choose to compress an entire drive because Windows won't compress open files.

The actual file compression methods aren't nearly as important for optimizing Windows as the results. Some files, such as documents and most graphics, compress quite well, but others, such as executable files (applications) don't compress much at all. Consequently, the amount of disk space savings you receive from using the techniques in the sections that follow depends on how well the files compress and on the technique you choose (many file compression utilities have a series of minimum to maximum compression settings).

TIP   If you want to learn more about data compression, the Internet contains a wealth of resources. This topic is extremely important because other technologies such as communication rely on compression. You'll find a good introductory overview of this topic on Howstuffworks at `http://www.howstuffworks.com/file-compression.htm`. If you prefer a question and answer format, check the Compression FAQ Index at `http://www.faqs.org/faqs/compression-faq/`. A more advanced compression reference (one that is technically precise but a tad hard to read) appears on the Introduction to Data Compression site at `http://www.faqs.org/faqs/compression-faq/part2/section-1.html`. You'll also find benchmarks for timing how long it takes compression utilities to work and discussions of the best compression technique to use for a particular need. All of these discussions are interesting to read, but the bottom line is that you still end up with more space on your hard drive.

Setting Compression Options for a Drive

Windows includes a compression setting for your files. You can choose to compress the entire drive, a single folder, or just one file. My recommendation is that you always compress the entire drive. The compression feature supplied with Windows works quickly and the advantages of compressing the entire drive are too great to ignore. Even on drives that only contain applications; you can always get some level of increased hard drive space from data compression. It's typical to see an increase in the 40 percent range, but the amount you see depends on the kind of files you want to compress.

NOTE   Before you read about it elsewhere, some people don't like data compression because they think it slows their system down. Truthfully, there's a small performance penalty from one perspective and a small performance gain from another to consider. The small performance penalty is the time required to compress or decompress files as needed in the background. When working with small files, you'll never even notice this time. The performance gain comes from the time saved reading the data from the hard drive. A compressed file requires fewer hard disk reads (which are somewhat slow compared to other data transfers), so you get a small performance gain. In general, these performance changes are so small that you won't notice them.

To compress an entire hard drive, right-click the drive and select Properties from the context menu. Choose the General tab. Check the Compress Drive to Save Disk Space option as shown in Figure 5.1. When you click OK, Windows will ask how you want the change applied. For example, you could apply it just to the root directory of the drive. Select the entire drive to obtain the highest optimization benefit.

NOTE Windows will likely report that it can't compress some files. When asked what to do about these files, select the Ignore option. Windows can't compress some files because they're always in use or because Windows needs them in the uncompressed state. For example, Windows can't compress the paging file because this file is always in use and it would be dangerous to compress paged memory that is constantly changing.

Make sure you set Windows to display compressed files in an alternate color so you can see the results of the compression. To set the alternative color, choose the Tools ➤ Folder Options command in Windows Explorer. Select the View tab of the Folder Options dialog box and check the Show Encrypted or Compressed NTFS Files in Color option. When you click OK, Windows Explorer will use the new color setting.

FIGURE 5.1
Compress the entire drive to obtain the maximum optimization benefit.

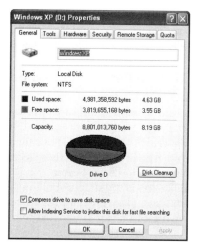

Compressing Individual Files

Sometimes you might not be able to compress all of the files on a machine due to company policy, bad experiences in the past, application compatibility problems, or any number of other reasons. I haven't actually seen or heard of any problems with compression on Windows XP, but it's conceivable that these problems do exist. Even when you run into a problem where you can't compress all of the files, you can compress individual files. For example, you might choose to compress all of the data files for your application but keep the application itself uncompressed.

You can use two levels of compression for individual files: folder level or file level. To compress a folder, right-click it and choose Properties from the context menu. On the General tab of the folder Properties dialog box, click Advanced. You'll see an Advanced Attributes dialog box like the one shown in Figure 5.2. Check the Compress Drive to Save Disk Space option as shown in Figure 5.2 and click OK twice to close the dialog boxes.

FIGURE 5.2
Compress individual files to gain a performance advantage when you can't compress the whole drive.

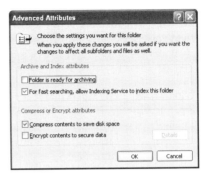

Compressing an individual file works the same as a folder. You'll find the Compress Drive to Save Disk Space option in the Advanced Attributes dialog box shown in Figure 5.2. The only difference is that you'll compress just one file, rather than all of the files in a folder.

TIP   You can also use the technique in this section to uncompress a folder or an individual file after you compress the entire drive. Perhaps a file has just the right content that file compression doesn't work very well, yet loading and unloading the file is slow due to the file compression. In this case, clear the check from the Compress Drive to Save Disk Space option shown in Figure 5.2. The rest of the drive will remain compressed—Windows will only uncompress the selected file.

Locating Hidden Data Compression Features

Many applications have data compression features. However, these features normally perform a different kind of data compression than reducing the size of the file using a compression technique. For example, a Database Management System (DBMS) can compress a file by removing empty records. The DBMS allocated these records at one time to fulfill a user request. However, at some point, the user deleted other records and now those record slots are blank. To recover the space used by the file, you must perform a file compression.

You'll find DBMS in the strangest places on your hard drive. For example, Outlook Express is a kind of DBMS. It includes a file compression feature, but you have to look to find it. In fact, this feature resides in two places: one for automated compression and the other for manual compression.

To tell Outlook Express to compress the folders automatically, select the Tools ➢ Options command. Select the Maintenance tab and you'll see the options shown in Figure 5.3. Pay particular attention to this dialog box because it's set up to work with my system—these aren't the default settings. For example, Microsoft assumes that simply because you place an item in the Deleted Items folder it doesn't mean you actually want to remove it. Check the Empty Messages from Deleted Items Folder on Exit option to ensure that these files actually go away at some point.

FIGURE 5.3

Select the options you want to use to compress files on your system automatically.

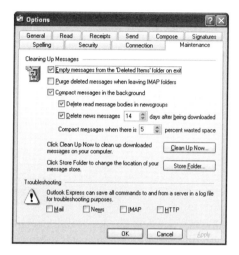

A few of the options are a little less straightforward. For example, the Compact Messages in the Background option looks like it's worthwhile because it lets you compact the messages without any added effort. The only problem with this option is that it takes the compression schedule out of your hands. You might be working on something important when compression begins and notice the drag on system resources. Generally, the performance loss isn't very big, so I keep it checked, but people with resource starved systems will probably want to clear this option and compress the files manually.

To perform a manual file compression in Outlook Express, select folder you want compress. Choose the File menu and look for the Folder submenu. You'll see two options: Compress and Compress All Folders. When you select Compress, Outlook Express removes excess space from the selected folder. On the other hand, when you select Compress All Folders, Outlook Express displays a Compressing dialog box and lists all of the folders as it compresses them.

Sometimes application-level data compression results from the kind of files you use. For example, when you work with a Tagged Image File Format (TIFF or TIF), you can store the image in uncompressed format or use one of several compression techniques. A committee standardized the compression techniques for the file so that everyone could read it. The application normally offers to compress the file for you using one of the acceptable compression techniques.

The only problem is that the option to compress a file isn't always obvious. For example, the Save As dialog box shown in Figure 5.4 shows four compression methods for the TIFF. Unfortunately, the field is labeled as Sub Type, not compression method, so some users will miss this option. Given that the default for this application is uncompressed, you'll find that most of these files will end up rather large.

FIGURE 5.4
Look for compression options whenever you save graphics files.

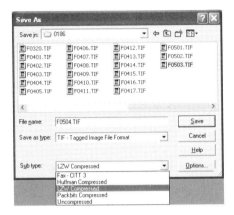

Making the compression picture murkier still is the fact that different compression methods have different results. In addition, the compression ratio can differ from image to image because each image has a different level of complexity. Some compression methods are also called "lossy" because you can lose some image details when using them. A typical user won't notice the loss in the image, but the loss of detail can eventually make the image unusable. Table 5.1 shows some statistics for a simple screenshot using different compression methods (including none at all) with a TIFF.

It's important to note that I selected a standardized file format that has been around for a long time. Other graphics file formats can become even more difficult to decipher. The point is that the application provides the resource required to compress the files, but hides it (in plain sight no less).

TABLE 5.1:   Comparing Compression Ratios Using Different Methods

COMPRESSION METHOD	FILE SIZE	AMOUNT OF COMPRESSION	LOSSES
Uncompressed	483KB	0%	None
Fax – CITT3	14.7KB	96.95%	Color and Detail
Huffman Compressed	14.7KB	96.95%	Color and Detail
LZW Compressed	41.5KB	91.41%	None
Packedbits Compressed	259KB	46.38%	None

Long-Term versus Short-Term Storage

The terms *long* and *short* are both ambiguous and changing. The reason I mention this is that I chose this section title with care. Most people have some idea of what they mean by long and short, but the definition for long and short for someone else might be different. In addition, long and short take different meanings based on content. A payoff period of 15 years is short for a mortgage on a home, but quite long for a credit card, even though both reflect some type of repayment option for a debt. Consequently, when you discuss the storage time frame for archived material, you need to use concrete terms such as five years—measures that don't leave the length of storage in doubt.

WARNING   Short-term storage often extends into long-term storage despite the best efforts of the people maintaining the archive. Sometimes legal requirements or other pressures dictate a longer storage cycle for archived data. Whenever you create an archive, note the time interval that the archive is intended to work as part of the package. Doing so ensures that anyone handling the archive knows the "expiration" date of the data the archive contains.

You'll also find that there aren't any perfect storage solutions. Every storage solution has special advantages and some equally terrible disadvantages. For example, when you work with tapes, you get a lot of storage space in an incredibly small space, but tape drives are incredibly slow. They're so slow, in fact, that network administrators are looking for something, anything, to replace them. So far, no solution has magically appeared to take tape's place. In short, don't assume that any of these solutions are better than the others—a solution is simply better in a given circumstance.

TIP   One of the more interesting sites for data backup and recovery is the USByte.com site at `http://www.usbyte.com/index_recovery.htm`. The site offers a number of interesting topics on everything from how to keep your media in good condition to fixing problems once they do occur. Of course, the focus of the site is the company's main business, recovering data from broken media.

The Amazing Disintegrating CD

Many people now consider the CD the best archive media on the planet aside from DVD. The CD is certainly the least expensive way to archive data (especially compared to DVD) and it requires very little storage space (hard drives are the bulkiest). CDs are also relatively fast, especially when compared to tapes and most people understand how to use them. However, the CD is also somewhat unreliable and prone to damage. A single mistake could corrupt the data from an entire project.

Several recent trade press stories have highlighted a number of problems with CD technology. The problem is that you can read these trade press stories and not come away with the whole story or become confused by conflicting claims. Obviously, scratches are a problem, so you should protect your CDs with the appropriate covers and handling. Most people understand this well-known problem with CDs, but think that with safe handing, their CD will last 100 years or more. For example, the MAM-A Gold Standard CD-R is supposed to last around 200 years (`http://www.inkjetart.com/mitsui/`).

However, other problems have become known that significantly challenge the idea of a CD that lasts 100 years (much less more). Some CDs are literally disintegrating. There are a number of reasons for this problem, but many of them come down to mild mishandling or simply age.

Here's the crux of the problem: the media can't decide where the problem lies or whether there's a problem at all. For example, the article at `http://peripherals.about.com/library/weekly/aa041701a.htm` makes it sound as if the people who are discussing this issue have gotten the story all wrong. Supposedly, the CDs are being mishandled, in every case, and they really will last a long time when handled properly. Even the article's author admits that some CDs are probably not good for more than five years when stored in the best conditions. This is a great article because it does provide solid advice on how to protect your CD investment.

TIP Sometimes an ounce of prevention is really worth a pound of cure. You can still use CDs for archives that will last five years or less. However, with the current problems with CD technology, it's better to make two archive copies of the data. This technique doubles the chance that one copy will survive, even if one does go bad. To reduce the potential for problems further, make one archive from a CD from one vendor and the second archive from a CD from a second vendor.

An eWeek article at http://www.eweek.com/article2/0,1759,1592925,00.asp appears to take the middle ground on the topic. Not only does this article discuss CD problems, it also discusses potential DVD problems. The author offers some excellent advice on how to avoid problems and even considers how future technologies could overcome the problems of today. If nothing else, make sure you read articles of this type with an eye toward understanding the issues and discovering possible cures.

The source of one problem is the glue used to hold the back of the coating on the top of the CD. Some people write on the top using a standard pen, which instantly destroys the data beneath the writing by damaging the glue and the media it holds. However, sometimes it's simply a matter of the glue letting loose. The second the glue loses adhesion, the silver coating used to store the data is damaged, resulting in data loss.

Another source of problems is fading dye. Leaving your CD out where the sun can hit it is definitely a bad idea, but the dye can also fade when you store a CD in the proper conditions. The article at http://www.rense.com/general52/themythofthe100year.htm explains how dye failure can occur with both CDs and to a lesser extent, DVDs. In short, a number of environmental problems beyond your control can damage the CDs you depend on for data storage.

Speed Issues Using Tape Drives

Tape drives are one of the oldest backup technologies available today. You can find tape drives in a number of sizes and capacities. In fact, tape drive vendors constantly work to increase the capacity of tape drives. You'd be hard pressed to find another media that can store as much data as a single tape drive. In addition, from a bytes per dollar perspective, tape drives are extremely cheap. Of course, because they hold so much data, tapes still cost considerably more than CDs. You can buy a CD for less than a dollar, but a tape will cost twenty dollars or more. Of course, the capacity of that tape is usually measured in GB (1,024MB) or TB (1,024GB) to the 650MB that the typical CD holds.

NOTE To give you an idea of how much data a tape can store, the older technology Digital Audio Tape (DAT) drive on my server holds 48GB on each tape. That's enough to store all of the documents on my system and the application settings as well (it's not enough to store the applications themselves). My DAT drive is an incredibly good deal from a cost per GB perspective—cheaper even than CDs. In addition, the package for this tape is incredibly small—smaller than a CD, so it packs a lot of data in a very small space.

Most people consider tapes one of the most reliable storage technologies when you want to create a backup for two years or less. Tapes have relatively long lives and known storage requirements. With good care, a tape can last ten years and sometimes more, but most experts agree that you should replace them within two years of first use for optimum performance. Using tape means that you won't run into anything unexpected because they have been in use for so long.

However, tape does require the proper storage conditions. You don't want to store tapes where there's high humidity or temperatures. Keeping dust at bay (usually with a good case) is also essential. The life of the tape depends on how often you use it and the conditions in which you store it.

Tape drives also experience wear that optical media such as CDs don't because the tape physically contacts the tape head, capstan, and other drive components. Because these parts wear, you theoretically need to replace them more often than other types of devices. In practice, however, technology changes faster than the drives wear out—you'll likely replace a tape drive because it has become outdated.

The biggest problem with tape is that it's incredibly slow. Tape vendors are also working on this problem, but there's only so much you can do with a media that requires physical contact between the tape head and the tape. In addition, tapes are a serial access device, which means you must read them from beginning to end. When you need data at the beginning of the tape, the tape reader searches from the current position to the very beginning of the tape before reading the data you need. Hard drives and other random access media go directly to the location of the data you need—no reading of the intermediate data.

Tapes are also approaching the end of the technology life cycle. For example, vendors have reduced the thickness of tapes so they can put more data into a smaller space. A thin tape consumes less space than a thick one. However, thin tapes are also easier to damage, so vendors have had to add all kinds of new technology to the drives to handle the tape properly. Many tape vendors now see an end to the technology advances they can make. The eWeek articles at `http://www.eweek.com/article2/0,1759,1583336,00.asp` and `http://www.eweek.com/article2/0,1759,1627778,00.asp` sum up many of the advantages of using tapes and some of the concerns for advancements in the future.

Reliability Issues Using Hard Drives

Hard drives represent the fastest method of backup today. A direct hard drive-to-hard drive backup gets the job done in minutes rather than hours. In fact, some home users actually have a second hard drive installed in their system for the sole purpose of backup. Obviously, this isn't the best way of doing things, but it does work and it points out the perceived speed advantages that a hard drive provides. Fortunately, you can install systems that combine the advantages of hard drive with the need to provide a removable media. For example, the Dual Drive Backup System (`http://www.jrwhipple.com/prod_dualdrives.html`) provides this feature.

For the most part, hard drives also represent the easiest method of creating a backup and because the hard drive is always in place, you can completely automate the entire backup process. Some people will view this ease of use as the main reason to use a hard drive backup system. It's true: the high speed, availability, and ease of use are very tempting.

From a cost perspective, hard drives are the most expensive way to backup your system—at least when you compare cost per MB of data saved. Hard drive vendors are constantly working on this problem, so you might eventually see a hard drive backup system that rivals CDs in the cost department. However, both technologies have a long way to go to reap the cost benefits of tape. Many large corporations still use tape for this reason—it's very inexpensive.

TIP   Make sure you consider hard drive–like solutions. In general, these solutions are slightly more reliable than a hard drive and offer slightly slower data rates (how fast the drive can move information to and from the machine). The cost of these drives is slightly higher than hard drives, but the benefits are often worth it. For example, Iomega provides a number of interesting drives—you can read about one of them at `http://www.graphics.com/modules.php?name=News&file=print&sid=2301`. also provides the well-known ZIP drive that you can read about at `http://www.iomega.com/zip/`.

Hard drives are also the least reliable method of backing up your system. They aren't very shock resistant—an unfortunate bump can cause you to lose your entire backup. Hard drives overheat easily, experience problems from myriad mechanical parts inside, and are generally fragile. Even with drives that vendors design to move from one location to another (such as the Olixir at `http://www.olixir.com/`), you have to exercise extreme care because the hard drive simply isn't very robust.

WARNING   Beware of the external hard drive solution. Yes, it appears that you'll get all of the speed benefits of a hard drive, combined with portability and the ability to use the same device on multiple machines, but it seldom works out that way. When an external solution relies on a common port type such as the Universal Serial Bus (USB), you're often limited in transfer speed, making the hard drive just a little faster than a tape backup. On the other hand, proprietary port solutions often come close to matching internal hard drive transfer speeds, but at the cost of portability—every machine has to have the proprietary port. In addition, external hard drive solutions can be extremely expensive. One indisputable value of an external device is that it doesn't run all the time, making it's life expectancy longer than devices that reside in your machine all of the time.

Compatibility is another problem for hard drives. The most compatible solution in the world today is the CD, followed by the tape drive. Both of these systems use standardized formats and the media readers are relatively easy to obtain. Hard drives rely on unique setups that are usually vendor specific. When you don't have a drive from a particular vendor available, you're simply out of luck.

PERFORMING BACKUPS THE CHEAP WAY

Someone is almost certainly wondering why I haven't mentioned something less expensive than CD burners, tape drives, or even hard drives in this chapter. There's a cheap solution, but it's also unreliable and quite painful to use—the floppy disk. Yes, it only stores 1.44MB at a time, but the floppy can backup your data with the right backup program. It can even perform the task inexpensively and could possibly provide a solution for someone who has only one machine to consider.

However, I don't recommend using floppies for backup. They pose a number of problems, not the least of which is finding a place to store them. A floppy backup can consume a large number of disks even on a single system when you perform a proper backup. Floppies are subject to more damage than other media described in this chapter, making them the least reliable option. Because you have to swap floppies in and out of the system, they're also time consuming, making it less likely that someone will backup a system faithfully.

At one time, long ago, people considered floppies an acceptable form of backup because data files were smaller, as were hard drives. Today, however, systems are larger and store a lot more data than ever before. Although you could use floppies as an extremely cheap backup method, I encourage you to try one of the other solutions described in the chapter.

Temporary Storage Online

Modern computer users have a solution that didn't exist in the past—temporary online storage. This solution requires you to set up an account with an online storage vendor such as IBackup (`http://www.ibackup.com/`) or XDrive (`http://www.xdrive.com/`). A few of these solutions are even free, such as Free Online Storage (`http://www.emailaddresses.com/email_storage.htm`). The main appeal of this solution is convenience. You don't have to install any special hardware, create backup schedules, or invest in a supply of backup media. There isn't anything special to learn and the vendor takes care of all the details for you. In fact, it can be a low cost solution to creating a backup so long as you don't have to pay for connection time to the Internet.

TIP Free might sound great, but it isn't necessarily a good deal. When you use an online storage solution, make sure you find one that guarantees specific levels of up time (a time frame when you can connect and work with the online data). In addition, make sure the vendor guarantees that your data will be safe, that you'll receive compensation when something damages your data, and that the vendor will protect the data from prying eyes. None of the free sites I checked will offer such guarantees, making them unsuitable for most data archiving needs. You could use such a site, however, as a temporary data store while on the road or for noncritical data stored on a home computer.

Although this sounds like a perfect solution to the problem of archiving your data, it isn't. You have a number of hurdles to overcome and some issues you can't solve—at least not easily. The biggest problem is security. Whenever you place your data on someone else's machine, you have to assume that they can access it. Even if you encrypt the data and protect it in other ways, you can't assume that data is safe. Consequently, you don't want to put the data for your latest invention on such a system, nor would you want to put your company's finances there. This kind of storage is only good for the kind of data that the public will likely know about anyway.

Another problem is reliability. If your system experiences a catastrophic failure, it's going to be very hard to get online to restore the data. You also can't guarantee that the online storage vendor won't suffer some type of connectivity problem. An Internet glitch or other problem could make the site unavailable, which means you're completely vulnerable during the time the communication problem persists. Any loss of connectivity can easily translate into lost employee productivity and a lot of wasted time.

Transfer speed is another problem. If you think tape is slow, even the slowest tape is going to be faster than an Internet connection. Even a high-speed connection is lower than any tape drive on the market. You'll spend considerable time making backups and restores will take even longer. Consequently, any savings you experience due to reduced hardware and maintenance costs could get eaten by the time required to perform simple archiving tasks.

Cataloging and Archiving Data

You need to provide some means of intermediate storage. For example, you might know that you don't need the data today, but you'll need it within the next six months. It might be easier to place that data in intermediate storage so that it's available quickly, but still consumes less space than normal. In addition to the intermediate storage, you also need to categorize the data to make it easier to find and store the information about it in a central location so that people know where to find it. Think about the system at a library. Without some form of catalog, it would take a long time to find a particular book even if you knew the name of it.

The dual tasks of cataloging and archiving data you don't need now, but will need later, are something you should perform together. It's easier to get all of the data for a specific project together and immediately archive it than it is to accumulate the data and hope it remains together until you get around to archiving it. The second method almost never works because some of the data is bound to get scattered, unintentionally deleted, or simply damaged in some way. The catalog provides a view into the data, while the archive provides a snapshot of the data at a specific moment in time. Even if you change the data later, you still have information about its origins and original content.

Unfortunately, most archive programs don't provide any kind of cataloging feature, so you should set up a database of some kind to hold the information. Anything will work. Some of the best catalogs I've seen reside in Excel spreadsheets or Access databases. Of course, making the catalog accessible and protecting its content are prime considerations when working in a group.

SAVING TEMPLATES AND OTHER DOCUMENT TOOLS

As you concentrate on various compression features and methods of making your documents ever smaller, it's also important to think about the support these files need. For example, many documents rely on templates for part of their content. I'm not necessarily talking about the words or other elements in the document, but the formatting for that information. The template defines how the words or other elements appear on screen and when you print them. In some cases, even though all of the elements you provided are still there, they're unusable once you remove the template. Consequently, when you archive the document, you have to consider any templates the document needs to appear properly on screen.

Here's a scenario to consider. A company archives a Word document for later use. Five years later, someone decides to take the company to court based, in part, on that document, so the document becomes a crucial piece of evidence. The problem is that no one can view the document anymore. Even though the company has a template with the same name, it has gone through so many changes that it no longer works with the old document. In short, when you archive, you take a snapshot of everything the involves the document so that you can restore the same setup later.

However, templates aren't the only document features you need to consider. Sometimes a vendor will stop supporting a specific version of a document when it updates an application. At this point, you have to consider archiving the entire application to ensure you can read the associated documents later. The tool that created the document becomes a resource that you must have in order to read it.

The document tool consideration extends to other kinds of tools too. For example, a word-processed document might have embedded graphics created with a second application. When the graphics are in a standard format, it's possible to open and view them with any application. However, specialized graphics formats require a specific tool to read, which means you also have to consider archiving the secondary tool as the need arises.

All of these document requirements point to the need to open the document, review the resources needed to work with the document, and then record those requirements before you archive the document. Placing this information in a central database ensures you can evaluate specific needs quickly and archive everything needed to work with the documents.

Using the MakeCab and Expand Utilities

The MakeCab utility creates a catalog (Microsoft called it a cabinet and the file normally uses a CAB extension) of your data files. It can also compress them, but it need not do so. The Expand utility retrieves files from a catalog. Here's the odd thing about the Expand utility—unlike other utilities like it, you don't have to use the same name for the output file as the internal file. For example, you might have created a cabinet with a file named `Test1.TXT`, but nothing stops you from changing the name to `Test2.TXT` during output. These utilities might seem archaic, but they're on your Windows drive by default and they actually provide a lot of functionality. The only down side is that you use them from the command prompt, rather than a nice comfortable GUI.

TIP Although most ZIP applications today will read CAB files as well, it pays to know how to use these utilities when your copy of Windows encounters a problem. You can use MakeCab to archive files that you suspect are damaged and obtain new copies from the Windows CD using Expand. Because these utilities work from the command prompt, you can use them when other utilities fail (there's no guarantee the GUI will work during an emergency).

USING MAKECAB FROM THE COMMAND LINE

The MakeCab utility creates a cabinet file from a file that you define. The two common outputs are either a cabinet file with a CAB extension or the file with the last letter of the extension replaced with an underscore (such as `Test1.TX_` instead of `Test1.TXT`). You can only place one file at a time into the cabinet, which makes for a slow archiving process. The MakeCab utility has the following command line switches:

/D *Variable=Value*   Defines a MakeCab variable that you want to change. You define which variable to change and what value to assign to it. For example, if you want to turn off compression, you would type **/D Compression=Off**. The command line can contain as many of these switches as needed to configure MakeCab.

/F *Directives*   Accepts the name of a file that contains the directives for compressing a file. Normally, you'd need to use this switch from the command line. Simply provide the name of a directive file and MakeCab will process it.

/L *Directory*   Defines the output directory for the cabinet. The default setting places the output in the current directory.

/V *Level*   Sets the verbosity level of MakeCab. The default level is 1. You can also set levels 2 and 3.

TIP Many application developers still use MakeCab as a basis for creating application installation programs. If you really want to learn all of the details about MakeCab and related utilities, download the Microsoft Cabinet SDK from `http://msdn.microsoft.com/library/en-us/dncabsdk/html/cabdl.asp`. Although this tool isn't for everyone, it does provide some interesting tidbits of information.

The /D switch is a bit of a mystery because there isn't any documentation for it included with Windows. MakeCab includes variables that you can modify to change its behavior. Some of these commands make sense when you use MakeCab from the command line, but others are better suited to working with MakeCab through a Diamond Directive File (DDF). (See the "Creating Cabinet Files with MakeCab" section for details on working with DDFs.) Table 5.2 describes the most important variables and tells whether you can use them in a DDF or at the command line.

TABLE 5.2: Common MakeCab Variables

VARIABLE	COMMAND LINE	DDF	DESCRIPTION
Cabinet		X	Use this variable to set the cabinet mode on or off.
CabinetFileCountThreshold		X	This variable defines the number of files that can appear in a cabinet before MakeCab creates a new cabinet.
CabinetName		X	This variable defines the name of the cabinet file, which always has a CAB extension. You can also assign a number to the cabinet name when creating multiple cabinets.
Compress	X	X	Use this variable to turn compression on or off. When compression is off, MakeCab creates cabinets that simply archive the data.
CompressedFileExtensionChar	X		Normally the command line version uses an underscore for a replacement character. For example, Test1.TXT would appear as Test1.TX_ as an archive. This variable lets you use a different replacement character.
CompressionType	X	X	The standard compression method for cabinets is MSZIP. Most ZIP archive applications can read this form of compression with ease, but the method is a little slow when you have a lot of files to compress. However, you can use the LZX method, in many cases, where speed is the factor and not the amount of compression. This method is not compatible with some ZIP archive applications.
DestinationDir	X	X	Set the destination directory using this variable. The default setting uses the current directory as the destination.

TABLE 5.2:   Common MakeCab Variables *(CONTINUED)*

VARIABLE	COMMAND LINE	DDF	DESCRIPTION
DiskDirectory		X	Defines the name of the directory used to store each disk in a multiple disk compression. For example, if you defined the name as MyArchive, then the first disk in the set would use a directory named MyArchive1.
DiskLabel		X	Set the printed disk label information using this variable. MakeCab uniquely labels each disk using a disk number. For example, when you set this value to My Archive, the label for the first disk is My Archive 1.
GenerateInf		X	Determines when MakeCab generates an INF (information) file for the archive. The INF lets you expand the cabinet and retrieve the files without using the Expand utility (see the "Retrieving Files from Cabinets with Expand" section for details). There are a number of INF variables you can also use, but these values are generally used for production installation programs, so you can safely skip them in this situation.
MaxCabinetSize		X	Use this variable to define the largest cabinet that MakeCab should create. When a file won't fit in a single cabinet, MakeCab fills the cabinet with as much of the file as will fit and then starts a new cabinet with the remainder of the file. The process continues until the file is complete.
MaxDiskSize		X	Set the disk size for a cabinet using this variable. The MaxDiskSize variable ensures that the content for each cabinet will fit on a separate disk. MakeCab doesn't currently support DVD recordings directly, but it does support CDs. Use the special CDROM, 1.44M, 1.2M, 720K, or 360K values to specify standard disk sizes, or you can define unique sizes by providing the number of bytes.
RptFileName		X	Use this variable to define the name of the report for the cabinet building process. The report tells you about any errors that MakeCab encountered and provides status information.

TABLE 5.2:   Common MakeCab Variables *(CONTINUED)*

VARIABLE	COMMAND LINE	DDF	DESCRIPTION
SourceDir	X	X	This variable defines the source directory for the files you want to archive. The default setting is the current directory.
UniqueFiles		X	Use this variable to determine whether the destination can include duplicate filenames. Normally, you want to set this option to On to ensure that the filenames are unique.

To try the command line version of MakeCab out, open a command prompt in a folder that contains a test file. At the command prompt, type **MakeCab /D Compress=On /D CompressedFile-ExtensionChar=# /D CompressionType=LZX /V3 Test1.TXT** and press Enter. This command line will produce a single file cabinet that uses compression, has an output name of Test1.TX#, and relies on the Lempel-Ziv-Welch (LZW) compression method. MakeCab will also provide verbose output so you can see the details of the compression. Figure 5.5 shows typical output from this command.

FIGURE 5.5
Use the command line version of MakeCab to compress single files quickly.

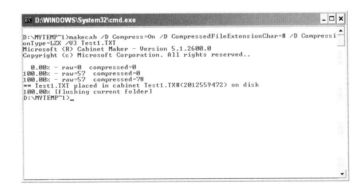

CREATING CABINET FILES WITH MAKECAB

From a usage perspective, MakeCab is a little limited when you use the command line approach. The greatest number of files that your cabinet will ever contain is 1. Although that's nice, creating cabinets with a number of files is better. To create a multiple file cabinet, you must create a DDF. Using a DDF opens all kinds of new possibilities. In fact, you might be surprised to find that many professional developers create installation programs and utilities based around MakeCab and the DDF. However, the purpose of this chapter is to demonstrate how to catalog and optionally compress files.

TIP   Microsoft provides limited documentation for working with CAB files and creating the DDF that extends MakeCab. You can find the one piece of arcane documentation that Microsoft does provide on the topic at `http://home.hiwaay.net/~pittman/archive/makecab.doc`. This document is a tad difficult to read—make sure you understand how the extended DDF features work before you use them on a real archive.

One significant advantage of MakeCab is that you can use it to build multiple disk archives. When a file is too large for a single disk, MakeCab automatically compresses the file in such a way that it spans the multiple disks. MakeCab also uses cabinet space efficiently by continuing to add files until the cabinet is full, even if this means that part of the file resides in one cabinet and part in the next. Finally, MakeCab performs the compression across file boundaries, which means that compression continues from one file to the next without stopping. Theoretically, this technique improves the compression ratio, but in reality you won't notice too much of a difference between the output from Make-Cab and other products.

The example in this section shows a simple DDF. The DDF can become quite complex, but usually you don't require that level of complexity for a simple archive. Listing 5.1 shows the DDF file I created for the sample files.

LISTING 5.1:   A Simple DDF for Archiving

```
; Set the various MakeCab variables.

.Set Cabinet=On
.Set CabinetName1=MyArchive.CAB
.Set Compress=on
.Set DiskDirectory1=CabinetStore
.Set DiskLabel="My Test Archive"
.Set MaxDiskSize=CDROM
.Set RptFileName=Archive.TXT

; Provide a list of files to archive.

Test1.TXT
Test2.INI
Test3.HLP
Test4.TST
```

When you create a DDF for archiving purposes, you essentially define two sections. The first section contains all of the MakeCab variable settings and the second contains all of the files you want to archive. You can also add comments as shown by preceding the line with a semicolon (;).

The keyword, .Set (always include the period), tells MakeCab that you're about to set a variable. Then comes the variable name, an equals sign (=), and the value. Most values are single words, so you don't need to enclose them in quotes. Some values are multiple words, however, so you need to enclose them in double quotes so MakeCab accepts the entire value as shown for the DiskLabel variable.

Generally, you'll place all of your archive files in the same folder, so you don't need to provide anything more than the filenames. When you want to include files in multiple folders, you can use a path as normal. For example, when the Temp.TXT file appears in the \Temp folder of the D drive you could include the file using D:\Temp\Temp.TXT as the DDF entry.

To create the archive, you use the /F MakeCab command line switch. For example, when your DDF file is named MyCatalog.DDF, you would type **MakeCab /F MyCatalog.DFF** and press Enter. Figure 5.6 shows typical results of using this command.

Notice that the output is far more complex than using the command line version of MakeCab. Using the /V2 command line switch tells you a lot about how MakeCab works without burdening you with too many details. In this case, you see all of the variable settings take effect along with the comments you provided in the code so it's easy to compare the output with the code you typed.

TIP   Creating the DDF file need not be a long and complicated task of typing filenames by hand. Use the Dir command to create the file for you. For example, when you want to archive all of the files in a directory, type **Dir *.* /B >> ACatalog.DDF** and press Enter. The ACatalog.DDF file will receive the list of files you want to archive. Simply open this file and place any variable declarations you want to use at the top and then feed it to the MakeCab utility.

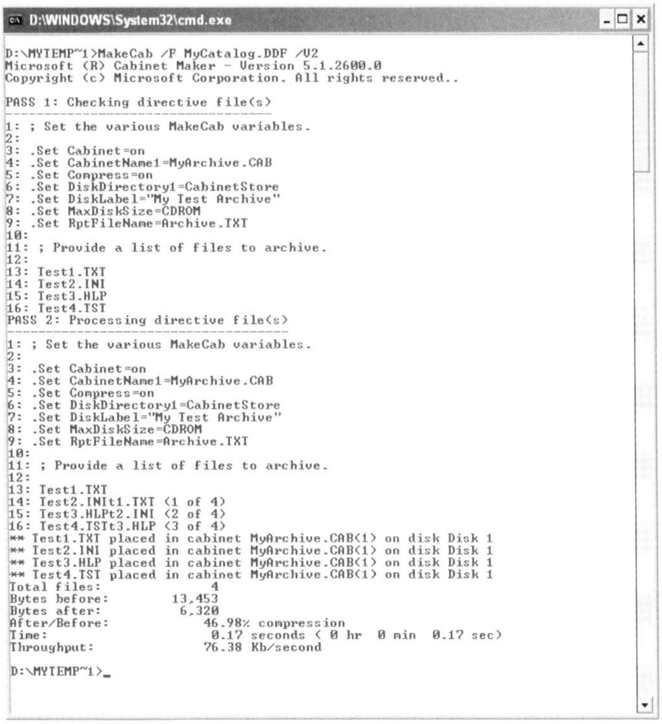

FIGURE 5.6
Using a DDF file creates a standard CAB file with multiple files in it.

RETRIEVING FILES FROM CABINETS WITH EXPAND

The Expand utility isn't nearly as complex as MakeCab. You use it to display or retrieve files archived in a cabinet. The Expand utility uses the following command line switches:

/R Rename the expanded files. The only problem is that this feature doesn't appear to work. The best way to rename the files is to ensure you place them in a separate directory and rename them by hand after you expand them.

/D Display a list of the files in the cabinet, but don't expand them. This command lets you review the content of a cabinet before you do anything with it.

/F *Files* Lets you selectively retrieve files from a cabinet. In some cases, you might want just one or two of the files, rather than expanding all of them. You must use this option when working with a cabinet that contains multiple files. When you want to expand all of the files in an archive, use the /F * command line switch.

To use the Expand utility on a single file archive, simply type the name of the archive. For example, if the name of the archive is Test1.TX_, you would type **Expand Test1.TX_** and press Enter. You don't need to provide a destination directory or any other information unless you want to.

When working with a multiple file archive, you must provide both a file list and a destination folder. For example, when you have a cabinet file named MyArchive.CAB and you want to extract all of the files, you type **Expand /F:* MyArchive.CAB** . and press Enter. Notice that I've used a wildcard character, the asterisk, to tell Expand to expand all of the files. In addition, I've specified the destination using a period (.). The period tells Expand to use the current directory. Figure 5.7 shows typical results from expanding files from a multiple file cabinet.

Notice that the output shows that Expand placed the files in the current directory as signified by the period. When you what to expand files into the parent (one level up) directory, you can use two periods (..). It's also possible to use wildcard characters in various ways to define the files you want to expand. For example, when you want to expand all files that begin with the word Test, contain a single character as a suffix, and have any file extension, you'd use Test?.* as the file definition. To put this all together, you'd type **Expand /F:Test?.* MyArchive.CAB** .. and press Enter.

FIGURE 5.7

Expanding a multiple file archive means including a file list and a destination directory.

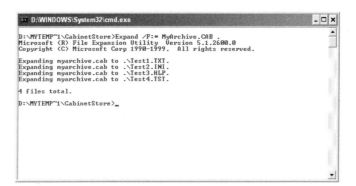

Using ZIP or Other Files

The ZIP file is perhaps one of the most popular file archive formats ever created. You can find utilities for working with ZIP files all over the Internet. Most of these utilities, such as WinZip (http://www.winzip.com) sport a GUI. However, you can also find command line utilities, such as Power-Archiver (http://www.powerarchiver.com/), that work with ZIP files. It's important to note that utilities that support the ZIP archive commonly support other archives as well.

The ZIP file is so popular, that Windows XP even includes resources for working with it as part of the operating system. However, the Windows XP ZIP support isn't going to be good enough for most uses because it doesn't provide a convenient means of creating an archive. The only real functionality is the ability to move files in and out of an existing ZIP archive as you would out of any other folder in Windows Explorer. Generally, you'll want to buy something better.

TIP   Many people find they don't like the ZIP support provided by Windows XP. Using the default setup, you can view ZIP files as a folder using Windows Explorer. Unfortunately, this feature slows down searches because Windows Explorer looks through every ZIP file on your system. It can also cause Windows Explorer to crash at times, seems to interfere with some backup utilities, and can cause other problems when you have a dedicated ZIP application installed. To remove this feature, open a command prompt in the \Windows\System32 folder. At the command prompt type **RegSvr32 -u ZIPFldr.DLL** and press Enter. You'll see a success message. Close and reopen any copies of Windows Explorer you have open.

The "Using the MakeCab and Expand Utilities" section of the chapter discusses the only true archiver that Windows supports. This utility creates cabinets that can exist across disk boundaries and provides all of the support required for application installations. When you need to create a permanent store for your data, you should consider using a product like MakeCab because it can help you organize the information into multiple disk sets. However, MakeCab isn't very good for creating compressed archives on the fly, which is why you need a product such as WinZip shown in Figure 5.8.

WinZip and other products like it serve a different purpose from MakeCab. I'll use WinZip as the example as the discussion progresses, but you can be sure that other products offer similar features. For example, you can't password protect an archive with MakeCab, but you can with WinZip. In addition, WinZip integrates directly into Windows Explorer. You can select one or more files, right-click, and choose a ZIP archive option from the context menu. In fact, you don't even have to create a permanent ZIP file when you want to email the file to someone because WinZip provides an option for creating the email with the ZIP attachment in place. (Depending on which version of Windows and the archive program you use, the archive program might create a disk version of the archive before it creates the email for you—you'll want to remove any disk files after you send the file.)

NOTE   Some people have gotten the idea that if they ZIP a file and then place it on a compressed hard drive that they'll double the amount of disk space they save. The problem is that this method doesn't work. A file you compress using a format such as ZIP doesn't compress much, if any, when you place it on a compressed drive because there isn't anything to compress. The file is already at the minimum size. Therefore, when you compress a series of files into a ZIP file, you need to remember that the file will consume the full number of bytes on a compressed drive.

FIGURE 5.8
You can create archives on the fly using products such as WinZip.

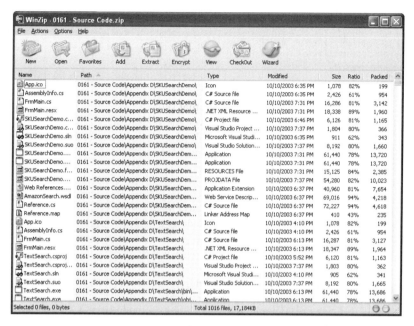

Most of these archive programs provide features you need to send data to someone else, such as data encryption and password protection. You may need these features in a local archive as well, but generally, you protect a local archive using physical security, so encryption and password protection isn't as important.

WARNING Beware of compatibility problems with ZIP files. Originally, everyone used the same version of the ZIP standard, so you could archive files using one ZIP program and expand them using any other application that supported ZIP. Vendors want to differentiate their products, so the ZIP standard has fragmented. One of the biggest areas of contention according to an InfoWorld article (http://www.infoworld.com/infoworld/article/03/06/10/HNzipsplinters_1.html) is the use of new encryption technologies (you must be an InfoWorld member to view the article, but registration is free). Another problem is the use of new compression methods that help you gain a little more disk space. You don't have to use these new features and most vendors will warn you about compatibility problems when using new features, but it never hurts to exercise a little extra care.

One of the most important features of GUI-based archive utilities is convenience. To add a file to an existing archive, all you need to do is drag it and drop it on the archive file in Windows Explorer. Most archive utilities display a dialog box similar to the one shown in Figure 5.9. Even if you don't understand all of the fancy options presented by the dialog box, you can click Add to add the file to the existing archive. When you use a utility such as MakeCab you always have to build the archive from scratch.

FIGURE 5.9
Many GUI archive applications provide a means to add files to an existing archive.

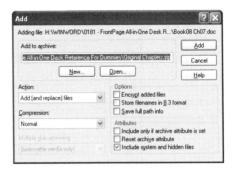

Notice that this product also lets you set a number of options. For example, you can choose the level of compression the utility employs. It's also possible to encrypt the data to protect it from prying eyes. A special feature saves only the DOS-formatted (8 letter filename and 3 letter file extension) filename. You can retain other features such as the name of the folder in which the file appears so you can restore the directory structure later. All of these features are available through a few clicks—no odd command line switches to memorize, no special configuration files to create.

Understanding Alternatives Like WinRAR

The world of archiving doesn't rest on the CAB and ZIP file. You have a wealth of other formats to choose from, each with their own advantages. For example, the Java Archive (JAR) file appears on many platforms, so you can use it when you need compatibility over functionality.

One interesting format is RAR. A few companies are using this format for public distribution of files. The main reason that companies use RAR is that like the CAB format, it provides good support for multiple volumes (learn more at `http://www.rarlabs.com/rar_file.htm`). The originator of this archive provides a special application for it named WinRAR (`http://www.rarlabs.com/`). However, other vendors have already added the RAR format to their repertoire.

The point you have to consider is which of these formats you should support as part of your archiving scheme. When you want to create a personal or company archive, you should focus on one archive and not confuse things by supporting other formats. However, it's important to know that these other formats exist when you work with other people.

Preventing Email Overload

Email has become the lumbering elephant of data storage for most people. It's slow, it's large, and it's hard to manage—just like the animal. Even with careful management, your email can quickly grow to gargantuan proportions because email has become central to many communications today. Don't get the idea that just business communication is affected either—email affects personal communication and even research to a great degree. One of my best research sources now are the trade press newsletters I received and carefully store in my email. In a matter of seconds, I can locate a story that I remember reading some time ago.

Despite careful management, my email often exceeds 360MB of storage space. That's a lot of space to devote to data. Yet, if I hadn't carefully managed it, my email could have easily ballooned to 1GB or more. In fact, email has become such a problem, that many administrators now consider 10GB or more of storage space, average. Imagine that—email consumes more space that many people have in all other kinds of data combined!

The following sections provide some ideas you can use to optimize your email. These sections provide great ideas, but I encourage you to experiment on your own because everyone's email needs are different. When you come up with some new ideas you'd like to share, let me know about them at JMueller@mwt.net. I'm always looking for new ways to manage my email and will definitely share them through my Web site.

Organizing and Categorizing Your Email

Email is going to consume a lot of space on your hard drive—get used to the idea because email isn't going to go away despite the ravages of spam. However, disorganized email is a waste of space because you'll never find what you need. The email lies about in heaps that you can't sort in any meaningful way. To ensure you can find what you need quickly, you need to organize and categorize your email.

One of the best ways to organize email is to create a folder for it. Unfortunately, there isn't one "best" way to perform this task. Because of the work I do, I have several kinds of organizational folders. Figure 5.10 shows the two most common types.

The folders on the top are project folders. When I start a new project, such as a new book or client relation, I create an email folder for it. All of the folders I create for that project have the same number, making them easy to differentiate and sort. When I finish the project, I archive the email files for that project (see the "Archiving Email Files" section for details). Consequently, the email for that project is always accessible, but it only consumes space on my hard drive while I work on that project.

FIGURE 5.10

Use folders as helpful aids for organizing your email.

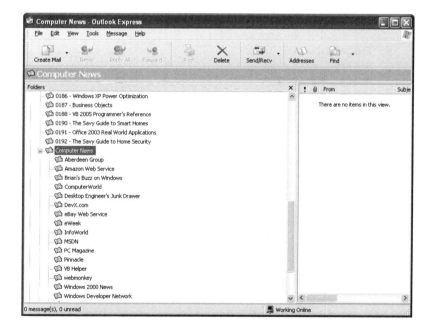

Sometimes a project folder will include subfolders. For example, I might find some interesting threads on a newsgroup, so I'll create a subfolder for them. Generally, I try to assign the folder a specific use. A book might contain information in a specific chapter, so I'll assign the subfolder to a specific chapter. When I complete that chapter, I decide whether any of the remaining information is useful and get rid of it when the information isn't useful. These folders are temporary and I never archive them.

The Computer News folder is a topical folder. In this case, it holds all of the trade press emails that I've saved for research purposes. Within this folder are subfolders—one for each trade press magazine I receive through email. Once a month my reminder program displays a message that it's time to remove the old messages from the trade press folders. Depending on the trade press folder, I remove messages that are either a year or two old. This section folder type is an example of one that doesn't end—it's continuous and you have to maintain it in order to maintain some kind of information viability.

Note that some email applications provide an automatic archiving feature. For example, when working with Outlook 2003, you can right-click a folder and choose Properties from the context menu. Select the AutoArchive tab and you'll see a number of archiving options for that folder as shown in Figure 5.11. In fact, you can simply tell Outlook to erase the messages in the folder after a specific time interval.

A third type of folder doesn't appear in Figure 5.10. It holds proposal information. Someone writes to me about an idea that they want to pursue. We haven't decided to proceed with the project yet, so I don't assign it a project number. Only after the idea becomes a project do I move it out of the proposal folder and into a project folder. About once a month, I also go through my proposal folder and remove old ideas that just didn't work out for some reason.

FIGURE 5.11
Some email applications help you keep your system clean through automatic archiving.

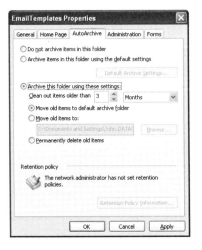

Archiving Email Files

Most email applications provide a method for archiving files. For example, when you want to export a folder from Outlook 2003, you choose the File ➢ Import and Export command and then follow the wizard to send the information to an archive file. In Outlook 2003, you choose the Export to a File option. Make sure you give the exported file the same name as the folder you're exporting. Afterward, you can simply delete the folder from the list of folders in Outlook and archive the exported file. This is the approach to use when you want to archive a project folder. Of course, Outlook 2003 also supports automatic archiving for topical folders.

Some email applications require a different approach. For example, many people use Outlook Express, which despite the name, has many differences from Outlook. Outlook Express stores each folder you create individually, rather than in a central database as Outlook does. To archive a folder in Outlook Express, you locate the storage location (normally in the \Documents and Settings folder hierarchy) and look for DBX file that has the same name as the folder. Archive this file and then delete it from Outlook Express. (Don't simply delete the file from the storage folder or Outlook Express will recreate it.) The DBX file will disappear from the storage location.

TIP   Archiving email files using the default Outlook Express setup can be difficult to say the least because even finding the email folder is hard. The default location for your email files places them deep within the \Documents and Settings folder hierarchy, which makes finding the file hard. To solve this problem, change the location of the email folder on your system. Select the Tools ➢ Options command to display the Options dialog box. Select the Maintenance tab and click Store Folder. You'll see the Store Location dialog box. Click Change and find a new location for the email files on your system. Moving the email files makes them much easier to locate and work with regularly.

When you have trouble locating the Outlook Express storage area, use the Dir command to locate it. Type the name of the folder with a DBX extension. For example, if the name of the folder is My Folder, you would type **Dir "My Folder.DBX" /S** at the command prompt and press Enter. Note that you must include quotes around a folder name that includes spaces and need to include the /S command line switch to tell Dir to search subdirectories. The Dir command will tell you the location of the storage area and you can use Windows Explorer to locate the file.

Restoring Email Files

Archiving email files is only useful if you can restore them later. Depending on the email application you use, you might receive help. For example, Outlook 2003 makes the process relatively easy. Use the File ➢ Import and Export command to display the Import and Export Wizard, select the Import from Another Program or File option, and follow the prompts to recover the file you created.

Other email programs make life a little more interesting. For example, to recover an Outlook Express archive, you need to make Outlook Express think the data was there all along. To begin, create a new folder in Outlook Express with precisely the same name as the archive you want to restore. For example, if the name of the archive is My Folder.DBX, you need to create a folder in Outlook Express named My Folder. Select My Folder after you create it and you'll see that it's blank. The act of selecting the folder creates a new file in the Outlook Express storage location (see the "Archiving Email Files" section for tips on locating the storage location).

At this point, close Outlook Express. Copy the archived file over the new file that Outlook Express just created. Windows will even ask if you want to copy over the existing file (if it doesn't, then you weren't successful creating the blank file). When you reopen Outlook Express and select the folder you created, you should see the archived data.

Using Free Email Accounts

One of the ways to keep email from cluttering your system is not to store it on your system. For example, you could get a Hotmail, Yahoo!, or Google email account and store your data online. You'll want to try out several of the online alternatives because not all of them offer the same features. In many cases, you can get the email account free so long as you're willing to view a few ads and encounter a few limitations. All of the free email vendors have paid versions that include some nice to add features, but try the free version first to ensure the email will work for you.

You do have a few problems to overcome when working with online accounts. Sure, you've optimized hard drive usage more than any local application would allow, but now you have to consider the fact that your data is online—on someone else's machine. It's not a very secure environment for the most part. In fact, Google's Gmail is going to search through your messages whether you want them to or not. Some of these privacy incursions should make you think twice about using free online accounts. You can read the full story on the Computerworld site at `http://www.computerworld.com/securitytopics/security/privacy/story/0,10801,92279,00.html?nas=PM-92279`.

Even though you do optimize hard drive usage, you also trade one performance problem for another. Now instead of just downloading your messages from the Internet, you also have to download all of the user interface elements. Consequently, viewing email online can be time consuming even with a high-speed connection. In addition, you can't count on the availability of the online service, so you might not have access to your email when you need to view it in a hurry.

All of these negatives aside, online email has proven very popular because it also has several advantages. For example, you can check your email from any location that has an Internet connection. In addition, online email lets you maintain several accounts (for different purposes such as business and personal) without incurring additional fees from your ISP.

Let's Start Cleaning

This chapter has discussed a number of file compression and archiving issues, most notably those involved with an increasing document resource, email. I'd love to tell you that there's a secret bullet that makes the decision of what strategy to use for archiving both automatic and simple, but there isn't. The best archiving strategy is the one that works for your particular needs. That might mean compressing your email and placing it on DVD for quick access later, but it also might mean freeing hard drive space from another resource so you can hold onto those email conversations a little long. The point is that you need an archiving strategy of some kind.

Now you're at the point where you need to do some work. The first step is to decide what to archive and consider how to archive it. You need to define the kind of archival you want to perform, whether you'll place the data in a ZIP file, and precisely how long you'll keep that file. The next step is to consider a storage media. Although CDs are insanely cheap, you might not want to trust your data to them when you plan to keep the information for several years. Sometimes storing the information to tape really is the best choice.

Chapter 6 opens a new vista into the inner workings of Windows—one that many people find quite scary, the registry. This chapter helps you discover that the registry is merely a database. Sure, the registry is complex and a misstep can cause problems, but when you approach it correctly, the registry is quite manageable. The secret is to perform specific tasks—just the ones you know about, and avoid changing anything you don't understand. The focus of Chapter 5 is to remove some of the mystery from the registry so that you can optimize it with greater ease and with less danger of doing something you'll regret later.

Chapter 6

Detecting Registry Leftovers

The registry is a special kind of database—it stores all of the settings for your system. For example, Windows consults the registry during startup so it knows which devices to install. Many of the applications that start automatically do so because of registry entries. The context menu you see when you right-click an item in Windows Explorer is the result of other registry entries. In short, editing the registry incorrectly can cause untold woe, but editing it correctly can make significant improvements to the way Windows works.

This chapter is all about discovering which areas of the registry you can edit and learning which areas to avoid. While you take your tour of the registry, you'll also uncover new techniques for cleaning the registry and keeping it working right. A registry clogged with old and useless entries makes Windows slow and could cause stability problems. Unfortunately, Microsoft doesn't provide much in the way of registry cleaning products, so to get out the last bit of dirt, you usually need to turn to a third party product.

Although optimization is a wonderful goal, the registry also serves another important purpose. Most applications store your personal settings in the registry. Consequently, when you want to optimize your hard drive by temporarily removing an application, you should save those personal settings so you can easily restore them later. In most cases, restoring the settings in the registry, along with any special files the application requires, will return the application to the same state that it was in before you uninstalled it.

WARNING Modifying the registry isn't something you should do without making a backup of the section you plan to edit and knowing precisely what the change will do. Never modify the registry unless you know how to make the required backup and you understand how the registry section works. The "Exporting Data" section of the chapter tells you how to make the required backup. Many of the other areas of the chapter discuss safe edits you can make. When in doubt, however, don't edit the registry.

Using the Registry Editor

The Registry Editor displays the content of the registry. You can use it to explore the registry, as well as add, remove, and modify entries. The following sections describe the techniques you use to edit the registry safely. These techniques include exploring the registry, and importing and exporting entries as needed. You also need to know about the data types (the kinds of data) that the registry can work with. Although this section doesn't provide an exhaustive registry reference, it does include enough information for beginning the optimization process.

Exploring the Registry Editor

Before you do anything else with the registry, you should explore it a little. It's important to become familiar with the various components the registry contains and see how Microsoft constructed it. In order to begin this process, you need some kind of viewer to see the registry, which is the Registry Editor. To start the Registry Editor, select the Start ➤ Run command. You'll see the Run dialog box. Type **RegEdit** in the Run field and click OK. Windows will start the Registry Editor shown in Figure 6.1.

This view shows several important registry features. All of the top-level entries that include an H in front of their name, such as HKEY_CLASSES_ROOT, are registry hives. Each hive contains a different kind of information that affects a particular part of the machine and can even appear in a different file from the rest of the registry. For example, the HKEY_CURRENT_USER hive appears in the D:\Documents and Settings*Your User Name* folder as NTUSER.DAT. However, for optimization purposes, it's not very important to know the location of the data.

Each of the hives contains one or more keys. For example, look in Figure 6.1 and you'll see that HKEY_LOCAL_MACHINE has a key named HARDWARE. All of the non-hive entries in the left pane are keys and each represents a data storage container of some type (even if it's only to store other keys).

When you select a key in the left pane, you see the values it stores in the right pane. A value consists of a name and value pair. The name of the value defines what kind of information the value contains. For example, in Figure 6.1 there's a value named SystemBiosDate with a value of 03/03/00. This value tells you that the Basic Input/Ouput System (BIOS) chip for this system was originally manufactured on 3 March 2000. It doesn't tell you about any updates to that chip, but at least you know when the manufacturer created the chip.

FIGURE 6.1

Use the Registry Editor to explore and to add, remove, or modify entries.

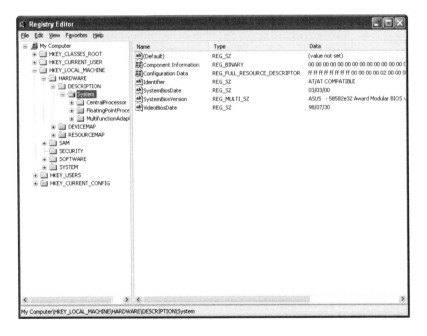

TIP   To keep track of registry sections that you visit frequently, use the options on the Favorites menu (not to be confused with Favorites in Internet Explorer). The Add to Favorites command displays a dialog box where you can add a new favorite to the list. The favorite will appear on the Favorites menu as an option you can select. When you find that you no longer need a favorite, select the Remove Favorite command to display Remove Favorites dialog box. Select the favorite you want to remove and click OK.

You'll find a lot of interesting information about your system in the registry just by exploring the various keys. The "An Overview of Interesting Registry Sections" section of the chapter tells you about areas that you'll want to look at carefully for potential optimization needs. For now, however, try looking at the upper levels of the registry to get familiar with the kinds of data that each hive contains. Look especially in the HKEY_CURRENT_USER hive because that contains your personal settings.

Exporting Data

The Registry Editor provides a convenient means of exporting data. The data appears in a REG (registry) file that you can read with any standard text editor such as Notepad. When you export a key, the Registry Editor also saves a copy of all the values contained in that key, along with any subkeys. The concept of saving the current key and anything lower in the hierarchy is saving a registry branch.

WARNING   Always save a copy of any key that you want to modify to disk—even when you're certain that you know precisely how the values in the key work. Everyone has accidents. Saving the current key values provides a quick method of returning the system to a known good state when you make a mistake. A little time exporting the registry key now will save you a lot of time reinstalling Windows later.

When you want to save a registry branch, highlight the starting key and choose the File ➢ Export command to display the Export Registry File dialog box shown in Figure 6.2.

FIGURE 6.2
Export registry settings to a registry file to save them for future use.

Notice the Export Range options shown at the bottom of the dialog box. You can use this dialog box to save the entire registry by selecting All or a particular piece of the registry by choosing Selected Branch. Within the Selected Branch option is the path to the starting registry key. The path looks like any path you might have used in Windows Explorer. However, instead of starting with a drive letter, this path starts with a hive name. The hive entries follow the same name structure, as shown in Figure 6.1. You separate each key level by a backslash (\).

To export a branch, select a location for the file, type a name for the registry file, and click Save. The Export Registry File dialog box will disappear.

It's interesting to look at the exported file to see how Windows saves the information. To view the exported registry file, find its location on the hard drive. Right-click the REG file and choose Edit from the context menu. Windows will open the REG file in a copy of Notepad (or another editor when you don't have Notepad installed on the system) as shown in Figure 6.3.

The file begins with the version of the Registry Editor used to create it. The first key in the branch you selected comes next. Notice that keys appear within square brackets in the file and include the entire path for that key. Directly below the key entry are the value entries. Notice that the SystemBiosDate value appears in the list and that it has the same value, as shown in Figure 6.1.

The subkeys appear in the same order in which they appear in the registry. The values for each subkey also appear in the file, so you end up with a complete view of that branch of the registry.

FIGURE 6.3

View the REG file you exported using Notepad or another text editor.

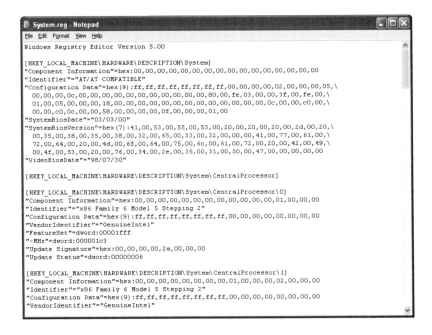

Importing Data

Importing data is extremely easy. If you don't care about reviewing the change to the registry, you don't even have to open the Registry Editor. Simply double-click on the REG file and Windows will display a message asking if you're sure that you want to include the registry information in the file in the registry, as shown in Figure 6.4. Click Yes and Windows will add the information to the registry. Note that adding the information to the registry automatically overwrites any existing values, so you need to exercise care when importing a REG file.

TIP   You can often use REG files as diagnostic aids. Export the branch of a problem registry entry on an operational machine and use it to compare entries on a machine that isn't working. In some rare cases, you can actually import the known good registry branch to fix the broken machine.

Sometimes you want to see a before and after picture of a registry change, so you import the REG file using the Registry Editor. To perform this task, open the Registry Editor using the technique found in the "Exploring the Registry Editor" section of the chapter. Choose the File ➢ Import command and you'll see the Import Registry File dialog box shown in Figure 6.5. Locate the folder that contains the REG files you want to import and select one. Click Open to import it. You can only import one REG file at a time using this dialog box, so working with a number of files can be frustrating.

FIGURE 6.4

Double-clicking a REG file in Windows Explorer displays this dialog box.

FIGURE 6.5

Select the files you want to import into the registry from the list provided.

The results of the import won't appear right away when you have the keys you want to monitor selected. Instead, you'll need to choose the View ➢ Refresh command to refresh the content. By comparing the before and after views of the registry, you can see the changes the REG file made.

Understanding the Data Types

The registry has a number of data types that it uses to hold information. It treats a numeric value differently from a text (string). Because each data type is different, you have to use the correct type when you make new entries. Microsoft Knowledge Base articles and other online tips will always tell you what data type to use when you create a new entry. However, it still pays to know what these data types are so you can view and understand the registry with greater ease. Here are the common registry data types.

String This is easiest data type to read. A string is simple text that you can read and normally understand with ease. The registry often uses strings for descriptive needs.

Binary This is a series of 1's and 0's. The binary values normally appear in a byte (8-bits), word (16-bits), or DWORD (32-bits) format, but the registry reads them as individual bits. The registry normally uses binary values for flags—essentially on/off switches for an application or Windows setting. In some cases, the registry will also use binary values for nonnumeric information, such as an application key or other complex information. You always need a map to read binary values to ensure you understand the individual switch settings or the overall value of the binary string.

DWORD This is a double word or 32-bit value. The registry normally uses DWORD values for numbers. A DWORD can store any value between 0 and 4,294,967,295. When you double-click a DWORD value, the registry displays a dialog box that lets you read it in hexadecimal (base 16 format) or decimal. Because a DWORD stores a number, you can usually read it directly as long as you know what the number means.

Multi-String This is a series of strings. Each string is a separate entry associated with the same value. The strings appear on separate lines when you double-click the value in the Registry Editor. Each string is separated by a null or 0 at the end of the string. The Registry Editor adds these nulls for you, but you still need to know they exist.

Expandable String This type is a string that includes a special expansion element. For example, the special text %WinDir% defines the location of the Windows folder on your machine. When a string contains this value, it can point to locations without having to know where these locations actually are on the machine. Windows automatically expands the special text when it reads the string from the registry. For example, %WinDir%\MyFlower.BMP might actually point to C:\Windows\MyFlower.BMP on your system. Although the registry normally uses expandable strings for data paths on your machine, they can expand to any environmental value. For example, the %OS% expandable string refers to the operating system installed on your machine.

TIP Most expansion strings appear as environmental variables on your machine. To learn what the expansion string means, right-click My Computer and select Properties from the context menu. Choose the Advanced tab and click Environment Variables. The Environment Variables dialog box contains a list of environmental variables on your machine—some are personal (only used by you) and others are system (used by everyone). Look near the bottom of the system list and you'll see the windir environmental variable.

It's important to note that you can only add common value types to the registry. The registry also includes specialized values that only an application can make. For example, the REG_FULL_ RESOURCE_DESCRIPTOR value shown in Figure 6.1 isn't accessible to you. When you open this value, you see a Resources dialog box similar to the one shown in Figure 6.6. Because these special values aren't easily to duplicate, make sure you save them before you make any changes (see the "Exporting Data" section of the chapter for details). In addition, use great care in editing such values—never edit them just to see what will happen.

FIGURE 6.6

It's best to leave special registry values alone, rather than risk a machine meltdown.

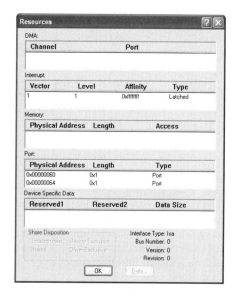

Securing the Registry

It's a little amazing that most people don't know that they can secure the registry. In fact, it's almost too easy to secure the registry to the point that just about no one can access it, but you don't want to go that far. What does this have to do with optimization?

By securing the registry, you make it more difficult for users to install just anything on the system or at least clutter the registry with the results of the installation. You can also reduce the risk of an over-zealous user removing or modifying settings that seem like they'll make all the difference in the world on system performance. Finally, you'll reduce the risk of adware and spyware finding a way to entrench itself in the system.

To work with registry permissions, open the Registry Editor using the technique found in the "Exploring the Registry Editor" section of the chapter. Highlight a key or value of interest. For example, the HKEY_CURRENT_USER\Software\Microsoft\Windows\CurrentVersion\RunOnce key is one point of interest for many crackers and other nefarious sorts. Choose the Edit ➤ Permissions command to display the Permissions dialog box shown in Figure 6.7.

The top of this dialog box contains a list of people and groups that can access the registry key. Administrators always have full access to the registry, but other groups don't. For example, you can set the user to have read access only, which means applications setup for that machine will start fine, but adding new values to the RunOnce key won't work—at least not with the user's account. Click Add to add new users or groups to the list and click Remove to remove the selected user or group from the list.

The bottom of this dialog box shows the permissions of the selected user or group. To change these permissions, click Advanced. You'll see the Advanced Security Settings dialog box shown in Figure 6.8.

FIGURE 6.7
Select the files you want to import into the registry from the list provided.

FIGURE 6.8
View, modify, and test permissions using the options in this dialog box.

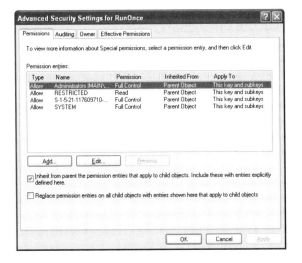

Use the options in the Advanced Security Settings dialog box as you normally would to set security on the registry key. Providing detailed security information is outside the scope of this book. However, you can learn more about auditing user actions in the "Auditing User Actions" section of Chapter 9. Here's a brief overview of the tab functions.

Permissions   This tab helps you set security for each of the users or groups that have access to the registry key or value. Click Add to add a new user or group. Click Edit to change the permissions of an existing group. Clearing the first option tells Windows not to allow inheriting of permissions from previous registry levels—Windows checks this setting by default as shown in Figure 6.7. Checking the second entry will copy any permission changes you make to subkeys.

Auditing   Even when you don't want to change the user settings, it pays to monitor certain keys, such as RunOnce, for changes. The options on the Auditing tab let you monitor activity on the various keys and take action as needed. All of the change notifications appear in the Event Log. In some cases, it pays to monitor everyone, even administrators. Activity on some registry keys is a definite indicator of virus infection or download of applications you don't want on your system.

Owner   Use this tab to change the owner of a registry key. Normally, there isn't a good reason to use this feature with the registry.

Effective Permissions   Testing permissions is very important because you don't know what permissions someone has acquired from previous registry areas. To use this tab, click Select to display the Select User, Computer, or Group dialog box and choose a user or group to test. Click OK. The entries on this tab tell you the true permissions of the selected user, computer, or group for the selected registry key.

An Overview of Interesting Registry Sections

You don't have to be a registry commando to optimize the registry. No one says that you have to delve into the innermost workings of the registry or perform mind-numbing registry surgery. In fact, it's better if you can stay out of the registry except for cleaning adventures. However, you can safely enter some sections of the registry and look for potential problems. The interesting sections of the registry don't affect how Windows loads device drivers, nor will you discover the information that Microsoft is hiding about your system. You'll discover why your application isn't working properly and can remove the entries made by old applications that you no longer use.

Working with Application Entries

The two application entry sections on your system are generally the easiest to understand because you made the entries while working with an application. Simple applications are generally the easiest to learn with, but you can eventually decipher the entries for any application. The first application entry section appears in HKEY_CURRENT_USER\Software, which stores all of your personal settings. The second application entry section is HKEY_LOCAL_MACHINE\SOFTWARE, which stores application settings that affect everyone who uses the machine (system settings).

Each application vendor will have a separate entry in this section, normally followed by the application name, and then the application version as shown in Figure 6.9. Drilling down into the registry information you need tells you a lot about the vendor and the application. For example, you might see entries for multiple versions of a product after an upgrade—you can usually delete the old version information even though the upgrade application didn't perform the task.

FIGURE 6.9
The registry organization tells you a lot about the entry that you see.

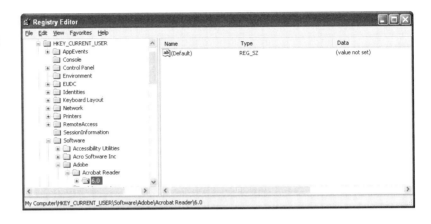

SAVING APPLICATION SETTINGS FOR LATER

When you intend to reinstall an application later, look for the registry entries for that application. In most cases, it's going to be very simple. Look for the vendor, then the application, and then the version keys. Use the method described in the "Exporting Data" section to save the settings for later. When naming your REG file, make sure you use unique names for the personal and system settings. Always save both the personal and system settings or you won't get a good restoration later. Applications use both sets of settings to create the application environment.

Some applications become almost devious in the way they save and restore settings to the registry, making it very hard to save your settings for later. For example, an application could come with what the vendor considers an add-in, even though you consider it part of the application. Office 97 comes with Microsoft Reference. Even though Microsoft Reference links appear as part of the application and you install both applications together, the registry entries are separate. When you want to reinstall Office 97, you must not only install the Office key settings, but also the Microsoft Reference key settings. Consequently, you have to check for four sets of keys (Office personal and system, and Microsoft Reference personal and system).

REMOVING THE ERRANT APPLICATION SETTINGS

This is also the first place you should look for entries to delete. Most applications are terrible about removing the entries they create. In fact, there are times when you'll see a note that the application is removing registry entries during an uninstall, only to find the entries are still there when you look in the registry even after a reboot to ensure the uninstall completes correctly. Consequently, after you uninstall an application and remove the folders it left behind (after archiving your data, of course), reboot the machine to ensure the uninstall program has a chance to remove any remaining Dynamic Link Libraries (DLLs) or other bits and pieces, and then check the registry for application entries. Always begin your search by looking for personal settings and then system settings—applications use both, so you have to check both areas to remove all of the registry entries.

RESTORING APPLICATION SETTINGS

At some point, you'll want to restore the application settings that you archive. You might think that the best course of action is to simply place the application files on your hard drive and restore the registry settings, but that technique won't work, in many cases, because application files are missing or the application isn't set up correctly in other ways. The best way to restore the application is to reinstall it. During installation, the application makes registry entries that will overwrite any archived settings you restored, so it doesn't pay to restore these registry settings until the application is ready for use.

After you reinstall the application, make sure you also install any service packs and updates you had installed at the time you archived it. This activity points out the need to maintain good archive notes. Don't install newer service packs or updates and don't open the application (either action can cause the restoration to work less effectively than you might want). At this point, use one of the techniques described in the "Importing Data" section to import the registry keys that you archived earlier. The act of importing the registry settings restores the application to its former state.

Your application still might not be ready to go at this point. Make sure you recover any templates or other special files from your archive and place them in the application folder. For example, Microsoft Word has a special template called `Normal.DOT`. To ensure the application works properly, you must restore this template after you reinstall the application. You'll want to restore any other templates you use, but `Normal.DOT` influences everything, so it's the most important file to archive.

You can open the application at this point. However, you shouldn't try to use it immediately. Before you begin working, check the application settings to ensure they really are in place. Check for settings that you might not have archived to ensure the application is ready for use.

Running Applications Automatically

You might have noticed that Windows runs some applications automatically whenever you start the system. The ability to run applications automatically makes Windows convenient because you don't have to set it up every time you use it. However, automation is also a source of problems. Even when someone isn't trying to run adware, spyware, or a virus on your system, the accumulation of automated applications can slow your system to a crawl, reduce reliability, and generally make it difficult to use your computer.

The only problem is that it isn't easy to find all of those automated programs. In many cases, it's a matter of knowing where to look for the required entries. For example, most people know to look in the Start ➢ Programs ➢ Startup folder for application entries. Windows automatically starts any applications found in this folder. When the application is located in the All Users Startup folder, rather than your personal Startup folder, Windows starts that application for everyone who logs into the machine. You can determine whether an application affects all users by right-clicking Start and choosing Explore All Users from the context menu. Windows will open a copy of Windows Explorer that displays the settings shared by all users on the machine.

TIP You don't have to look all over the system for most startup settings. Microsoft includes the MSCONFIG utility to make it easier to locate startup settings. The "Using MSCONFIG" section of Chapter 7 describes this utility in detail.

Another source of automatic startups is services. Although a service doesn't usually support any kind of user interface other than the one that Microsoft provides, vendors often couple services with applications. For example, when you install support for an Uninterruptible Power Supply, you see an application, but the application relies on an underlying service. Without the service, the application won't start. You can learn more about getting rid of annoying services in the "Clearing Unnecessary Services" section of Chapter 7.

Device drivers can also cause applications to run automatically. For example, when you install a new display adapter, the associated software disk includes a combination of applications and device drivers that help you make better use of the new display adapter. Unfortunately, especially in the case of display adapters, the new software can actually decrease system performance. The "Locating Unnecessary Drivers" section of Chapter 7 describes how to manage this source of performance killing software.

At this point, you might wonder where the registry connection is in all this. For one thing, the registry normally holds all of the settings for the previously mentioned sources of irritation. Unfortunately, uninstalling the software might not clean up the settings. Forever afterward, your system takes on the appearance of a punchy boxer on the ropes, but it doesn't have to be that way. The "Relying on Registry Cleaning Products" of this chapter tells you how to rid yourself of these nasty remainders.

This leaves the one contribution that the registry makes to the overall filth of your system. Anyone can store automatic execution settings in the registry in one of two main areas: one for personal settings (HKEY_CURRENT_USER\Software\Microsoft\Windows\CurrentVersion) and another for system settings (HKEY_LOCAL_MACHINE\SOFTWARE\Microsoft\Windows\CurrentVersion). Both of these keys contain three subkeys that automatically execute applications of all types:

Run This is the most common place to find applications you don't want running on your system. Applications listed as values in this key run every time someone logs into the system. When you look through the list of applications stored as values in this key, you should only see applications that you installed or recognize as part of device driver installation. When spyware or adware wants to hide on your machine, it commonly uses this registry key to ensure it gets started.

RunOnce The only values you find in this key are those for applications that run one time and then don't run again. When a value appears within this key, Windows looks for the application, runs it, and then removes the entry from the registry. A good example of an application that could appear here is a registration or activation application. A few nefarious applications also use this key to help avoid detection. When you log in, Windows runs the application and removes the entry as normal. However, before the application ends, it adds the entry back in. Consequently, the key ends up acting like the Run key, even though it theoretically only allows the application to run one time.

RunOnceEx This key only appears in the system area (HKEY_LOCAL_MACHINE\SOFTWARE\ Microsoft\Windows\CurrentVersion). Some applications require extended settings to work properly and this key allows applications with those extended settings. Generally, you'll never see a value in this key.

Not all entries in the Run key are from undesirable sources. Sometimes an uninstall application leaves a key behind. For example, Figure 6.10 shows the results of an upgrade performed on a machine. Notice the two copies of MBM.EXE in this list: the first is version 4 and the second is version 5. The uninstall program left the MBM 4 entry behind after an upgrade, so now, every time the system starts, it looks for that entry. Windows ends up searching the entire system for that entry every time a user logs in, creating a performance problem. You should look for and remove this type of entry to improve system startup time.

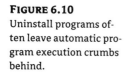

FIGURE 6.10
Uninstall programs often leave automatic program execution crumbs behind.

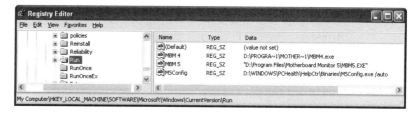

Working with Components

Components are special pieces of application code that reside in a DLL. In a few cases, components are pieces of application code that are separate from anything else, but lack a user interface. The user interface appears as part of a host application. In fact, Windows provides three common ways to work with components from an optimization perspective (Windows supports many other uses for components that you need not worry about).

Application Subcomponent   When you embed a picture in a Word document and then use the controls from the application that created the picture within Word to make additional changes, you're seeing the effects of a component. In this case, the component is associated with Word through the special file you embedded within the Word document. The component is tightly associated with the server application, rather than the host application.

Stand-alone Component   Another example of a component is the ZIPFLDR.DLL file that lets you look at ZIP files from within Windows Explorer, rather than using a separate application to perform the task. In this section case, Windows Explorer acts as a host for the ZIPFLDR.DLL file. A component is usually part of an application solution, not an application itself. Using a component is akin to working with just the part of an application that manages a resource, instead of interacting with the user interface. The association between the component and the application is loose—the only way the application knows to host the component is through registry settings. In addition, a component of this type could execute within more than one host container because the vendor designs the component to work as an augmentation, rather than as a strict enhancement to the application environment.

Standardized Add-in Component   Vendors design certain kinds of applications to provide a hosted environment for specially designed components. The application may have functionality beyond hosting the component, but sometimes it doesn't. The component never has any functionality beyond the hosted environment the vendor designed it to occupy. One common example of such an application and component environment is the Microsoft Management Console (MMC). This application relies on specially designed DLLs to provide access to Windows settings. Every console within the Administrative Tools folder of the Control Panel executed a copy of MMC with one or more snap-in components loaded. Another good example of this component type are the add-ins used with a browser.

Unlike applications, components wind their way throughout the registry in more ways that you'll ever want to know. Generally, when you remove an application from your system, the uninstall program also removes the associated components. The uninstall program also removes the registry entries that make the component function—that attaches it to a particular file extension or makes it part of a host application.

Unfortunately, in some cases, the uninstall program only performs part of the task and leaves a few of the registry entries in place. In fact, in some cases, the application stores the component in the \Windows\System32 folder and the uninstall program leaves both the registry entries and the component. You might also find that the registry and your hard drive are clean. The only reminder of the component is an errant menu entry.

The easiest of these three issues to resolve is the errant entry. Some applications will actually help you to remove them. For example, when you try to execute the add-in, some applications will note that the add-in is no longer available and ask whether you want to remove the entry, as shown in Figure 6.11. In other cases, you can remove the remnant by using one of the customization options the application provides. For example, when working with Word, you can right-click anywhere in the toolbar area and choose Customize from the context menu. Now, simply drag the errant entry off the affected menu or toolbar to get rid of it.

The second easiest problem to remedy is one in which the registry entries and the component remain intact on the system. Getting rid of the component and the entries is easy. Simply type RegSvr32 -u ComponentName.DLL and press Enter at the command prompt in the directory where the component appears. This action removes the registry entries. You can then simply delete the component. The problem is in finding the name and location of the component in the first place. If you know enough about the component, you can use the methods discussed in the "Using Find and Find-Str" section of Chapter 3 to locate the DLL. When you aren't sure about the add-in, you need to use the "Following the Flow of Registry Entries" section of this chapter to trace the component through the registry. As a last ditch effort, you can use the techniques in the "Relying on Registry Cleaning Products" section to locate the name and location of the DLL, but never remove the DLL using this technique. Always rely on the RegSvr32 utility to remove the registry entries for you.

The third problem is going to be difficult to solve. The only way to clean up the mess is to rely on the techniques found in the "Relying on Registry Cleaning Products" section of the chapter. This is a strong measure, but it's the only option you have. Don't attempt the remove the entries by hand—you'll definitely miss some entries and could end up damaging the system.

NOTE After a long time, even if you maintain a clean system, these extra little registry entries accumulate and begin to cause system glitches. At some point, you need to reinstall Windows to counteract the damage created by the entries. How long you can go before a reinstall depends on your system, how much you use it, and how well you maintain it. One test system I own lasted 6 years before it required a new Windows installation. Most organizations get rid of their computers before 6 years are up, so with proper maintenance, you might never have to reformat your drive. Typically, you can expect a Windows installation to last about a year if you don't maintain it and four years when you do, so it really is worth the effort to maintain your system.

FIGURE 6.11
Some applications ask whether you want to remove errant add-in entries.

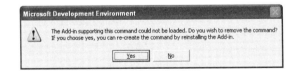

Following the Flow of Registry Entries

Every registry entry is important. The keys and the values work together to define the settings for applications, components, device drivers, services, and hardware. In some cases, the registry defines more than just settings. The registry creates a sequence of events that define how Windows reacts to a particular user action. For example, have you ever considered what happens when you right-click or double-click a file? The registry tells Windows how to react. By following this well-known sequence of events, you can discover more about how the registry works and begin solving complex registry problems.

Looking for Simple Files

The example in this section discusses the flow of the TXT file extension. You can use this same technique to discover the events behind any file extension. More importantly, you can use the techniques you discover here to learn more about any complex registry entry. Obviously, the place to start is looking for the .TXT extension in the registry (note that the period before the TXT extension is important, but the capitalization isn't). Highlight My Computer, found at the very top of the registry, to ensure you search the whole registry. Choose the Edit ➤ Find command to display the Find dialog box. Type **.TXT** in the Find What field and click Find Next. The Registry Editor will take you to the .txt entry shown in Figure 6.12.

The .txt key contains three values. The first tells you the registry file type, so that's the one you'd follow in this case. The second entry, Content Type, tells you the Multipurpose Internet Mail Extensions (MIME) type, which is how Internet Explorer views the file. The third entry, PerceivedType, tells you how Windows sees the file. In some cases, this entry tells Windows to use a special add-in application. For example, when you right-click on a MID file, Windows perceives it as audio and offers additional context menu entries for using the Windows Media Player. Likewise, some graphics files will include context menu entries for previewing the image in the Windows Picture and Fax Viewer. This key contains a number of subkeys, all of which are important, but aren't necessary for this discussion.

TIP   Notice that the .txt key includes a ShellNew subkey. This subkey tells Windows to place this kind of file on the New context menu entry you see when you right-click an open area in Windows Explorer. You use these entries to create new files using Windows Explorer. Unfortunately, this menu can get clogged with a bunch of entries you don't want and it often seems like some of the entries you do want are missing. To remove a file from the menu, highlight the ShellNew key and press Delete. To add a new entry to the menu, right-click the file extension key and choose New ➤ Key from the context menu. Name the key ShellNew. Select the new ShellNew key and right-click in the right pane. Choose New ➤ String Value from the context menu. Name the new value NullFile. Close and reopen Windows Explorer to see the new entries or delete old ones.

FIGURE 6.12

Always search from the top of the registry down, unless you know a search term lies in a particular hive or branch.

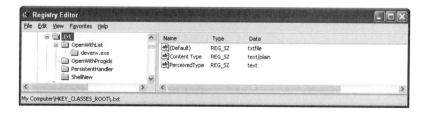

From the current location, choose the Edit ➤ Find command to display the Find dialog box. Type **TXTFILE** in the Find What field and click Find Next. You might have to press F3 several times to locate the `txtfile` key shown in Figure 6.13.

This registry key defines the file type information. You can assign this file type to more than one file extension. For example, I use Paint Shop Pro for editing graphics images, so many of the image file extensions on my system are of type `PSP.Image`. The file extension entry defines what to do with a particular file extension, while the file type entry provides details about a particular kind of file. As you can see, the `txtfile` file type defines which application to use to open the file, the default icon to display for these files, and the actions someone can perform on the file type, which includes open, print, and printing to a nonstandard location.

Looking for Complex Files

It turns out that the `txtfile` file type is relatively simple. Some entries become quite complex because you expect more out of that file. For example, a Word document is complex because you can embed it in other documents and perform a wide variety of tasks with it. Figure 6.14 shows the `Word.Document.8` file type. Notice that this file type doesn't define an application for opening the document.

FIGURE 6.13
Each file type entry defines actions for a particular kind of file.

FIGURE 6.14
Complex file types define a number of entries that are unique to that file.

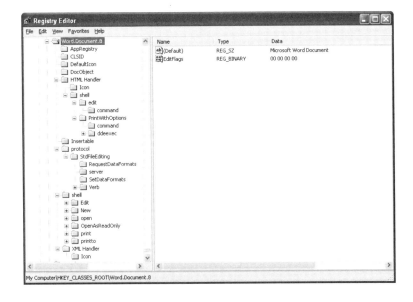

The "Working with Components" section tells you that some applications separate the user interface from one or more components that perform the actual work. A Word document is one such file type. Notice the CLSID key in Figure 6.14. This key tells you about the component used to interface with Word documents. It includes a special number called a Globally Unique Identifier (GUID) that identifies the component within Windows—no other component has that number. Consequently, a GUID is a very easy way to track components and trace them in the registry.

To search for a GUID, highlight the CLSID key and double-click the (default) value it contains. You'll see an Edit String dialog box and a number inside it highlighted that looks like {00020906-0000-0000-C000-000000000046} for a Word document. Press Ctrl+C to copy the number to the clipboard and then press Cancel to exit the Edit String dialog box without changing any entries. Highlight the My Computer entry at the top of the registry. Choose the Edit ➢ Find command to display the Find dialog box. Press Ctrl+V in the Find What field to paste the GUID from the clipboard to the search field and click Find Next.

You'll find that the first occurrence of this number selects a key that tells you it is a Microsoft Word Document. Additional searches will locate additional information about the key. As you search through the registry, you'll discover many things about Microsoft Word documents that you never knew before, such as the sequence of events that occurs when you convert an older document to the new format. However, the most important entry appears in Figure 6.15. Notice that this entry tells you about the various servers (components) that fulfill specific Word needs, such as when you embed a document in another application. The bottom line is that all file types eventually tell you about the application or component used to manage that file. You can use this information when searching for details about the application. These details define how the application works so you can extricate it from your system or augment it as needed.

The point of this particular part of the exercise is that the Word document GUID appears all over the place in the registry. That's why you need a registry cleaning kit to remove especially nasty entries that include components and file types when the uninstall program fails to do it for you.

FIGURE 6.15

Components make it easier to perform a number of tasks with a single file type.

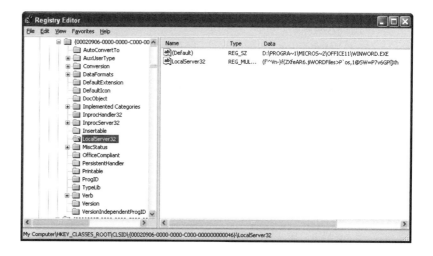

Removing Application Tidbits

Many applications leave tidbits behind. Previous sections of the chapter have already told you how to manage some of these tidbits. For example, the "Working with Components" section discusses application components and the "Following the Flow of Registry Entries' section describes the inner workings of file associations. This section provides some additional pointers on getting rid of applications you no longer need. It's important to remember to save these application settings, should you need them later, by exporting and archiving them.

Deleting Old Setup Data

Even after you uninstall an application, many applications leave registry settings in place. The most common registry entries are user or system settings. The "Working with Application Entries" section of the chapter describes how to work with these settings. However, once you get past these settings, you'll often find other settings left behind. These settings can cause any of the following problems:

Inefficient Use of System Resources   As with many other elements of the registry, Windows believes everything it has to say. When the registry tells Windows that there's an application available to handle a particular file or other need, Windows believes it. Even when the application folder for the application is missing, Windows will faithfully search for it, consuming your time, system processing cycles, and memory. Anything you can do to keep old setup information out of the registry optimizes Windows.

System Reliability Problems   Old registry settings cause more grief than you can imagine. It's possible for these settings to affect system stability. When your machine thinks it has a resource that no longer exists and the machine tries to use that resource, reliability problems begin to manifest themselves. You won't always see an outright crash. For all its flaws, Windows does recover remarkably well from single or even double errors. However, as the number of registry errors increase, the fixes for the problem become more problematic and you begin to notice system glitches. At some point, the recovery system becomes overwhelmed and your system begins to crash or exhibit other strange behavior.

Application Reliability Problems   Applications receive input from a number of sources in Windows. You don't see most of the activity that goes on behind the scenes, but your application is constantly interacting with Windows, device drivers, and even other applications. As the number of resource or application interaction errors increases, the reliability of your application decreases. Imagine this scenario. You open a document that contains an embedded document from another application. The application requests server support from the other application through Windows. Unfortunately, you have already uninstalled the other application. Unless the requesting application has good error handling (most don't) the application will crash—all because a leftover registry entry led the requesting application to believe a server was available for the embedded file.

Security Issues   All of the accumulated dirt in a registry can also lead to security problems. For one thing, all of those old entries provide more places for virus, adware, and spyware application entries to hide. The extra registry entries make it harder for antivirus and other helpful applications to locate the applications you don't want. In addition, older files often contain bugs that let these unwanted applications in the door. For example, even if you aren't using an older DLL, a registry entry could tell Windows to load it into memory. The second this event happens, your system becomes vulnerable to the attacks the older DLL allows.

In many cases, a registry cleanup aid will help locate old setup data, but even then you might not locate all of the settings. Most registry cleanup aids look for broken settings and these settings might still provide a cohesive line of associated entries akin to those discussed in the "Following the Flow of Registry Entries" section of the chapter. Fortunately, you can search the registry to locate these additional entries using the following criteria.

◆ Vendor name

◆ Application name

◆ Application executable filename

◆ Application-specific file extension

◆ DLL filenames

◆ Component GUIDs

◆ Application URLs

◆ Unique application setting data

You can also check for several symptoms of old setup data with certain types of applications. For example, some types of complex applications and device drivers will leave Control Panel entries behind. The application file appears in the \Windows\System32 folder with a Control Panel (CPL) file extension. You can normally verify that the file is the correct one by double-clicking the CPL file—you'll see the familiar Control Panel applet appear. However, removing the CPL file doesn't get rid of the problem. The registry keys that affect the Control Panel appear in the HKEY_CURRENT_USER\Control Panel branch for each user as shown in Figure 6.16. There aren't any system level Control Panel settings.

FIGURE 6.16

Make sure you remove any old Control Panel settings as part of removing an applet.

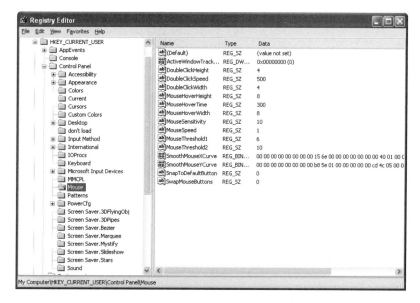

Notice the settings in the right pane in Figure 6.16. Like any other part of the registry, you always want to export Control Panel settings and archive them for future use when you remove an applet you no longer need. Saving this information will reduce the work needed to configure your system later.

One of the interesting things about spending time looking through the registry is that you can sometimes find interesting entries that lead to the source of a problem or at least some additional dirt. For example, many applications today register a special set of events in the HKEY_CURRENT_USER\AppEvents branch shown in Figure 6.17.

The Schemes key can lead you to some interesting discoveries. A client was having a mysterious glitch that occurred when using an online communication program. The glitch didn't damage anything; the system would simply take a break. In this case, the system didn't have NetMeeting installed, yet many of the entries in the event system pointed to a nonexistent NetMeeting folder on the target machine. Somehow, this other communication application was triggering a NetMeeting event. Removing the NetMeeting-related Conf key resolved the issue—no more glitches. The moral of this story is that careful observation and knowing what the "user" sections of your registry contain can help you localize and fix many Windows problems.

FIGURE 6.17
Errant event entries can cause system glitches, so you need to remove them.

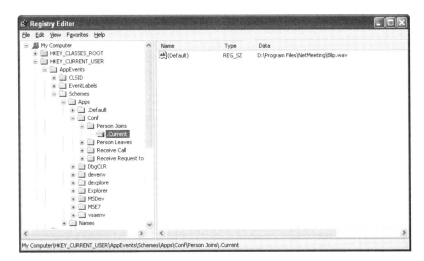

Reassigning File Associations

The most common application tidbit problem is the file association. Most applications leave their file associations in place. Personally, I think it's a secret plot by vendors to remind you of their missing application, but none of the vendors I talked with would admit to this subtle advertising scheme. No matter the reason for the leftover file associations, they can cause a number of problems for you, most of which are convenience-oriented.

You can reassign file associations in many ways. Using the registry is the most precise and fastest technique, but you could make a mistake. To change a file association using the registry, simply modify the (Default) value of the file extension key (see Figure 6.12) to point to a different file type. Double-click the (Default) entry and you'll see the Edit String dialog box. Type a new file type name in the Value Data field and click OK. When you don't have a new file type to assign to the extension, clear the Value Data field and click OK. The registry will display (value not set) as the value. Make sure you clear any subkeys from the file extension key to ensure Windows Explorer handles the file extension properly.

An easier way to perform this task, in many cases, is to choose the Tools ➤ Folder Options command in Windows Explorer. When you see the Folder Options dialog box, select the File Types tab. Windows Explorer will display the hourglass for several seconds (up to a minute) as it searches the registry for file types to display—be patient. When Windows Explorer displays the file type list, you can select the file extension you want to change as shown in Figure 6.18.

To modify the application used to work with the file extension, click Change. You'll see an Open With dialog box where you can choose a new application to service the file extension. When you don't have a new application to service the file extension, click Delete in the Folder Options dialog box. This act removes the file extension completely from the registry. The only way to set a file extension to a null (no application support) setting is to use the Registry Editor.

FIGURE 6.18
Use Windows Explorer whenever possible to modify old file associations.

Avoiding Common Application Cleansing Mistakes

Given that the registry has so much control over Windows, you'll want to avoid making any mistakes editing it. However, editing the registry need not be the end of life as we know it. Some people will make a terrifying mistake on their first visit to the registry and never visit it again. Avoiding mistakes is important, but don't give up on your first try either. Nothing you do will damage your machine to the point that it's unusable—the worst-case scenario is that you'll have to reformat the drive and reinstall everything from scratch. (Even if you don't have the skills required to reinstall the operating system, the fact that the hardware is undamaged means that someone can reinstall it for you.) Although formatting your drive and reinstalling Windows from scratch isn't something to savor, it certainly isn't life threatening.

If you truly want to avoid reinstalling Windows, make sure you create a backup of any registry branches you modify using the procedure in the "Exporting Data" section and archive them safely before you make the change. Try to test the change as thoroughly as possible before you reboot the machine. When you reboot the machine, check for possible errors. Don't continue using the machine if you spot any problems—reverse the registry edit instead and reboot the machine again. Make sure that reversing the registry edit actually fixed the problem.

Never modify a registry setting that you don't understand thoroughly. This might seem like a straightforward bit of advice, but many machines end up unusable because someone wanted to see what a registry change would do. Professionals who dig up the interesting registry edits that you seemingly find everywhere commonly use an experimental machine for their work. It doesn't matter if the machine dies and they have to reinstall Windows to revive it because the machine doesn't have anything of value installed on it. You can't afford to experiment with your machine because it contains a wealth of personal information that you can't easily replace.

Experiment on a test machine if you have that luxury. Sometimes, even the best advice from experts will backfire on a particular machine configuration because of interactions between registry settings. Whenever possible, test a new setting on an experimental machine configured precisely like the one you normally use. In most cases, you can move successful changes to your production system without any harm.

Always perform a backup of your system before you optimize it, but especially before you change anything in the registry. A failed registry change can cause significant problems, but the when you have a backup to use to restore your system the problems are greatly reduced. Yes, you'll still spend several hours fixing the error, but you won't lose any data and might even save time reconfiguring applications and performing other tasks required for a complete restoration.

Relying on Registry Cleaning Products

One of the more valuable tool investments you can make for optimizing your system is a registry cleaning product. A good registry cleaning product can take much of the pain out of locating errant registry entries and make it less likely that you'll remove something you really need. The following sections describe three registry cleaning utilities. Although these utilities worked fine on my system, I'm not advocating a particular registry utility.

Using RegClean

Microsoft produces RegClean (`http://www.majorgeeks.com/download458.html`). When you first start this utility, it scans the entire registry on your system. After what seems like an eon, the Reg-Clean utility completes the scan and tells you that it's ready to fix errors. This is where you have to take it on faith that RegClean has not only done its job, but can fix your registry without any help. The only option is to click Fix Registry (to fix the errors that RegClean found) or Cancel (assuming you don't believe that RegClean can do the job).

This particular utility has been around for years and many people, including myself, have used it with numerous versions of Windows with good success. However, it's a little disappointing that you don't get to see a list of fixes it will provide. In general, RegClean is extremely safe, but won't do more than repair problems it finds and get rid of a little of the grime. RegClean skips any registry entries it doesn't understand and concentrates its efforts in the HKEY_CLASSES_ROOT hive.

One of the features that you could easily miss about this product is that it creates an UNDO.REG file. To restore the registry to its previous state, all you do is double-click this file. Consequently, even if RegClean makes a change you don't like, you can easily reverse it.

Using Registry Mechanic

Registry Mechanic (http://www.winguides.com/regmech/) has the look and feel of a major cleaning tool. During installation, you can even choose to have Registry Mechanic scan your registry for potential problems every time you start Windows. This level of scanning verges on overkill and is probably more than most users will ever want, but it's nice to know the option is available. Fortunately, you can try this product before you buy it—the vendor includes a free trial download version.

When you open Registry Mechanic, you'll see a display similar to the one shown in Figure 6.19. The first thing to look at is the impressive list of items that Registry Mechanic scans. This comprehensive list covers most of the issues described in this chapter and the common issues that cause major Windows problems. Second, notice that this utility lets you create a backup of the registry before you even scan the system. You can set Registry Mechanic to create a new backup every time you perform any repairs using it. Restoring a backup is simply a matter of clicking Backup and choosing the registry version you want to restore.

TRACKING THE REGISTRY SIZE

When working with Windows NT and Windows 2000, you can set the registry size using a special option on the Virtual Memory dialog box. When Windows begins running out of registry space, you see an error message on screen that tells you about it. This is a good indicator that the registry is too full and that you need to clean it. You access the Virtual Memory dialog box by opening the System Properties applet of the Control Panel, selecting the Advanced tab, clicking Performance Options, and clicking Change in the Virtual Memory area of the Performance Options dialog box.

Unfortunately, Windows XP doesn't include this easy method of determining the registry size and Microsoft seems to imply that it doesn't matter (don't believe them). Check the Microsoft Knowledge Base article at http://support.microsoft.com/?kbid=292726 and you'll see that Microsoft has simply removed the size limit on the registry, rather than fix the problems of keeping it lean and trim. The Microsoft Knowledge Base article at http://support.microsoft.com/?kbid=124594 provides some tips you need to know, but it's in language that only a computer junkie would love.

Windows 98 users have access to a special utility called ScanReg. Simply type **ScanRegW /Fix** at the command prompt and press Enter to remove excess space from the registry. You can get a very good overview of the Windows 98 registry at http://www.microsoft.com/resources/documentation/windows/98/all/reskit/en-us/part6/wrkc31.mspx. The Microsoft Knowledge Base Article at http://support.microsoft.com/default.aspx?scid=kb;EN-US;183887 describes the ScanReg utility in detail. Note that the Microsoft Knowledge Base Article includes links for a number of helpful articles for ScanReg, including complete documentation for the command line switches.

FIGURE 6.19
Registry Mechanic performs a major exploration of your registry and comes up with detailed results.

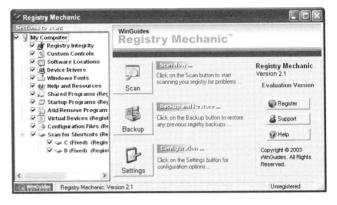

Once you get Registry Mechanic set up, click Scan and you'll see Registry Mechanic go to work. It takes a long time to scan the registry. My advice is to get a cup of coffee and read a magazine—a scan on one machine required more than an hour, which is why the scan during startup feature is of dubious benefit. However, the scan is incredibly comprehensive and it's unlikely that you'll find a better utility. To repair all of the errors that Registry Mechanic can find, you do need a registered version, which means you'll need to spend a little to get full use from this utility.

Using TweakNow RegCleaner

TweakNow RegCleaner (`http://www.tweaknow.com/RegCleaner.html`) is one of the free registry cleaners you can get on the Internet—at least it's free for noncommercial use. This utility scans for the most common registry errors as shown in Figure 6.20, which is more than sufficient for home use and probably meets the needs of business users. This utility probably won't meet the needs of developers because developers tend to create a wealth of registry entries in the "other" category. Testing TweakNow RegCleaner on a development machine that hadn't seen a registry cleaner for a year found 104 errors to the 114 found by Registry Mechanic, so either utility does a very good job.

FIGURE 6.20
TweakNow RegCleaner will locate and fix the most common registry errors.

Because this utility doesn't look for quite as many registry faults, it's significantly faster than Registry Mechanic. Interestingly enough, it's also faster than Microsoft RegClean. One of the features that I especially like about this utility is that it provides indicators to show that a registry entry is either safe or not safe to delete. This feature is lacking in the other two products.

TweakNow RegCleaner automatically creates a backup before you delete any errant registry entries. It only keeps the most current version of the registry, so you have to test between cleanings. However, this feature is possibly less confusing than the multiple backups that Registry Mechanic supports for novice and even intermediate users, so I don't consider the single backup a problem.

TIP   RegCool (`http://home.tiscali.de/zdata/regcool_e.htm`) is a full-featured registry editor and manager. This program adds a variety of powerful features such as the ability to export multiple keys into one REG file and a special feature that lets you work with secure registry keys. When combined, the special features help you to work faster and more efficiently when performing registry-related tasks. In addition, RegCool helps you carry out common tasks such as cutting, copying, pasting, moving, deleting, and renaming keys and values with greater ease. Unlike RegEdit, this product offers a Windows Explorer-style interface. An address bar helps you access registry keys and values quickly. Especially practical is the option to compare registry hives—a feature that can help you fix the registry when needed (see the "Restoring Registry Settings Using Comparison" section of Chapter 12 for details).

Performing Registry Tweaks that Make Sense

Some users are looking for every possibly means to increase the performance of their machine—nothing is off limits, even tricks like overclocking (a method of gaining better performance from a system by increasing the clock speed over the recommended value) their systems aren't out of the question. In at least a few cases, these performance tricks end up costing the user their machine or at least severely shortening its life. This section doesn't contain any tweaks of that sort. These are optimizing tips that you can use within the constraints provided so long as you're extremely careful. These tweaks often make sense in the context provided because Microsoft optimizes Windows for a standard machine and your machine is most definitely unique.

Disabling the Paging File

If you have at least 256MB of RAM and don't run many applications at once, you can get a performance boost by disabling the paging file. The paging file acts as extra memory when your system runs out of physical memory. When you use this tip, you're reducing reliability to gain speed. The best way to gauge whether this tip will work for you is to monitor how much memory Windows currently uses on your system—if you have a 40 percent or higher surplus, this tip should work. If you receive out of memory messages, however, restore the paging file setting to normal or get more physical memory.

This is a three-step process. You'll find all of the required values in the `HKEY_LOCAL_MACHINE\ SYSTEM\CurrentControlSet\Control\Session Manager\Memory Management` key of the registry.

Begin by opening the Registry Editor. To change any entry, double-click its value and type the new value in the dialog box provided.

1. Disable the paging executive by setting the `DisablePagingExecutive` value to 1. Changing this setting tells Windows XP to keep data in memory, rather than page it out to the hard drive.

2. Disable the large system cache by setting the `LargeSystemCache` value to 1. Changing this value tells Windows XP to keep the kernel (the main part of Windows) in memory.

3. Create a new DWORD value named `IOPageLockLimit`. Set this value to 10000 if you have at least 256MB of RAM or 40000 when you have more than 512MB of RAM.

Try the new settings during work to ensure you don't experience any out of memory errors. Once you've worked with the settings for a while reopen the Registry Editor and locate the `PagingFiles` value. Remove the text from this entry and reboot. This change effectively sets the paging file size to 0 (a change you can't make using any other method). After you reboot the system, manually erase the `PageFile.SYS` file on your hard drive—the file won't return unless you set a new paging file entry.

Setting Internet Explorer Automatic and Optional Searches

When you type an incomplete URL in the Internet Explorer Address field, Internet Explorer uses the automatic search site on the Internet to locate the missing information, the protocol for example, or at least provide a list of possible sites based on the value you type. Unfortunately, Microsoft makes it very difficult to change this value to something you like and many ISPs distribute software that change this entry. Although you can use products such as TweakUI (see the "Using TweakUI" section of Chapter 8 for details) to add extra searches, you must use the Registry Editor to modify the automatic search URL.

To make this change, locate the `HKEY_CURRENT_USER\Software\Microsoft\Internet Explorer\ SearchUrl` branch of the registry. You'll see a display similar to the one shown in Figure 6.21. What you're seeing are the automatic and optional searches for Internet Explorer. The automatic search relies on the values in the `SearchUrl` key and the subkeys hold optional searches. To use an optional search, type the key for that search in Internet Explorer, followed by the search value. For example, `af` in Figure 6.21 is associated with Acronym Finder. When I want to search Acronym Finder for an acronym, I type *af Acronym* in the Internet Explorer Address field and press Enter.

FIGURE 6.21
Adjust your Internet searches to meet specific needs.

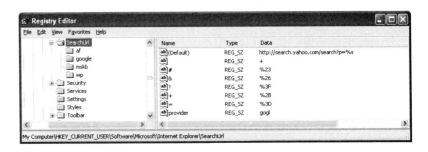

Constructing a search requires two kinds of values in most cases. The (Default) value for the key is the URL of a search engine. You provide the URL and a special %s entry that Internet Explorer substitutes with the search term you provide. For example, for Acronym Finder, you would use http://www.acronymfinder.com/af-query.asp?String=exact&Acronym=%s as the (Default) value. Beneath this value are several character replacement values. For example, you'll normally need to replace a space with a plus sign (+). Figure 6.21 shows the most common replacements you need to make. However, some search engines could require other replacements.

Choosing between Security and Shutdown Speed

Some registry edits let you choose between two different goals. For example, the page file on your system contains information that appeared in memory. Windows doesn't clear this file at any given time (not even at shutdown), so a cracker could view it and learn more about you. For example, the passwords you think are so secure aren't, because the page file stores the plain text password that you thought was in memory. Consequently, many people want Windows to clear the page file before they shut down the system. This act ensures that no one can see what was in memory, not even a fellow employee who uses your machine when you're not around.

Unfortunately, clearing the page file is a time-intensive process. When you have a relatively large page file, clearing it can take a long time. It might not be practical to clear the page file before you go home each evening and it's probably not even necessary for most home systems.

You'll find this setting in the LOCAL MACHINE\SYSTEM\CurrentControlSet\Control\Session Manager\Memory Management key of the registry. Setting the ClearPageFileAtShutdown value to 1 tells Windows to clear the page file, while setting it to 0 tells Windows to shut down faster.

Clearing the Open With List

Whenever you right-click a file in Windows Explorer, you see a list of standard operations for that file such as opening or printing it. You can also send the file to another location (such as an email message or a floppy disk). Another useful option is to open the file using an application other than the standard application—these options appear as part of the Open With menu. One option always appears in this list, Choose Program. All of the other options are optional.

Sometimes this list is filled with applications for popular files. As you remove older applications from the machine and add new ones, the list gets longer because Windows Explorer doesn't remove the old applications from the list. At some point, it becomes a chore to decide which application to use. The only way to clear this list and make the system efficient again is to perform a registry edit beginning at the HKEY_CURRENT_USER\Software\Microsoft\Windows\CurrentVersion\Explorer\ FileExts branch.

The subkeys in this branch are file extensions. To edit the Open With list, locate the file extension you want to modify and click the plus (+) sign next to it. You'll see several subkeys, one of which is OpenWithList. The values in this key tell which applications to use to open the file. Simply delete the values that you no longer need and they won't appear in the Open With menu of Windows Explorer any longer.

Let's Start Cleaning

This chapter hasn't explored the registry in detail, but it has provided you with ideas of where to look for problem entries. More importantly, this chapter helps you understand how to trace registry entries and provides a number of techniques for searching for specific registry entries. Even though the registry can cause problems when you don't understand how to work with it, careful removal of stubborn entries with the right cleaning product keeps your registry in great shape.

It's time to work with the registry. Open the registry and carefully explore the areas discussed in this chapter. Remember that simply looking at the registry doesn't modify it in any way. When you do decide to edit the registry, make sure you create a backup. In fact, you might want to practice exporting and importing simple registry entries before you perform any editing. Finally, remember the simple principle of using a tool designed to work with the registry whenever possible. Try one or more of the cleaning products discussed in this chapter on your registry.

Memory has gone down considerably in price since computers first appeared on the market, but it's still a relatively expensive part of your system. Consequently, you'll want to ensure that your system uses memory for tasks you want to perform, rather than wastes it on applications you don't know or care about. Chapter 7 looks at memory and various ways to ensure your system uses it properly. Memory optimization isn't difficult, but you'll want to check for any memory-eating beasts on your system.

Chapter 7

Memory Hogs and Other Vicious Beasts

You might not know it, but vicious beasts roam your computer devouring resources that kindly applications require. These evil manifestations from gizmo hell disrupt system operations and make it impossible for you to complete your work in a timely manner. If you didn't know better, you might think there was a conspiracy to make you look bad. However, the problem is more subtle than you think—the source of the problem is the perceived need for something that ultimately doesn't deliver anything at all and is ultimately forgotten—left to forage on its own.

Fortunately, you can hunt the beast down, assess its threat, and remove it from your system. This chapter discusses a number of unruly beasts that attack computer systems—everything from device drivers to gizmos that you installed, at some point, because they looked interesting. In fact, many useful applications turn into beasts through neglect. Often, someone thought they would use the application, found out later that the application really didn't do the job, and then failed to remove the application from the system.

Understanding How Much an Application Costs

Every application you start costs something in system resources. You can't start an application without using memory and processing cycles at a minimum. Applications also require hard drive space, network bandwidth, and access to various connections (such as the serial or parallel ports). Without resources, applications can't run and perform useful work. Unfortunately, this simple principle eludes many people and they stare in horror at the message that's bound to appear—the one that tells you that Windows has run low on a particular resource, usually memory. In fact, memory is one of the most used resources on your system, so managing it is especially important. However, before you can manage something, you need to know how much it costs and this information is surprisingly difficult to track down.

NOTE   Many application packages tell you how much memory the vendor recommends for a particular application. Unfortunately, these numbers rarely reflect reality. You really don't know how much memory an application requires based on these recommendations. The only way to understand how much memory an application requires is to measure the memory in some way and then write the value down for future use.

Using Task Manager

The Task Manager might not seem like the most capable tool, but it's fast, easy to use, and easy to understand. Because it's part of Windows, you don't have to do anything to install it, so Task Manager is always available. In many cases, Task Manager is all you need to get the job done because it provides the information necessary to identify and track down vicious memory beasts. To activate Task Manager, right-click the Taskbar and select Task Manager from the context menu. Choose the Processes tab and you'll see a list of applications running on your machine, as shown in Figure 7.1.

TIP   Clicking the columns in Task Manager will sort the list. You could set Task Manager to display the running processes in alphabetical order (for verification) or by the percentage of CPU time used (for performance tuning). You can also add new columns to the list using the View ➢ Select Columns command. You'll see a Select Columns dialog box that lets you choose all kinds of interesting information including the Process IDentifier (PID) and performance features such as the number of I/O Reads the process has performed.

You'll find that the Task Manager display isn't quite complete. It's enough to help you optimize your system, but you can do better with other utilities. Here are the limitations you need to consider.

The List of Processes Isn't Complete   Task manager only displays the applications that register themselves with Windows. Generally, the list includes applications you run, some low-level Windows applications, and any services that have a user orientation. Not included in the list are device drivers and some services that have a system orientation.

Memory Requirements Reflect Current Conditions   You can run into problems with the memory values listed in the display because they reflect the amount of memory the application is currently using, not the amount that it could use. For example, as you load more documents into a word processor, it uses more memory. Always remember to check your applications when they're in the state that you normally use them or you'll obtain false memory readers—never just load the application without opening documents or getting it into a working state.

FIGURE 7.1

Task Manager provides a list of applications running on your system and their current memory cost.

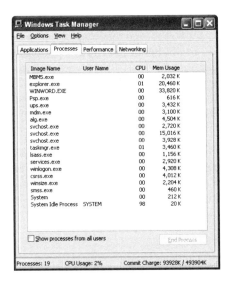

Lack of Historical Data Application memory requirements can vary quite a bit over time based on background processes and other needs. Because the Task Manager lacks a historical display, you only get a snapshot of current memory usage, which might not reflect the application's use of memory over time. Even so, application memory use won't vary enough to make the reading useless and Microsoft designed Task Manager to provide an overview.

You should know the purpose of every application in the list in Task Manager. In fact, you should know these applications on sight. When you see an application you don't know about, it's time to check it out. The application could be a virus, adware, spyware, or other unwanted memory hog. Generally, the best way to locate the executable is to open a command prompt at the root folder of your hard drive and use DIR to look for it. Table 7.1 tells you about the applications listed in Figure 7.1.

TABLE 7.1: A Sample Listing of Applications and Services

EXECUTABLE	PURPOSE	REQUIRED?
MBM5.EXE	This application monitors my motherboard for potential problems such as overheating or a nonfunctional fan.	This isn't a standard Windows application, but you should have something like it.
EXPLORER.EXE	This is a copy of Windows Explorer running on my system while I perform some file-related tasks.	No
WINWORD.EXE	I'm using this word processor to write the book—it's an example of a major application.	No
PSP.EXE	I'm using Paint Shop Pro to capture screenshots on my system.	No
UPS.EXE	This generic Uninterruptible Power Supply (UPS) service monitors system power as well as the UPS condition.	This isn't a standard Windows application, but you should have something like it.
MDM.EXE	This is the Machine Debug Manager (MDM) used with Visual Studio .NET, one of the programming language products that I use. Theoretically, I could turn it off between uses to save memory, but I develop a lot of applications so it saves time to leave it on.	No
ALG.EXE	This is the Application Layer Gateway (ALG) service provided by Windows. You need it to run certain kinds of applications. This is also the basis for features such as the Internet Connection Firewall and Internet Connection Sharing.	Only if you're using one of the affected Windows XP system features.

TABLE 7.1:   A Sample Listing of Applications and Services *(CONTINUED)*

EXECUTABLE	PURPOSE	REQUIRED?
SVCHOST.EXE	The service host executable isn't a standard application or service; it's actually a container for hosting services. The text that follows this table describes this particular executable in more detail.	It depends on the service that the service host executable is hosting.
TASKMGR.EXE	This is the Task Manager application.	You only need Task Manager to view the applications running on your machine.
LSASS.EXE	This is the Local Security Authority (LSA) Service Shell (LSASS) used to manage security on your system. This application also works with the WINLOGON.EXE to verify user logons and other user security concerns.	Yes
SERVICES.EXE	This application manages the services and controller applications on your machine. It's also associated with the Event Log and Plug and Play services.	Yes
WINLOGON.EXE	You use this application to log onto Windows and it monitors certain security aspects of your machine.	Yes
CSRSS.EXE	This is the Client Server Runtime Service Shell (CSRSS). This application handles all of the graphics and windows on your system, along with some other low-level process management.	Yes
WINSIZE.EXE	This is a special Notification Area application used to resize windows without having to drag the borders.	No
SMSS.EXE	This is the Session Manager Service Shell (SMSS). You rely on this application to start, manage, and delete your user sessions. In addition, Terminal Services uses this application to work with client sessions.	Yes
System	This is a theoretical measure of memory used by other system processes.	Yes
System Idle Process	You really don't have to worry about this entry. This entry tells you about the special process that soaks up any unused resources. Whenever you need more resources, this application gives them up.	This process is always present; you can't delete it, but theoretically, you don't need it either.

Some services on your machine rely on SVCHOST.EXE as a container application, as a means of executing without having to provide anything in the way of a user interface even in the Services console. You can't tell which of the services rely on SVCHOST.EXE just by looking at them—you need to open up the service in the Services console (found in the Administrative Tools folder of the Control Panel). Right-click the service you want to inspect and choose Properties from the context menu. You'll see a Properties dialog box, as shown in Figure 7.2. Look at the Path to Executable field in this figure and you'll see that SVCHOST.EXE is the executable.

Unfortunately, the technique of using SVCHOST.EXE makes it difficult to determine which Task Manager entry belongs to which service. Generally, because you need all of these services or would turn them off using entries in the Services console (see the "Clearing Unnecessary Services" section for details), you don't really need to know the specific service name. Seeing that it's a SVCHOST.EXE entry is enough to tell you that it's probably not a virus, adware, or spyware. Note that you can use the TaskList utility to make a finer determination of precisely what each SVCHOST.EXE entry does (see the "Using the TaskList Utility" section for details).

TIP   Many people don't trust Microsoft and with good reason—it seems as if Microsoft is always poking around on their systems. The reason for all of this information searching isn't important. Services such as Automatic Updates use resources and could expose information that you don't want exposed. You could manually remove all of these suspicious services by hand, but the process is time consuming and error prone. Products such as XP-Antispy (http://www.majorgeeks.com/download2062.html) can perform the task for you in an incredibly short time frame. The XP-Antispy utility looks for suspicious services on your system, stops the service, and then disables it. You can always start the service temporarily when necessary.

FIGURE 7.2

Some services rely on SVCHOST.EXE to execute.

Using the TaskList Utility

The TaskList utility provides a lot more information than Task Manager, but it's also harder to use. You can use TaskList to find specific information about services and applications running on your system. For example, you can determine which services are running or perhaps locked up (not responding). To get a display similar to the one shown in Task Manager, type **TaskList** at the command prompt and press Enter. Figure 7.3 shows typical output.

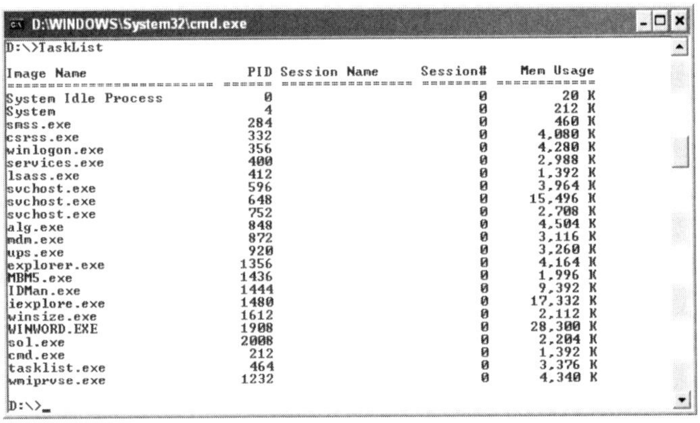

FIGURE 7.3

Use the TaskList utility to determine basic memory usage and process details.

```
D:\WINDOWS\System32\cmd.exe

D:\>TaskList

Image Name                   PID Session Name        Session#    Mem Usage
========================= ====== =================== ========== ============
System Idle Process            0                             0         20 K
System                         4                             0        212 K
smss.exe                     284                             0        460 K
csrss.exe                    332                             0      4,080 K
winlogon.exe                 356                             0      4,280 K
services.exe                 400                             0      2,988 K
lsass.exe                    412                             0      1,392 K
svchost.exe                  596                             0      3,964 K
svchost.exe                  648                             0     15,496 K
svchost.exe                  752                             0      2,708 K
alg.exe                      848                             0      4,504 K
mdm.exe                      872                             0      3,116 K
ups.exe                      920                             0      3,260 K
explorer.exe                1356                             0      4,164 K
MBM5.exe                    1436                             0      1,996 K
IDMan.exe                   1444                             0      9,392 K
iexplore.exe                1480                             0     17,332 K
winsize.exe                 1612                             0      2,112 K
WINWORD.EXE                 1908                             0     28,300 K
sol.exe                     2008                             0      2,204 K
cmd.exe                      212                             0      1,392 K
tasklist.exe                 464                             0      3,376 K
wmiprvse.exe                1232                             0      4,340 K

D:\>_
```

Notice that TaskList doesn't provide any information on CPU usage, but it does provide a mysterious Process Identifier (PID) column. Windows assigns a PID to every application that executes and uses this number to identify the application. When multiple copies of an application run, each copy has a unique PID. Other utilities rely on the PID as well for identification purposes, so knowing the PID when you want to perform detailed research is important.

Using TaskList without any arguments does net you some useful information, but it's the command line switches that make TaskList most useful. Here's a list of the switches with explanations of how to use them.

/S *System*   You can use TaskList to monitor the tasks on any system to which you have access and the proper rights. An administrator could use this feature to check which machines on the network are currently running Solitaire, if desired. In many cases, you'll need to combine this switch with the /U and /P switches to log into the system using an account with the correct privileges.

/U [*Domain Name/*] *User Name*   Use this switch to specify a user name and optionally, a domain name, for running TaskList. You need to include the /P command line switch when using this switch to provide a password. When you call TaskList without the /P switch, it will prompt you for the password. The only time you need to supply a domain is when you're working on a network with a domain controller.

/P *Password*   This command line switch lets you provide a password to go along with the username supplied with the /U switch. Don't use the /P switch alone.

/M [*Module*]   Most applications require use of one or more modules (usually DLLs) for support. When you use this switch alone, TaskList displays a list of every module used by every loaded application. It's quite a list, so you'll probably want to redirect the output to a file using the > or >> redirection symbols and adding a filename. The switch also lets you optionally specify a specific module name. You can use this option to determine which applications require a specific module to execute. Often, this process can help you understand why a particular application glitches when another application is loaded (sometimes they rely on a shared module, but each application requires a different version of that module).

NOTE   The list of modules TaskList provides are the modules the application has loaded. Some applications load modules optionally when they need them to save system resources. For example, a word processor might load a spelling module only when a user has requested a spelling check. Consequently, you can view this list as the modules the application must access to run, not the list required to enable all application features.

/SVC   Task Manager won't tell you which services each of the SVCHOST.EXE entries hosts. Use this command line switch to display that information. You'll find that each SVCHOST.EXE entry supports one or more services. Figure 7.4 shows typical output with this switch. Now compare this output with Figure 7.1 and you'll discover why one of the SVCHOST.EXE entries is so much larger than the other entries.

/V   This switch adds information to the display shown in Figure 7.3, including the application status, name of the user running the process, the amount of processor time the application is using, and the name of the application window. You might be surprised at how many of the applications listed are run by the system on your behalf or to maintain Windows. One of the most useful columns for optimization purposes is Window Title, which tells you the human readable name of the application. The connection between the executable and window names can help you locate viruses, adware, and spyware on your system.

/FI *Filter*   It's possible to filter the information TaskList provides so you see just the entries you want. The filters can become complex, so read the text that appears after this list for additional information. Table 7.2 describes the filter criteria.

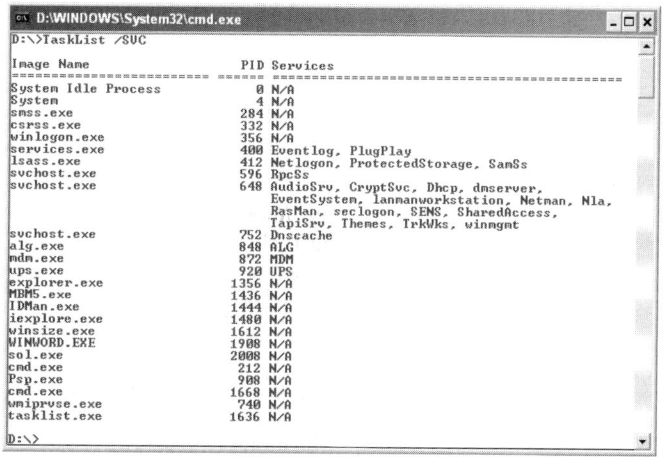

FIGURE 7.4

The /SVC command line switch tells you how the services are loaded.

/FO *Format* You don't have to display the TaskList output as a formatted table (TABLE format), as shown in Figures 7.3 and 7.4. In fact, you can use the LIST format to display the entries as single entries and the CSV format to display the entries in Comma Separated Value (CSV) as input for a database. Combine the /FO CSV and the /NH switches to create output that you can place in a file and output to a database. For example, to create a complete view of the current tasks, type `TaskList /V /NH /FO CSV > InputData.CSV` and press Enter.

TIP You'll be able to import the CSV file that TaskList creates directly into databases such as Access and SQL Server, or an application such as Excel without any problem. These applications can help you maintain a history of task lists and perform comparisons of various application loads on your system. Keeping track of the task list also makes it easier to detect when another application has "magically" appeared on the list.

/NH Tells TaskList to display the output without any header information. This switch only works for the TABLE and CSV formats.

TaskList also supports a number of filters. A filter helps reduce the number of outputs by comparing the entry against criteria you provide. The filters can use comparisons such as equal (eq), not equal (ne), greater than (gt), less than (lt), greater than or equal to (ge), and less than or equal to (le). You just use the two-letter comparison when working with TaskList. Table 7.2 lists all of the filters, describes them for you, provides a list of comparison operators for that filter, and tells you which values are valid.

TABLE 7.2: An Overview of TaskList Filters

FILTER	DESCRIPTION	COMPARISON OPERATORS	VALID VALUES
STATUS	This filter can help you locate any applications that are no longer responding so that you can manually end them.	eq, ne	Running or Not Responding
IMAGENAME	Use this filter to locate a particular application in the list based on its file name.	eq, ne	The executable file name
PID	Use this filter to locate a particular instance of an application when there's more than one copy of the application running.	eq, ne, gt, lt, ge, le	Program Identifier
SESSION	Unless you're using a sharing application such as Terminal Services, this filter is useless because every application running is for the current session.	eq, ne, gt, lt, ge, le	The session number

TABLE 7.2:   An Overview of TaskList Filters *(CONTINUED)*

FILTER	DESCRIPTION	COMPARISON OPERATORS	VALID VALUES
SESSIONNAME	Unless you're using a sharing application such as Terminal Services, this filter is useless because every application running is for the current session.	eq, ne	The name of the session
CPUTIME	This filter can help you locate applications that have just started or have been running a long time. For example, you might notice a sudden drop in system performance and can use this filter to locate applications that have just started to help determine which application might have caused the performance problem.	eq, ne, gt, lt, ge, le	The amount of time that the application has used the CPU in hours, minutes, and seconds since the session has started
MEMUSAGE	Sometimes you have more applications loaded than the system can comfortably support. This filter helps you locate applications that you can end or possible candidates for removal from the system.	eq, ne, gt, lt, ge, le	The amount of memory the application uses in KB
USERNAME	Use this filter to separate applications that the user starts from those the system starts.	eq, ne	The name of the user who started the application
SERVICES	Use this filter to locate the application hosting a particular service on the system.	eq, ne	A service name
WINDOWTITLE	This filter can help you locate a particular application based on the name it displays to the user.	eq, ne	The name the application displays to the user on the title bar
MODULES	This filter can help you locate applications based on the modules they use. You can use this filter to help locate a variety of problems, including DLL conflicts (when two applications use the same DLL, but they each need a different DLL version).	eq, ne	The filenames of any modules that an application uses

Using System Monitor

System Monitor is the medium-term performance monitoring tool. This tool provides better monitoring capabilities than Task Manager because you can view it for a longer time frame—the history is more complete and easier to manage. System Monitor provides all of the displays used for analysis of performance data. To view System Monitor, open the Performance console found in the Administrative Tools folder of the Control Panel. The Performance console actually contains two snap-ins (applications): System Monitor and Performance Logs and Alerts (described in the "Using Performance Logs and Alerts" section of the chapter), as shown in Figure 7.5. The following sections describe some essential areas of System Monitor usage.

Using Counters

System Monitor lets you track a performance characteristic of your system over an extended time frame. For example, you might want to track how well the hard drive is performing by checking the number of disk accesses. Every characteristic you track is a counter. A monitoring session begins with the selection of performance counters. The easiest method to add counters is to click the Add button (the plus sign) on the toolbar. You'll see an Add Counter dialog box like the one shown in Figure 7.6.

The dialog box shows that you choose performance monitoring at four different levels. Each level refines the one before it. The following list describes each level in the order that you would select them.

Machine   The machine you choose to monitor depends on the circumstances. For example, one performance monitoring scenario is to compare two machines with the same characteristics and application load. If one machine performs substantially slower than the other, the statistics might indicate the presence of a problem on the slower machine. Normally, you'll choose your machine to perform local monitoring.

Performance Object   System Monitor uses special bits of code called performance objects to monitor each area on your machine. In addition, vendors can add other performance objects to System Monitor so you can monitor larger applications such as SQL Server. There's a performance object for each major category of device or application on your machine. For example, Figure 7.6 shows the Process object. You'll also find objects for the physical and logical disk drive, memory, and network. Applications appear in objects such as browser, job, and thread.

Counter   A counter is a specific performance measure within the object. The counter is the portion of the performance monitor that acquires the data. The term *counter* is accurate in this case. The counters actually do count the number of occurrences of an event within a given time interval. For example, when determining the percentage of CPU cycles used to handle user requests, the counter counts both the total processor clock cycles and those used to handle user needs. It then performs a mathematical computation to calculate the percentage.

Instance   In some cases, saying you want to count something such as the percentage of processor time used to handle user needs doesn't define the problem. For example, if you have two processors and want to determine the percentage of user time, you have to indicate whether you want the user time for one or both processors. You also need to indicate which processor you want to work with if you choose only one.

As you can see, the potential number of performance monitoring combinations for a single system is immense. A typical system provides a minimum of 40 performance objects. Each of these objects have a number of counters (2 is a minimum and 30 is common). Many of these counters have at least two instances and a _Total instance (the combination of all instances of a counter). After you add the counters, click Close. You'll return to the Performance console and see the counters you selected displaying data.

FIGURE 7.5

The Performance counter actually contains two performance monitoring tools.

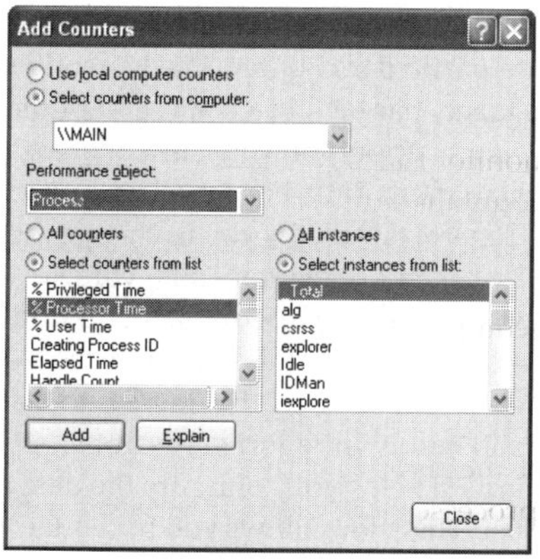

FIGURE 7.6

The Add Counter dialog box is the starting point for every System Monitor session.

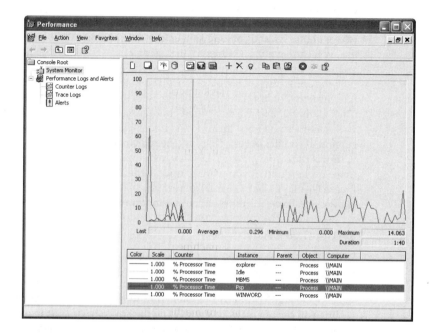

TIP Click Explain in the Add Counters dialog box if you want to know the meaning behind a particular counter. The explanation is relatively short, but usually helpful. It will always provide you with enough information to conduct additional research into the counters.

This brings up an important point. You don't want to overload a single display with too many counters. Tracking five or six of these counters is difficult on some displays. Adding more than that makes the information hard to track. Select carefully the counters you want to see. If you find that you've selected too many counters, remove a few by highlighting them in the listing shown at the bottom of Figure 7.5 and clicking Delete (the X next to the Add button). Once you find settings that you like, you can save the settings to disk using File ➤ Save As and reopen them later.

Even with the few counters displayed in Figure 7.5 (the counters show the amount of processor time the applications I have open use), you still might have a hard time seeing a particular counter line. System Monitor fixes this problem with the Highlight button, which looks like a little light bulb. Click Highlight and the associated counter line will become wider.

Sometimes you need to study the information you're seeing on screen for a while without interruption. If so, click Freeze Display (the red circle with an X in it). Click Freeze Display a second time to restart the display. Freeze Display just stops the display; System Monitor continues to collect data in the background. If you want to update the display quickly, click Update Data (the camera next to Freeze Display). Click Clear Display if you want to start the entire sequence over again. This method allows you to see an entire screen without interruption.

SETTING GRAPH PROPERTIES

Graph appearance is important. For example, you might want to add horizontal or vertical graph lines. Click Properties on the System Monitor toolbar when you want to change any of the settings. Figure 7.7 shows the General tab of the System Monitor Properties dialog box where you can choose many of the graph properties. System Monitor supports three views including graph, histogram, and report. You can also select a view using the appropriate button on the toolbar.

Below the views are three options for displaying the Toolbar, Value bar, and Legend. The toolbar contains all of the buttons we've discussed to this point. The Value bar contains a list of all the vital statistics for the counter highlighted in the Legend. For example, you can learn the minimum, maximum, and average values for a particular counter. The Legend lists the selected counters. Each counter entry includes the instance, parent, object, and computer information.

The report and histogram views support only instantaneous data values. Sometimes it's beneficial to see something other than the default data. For example, you might want to see the average data value. The next section of the General tab allows you to change the histogram and report view values. The default setting displays the current (instantaneous) values.

"The Sample automatically every setting" permits you to update the display more or less often than the default setting of 1 second. Clearing this entry will freeze the display. The "Allow duplicate counter instances" option tells System Monitor that it's OK to display more than one instance of the same data. This feature comes in handy in report view, but is actually detrimental in other views.

The Data tab shown in Figure 7.8 helps you configure the data display. You begin by selecting one of the entries in the Counters list. This view allows you to change the color of the data, along with the width and style of the line. The scale determines how the lines scale in comparison with the rest of the lines on screen. Using a larger scale can often bring out details about the data, especially if variations are small.

The Graph tab contains settings that change graph display elements. The display elements include the use of a vertical and horizontal grid. You can also give your graph a title and assign a name to the vertical element (the horizontal element is always time). The Vertical Scale properties offer another chance to optimize the graph display. You can set the graph so it displays the data a little larger or smaller than the default settings allow.

Finally, the Appearance tab contains settings that change the colors used to display certain elements such as the graph background and time bar. This tab also enables you to choose a new font for the display. The use of a different font may make the information more legible or easier to print.

FIGURE 7.7

The General tab allows you to set graph elements such as the graph type.

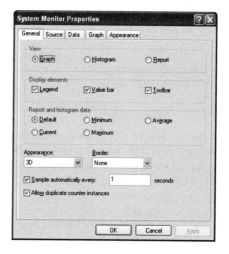

FIGURE 7.8

Use the Data tab to change the appearance of the data on screen.

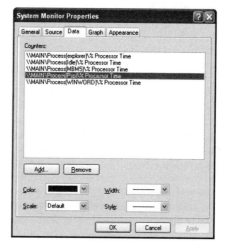

Using Performance Logs and Alerts

The Performance Logs and Alerts snap-in performs long-term performance monitoring. The reason you need long-term performance monitoring is that some changes aren't apparent right away. You might make a change to the registry and not see the effects for a while. In addition, many performance changes are subjective—you can't really trust your senses to verify the change (sometimes a good dose of hope makes a nonexistent change seem quite substantial)—you must measure it to be sure. This snap-in performs three different tasks, using three folders: Counter Logs, Trace Logs, and Alerts. The following sections describe each of these folders.

CREATING COUNTER LOGS

The Counter Logs folder performs essentially the same task as System Monitor. It relies on the same counters as the System Monitor, but stores the data it collects on disk, rather than displaying it immediately. You'll view the data created by this snap-in using the System Monitor and a few special settings that we didn't discuss earlier.

Storing the Counter Information

You begin creating a log by right-clicking Counter Logs and choosing either New Log Settings or New Log Settings From. When you choose New Log Settings From, you'll see an Open dialog box from which you can choose an HTM or HTML file containing the appropriate settings. You'll generate this HTM or HTML file by right-clicking an existing Counter Log entry, then selecting Save Settings As from the context menu.

The New Log Settings entry displays a New Log Settings dialog box. Type a name for the counter log and click OK. You'll see a properties dialog box like the one shown for My Counter Log in Figure 7.9. Notice that I've already added a counter to this dialog box. Normally, you'd see a blank dialog box and would need to add counters to it.

The counters and objects used with the Counter Logs are the same as those used for System Monitor. In fact, when you click Add Counters, you'll see the same Add Counters dialog box, as shown in Figure 7.6. Click Add Objects and you'll see a dialog box that only allows you to select a machine and a performance object. If you select a counter, then you're selecting just that counter or even a counter instance. When you select an object, it includes all the counters within that object.

TIP   You need to consider the trade-offs between counters and objects. An object will require more hard drive space to store and will consume more processing cycles. However, you'll have all of the counters for that object, so you don't need to worry about finding a particular piece of data. Using counters is more efficient, but lacks flexibility. If you don't think to store a critical piece of data, it won't appear in the log later for analysis. Generally, it's best to use objects when you can spare the hard drive space and lost processing cycles.

After you select some objects or counters, you can set the sampling interval. Short intervals produce more data, so you'll get results that are more precise. However, using short intervals also makes the impact of performance monitoring more severe. Again, it's a matter of balancing system resources and performance against the performance monitoring requirements.

FIGURE 7.9

Use the report view to organize large numbers of counters into an easy-to-read report.

Notice the Run As field on the dialog box. In some cases, the person running the performance monitoring software won't have the credentials required to perform all tasks. The monitoring will fail, in this situation, preventing you from obtaining good readings. To overcome this problem, type the name of a person with the correct rights, click Set Password to display the Set Password dialog box, type the password twice, then click OK. The counter can run now because it isn't relying on the user's credentials.

The Log Files tab of the properties dialog box contains fields that adjust the output log. You can choose from several output formats including text, binary, and SQL Server. The last entry is helpful if you want to store the results in a database for complex analysis and archiving. The Example field shows what the output filename will look like; you can monitor this entry as needed. Finally, you can add a comment to the file and choose to overwrite the old log file each time you restart the Counter Log.

You'll use the Schedule tab to define a starting and ending time for the Counter Log. The Start Log field contains entries that start the logging manually or on a specific date and time. The current time is the default setting. The Stop Log field contains entries that will stop the logging manually, after a specific time interval (seconds, minutes, hours, or days), a specific date and time, or when the log is full. The default setting stops the logging manually. Finally, you can set the Counter Log to perform a task automatically when the log file closes. This parameter includes creating a new log and running an application.

After you set up everything, click OK. If you're using the default Start Log settings, the Performance Logs and Alerts snap-in will begin the logging immediately. Otherwise, you'll need to start the logging manually by right-clicking the Counter Log object and selecting Start, or waiting until the predefined conditions occur. Active counter log entries have green icons, while stopped entries have red icons.

Viewing Counter Logs

You have a log that you created of processor activity or some other performance object. Having the log and doing something with it are two different things. You need to know how to view the log after you create it.

To view the content of a log file, open System Monitor and click View Log Data (the icon that looks like a database symbol). You'll see the Source tab of the System Monitor Properties dialog box. Click Log Files (or database, if you saved the data in that form). Click Add, and then select the log file(s) you want to view. Note that you can add more than one log file to the list to see a longer interval. Make certain that all the logs come from the same Counter Log. If you think you might want to limit the interval viewed on screen, click Time Range.

Click OK and you'll see the static data collected in the log. Of course, this means you won't see the Time Bar moving across the screen—System Monitor only uses the Time Bar when it has active data to read. All of the other options that you use for active data apply when working with a log. For example, you can display a graph, histogram, or report version of your log.

NOTE One change that you'll notice is that the content of the Add Counters dialog box will change. You can only view data that you've recorded, which means the list of objects and counters will change. In addition, you can only select counters for computers that you logged. Any other computers will fail to appear on the list.

CREATING AND CONVERTING TRACE LOGS

Trace Logs perform detailed system monitoring. It's almost never necessary to use this level of monitoring to optimize your system. In fact, you normally use this level of monitoring to fix major system problems—the type that give network administrators nightmares.

You can choose the types of events that a Trace Log monitors. A Trace Log can help you see the flow of data on a system or determine when an application is creating too many threads. By knowing that an application is creating too many threads, you can begin optimizing it for better performance and behavior (too many threads can cause crashes) by reducing the number of simultaneous tasks the application performs.

This part of the Performance Logs and Alerts snap-in creates special logs that you have to convert into human readable format using the TraceRpt utility. You can read the resulting output in System Monitor or within an application such as Excel (the preferred method in this case).

Saving the Trace Log

The process used to create a Trace Log is similar to that of a Counter Log. You begin by right-clicking Trace Log and choosing New Log Settings From or New Log Settings from the context menu. I'll assume you've selected New Log Settings in order to create the Trace Log object from scratch.

When you see the New Log Settings dialog box, type a name for your Trace Log and click OK. You'll see the properties dialog box shown in Figure 7.10. Note that I've selected Events Logged by System Provider to show those options clearly in the figure. You can also choose nonsystem providers to track. In most cases, you'll need to provide a Run As entry to ensure the Trace Log works as anticipated because few users have the rights required to perform this low-level work.

FIGURE 7.10
You'll need to define what type of system events you want to trace.

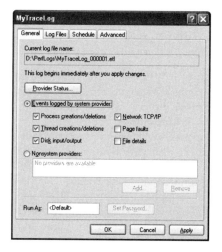

The Log Files and Schedule entries work just like those for the Counter Log. One difference that you'll note is that Trace Logs use different log file types. You can't read either log file type directly; both require the use of the TraceRpt utility.

The Advanced tab contains the buffer settings for the Trace Log. A Trace Log gathers a large amount of data. The log service saves data to temporary buffers in order to improve performance. If the settings you choose don't meet minimum requirements, the log service will override them. Normally, the log service saves data in the buffers to disk when the buffers are full. However, you can also set the number of seconds between data transfers to reduce the risk of losing data.

TIP The settings you use for the buffers will affect the performance of your machine and the activities of the Trace Log. In some cases, providing a larger number of buffers or using a larger buffer size will allow the log service to work more efficiently and reduce system load. However, adding too many buffers increases the risk of data loss or corruption should the machine freeze or act in other unexpected ways.

Click OK. Performance Logs and Alerts will attempt to start the Trace Log if you used the default settings. Otherwise, you'll need to start the logging process manually, or wait for the conditions you set to occur. If the Trace Log lacks the proper permissions to start, the indicator will remain red and you'll see a warning message in the Applications folder of the Event Viewer indicating the problem. Fix any problems and restart the Trace Log manually.

Viewing the Trace Log

After you collect the required data, stop the Trace Log from running. Right-click the Trace Log entry, and then select Stop from the context menu. The indicator will turn red. Open a command prompt in the \PerfLogs directory. Type **TraceRpt <Name of Trace Log>**, and then press Enter. TraceRpt will process the files and create two outputs for you. The first is SUMMARY.TXT, which contains a summary of the number and type of events. You can read SUMMARY.TXT with any standard text editor such as Notepad. The second is DUMPFILE.CSV, which contains the detail data. Note that you can use wildcards in your arguments to TraceRpt in order to process more than one file.

NOTE TraceRpt accepts other command line switches, but you normally won't need to use them unless you perform multiple traces on one system and don't want to overwrite the default files. Use `TraceRpt /?` to see a list of other command line arguments and switches.

You can open the `DUMPFILE.CSV` file in a number of ways, but the two best ways are with a spreadsheet or database manager. This file will contain a lot of information and working with it any other way will prove difficult. Sorting the data is going to be a necessity. Figure 7.11 shows a typical `DUMPFILE.CSV` file output.

This log shows what happens when you select the default monitoring options. As you can see from the figure, I created a few new processes, but the system generated a lot more. Much of the trace data remains hidden in the figure. For example, you can't see the event name or type columns.

One column contains the Thread IDentifier (TID) for the process. Windows XP assigns every instance of an application a unique TID. For example, if you open two copies of Notepad, they'll both have a different TID. It's safe to ignore this column for troubleshooting and performance needs.

You'll also see columns for clock time (indicates the process priority), user time, and kernel time. These are the three columns of most interest for performance needs. The priority tells you how the application shared CPU cycles with other applications. If you see an application that sets a high priority, you might want to explore further and ensure the application warrants the extra processing cycles. The user time indicates how much time the application spent in user mode, generally serving user needs. The kernel time shows how much time the application spent in protected mode accessing system resources.

FIGURE 7.11
The `DUMPFILE.CSV` file contains the detailed trace information.

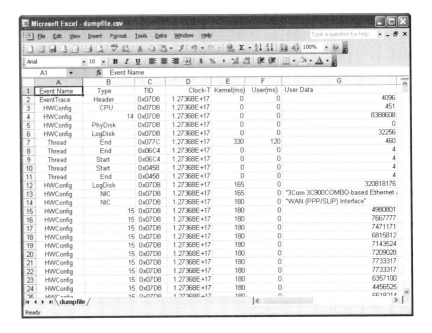

CREATING ALERTS

You'll use the Alert folder to warn you of system conditions or to tell you when an optimization event has occurred. For example, you can use it to warn you that system memory or hard drive space is low. The alert could occur because an optimization you performed left the system too short on a specific resource. Disabling the paging file makes your system faster and reduces hard drive resource use, but at the cost of memory. When you use the technique located in the "Disabling the Paging File" section of Chapter 6 to disable the paging file, you might also want to set an alert to tell you whether the cost of the optimization is too high. Here are the techniques that an alert can use to warn you of impending disaster.

◆ Create event log entries

◆ Send you a console message

◆ Run an application as part of the alerting process

To create an Alert, right-click Alerts, and then choose New Alert Settings From or New Settings Alert from the context menu. Type the name for your Alert in the New Alert Settings dialog box and click OK. You'll see a properties dialog box.

Alerts work by monitoring performance counters on your system, so you need to add at least one counter to the Counters list before you can do anything else. Click Add and you'll see an Add Counters dialog box. I chose processor idle time as an example because it's easy to generate an Alert using this counter. Figure 7.12 shows the General tab for the sample Alert. An Alert can rely on more than one counter, but you should create one Alert for each major event so that you can detect which Alert went off.

You also need to select an Alert condition. For example, if you're monitoring memory, you might want to set an Alert when the amount of available memory falls below a certain level. As you can see, this tab also allows you to set the monitoring frequency and the Run As field.

FIGURE 7.12
The General tab helps you configure the alert conditions.

The Action tab contains options for telling you when an event occurred. The following list discusses each option and explains what they mean.

Log the Event to the Application Event Log   This is the best solution for noncritical alerts. You want to know the event happened, but you don't have to fix the condition immediately.

Send someone a message   Reserve this option for critical alerts that require immediate attention. For example, if a lack of memory or hard drive space will cause the system to fail, then you want to send someone a message. There are two odd requirements when sending a message. First, the message must go to a machine other than the current machine. Second, the message must go to the machine and not the person. If more than one person uses a machine, this second requirement could become a problem. If the message sending option looks like it won't work, then you could always write a script to send the message in another way.

Start a Performance Data Log   Some events require monitoring because you know they already exist, but don't know how to fix them. Starting a performance data log can give you the information needed to track the problem and fix it.

Run an Application   You'll reserve this action for situations when an application can fix the problem automatically. For example, you might set an alert for a condition when a hard drive nears its capacity. The alert could start an application to clean up temporary and other unneeded files. A higher-level alert could tell you that the action was ineffective and you need to look at the machine.

The final tab, Schedule, works the same as every other performance monitoring tool discussed in this section. Just set a starting and ending time. You can also set the Alert for a manual start or stop. Once you complete the Alert setup, click OK, start it, and hope you don't see a message.

Using the TypePerf Utility

The TypePerf utility is a kind of System Monitor in text, rather than graphic format. Both of these utilities let you monitor system performance in real time and you can discover counters using either utility. Although the TypePerf utility doesn't display data in graphic format as System Monitor does, you can use it to produce text output suitable for a database or other archiving application. In short, both utilities perform essentially the same task using a different output technique.

NOTE   You never use the TypePerf utility by itself—you always include command line switches or other information with it. When you attempt to use TypePerf by itself, the application displays an error message.

To use the TypePerf utility, you need to decide on which task you want to perform: list the counters and instances for a particular performance object or to track performance. The two tasks are mutually exclusive and you use the utility in different ways to perform each task. The following sections describe how to perform each task.

LISTING PERFORMANCE OBJECT COUNTERS WITH TYPEPERF

You might initially think that you can't use System Monitor and TypePerf together, but listing object counters is one place where TypePerf excels and makes it easier to work with System Monitor. When working with System Monitor, you have to spend time looking through the various counters and instances that a particular object provides. Using TypePerf, you get comprehensive list that you can scan quickly for the information you need. Here are the TypePerf command line switches you need to perform this task.

/Q [*Performance Object*] Use this command line switch to list just the counters provided by an object without the instances. Note that you can use this switch by itself to retrieve a list of all of the objects and counters supported on the current machine. This switch works best when you need to research an object for use with System Monitor and already have a good idea of which instances the object supports. The output from this option is also shorter than using the more complete /QX switch. Consequently, you can often display the counters on screen, rather than send the output to a file.

/QX [*Performance Object*] Use this command line switch to retrieve both the counters and the instances for the requested performance object. When you use this switch by itself, you receive a list of every instance of every counter of every object on your machine—the list is immense, so only use this option when you have time to wait. Always use this command line switch with the /0 option to output the data to a file. This option works best when you want to obtain the full syntax for tracking performance with TypePerf or you want to research objects used with System Monitor fully.

/0 *Filename* Use this command line switch to redirect output from the screen to a file. The output remains the same listing format as you see on screen.

To use TypePerf to list objects, you need to decide on an object name, which might means using the /Q command line switch by itself. Once you do decide on a TypePerf object, use it along with the listing option you want to use. For example, when you choose the Job Object performance object, you type **TypePerf /Q "Job Object"** or **TypePerf /QX "Job Object"**. Always place quotes around objects that have spaces in their name. Figure 7.13 shows the results of using both commands.

FIGURE 7.13

Use TypePerf to list the counters and optionally the instances for a performance object.

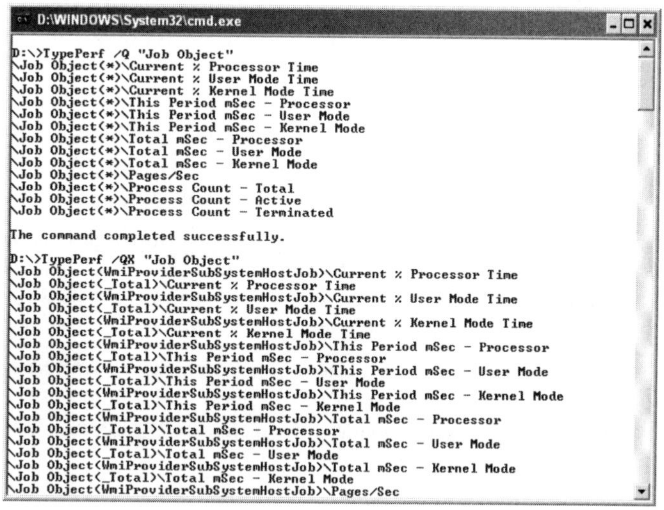

The upper half of the display shows the results of the /Q command line switch. This listing shows just the counters. The lower half shows the results of using the /QX command line switch. The performance object name appears first, followed by the instance name in parenthesis. The counter name appears after the first slash. So, the first entry on this list is for the Job Object performance object, the Current % Processor Time counter of that object, and the WmiProviderSubSystemHostJob instance of that counter. This is the same formatting you use when you want to display the performance statistics on screen.

TRACKING PERFORMANCE WITH TYPEPERF

Let's face it, the output from TypePerf is a little bland compared to System Monitor for real time viewing. However, TypePerf makes the perfect low cost method of gathering statistics for later analysis. From a resource perspective, TypePerf has a much lower impact on system resources than System Monitor does and you can run it as a scheduled task. You can even manage it using a script—all good reasons to use TypePerf for automation. With this in mind, here are the command line switches you use for working with TypePerf to accomplish performance tracking.

/F CSV **or** /F TSV **or** /F BIN **or** /F SQL   These four command line options let you choose the output format of TypePerf including Comma Separated Value (CSV), Tab Separated Value (TSV), binary, or Structured Query Language (SQL). The only option that works well for a screen display is CSV, the default format. Use the TSV, BIN, and SQL formats for file output only.

/CV *Filename*   You might want to monitor more than one counter at a time. This command line switch lets you create a list of all the counters that you want to monitor. Supply the filename as part of the input and TypePerf will monitor all of the counters you requested. This command line switch also reduces the work required to automate the use of TypePerf because you simply change the content of the file to change what TypePerf automatically monitors on the target system.

/SI [[*Hours:*]*Minutes:*]*Seconds*   Use this command line switch to change the interval between samples. You must provide the number of seconds, but can optionally provide the number of minutes and even hours between samples. The default setting is 1 sample per second, which is too fast for many measurements. You might only need to sample a particular counter once an hour to ensure it remains within a specific range of values.

/O *Filename*   Use this command line switch to redirect output from the screen to a file. When using the /F SQL option, you can also supply the name of a SQL Server database as an output. The output appears in whatever format you choose using the /F option.

/SC *Samples*   Normally, TypePerf continues gathering samples until you press Ctrl+C to stop it. However, you can use this command line switch to define the number of samples to collect. You should always use this option when working in an automated setup to ensure TypePerf doesn't continue to use resources any longer than necessary to collect the required information.

/CONFIG *Filename*   Use this option to specify the name of a file that contains all of the required configuration options. This is a good option to use when you rely on Task Scheduler to start TypePerf. All you need to do to change TypePerf behavior is modify the configuration file. The Task Scheduler entry remains the same.

/S *Computer Name*   This option lets you monitor a computer other than the local computer. To use this option, you must have the required rights on the remote computer.

/Y   Tells TypePerf to answer yes to any questions it might ask.

TIP   You can monitor several computers at once by specifying the name of the computer as part of the performance counter declaration. For example, "\\Main\Process(_Total)\% Processor Time", would tell TypePerf to monitor the _Total instance of the % Processor Time counter of the Process object on a server named Main. To change monitoring to a different machine, you simply change the name of the server. This technique lets you monitor several machines for the same statistic at one time.

Using MSCONFIG

The Microsoft Configuration (MSCONFIG) utility lets you look at how Windows boots and optionally changes the features that it automatically loads during the boot process. This configuration utility can help you locate applications and low-level services you don't need without any potential for damage. In addition, it helps you look in areas that none of the utilities discussed so far cover.

Understanding the MSCONFIG Basics

You might find it interesting that some Windows XP machines are still running older Windows 9*x* applications, some of which are 16-bit and require entries in two special configuration files: WIN.INI and SYSTEM.INI. One major hint here, 16-bit applications are excessively slow and you should do everything possible to get rid of them. These two files were the original receptacles for system information before the registry took center stage. The WIN.INI file concentrates mainly on user settings, while the SYSTEM.INI file concentrates mainly on system settings. Windows XP supports, but doesn't need either WIN.INI or SYSTEM.INI. However, it's important to know that these two files exist because some applications hide there hoping you won't find them.

It's also possible to use MSCONFIG to view and configure other startup options. For example, all of the services appear here, as well as the startup applications your system runs. MSCONFIG retrieves information from several sources to provide you with a complete picture of your startup situation. That's why this utility is so important; it helps you overcome configuration problems in a safe environment.

When you want to check for potential problems in these two files or monitor how Windows XP uses other boot options, run the MSCONFIG utility. Select Start ➢ Run to display the Run dialog box. Type MSCONFIG in the Open field and click OK. You'll see the System Configuration Utility dialog box shown in Figure 7.14.

Notice that this utility offers several startup options. The Normal Startup option lets your system start normally. Use the Diagnostic Startup option when your system suffers a severe setback that you need to reverse, such as installation of an incompatible device driver that prevents a normal startup. The Selective Startup option is the one you should try for optimization because it lets you choose the setup of startup commands that Windows XP uses. To modify the boot sequence, simply clear the check next to the major feature that you want to disable. You can also go to the individual tabs and disable one or more of the boot elements.

FIGURE 7.14
Use MSCONFIG to dis-
able compatibility file
processing if desired.

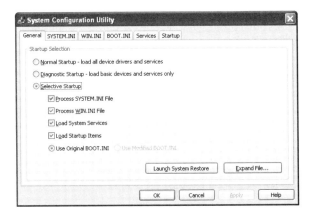

TIP   You're looking at a friend's machine. The machine is running a common application faster than
your machine will run it despite having the same processor and amounts of memory in both
machines. Your machine might not simply be slow, you might be the victim of a problem with vendors who say they're providing a high performance part, but use a lower cost part instead. Fortunately, you can verify that you received the processor you paid for using the Intel Processor
Frequency ID Utility (`http://www.majorgeeks.com/download2343.html`). The application
will tell you all about your processor, such as the frequency at which it runs. All of this information
helps you decide whether you received the processor that you paid for.

Understanding *SYSTEM.INI*

The SYSTEM.INI tab shown in Figure 7.15 contains device driver entries and settings needed to configure them. For example, you'll find both the wave file and windows timer entries on this tab and in
the associated file. In general, these settings are for 16-bit applications. When you don't have any 16-
bit applications on your system, you can free memory and improve system performance by removing
these entries. Unbelievably, Windows XP loads these drivers when you start the system even if you'll
never use them.

Generally, you don't want to get rid of these entries because you might need them sometime in the
future. However, when you clear the check in front of the two entries, so Windows XP doesn't load
them, the system will ask you about using the Selective Startup option every time you start your
machine. A good alternative to this problem is to place a semicolon (;) and a space in front of each
entry that you don't want to use in SYSTEM.INI. This way, the entry is still there, but Windows XP
ignores it. Adding the semicolon disables the entry. To perform this task, select the entry and click
Edit. Place the semicolon and space in front of the entry, as shown in Figure 7.15. The entry is now disabled, but still present should you need it later.

TIP   Windows XP Service Pack 2 (SP2) enhances security to the point of strangulation in many cases.
Microsoft purposely ignored backward compatibility when creating SP2 because the cries of people
suffering from the poor security of previous Windows versions were so loud. The worst thing you
can do for your system is install SP2 if you need to run any 16-bit applications. When you see entries
in SYSTEM.INI other than those displayed in Figure 7.15, watch out, SP2 isn't for you.

FIGURE 7.15

Modify the SYSTEM.INI file to remove unnecessary 16-bit drivers from your system.

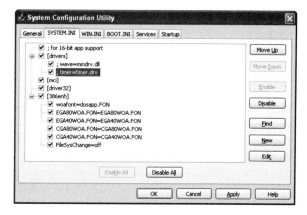

You don't really need to remove the font entries from the list. They do consume a small amount of system memory, but you need them in some cases. The important issue is that you want these fonts available in case you do have a 16-bit application that needs them. The application can then tell you that any drivers you disabled are missing. It's not a perfect optimization technique, but it works.

Understanding *WIN.INI*

Windows XP can theoretically get along just fine without WIN.INI. However, before you get rid of your file, you might want to check it out first. A few applications, especially screen savers, load themselves by using the LOAD= or RUN= lines of this file. You can get around this limitation by adding the filenames to your Startup folder and changing the application settings as needed. (You may want to get rid of a screen saver that uses these WIN.INI entries if it's a 16-bit application. A 32-bit screen saver will be more responsive and less likely to crash your system.)

Many applications also store their file-association information in WIN.INI. Windows XP applications don't need these entries because they already appear in the registry. Any new 32-bit applications will know to look in the registry for file association information, but some older 16-bit applications won't. You might want to check for problems by disabling the [Extensions] section using MSCONFIG and rebooting the system. If all your applications seem to work properly, you might be able to remove this section for good.

NOTE Windows XP always checks for new entries in both WIN.INI and SYSTEM.INI. It automatically adds any new entries that it finds to the appropriate section of the registry. This is the reason why you can get rid of these two files if you have a stable system and none of the 16-bit applications that used to rely on them.

You have to exercise care when working with WIN.INI. Microsoft has decided to change course yet again and is trying to get developers to use external storage files again so their application settings aren't in the registry. This technique allows for what Microsoft calls XCOPY compatibility—someone can copy an application from one machine to another using the XCOPY utility (described in the "Using XCopy" section of Chapter 3). Consequently, I recently found settings for the scientific calculator that comes with Windows XP in WIN.INI, along with settings for WinSize (a program I used for sizing application dialogs precisely) and my hexadecimal (programmer's) editor. I have no doubt that INI (initialization) files will become popular again, so you need to work with them carefully.

Avoiding *BOOT.INI*

The BOOT.INI tab might look like it contains interesting settings, and it does for diagnostics, but you should probably avoid it when optimizing your system. This tab shows the basic startup process for Windows XP and contains some special check boxes for performing diagnostic tasks. For example, you can check /BOOTLOG and Windows XP will record every event during the startup process. The only problem with the resulting boot log is that it's huge and very hard to understand. You can even select the /SAFEBOOT option, but these features are available using other, less intrusive techniques, such as pressing F8 when you start your machine.

Selecting Services

Windows services are normally very stable and you won't have any trouble with them. However, it's possible that you'll run into services that you really don't want or need. You can't remove a service using MSCONFIG, but you can disable it, reboot the machine, and discover how the machine will operate without that service. The "Clearing Unnecessary Services" section of the chapter tells you a better way to work with services on your machine. In general, the features on the Services tab are nice and you can use them for experimentation, but it's better to work with the services directly. To remove a service temporarily, clear its entry. Check the entry again when you want to enable the service.

Exercising Startup Options

The Startup tab might be the most important tab the MSCONFIG provides because it shows all of the applications that get started when you log into Windows XP. Figure 7.16 shows a typical view of this tab.

You should know every entry on this tab because somewhere along the way, you installed every item on this list. When you don't know an entry, clear its entry, reboot the machine, and see if anything is missing. Sometimes, you'll encounter spyware, adware, or even viruses using this simple tab because it draws information from every startup location on your system.

The Startup tab includes three important pieces of information. First, it provides the human readable form of the application name. This isn't the name that appears on the application title bar, in many cases, but the name that appears when you view the application's properties. Second, it shows the location of the application on your hard drive, which is especially important to know when you want to remove the application. Third, you'll see the location of the startup entry—even when it appears in the registry. This information helps you disable the startup application permanently, rather than the temporary fix that MSCONFIG provides.

If you accidentally disable a startup application you need because you don't recognize its name, simply check the entry in MSCONFIG again and reboot your system. That's one of the best parts about using MSCONFIG—any change you make is fixable because the entry is only disabled, not removed.

FIGURE 7.16
Use the Startup tab to
check the applications
that start when you log
into Windows XP.

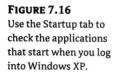

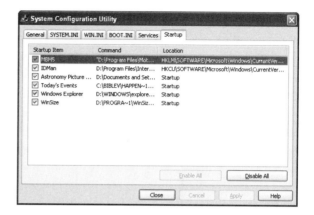

FIGURE 7.16
Use the Startup tab to
check the applications
that start when you log
into Windows XP.

Clearing Unnecessary Services

Windows services (called just services for the rest of this chapter) are indispensable parts of the operating system. They wait in the background until an application makes a request and then they perform a task. Afterward, the service waits again until another request appears. For example, whenever you make a request for an online resource, the Telephony service makes sure you can access it. You can't connect to the Internet without this service. You'll find all of the services on your machine listed in the Services console located in the Administrative Tools folder of the Control Panel. Figure 7.17 shows a typical view of this console.

Notice that this console displays the status of the service—whether it starts automatically and whether it's running now. When a service is marked as stopped, it means that you don't have to worry about the service using any memory or processing cycles because the service isn't loaded. Services marked Automatic always start; those marked Manual can start when an application needs them; those marked Disabled can't start for any reason.

The biggest problem with services is that Microsoft assumes that everyone works in a large corporation with a complex network and a brutish administrator who is also a control freak. Consequently, Windows XP enables every service that provides even a dubious connection to some form of control or network connection during initial installation. In fact, when you run a stand-alone machine, you can't even use some of these services.

NOTE Most services are obedient application slaves that wait for a request, but some are hungry monsters waiting for an excuse to gobble up system resources. For example, the Automatic Updates service will grab processing cycles and network bandwidth at regular intervals to look for Windows updates even if you disable this Windows feature. This particular service has become such a problem for gamers and others who need uninterrupted network bandwidth that you can find mentions of it all over the Internet. The only way to get the processing cycles and network bandwidth back is to disable the Automatic Updates feature. Unfortunately, Windows XP SP2 insists on turning this service back on, so you have to reconfigure your system yet again after you install SP2.

FIGURE 7.17
The Services console contains a complete list of the services on your system.

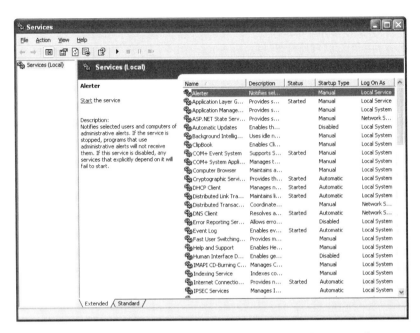

Although services don't necessarily use any processing cycles unless an application makes a request and you can't easily remove them to recover the hard drive space they use, services do use memory that you can recover. Because services can become very large and memory is a precious commodity, removing the services you don't need is a good idea.

You need to consider the ramifications of removing some services, but disabling others is a no brainer. For example, disabling the Messenger service (not related to Windows Messenger) is a no brainer because this service has been linked to a number of viruses and few people seem to use it, even on those large corporate networks. However, you wouldn't want to disable the Internet Connection Firewall (ICF) / Internet Connection Sharing (ICS) service unless you have a third party firewall and don't need to share your Internet connection with anyone. Unfortunately, running a firewall is going to slow your online game—you have to make a choice between a secure connection and a fast connection.

NOTE   It's possible that a service you didn't need in the past suddenly becomes necessary after an update. For example, Windows Update version 4 will scan your system and download updates to it without having either the Automatic Updates or Background Intelligent Transfer Service services started. However, once you upgrade to Windows Update version 5 (an automatic update when you install Windows XP Service Pack 2) these two services become mandatory because Microsoft checks for them. Windows Update will complain when you try to access it without the services started. To ensure your system can remain updated and yet not use precious resources needlessly, you can keep these two services set to manual and only start them when you want to perform an update of your system.

To modify a service, right-click the service and choose Properties from the context menu. You'll see a Properties dialog box like the one shown in Figure 7.18. You'll seldom need to use anything other than the General and Dependencies tabs. Always check the Dependencies tab before you stop a service to ensure that no other services (ones that you need) rely on the current service. Stopping a service that has dependent services always stops the dependent services as well.

The Startup Type field is very important for operation. Set this field to Automatic for services that you always want to start, Manual for services that you might want to start manually, at some point, and Disabled for services so dangerous that you never want them to start for any reason. The Service Status field tells you the current service status. Click Stop to stop a service that you no longer need.

The complexity of configuring a machine to use an optimal number of services has led to a number of lists online. Black Viper presents one of the better lists at `http://www.blackviper.com/WinXP/servicecfg.htm`. This list considers a number of factors, including how you use your system. However, no one list is perfect. You might find that you need some services that other people don't need.

FIGURE 7.18
This dialog box helps
you modify service
operation.

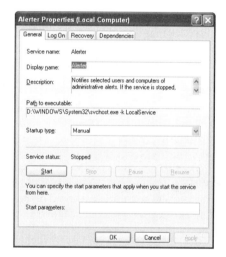

Modifying Network Connections

Network connections can be a source of unseen optimization issues. Some of the costs are evident. For example, every network connection costs memory because Windows maintains facts about the connection and processing cycles because Windows updates the connection information it possesses as needed. These housekeeping tasks ensure that you see the most current information when you access the network with an application or perform a search.

The visible costs of network connections make it well worth the effort to remove unneeded connections from your machine. To remove a network connection, right-click the connection in Windows Explorer and choose Disconnect from the context menu. You can easily reconnect later if needed. Likewise, to remove a printer, fax, or other equipment connection, open the Printers and Faxes applet in the Control Panel, right-click the connection you want to remove, and choose Delete from the context menu. The act of deleting the connection doesn't make the printer inaccessible.

TIP If you're like me and print only about once a week, you can save additional system memory by setting the Print Spooler service in the Services applet of the Control Panel to manual. Stop the service until you actually need it (stopping the service also releases all printer and fax connections). Start the service and create a connection to the network printer you want to use before you print. The "Clearing Unnecessary Services" section of the chapter tells more about working with services. This particular system change not only reduced memory use and made my system faster, it also reduced the amount of paper I use by about half—I find that I make fewer frivolous printouts that end up in the recycle bin.

The hidden costs of excess network connections depend on how you use your system. For example, when you use Windows Explorer to search, you could end up looking through every network drive on your system every time you perform a search unless you search carefully.

Windows Explorer automatically causes some optimization problems in the way that it works. For example, open the Folder Options dialog box using the Windows Explorer Tools ➢ Folder Options command. Look at the Automatically Search for Network Folders and Printers option on the View tab. When this option is checked, Windows Explorer searches all of the network drives every time you start it up. It's better to clear this option to save time when opening the application, but some people prefer to leave it on because it does provide a small performance boost when you search network drives. However, even if you keep this option checked, you can reduce its impact by removing excess network connections.

One source of network connections you might not know about is in My Network Places. As you roam the network, Windows XP helpfully creates links such as those shown in Figure 7.19 to places you visit regularly to make it easier for you to find these locations again, even when you'll never visit them again. The My Network Places folder appears on your Desktop, but it also appears within Windows Explorer. In fact, when you look at these links in Windows Explorer, they appear as specialized folders. Whenever you open Windows Explorer, Windows also tends to update these links. It's possible for a system to accumulate a hoard of these helpful links that the user doesn't even know about that end up slowing the system to a crawl.

NOTE The My Network Places links problem is especially severe when some of the links point to locations online and the user has an inactive dial-up connection. Users have reported that Windows appears to connect to the Internet for seemingly no reason at all—this is one source of that problem. Of course, features such as Automatic Updates also play a part in the mysterious Internet connection problem.

FIGURE 7.19
The links Windows adds to My Network Places are of dubious value.

Of course, like any tool, My Network Places does have a use. You can optimize your network browsing by adding your own custom links. Simply double-click the Add Network Place icon that appears in My Network Places. Follow the prompts to add the kind of connection you want to create (there are several). The difference between the custom links that you create and those that Windows creates arbitrarily is that you know about them, so you're likely to use them. In addition, these custom links actually point to locations that you want to view. Consequently, the arbitrary links are a source of system resource drain, while the custom links are an example of network connection optimization.

Working with Device Drivers

Generally, when you want to access a device on your system, Windows must have a corresponding device driver installed. Windows has generic device commands such as telling a CD drive to open its door. The device driver translates these generic commands into the specific commands that the device requires. Consequently, even though every CD drive has a different set of instructions for opening the door, Windows only needs to know one command.

Your system could contain all kinds of unnecessary drivers and Windows XP might hide some of them from sight. For example, the "Understanding *SYSTEM.INI*" section of the chapter tells you how to remove some of the remaining 16-bit drivers from your system. That's right, Windows XP, the 32-bit operating system, could have 16-bit drivers still hanging around for compatibility purposes. Those older drivers are going to slow down your system.

Sometimes, a 32-bit device driver also hangs around long after the device is gone. These device drivers consume memory and other resources, can cause system instability, and make life interesting in other ways. Always remove any custom third party software before you remove the device by using the entry the software provides in the Add or Remove Programs applet (look at the "Removing Unneeded Applications" section of Chapter 4 for details). Common devices can come with any number of device drivers for it. For example, my DVD drive works best with a third party DVD driver—the original vendor device driver is fast, but it's unreliable and makes my system unstable, while the Windows driver is both generic (it doesn't use all of the device features) and slow. You usually find out about these third party device drivers from newsgroups or list servers on the Internet. As with the vendor driver, remove the third party driver before you uninstall the device using the Add or Remove Programs applet.

TIP Deciding on which device driver to use for your system can be a time-consuming task. Vendor device drivers tend to provide the best access to every device feature and the fastest access speed, but at the cost of resource usage and system reliability. Choose this driver type when you need the most from the driver. Windows drivers are generic, so they tend to ignore any special device features. However, Windows drivers are generally very reliable because Microsoft tests them thoroughly and they use resources more efficiently. Use the Windows drivers when you want to optimize the system as a whole and don't need access to special device features. Third party drivers, when you can find them, tend to be somewhere between these two extremes. However, you also have to consider third party driver risks such as potential compatibility problems.

Drivers supplied with Windows require a different process for removal. Begin by opening the System applet of the Control Panel—you'll see the System Properties dialog box. Select the Hardware tab and click Device Manager. The Device Manager dialog box shown in Figure 7.20 tells you the status of every device driver on the system (at least those that you need to know about). Notice that the Multimedia Controller entry in the Other Devices folder has an exclamation point next to it (some people say that the entry is banged). This entry is a Windows driver that was left over when I removed a device from my system (in this case, for experimentation because I really do need the device). To remove this driver from the system, right-click it and choose Uninstall from the context menu. Windows will remove the driver from the list.

FIGURE 7.20
Old drivers can hang around after you remove the device from the system.

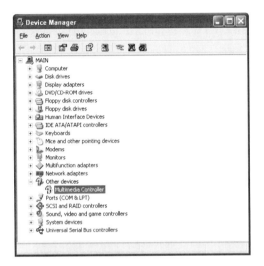

Removing Gizmos from Your Systems

One of the most vicious memory hogs is the one that people are least likely to give up. Everyone loves gizmos. They help make the system feel friendly and special, even though they contribute nothing to the computing experience. Gizmos add pizzazz, the ooh and ah of computing, but other than that, they're a waste of system resources and time for the most part. A few of these gizmos really are helpful and the following sections tell which ones.

Understanding Themes

You might be under the impression that themes are a complete waste of time, but they aren't necessarily. To see for yourself what features themes control, disable the Themes service found in the Services applet of the Control Panel and reboot your machine. The rounded corners and other aesthetic features that Windows XP offers are noticeably absent, but so are some features that some people need to use the computer successfully. For example, font smoothing, a feature that makes the screen easier on the eyes, is gone. Even though the best option from a system performance perspective is to get rid of themes completely, the human using the machine probably needs a few of those features to remain comfortable.

Unfortunately, Microsoft didn't place all of the theme support in one place. To optimize themes, you need to look in at least two places. First, right-click the Desktop and choose Properties from the context menu. The Themes tab doesn't offer much in the form of direct optimization. However, remember that themes can consume a lot of disk space, so deleting any themes you aren't using from the list can optimize hard drive use. Simply select the theme and then click Delete to remove it from the drive. Windows does a good job of removing the bits and pieces of the theme for you, so this is one case where a look at the hard drive probably isn't necessary.

The Desktop tab offers a few places for optimization. You can do things like rely on a plain background or one with patterns, rather than a picture, to save memory. This option doesn't save it a lot, but it does save some and admittedly, most people don't see the background on their monitor anyway. Click Customize Desktop and you'll see the Desktop Items dialog box. Removing all of the checks next to items on the Web tab can save considerable memory, hard drive space, and network bandwidth. Make sure you delete any items you won't use.

One of the best places to save system resources is on the Appearance tab. One simple change from Windows XP Style to Windows Classic Style in the Windows and Buttons field can make a big difference in system performance. Click Effects and you'll see the Effects dialog box. Clearing all of the options except font smoothing will net another big performance boost.

The second place to look for themes settings to optimize is in the System Properties dialog box that you access by right-clicking My Computer and choosing Properties. Select the Advanced tab and click Settings in the Performance section of the dialog box. You'll see the Performance Options dialog box. The Visual Effects tab contains a number of special effects that you can remove to improve system performance. Again, make sure you keep font smoothing to help the user see well.

Understanding Screen Savers

Theoretically, screen savers are one of the least intrusive forms of glitz you can add to a system. The diminutive SCR files you can find in the \Windows\System32 folder containing the screen savers range in size from 8KB to 652KB for a default Windows installation. The default setup only contains 11 files for a total of 2.46MB. In short, even if you remove the screen savers you don't want, you'll save little hard drive space. Because screen savers run when you aren't using the system, you don't have to worry too much about how many processor cycles they use either. The only way that you'll save much is by disabling screen savers completely to save the memory they use.

Screen savers do offer quite a bit to the user. The obvious benefit is that the screen saver reduces "burn in" the effect that occurs when a monitor displays the same information repeatedly. Of course, you can avoid this problem by shutting the monitor down after a period of inactivity. Many corporations prefer this course because shutting the monitor down also reduces the power bill for the system.

Most screen savers also provide password protection. When the screen saver activates, you can't get it to go away unless you enter your name and password. You can avoid this cost by logging out of the system whenever you leave the room. The time required is the same, but it's a little more work for the user. In addition, the user might forget to log out and the screen saver is automatic.

The bottom line is that screen savers are a cheap piece of glitz and they serve a useful purpose. Generally, it's not worth your time to remove them unless you have significant performance problems to overcome.

Let's Start Cleaning

This chapter has helped you locate and identify the memory hogs invading your system. It doesn't take much to realize that some memory hogs are flamboyant affairs that some people refuse to remove because they're amusing, while other memory hogs lurk in the darkness hoping you won't find them. No matter what memory hog you decide to pursue, it's always important to consider the point of balance. Always ask what you'll give up when you remove the memory hog.

Besides helping you understand the costs associated with various memory hogs and other resource beasts, this chapter provides instructions on how to deal with them. Only you can decide whether to keep that memory hog or not. Sometimes you do need a pet to keep you entertained. As long as you understand the cost, it's probably not that big of a deal. What you should do is inventory your system and see what you can do without and what you want to keep. Getting rid of the resource issues that cause problems could be all you need to restore your system to its youthful vigor.

Figuring out what to remove based on scientific study and observation is a good first step. Getting rid of the vicious beasts lurking on your system is the second. However, now it's time to take the third step—keeping those vicious beasts at bay. Chapter 8 discusses various tactics you can take to keep your system in great shape so it always works as you expect it to. Keeping Windows clean and free of resource issues is a lot better than having to optimize it from scratch.

Chapter 8

Keeping Your Windows Clean

Cleaning Windows can take a long time and a lot of effort. Once you complete the task, you'll notice that you've gained a lot in system stability, reliability, performance, and usability. However, getting Windows clean and keeping it clean are two different matters. Sitting back and gazing at what you've accomplished will eventually lead to Windows getting dirty again. What you really need is some method of keeping Windows clean after you get it to a good working state.

Many of the tasks you performed to clean Windows also apply to keeping it clean, but the tasks are less time consuming when you perform them as maintenance. Instead of removing five or six errant applications, you'll remove one at a time. You need to perform other tasks as part of a good maintenance plan, however, and that's the purpose of this chapter. For example, instead of having to search the registry for all of the entries related to a particular application that won't uninstall properly, wouldn't it be nice to roll back the system to its state before you installed the application? Using this technique uses the operating system features to perform all of the manual work for you.

Some of the maintenance tasks make sense for more reasons than keeping Windows clean. For example, backing up your data regularly is a task that you need to perform to ensure you can recover from any cleaning chores gone wrong, but it's also a requirement to keep your data safe from other disasters.

A few of the methods described in this chapter represent new optimization techniques that you perform after you complete the initial cleaning process. Defragmenting your hard drive is an important way of optimizing the hard drive, but you can't really perform it until you get all of the junk cleaned off the hard drive and you can't perform it quickly until the system uses memory efficiently.

This chapter also looks at ways to detect potential problems before they become an issue. Simply checking the event log after a boot cycle can tell you a lot about your system. For example, you can quickly discover whether a change you made affects the system negatively or if a piece of adware has begun affecting the system in a negative way. Locating problems and fixing them as they arise greatly reduces the work you have to perform at any one time.

Rolling Back Bad Installations

Some people don't differentiate between an initial system setup and maintenance application setups after the fact, but there's a big difference. During an initial system setup, you install applications that you know work on the system. Even if the applications don't work on the target machine for some reason, reinstalling the applications doesn't cost anything but a little time. However, once you have a system established, you can lose a lot when a new application setup fails to work as anticipated.

WINDOWS XP SERVICE PACK 2 ISN'T A BAD INSTALLATION

Despite what you might think after you install it, Windows XP Service Pack 2 (SP2) really isn't broken, nor is it simply bad. The ongoing rash of security problems facing Microsoft because of security holes in Windows XP requires drastic measures. In the past, Microsoft concentrated on making updates backward compatible (not breaking older operating system behaviors) in favor of making Windows secure. That's no longer an option. Events have made it necessary that Microsoft concentrate on security, rather than on backward compatibility. The result is that applications that break the rules often fail.

Microsoft even discusses the issue in a special Knowledge Base Articles entitled, "Some programs seem to stop working after you install Windows XP Service Pack 2" (`http://support.microsoft.com/default.aspx?kbid=842242`) and "Programs that may behave differently in Windows XP Service Pack 2" (`http://support.microsoft.com/default.aspx?kbid=884130`). The problems are severe enough that some companies have simply recommended that users not install SP2, according to the ComputerWorld article at `http://www.computerworld.com/softwaretopics/os/story/0,10801,95130,00.html?nas=AM-95130`. Users who have tried SP2 give it mixed marks, which is probably reasonable considering how many changes SP2 makes (see the eWeek article at `http://eletters.eweek.com/zd1/cts?d=79-984-2-3-67152-112048-1`). The point that all of these sources make is that installing SP2 is going to better optimize your system for security at the expense of application compatibility. You'll also give up some application speed, especially for those applications connected to the Internet, to improve your ability to survive attack.

However, not just the broken applications are causing people concern. Windows XP SP2 is a huge download at 266MB and time consuming to test. Once you do test it, getting it installed on more than one machine could be a problem because of the sheer size of the service pack. With this in mind, some Web sites are showing how to slipstream (create a single Windows XP CD that has everything you need on it) this update. You can find instructions on the PCStats site at `http://www.pcstats.com/articleview.cfm?articleID=1626`. Creating a slipstreamed version of Windows XP SP2 when you have more than one machine to maintain optimizes the entire installation process. When working with a single machine, you can get a smaller single download using Windows Update. Some people have expressed concern over this approach, but many others (including myself) see Windows Update as the optimal approach for a single machine (see the eWeek article at `http://www.eweek.com/article2/0,1759,1634992,00.asp?kc=ewnws081304dtx1k0000599` for another opinion).

Now that you have Windows XP SP2 installed and your system no longer runs as many applications as it used to, you're supposedly more secure. You are, in fact, more secure, but as usual, people have an opinion on just what "more secure" means. Some people say that some of the main features such as the new firewall simply don't go far enough (see the PCWorld article at `http://www.pcworld.com/news/article/0,aid,117380,00.asp` for details). In addition, your friendly neighborhood cracker is already at work looking for flaws in SP2, according to the InfoWorld article at `http://www.infoworld.com/article/04/08/13/HNhuntforsp2flaws_1.html`. The bottom line is that SP2 is probably an optimization you shouldn't forgo, despite the hardships it can cause.

The loss of an established system makes the rollback feature of Windows XP important. You create a restore point before you install the application. A restore point creates a picture of the operating system and the associated applications, and places this picture on the hard drive. Next, you install the application and begin testing it. It's important that you don't install anything else until the new application is fully tested and you assure that the system will retain all of the good attributes you worked so hard to create. When the worst-case scenario does occur, you can uninstall the application. If the uninstall doesn't work, or you aren't sure that it worked as planned, you can use the restore point to roll the operating system back to its previous state.

This technique does restore the operating system, but it doesn't restore the hard drive. The hard drive still contains the application files, and you must remove them manually. However, getting rid of files you no longer need isn't nearly as hard as getting rid of a stubborn application. (See the "Removing Application Installation Crumbs" section of Chapter 4 for details on removing application leftovers.) The important technique that this chapter provides is to make it easier to get rid of the application you don't want on your system after an initial test period.

Verifying You Can Create a Restore Point

One of the performance enhancing tips that you'll often see is turning off the System Restore feature. It's a good tip because you don't need to have this feature on all the time—just when you're testing a new application or an update such as a Windows service pack. After the testing phase is over, you can turn the System Restore back off to save the hard drive space, memory, and processing cycles it uses. However, this means you have to verify you can perform a system restore before you attempt to create a restore point.

To check the status of the System Restore service, right-click My Computer and choose Properties from the context menu. Select the System Restore tab and you'll see a System Properties dialog box similar to the one shown in Figure 8.1.

Notice that the Turn Off System Restore on All Drives option is cleared. When this option is checked, you can't create a system restore point, but you also aren't using the resources to run the System Restore service. In this case, the system is set to use drive D for the system restore point—drive C has the System Restore service turned off. To change the settings for an individual drive, highlight the drive and click Settings. The Settings dialog box not only allows you to turn monitoring on or off, but it also lets you set the amount of hard drive space set aside for system restore points.

FIGURE 8.1
Verify that the System Restore service is running before you attempt to create a restore point.

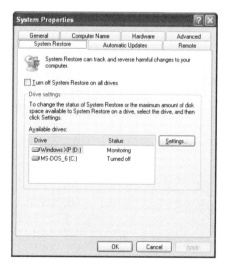

Defining a System Restore Point

Windows theoretically creates restore points automatically when you perform certain tasks on your machine, such as installing a service pack. However, experience shows that it's always better to create a restore point manually so you know the restore point name and ensure that you actually have one to use after a failed application test.

Use the System Restore wizard to create a restore point. You can access this wizard using the Start ➤ Programs ➤ Accessories ➤ System Tools ➤ System Restore command. Figure 8.2 shows the initial System Restore dialog box where you choose between creating a restore point and using one to restore the system.

Once you open the System Restore wizard, select the Create a Restore Point option and click Next. Type a name for the restore point and click Create. Creating a restore point can take several minutes, during which time the hard drive will sound like it's going to take off. Be patient—the process will eventually end and you'll have a restore point to use while testing a new application. The wizard will display a final dialog box with the name and date of the restore point when it completes the process. You can click Home to go back to the original screen shown in Figure 8.2 or click Close to close the dialog box.

Restoring the System

The biggest reason to create a restore point for your system is to ensure you have a fallback position should a new application, update, or patch fail to perform as anticipated. Once you use a restore point several times, you'll find that it works precisely as advertised—the system removes the errant application settings, but the hard drive additions remain.

FIGURE 8.2
Use the System Restore wizard to create a restore point for your system.

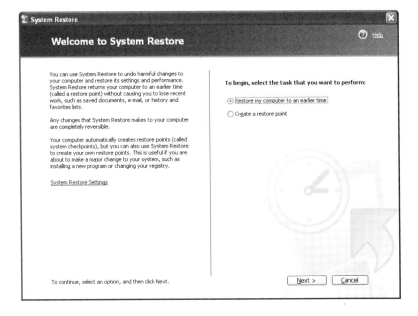

WARNING   Some people view a restore point as a cheap kind of backup, but it isn't. To ensure the safety of your data, you must create regular backups of your system. A complete backup will restore your system to its saved state once you install a basic Windows setup, along with any applications you need.

This lack of hard drive restoration means that a restore point isn't the same as uninstalling the application—you still have those hard drive additions to consider. Consequently, the best policy to follow is to uninstall the application first, and then use the restore point to clean up any mess the application creates in the registry or with other applications.

To restore a previously saved restore point, access the System Restore wizard using the Start ≻ Programs ≻ Accessories ≻ System Tools ≻ System Restore command. Figure 8.2 shows the initial System Restore dialog box where you choose between creating a restore point and using one to restore the system. Select the Restore My Computer to an Earlier Time option and click Next. You'll see the Select a Restore Point dialog box shown in Figure 8.3.

Choose one of the restore points from the list. The latest restore point should be the one that you use because it should be the last one you created prior to installing the application. The name of the restore point will help you ensure you select the correct one from the list. Click Next. The System Restore wizard displays a dialog box that tells you how the restore point will affect your system. Notice that it specifically mentions that none of your documents will change—they will all retain any changes you made. This feature ensures you don't lose any data, but it also limits the usefulness of this particular utility.

FIGURE 8.3

Choose a restore point from the list provided.

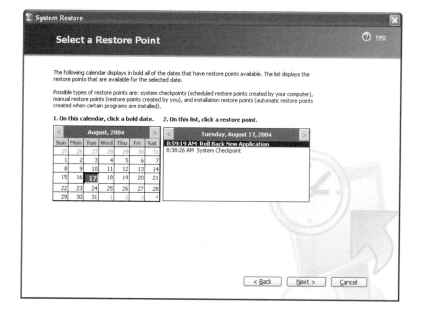

At this point, you're ready to restore your system. Make sure you close all other applications before you begin. Click Next. After what seems like hours, the hard drive will finally stop, everything will close, and you'll see a System Restore dialog box. The system will restore itself and then reboot. After the reboot, you'll see the System Restore wizard telling you which restore point it used and letting you know that you can undo the restoration if things don't work out as you expected.

Performing Regular Maintenance

It might be hard to understand that a computer requires regular maintenance. After all, it doesn't have any moving parts to speak of except the hard drive and the fans that go whirr in the night. However, a computer system does require regular maintenance, more than most people give it. The following sections don't get into the physical cleaning you should do (such as removing those dust bunnies from the front of the cabinet), but it does consider the kinds of cleaning that result in an optimized system. Each of the cleaning aids listed in the sections that follow will not only help you maintain your system, but they also make it run better.

Using Disk Cleanup

Once you get your system cleaned, Windows does everything it can to make it dirty again. On your first visit to the Internet, Internet Explorer will dump a bunch of temporary files on the hard drive. Applications continue to create temporary files as they help you create the documents that define your work and play. In short, your system is like any home—yes, it looks clean now, but the mess returns soon enough during the act of simple computing. That's why you need to continue looking for temporary files in an effort to keep your hard drive clean. The Disk Cleanup utility comes with Windows. It helps you locate and remove those temporary files that keep clogging the system.

TIP   Although Disk Cleanup is free and very useful, it's also not complete. This utility will make a difference, but third party utilities such as Empty Temp Folders described in the "Using the Empty Temp Folders Utility" section of Chapter 4 do a better job.

Use the Start ➢ Programs ➢ Accessories ➢ System Tools ➢ Disk Cleanup command to start the Disk Cleanup application. The initial dialog box will ask which drive you want to clean (you have to clean them one at a time). Select a drive and click OK. Disk Cleanup displays a dialog box that shows the scanning progress of your drive—this process can take a very long time, depending on the size of your drive, so be patient. After Disk Cleanup completes the scan, you'll see a Disk Cleanup dialog box similar to the one shown in Figure 8.4 (this is the Windows XP version, the dialog looks almost the same in other versions of Windows).

After you look through the list of files that Disk Cleanup provides, you'll notice some pros and cons compared to the third party utilities. For example, Disk Cleanup won't find all of the temporary files on your system and doesn't help you clean backup files that applications create. However, unlike most third party products, Disk Cleanup locates the Office setup files that you normally have to remove by hand. It also finds all the log files—at least those that Windows creates—that you normally remove by hand.

FIGURE 8.4
Select one or more file categories to remove from your system in order to keep it clean.

Most important of all, Disk Cleanup lets you remove extra restore points—a task you can't perform using the System Restore utility described in the "Rolling Back Bad Installations" section of the chapter. This option appears on the More Options tab. Click Clean Up in the System Restore section. Because a restore point can consume several hundred MB of hard drive space, removing all but the most recent restore point is important.

Once you choose one or more file categories, click OK. Disk Cleanup displays a status dialog box as it removes the files you requested from the system.

Scanning Hard Drives for Errors

Many people will tell you that a hard drive suddenly fails just to make life difficult for the computer user. Actually, hard drives are hard working—they usually provide plenty of notice about impending failure. All you need to do is listen for the signs. Fortunately, Windows provides two free utilities you can use to check your hard drive for potential problems. Although these utilities aren't quite as good as third party alternatives, they are relatively simple and fast.

The utilities check general drive health and can help you recover lost space (measured in clusters of sectors, which is a single unit of hard drive storage). For example, when an application terminates unexpectedly, it can leave behind inaccessible areas. You can use these utilities to recover lost hard drive areas. In addition, you can use them to monitor the hard drive for failed areas—places you can't use to store information because they have gone bad or the drive has suffered some kind of mechanical problem.

As a drive ages, the number of failed clusters begins to increase and you'll notice a performance drop off. When you begin seeing these signs, then you know the hard drive is beginning to fail—it hasn't failed yet, but failure will usually occur sometime soon. An optimized system management approach means planning for the drive failure and replacing the drive before it does fail.

Unfortunately, Windows doesn't provide utilities that perform a complete check. For example, you can't determine whether the drive mechanics are in good shape or if there are other problems with the drive electronics. Consequently, even though you can monitor the drive media and make optimization decisions based on what you find, you can't monitor every potential source of failure.

NOTE This section describes two file formats: File Allocation Table (FAT) and New Technology File System (NTFS). Microsoft changes the meaning of NTFS regularly, so I've decided to use the original meaning. The FAT file system is older—it was originally used by DOS and updated for use with Windows 9x. The FAT file system can use 12-bits (floppy disk), 16-bits, or 32-bits for directory entries. The FAT32 (32-bit) version is available only with Windows 9x. The advantage of this file format is that every version of Windows can read it. Consequently, FAT32 is the optimum choice when you need to support multiple operating systems on one machine. NTFS also relies on 32-bit directory entries, but uses them more efficiently. From an optimization perspective, NTFS provides better security, file compression, and better performance.

USING CHKDSK

The ChkDsk utility has been around in various forms from the days of DOS—before Windows appeared on the scene. Of course, Microsoft keeps adding features to this utility and it now runs as part of Windows, instead of part of DOS, but the concept remains the same. You use ChkDsk to perform a basic check of the hard drive. In addition, you can optionally use it to recover lost clusters and attempt repairs on damaged clusters.

To use ChkDsk to perform a basic check, type **ChkDsk** at the command prompt and press Enter. ChkDsk always assumes that you want to check the current drive. When you want to check a different drive, add the drive letter to the command. In addition, when you're working a FAT-formatted drive, you can specify a specific file. For example, you could type **ChkDsk C:\DRVSPACE.BIN** to check the DRVSPACE.BIN file on drive C.

ChkDsk also provides access to a number of command line switches. The following list describes these switches. Note that some of them work only on drives with a specific file format.

/F   Adds fixing media errors to the list of tasks to perform. This switch differs from /R, which recovers clusters lost when an application terminates unexpectedly.

/R   Adds recovering lost clusters to the list of tasks to perform. Using this switch also adds the /F switch automatically.

/V   Use this switch only on FAT or FAT32 formatted drives. It tells ChkDsk to display the full path and name of every file on the disk.

/L [*Size*]   Use this switch only on NTFS-formatted drives. When you use the /L switch alone, ChkDsk outputs the current size of the log file used to track drive activity. Including the optional log file size modifies the size of the log for the current drive. Theoretically, a larger log could help improve drive reliability, but in practice, the default size normally works well.

/X   Use this switch only on NTFS-formatted drives. The operating system must mount a drive before you can access the drive contents. This switch forces the operating system to dismount a drive before performing a check. Dismounting the drive makes all drive resources unavailable, but also ensures uninterrupted access by ChkDsk, which can help improve the results of any tasks performed.

/I   Use this switch only on NTFS-formatted drives. This switch tells ChkDsk to perform a less robust check of the drive indexes (the portion of the drive used to locate files). Normally, you won't use this switch when you want to check a drive for optimum performance. However, you can use this switch to reduce the time required to check the drive.

/C   Use this switch only on NTFS-formatted drives. This switch tells ChkDsk to skip checking cycles within the drive folders. When a folder contains cyclical references, damage to the files can result. Consequently, even though this switch does reduce the time to check the drive, you want to avoid using it because ChkDsk doesn't thoroughly check the drive otherwise.

NOTE   You can't use ChkDsk directly on the Windows (boot) drive with either the /F or /R options because Windows needs access to specific files at all times. Use the ChkNTFS utility to repair the Windows drive. It's possible to use ChkDsk in the read-only mode to look for potential errors without fixing.

USING CHKNTFS

The ChkNTFS utility works with ChkDsk to ensure your system remains problem free. You won't see the effects of this utility right away in most cases. This utility sets up your drive to use ChkDsk during the boot process, rather than after Windows has booted, to ensure you can gain full access to the drive. The drive repair can occur without Windows interference. When you select a drive for a scan, ChkNTFS says that it's dirty. Therefore, when you see that the drive is not dirty, that means ChkNTFS hasn't scheduled it for a check. A drive can also become dirty when Windows detects an error on it.

TIP   You don't have to use ChkNTFS to perform some tasks. For example, when you want to set up a drive for a scan, right-click the drive in Windows Explorer and choose Properties from the context menu. Select the Tools tab and click Check Now. You'll see a Check Disk dialog box. Check both of the repair options and click Start. When working with a boot drive, Windows Explorer will display an error saying that it couldn't complete the check. It then offers the chance to perform the check later during the next boot. Click Yes and Windows Explorer will set up the check.

To use ChkNTFS, you must provide a drive argument or one of the command line switches at a minimum. When you supply a drive argument, ChkNTFS tells you the drive format and determines whether Windows has scheduled it for a check. The command line switches work as follows.

/D   Use this switch to place all of the drives in the default state. You can use this switch to remove a drive from the checklist when you schedule the check. This switch won't reverse a mandatory check due to an error detected by Windows.

/T[:*Time*]   When you use this switch by itself, ChkNTFS tells you how much time it allows before it begins the check sequence during boot time. The automatic countdown lets you decide at boot time whether to run ChkDsk as planned. Supplying the optional time value modifies the countdown timer to give the user more or less time to make the ChkDsk decision. The default automatic countdown value is 10 seconds.

/X *Volume*   Use this switch to exclude one or more drives from a check. You use this option when you set up the system to perform ChkDsk every time it boots. This is a one time switch—Windows excludes the drive for one boot cycle.

/C *Volume*   Use this switch to schedule a drive for a check during the next boot cycle.

Performing Backups

Creating a backup of your hard drive is one of the more important maintenance tasks you can perform. If your machine fails or a disaster occurs, the backup protects your data investment, which is often more than the cost of your machine and associated software. From an optimization perspective, backups are always a required prerequisite to testing new settings, installing updates, or performing other optimization tasks. Creating a good backup is akin to buying insurance. Just as you wouldn't drive your car without insurance, you shouldn't work on your computer without a backup.

NOTE Make sure you clean your tape drive regularly and inspect it before each backup. Open the tape drive door with a nonmetallic screwdriver or other small nonmetallic implement. Peek inside at the mechanism to ensure everything is intact. One company I knew faithfully made backups of their system, only to discover that the tape head had detached from the tape transport. None of the tapes had any data on them.

The first time you start Backup, it will ask if you want to use the Backup Wizard (described in the "Creating a Backup with Backup Wizard" and "Restoring a Backup with Backup Wizard" sections). Advanced users will want to clear the Always Start in Wizard Mode option, and then click the Advanced Mode link. Windows XP displays the Welcome tab of the Backup Utility dialog box. At this point, you can create a backup, restore and manage media, and schedule backup tasks. These options appear in the sections that follow the Backup Wizard section.

UNDERSTANDING BACKUP REQUIREMENTS

For many people, the act of backing up a system is one of those tasks they'd rather not perform. However, putting a backup off or not performing it properly is always going to cost you something in the end. Data is too valuable to ignore or treat improperly. Backing up your system once a year probably isn't sufficient. Using a single tape to store everything probably isn't a good idea, either.

It's impossible for a book to tell you how often to back up because it largely depends on the value of your data. Some businesses could back up their systems every second of the day and not have enough insurance to cover every need. In fact, there's a system called Redundant Array of Inexpensive Disks (RAID) that provides reliability in multiple copies of the same data spread across multiple drives. When one drive fails, one of the others takes its place. However, not everyone needs such as system and even when you have it, you still need a backup to recover from disasters where the entire RAID system is disabled.

A good rule of thumb is to back up your system on a schedule that you can maintain and that makes sense given the value of the data. A home user who works with nonessential data daily can probably get by with a weekly backup. Many business users can rely on a daily backup—the loss of one day's data usually isn't critical enough to cause problems. However, some business users work with data so critical and that changes so rapidly that backing up twice a day might become practical. This book doesn't discuss the variety of backup systems or schemes on the market, but you should consider the value of your data and back it up accordingly.

Another problem is the life expectancy of the backup media. The "The Amazing Disintegrating CD" section of Chapter 5 describes what can happen to optical media. Tapes are just as vulnerable.

Replace your tapes when they become too old or you've used them too often. Most tapes wear well through 20 uses, but you need to monitor signs of problems such as an uneven tape pack, which usually indicates stretching. The adhesive on tapes also fails after a while. Most tapes last about two years under perfect conditions. DAT tapes last about five years. Some tapes reportedly last up to 10 years, but most professionals consider such extended use marginal at best. Check your tape vendor specifications for tape storage requirements.

Some people fall short when it comes to discovering what to back up. When you have doubts or simply don't know what you might need, back up the entire drive. It's easier to wade through what you don't need than to conjure up what you don't have on the backup. However, a practical backup normally includes all of your data, any required application settings (just back up the entire \Documents and Settings folder if necessary), and any special application data such as INI files. It usually isn't necessary to back up the applications.

Make sure you test your backup system. For one thing, make sure that you verify the backup. All backup programs include this feature and many turn it on by default. In addition, test your backup system by restoring some test files to a different folder. Use the file comparison utilities, such as FC (explained in the "Using Comp and FC" section of Chapter 3), to compare the original file against the restored backup. If the files don't compare, then you probably have a backup system problem and need to fix it. Performing this test every three or four months will save you a lot of grief later because you'll know that your backups are good.

CREATING A BACKUP WITH BACKUP WIZARD

The Backup Wizard is a great choice if you have no experience at all creating backups. The Backup Wizard starts automatically when you start the Backup utility. You can also access it from the Welcome tab of the Backup Utility dialog box. The following steps tell you how to use the Backup Wizard to create a backup. I'll assume you can see the Welcome screen.

1. Click Next. Backup Wizard will ask if you want to create a backup or restore previously backed up files.

2. Select Backup, and then click Next. You'll see a What to Back Up dialog box. Select one of the four options. If you select the Let me choose what to back up option, Backup Wizard will display an Explorer-like dialog box that lets you choose the backup files. Select the files you want to back up, and then click Next. Backup Wizard will ask which device you want to use for backup purposes. You can use a dedicated tape drive, a floppy drive, or an area on another hard drive. (In some cases, you might also be able to use a CD as backup.)

3. Select a backup device, and then click Next. You'll see a completion dialog box. Notice the Advanced button at the bottom of the dialog box. This enables you to choose advanced backup features such as type of backup and the use of verification after the backup.

4. Choose advanced features if desired. Follow the prompts to make any changes to the standard setup. Click Finished. Backup will perform the backup you created.

RESTORING A BACKUP WITH BACKUP WIZARD

As previously mentioned, backups are like insurance. You know you need to have them, but you hope never to use them. Unfortunately, you'll eventually need the backup you created. That's when you perform a restore using the Backup Wizard. The following steps show how. I'll assume you can see the Welcome screen.

1. Click Next. Backup Wizard will ask if you want to create a backup or restore previously backed up files.

2. Select Restore, and then click Next. You'll see a What to Restore dialog box that looks similar to a two-pane view of Windows Explorer.

3. Select an entire backup, or just a single file in a backup, using the same techniques you've used to choose files in Windows Explorer.

4. Click Next. You'll see a completion dialog box. Notice the Advanced button at the bottom of the dialog box. This enables you to choose advanced restore features such as restore location and whether Restore should overwrite existing files.

5. Choose advanced features if desired. Follow the prompts to make any changes to the standard setup. Click Finished. Restore will restore any required files on your system.

CREATING A BACKUP

Advanced users will want to use the manual method for creating backups because it provides better control over the backup settings. Always create backup jobs for your system. You'll perform the same backup process more than once, so saving your settings is always a good idea. Even if you have to modify the default settings, making small changes usually requires less time than creating a new backup.

It's important to create a backup strategy for your system. For example, many companies will store some tapes in a vault and others in an offsite location to ensure they always have a viable backup of their system. The following steps show how to create a backup job and start it. Begin the job creation process on the Backup tab of the Backup Utility.

1. Use the Explorer-like display to select the files you want to back up. Note that it's better to use My Network Places entries than to use network shares when selecting network files. You never know when a network share (a connection to a remote drive) will go away or change—making your settings obsolete.

2. Select a backup destination and a backup media or filename. The backup destination can include a backup device or a file. You can use any accessible location when working with a file. It's best to use another machine for the purpose so you won't have the data stored locally.

3. Use the View ➢ Options command to display the Options dialog box. Select a backup type on the Backup tab.

4. Select the Backup Log tab and choose one of the three logging options. You'll normally want to create a log to ensure Backup can record any backup errors.

5. Select the Exclude Files tab and add or delete file specifications as needed. Backup always includes files and directories that are active during backup. However, you'll want to add file specifications such as *.BAK to reduce backup time.

6. Select the General tab and perform any required configuration. For example, Microsoft assumes you don't want to verify data after the backup completes; yet, this is an extremely important feature.

7. Click OK to close the Options dialog box.

8. Use the Job ➤ Save Selections command to display the Save As dialog box. Give your job a name, then click Save.

9. Start the backup by clicking Start Backup. You'll see a Backup Job Information dialog box.

10. Click Start Backup. You'll see a Backup Progress dialog box. The Backup Progress dialog box will eventually tell you the backup is complete and allow you to view a report if desired.

11. Click Close to complete the backup process.

RESTORING A BACKUP

Disasters happen to the best of us, which means you'll eventually need to restore a backup. Unlike backups, you'll seldom perform a restore. For this reason, the Backup Utility doesn't provide the means to create a job for restores. The following steps show you how to restore a backup.

1. Select the Restore and Manage Media tab of the Backup Utility dialog box.

2. Select the backup media you want to use from the Explorer-like display. Choose one or more files from within that media. The Backup Utility won't restore files from more than one media at a time, so if you try to choose files from more than one media, it will ask if you want to clear the previous selections.

3. Select the files you want to restore. Make sure you choose all of the required files so you restore everything needed on the first pass. Restores take longer than backups, so you'll want to get this step right.

4. Select a restore location. If you choose anything but the Original Location option, you'll also need to provide a directory name.

5. Use the Tools ➤ Options command to display the Options dialog box. Select a restore option from the Restore tab. Microsoft recommends that you never replace an existing file with one from the backup. You do have the choice of replacing older files only, or replacing all files.

6. Click Start Restore. You'll see a Confirm Restore dialog box. The Advanced button on this dialog box enables you to change additional restore options, such as the restoring security. Generally, you want to leave these options alone.

7. Click OK and you'll see a Restore Progress dialog box. This dialog box will tell you when the restore is complete and provide you with restore statistics. As with the backup, you can view a report containing any restore anomalies.

Defragmenting the Drive

The first question many of you will have is "What is disk fragmentation?" As you work with a disk drive, Windows XP has to find new places to put files. At some point, all of the spaces available for holding files will get too small for the file you want to save and Windows XP will have to place the file in two sections of the hard drive. The act of placing the file in two or more places is fragmentation.

Fragmentation affects performance in a big way. Every time the system needs to access a fragmented file, it will have to move the drive read head to two (or more) locations, which is expensive in computer time. Of course, this problem will begin affecting more than just one file. After a while, many of the files on your drive will experience some level of fragmentation and you'll definitely see the performance drop.

Defragmenting your hard drive is one of the most important performance-related maintenance actions you can do. The Disk Defragmenter utility reorders the content of your hard drive. It places the files back into one section of the hard drive and frees continuous space by moving all of the files to one end of the hard drive. A defragmented hard drive runs much faster. Unfortunately, this fix doesn't last forever; you have to defragment your hard drive on a regular basis.

NOTE There are some problems with the Microsoft solution to disk defragmenting. The biggest one is convenience. Disk Defragmenter only works on local drives; you can't start it on a local drive and hope to defragment remote drives. Disk Defragmenter is also Windows version specific. You need to use the version of Disk Defragmenter that comes with your system (or a compatible third party product).

Drive fragmentation also affects the life of the drive. The more Windows XP has to move the drive head, the faster the components will wear. The optimum setup would be one in which the drive head never moves, but there isn't any way to accomplish that goal. Even so, you want to reduce head movement whenever possible by defragmenting the drive. Windows XP provides both graphical and command prompt methods for defragmenting a drive, as described in the following sections.

TIP The market for third party disk defragmenter utilities is huge. This is an extremely important computer maintenance task, so administrators want to be sure they have the right tool for the job. Unfortunately, Microsoft changes the format of their drives every time they release a new product. This means you need a new version of the third party product if you want to run it on Windows XP. Unlike Microsoft, most third party vendors make their product usable with all previous versions of Windows. They support features such as remote defragmenting and they provide you with statistics that show the results of your activity. In short, while the Microsoft-provided utility is good, the third party products tend to be better.

USING THE STANDARD DEFRAGMENTER

The graphical disk defragmenter appears in two places. You can use the Disk Defragmenter utility located in the Start\Programs\Accessories\System Tools folder or you can use the Storage\Disk Defragmenter tool that appears in the Computer Management console found in the Administrative Tools folder of the Control Panel. The tool works the same in either case, but this section will rely on the Disk Defragmenter utility. The following steps show you how to perform a typical disk defragmentation.

NOTE   The Disk Defragmenter utility might not run when you have less than 15% free drive space on your system. When the Disk Defragmenter fails, clear any temporary files and archive older files to free the required space.

1. Start the Disk Defragmenter utility. You'll see a list of the drives on your machine. The statistics include the formatting method, capacity, amount of free space, and the percentage of free space. The first phase of defragmenting the drive is to make sure you actually need to defragment it.

NOTE   You can perform two tasks using Disk Defragmenter: analyze and defragment. Performing analysis first on large hard drives can save time. It pays to defragment drives smaller than 1GB each time you perform maintenance.

2. Click Analyze. The Disk Defragmenter display will change, as shown in Figure 8.5. Disk Defragmenter will check each file on the drive for fragmentation. When the analysis process is complete, you'll see a dialog box that either recommends you defragment your drive or leave it alone for now.

FIGURE 8.5
Disk Defragmenter helps you check your drive for fragmentation.

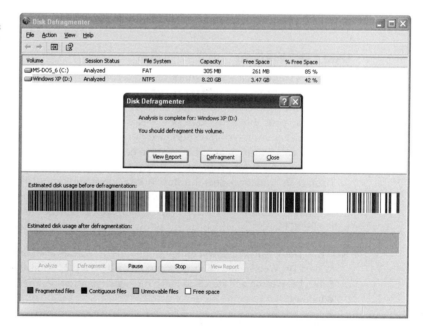

3. Click View Report. You'll see an Analysis Report dialog box. This dialog box provides information about the volume and lists the most fragmented files. Even if your drive doesn't require defragmentation, you may want to defragment the drive if one or two files have an exceptional amount of fragmentation.

4. Click Defragment if you need to defragment a drive. Disk Defragmenter will perform a quick analysis, then begin the defragmenting process. You'll see the areas of fragmentation disappear as the program moves files around on your system.

USING DEFRAG

Defrag is the command line version of the Disk Defragmenter utility described in the "Using the Standard Defragmenter" section. The advantage of using this utility is that you can call it from a script. In addition, it tends to be a little faster because it isn't updating the display all the time. The disadvantage is that the Defrag utility is harder to use and you don't receive any feedback on the defragmentation process. The Defrag utility relies on the following command line switches.

/A   Use this switch to analyze the drive without defragmenting it.

/F   The defragmenter will ask whether it should continue when the drive space is low. The defragmenter needs drive space to move the files around—when this space is limited, the defragmenter takes longer to accomplish the task. This switch forces the defragmenter to continue.

/V   Use this switch when you want verbose output—to see all of the details of the defragmentation process. Even though this display doesn't provide as much feedback as the graphical interface does, you can use the output for later analysis when you save it to a file.

Using Dr. Watson

Sometimes you need a way to monitor and record errors that occur on a system so that you can look for patterns. A problem might not occur after a specific repeatable set of steps or it might only happen when just the right environmental conditions exist on the system. Dr. Watson is an unusual tool in that you can probably better describe it as a service, or perhaps a monitor, than as an actual application. Whenever your system experiences an error, even one that you might not see, Dr. Watson records it. This feature makes Dr. Watson equally good as a diagnostic aid and as a means for monitoring your system for problems that require maintenance.

To start Dr. Watson, select the Start ➤ Run command. Type **DrWatson** in the Open field of the Run dialog box and click OK. Dr. Watson will start, but you might not notice immediately because it doesn't have an interface. The Dr. Watson icon appears on the Taskbar. Click this icon and Dr. Watson will tell you the status, which, at this point, is a message box saying that it hasn't detected any errors.

NOTE   The default Windows configuration runs Dr. Watson at all times in the background. If you try to start Dr. Watson and an error occurs, type **DrWtsn32 -i** at the command prompt and press Enter. Dr. Watson will start and make the registry entries required to start each time you log into Windows.

When Dr. Watson finally does detect an error, clicking the icon will display the error information. You can also view the DRWATSON.LOG file in the \Windows folder. This log tells you the start and end times for Dr. Watson. The DRWTSN32.LOG file contains the actual error information. You can learn more about this log file at http://www.microsoft.com/resources/documentation/windows/xp/all/proddocs/en-us/drwatson_logfile.mspx. The location of any crash data depends on the

Dr. Watson settings, but you'll normally find them in the \Documents and Settings\All Users\ Application Data\Microsoft\Dr Watson folder. The interesting feature of the log file is that it tells you which applications were running at the time of the error, which helps you better understand the environment in which the application was running and could help you locate the error.

The Dr. Watson configuration utility is different from the icon that you see displayed on the Taskbar. To configure Dr. Watson for use, select the Start ➤ Run command. Type **DrWtsn32** in the Open field of the Run dialog box and click OK. You'll see the configuration dialog box shown in Figure 8.6.

Normally, the settings shown in Figure 8.6 work fine when you want to monitor the system—especially if you don't want to cause user frustration with the Dr. Watson display. However, when you're optimizing your system and want to learn about problems immediately, you can set Dr. Watson to provide both a visual and audio alert. In some cases, you might want to use a special optimizing folder for the dump file (the one that tells about the application that crashed), so you can change the Log File Path and Crash Dump entries. The dump file is a binary file that a programmer can use to locate the source of a fault quickly—you won't get any usable information from this file unless you're an application developer. However, sending this file to the support department for your application can help you locate optimization problems. Some vendors, such as the Panorama Factory, are quite proactive about receiving the Dr. Watson logs (learn more at http://www.panoramafactory.com/ drwatson.html).

TIP You can stop Dr. Watson from automatically starting by modifying the Auto value of the HKEY_ LOCAL_MACHINE\SOFTWARE\Microsoft\Windows NT\CurrentVersion\AeDebug key. Setting Auto to 0 means that Windows won't start Dr. Watson automatically when you log in. What will happen instead is that Windows will display a dialog box with two buttons—OK and Cancel—whenever an application error occurs. When you click OK, the application will simply terminate. Clicking Cancel starts Watson and lets you make a log file entry about the error. See Chapter 6 for details on working with the registry. Making this change can improve system performance, but it also means that errors won't get recorded in the background and users could thwart efforts to locate an errant application.

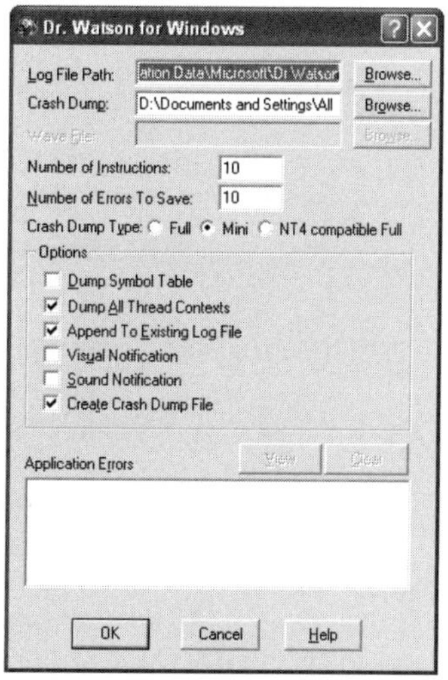

FIGURE 8.6
The default Dr. Watson configuration normally works well, but you can change it to meet specific needs.

When you don't want to send Dr. Watson information to a support person and you don't have the code required to diagnose application errors, you can save a considerable amount of hard drive space by clearing the Create Crash Dump File option. Every one of these entries consumes 100KB or more of disk space using the default settings. When you check expanded options, such as Dump Symbol Table, the file can become immense and quickly chew up hard drive space. When you want to maintain a dump file, but only the current one, clear the Append to Existing Log File option.

Using jv16 Power Tools

Some cleaning products help you get rid of initial grime—others help you keep your system in its now clean state. The jv16 Power Tools package from Macecraft Software (`http://www.macecraft .com/brief_pt/`) helps you maintain a clean state. This application includes some of the registry cleaning features found in products like Registry Mechanic and TweakNow RegCleaner described in Chapter 6. It also includes some of the features of the Empty Temp Folders utility described in Chapter 4. Although the tools jv16 Power Tools provides are well designed and useful, they lack some of the functionality provided by the single purpose tools. Figure 8.7 shows how this utility appears when you first start it.

The jv16 Power Tools package does include some features that make it especially useful for maintenance. The file tools include an excellent search engine for your system that helps you locate files of all types. Unlike Windows Explorer, this search engine actually tells you what your hard drive contains. The DLL Cleaner is also a nice addition because it locates DLLs that don't appear to have any application connections and helps you remove them.

Automation goes a long way toward making maintenance palatable for many people, which means scripting in many cases. You'll find a full-fledged scripting environment, including security features that make using scripts a little safer. These scripts use a JVB extension, so they don't tend to suffer from the same problems as the more popular Visual Basic Script (VBS) and JavaScript (JS) files. The scripting environment includes a script manager so you can see the scripts you create at a glance and edit them as needed. You can even execute the scripts without leaving the jv16 Power Tools environment. The scripting environment even includes a script wizard to reduce the effort required to create a script.

FIGURE 8.7
Use jv16 Power Tools as a means to keep your system clean.

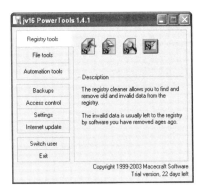

You'll also find a number of maintenance features in jv16 Power Tools that make it easier to use over a long time frame. For example, a single click will tell the application to check for updates online. A second click downloads and installs the update, all without having to use a browser. You also have great control over how jv16 Power Tools works, which means that you can set it up to meet personal needs. It's these long-term usage features that set jv16 Power Tools apart as a maintenance tool, rather than a heavy duty, short-term cleaner.

Utilities You Didn't Know About

Windows contains a wealth of utilities, and Microsoft constantly adds more to the package. In some cases, third party vendors also add new utilities that you could find useful for a number of tasks other than the ones the third party vendor originally intended. The only problem is that some of these utilities are such secrets that few people know they exist, much less how to use them. These utilities await discovery on your hard drive, and the following sections tell you how to find them. Not only that, but the following sections discuss a few of these hidden gems that you can use to clean and optimize your system as well.

Techniques for Discovering Unknown Utilities

Many hidden utilities are hiding in the open. You'd see them if you were looking for them, but you really aren't looking, so they remain undiscovered. For example, open a copy of Windows Explorer now and look in the `\Windows\System32` folder of your system. Change the Views setting to Details and click the Type field to sort the display by type. Figure 8.8 shows typical results.

FIGURE 8.8
Utilities often hide in plain sight—you just have to look for them.

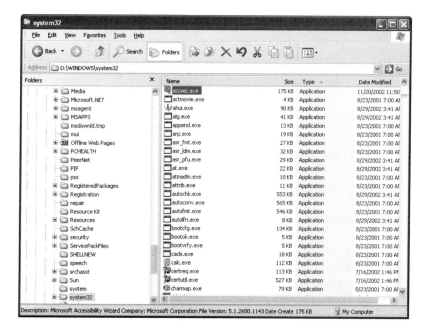

Look at all the of application files in Figure 8.8. Just going through this list should provide you with a wealth of new utilities to try. Some of the executables are familiar, but some of them are going to be new. (Many of these utilities already appear somewhere in the book.) The entries in this folder alone could keep you busy for weeks. The subdirectories also contain executables in many cases—any of which could prove to be the best time-saving utility you've ever found. The idea is to look for the things that Microsoft hasn't really discussed.

WARNING   Never assume you can simply execute a utility to see what it does. This technique often results in disaster when the utility does something unexpected like erase your hard drive. Always research the utility, online if necessary, to discover what tasks it performs before you use it. Often, you can simply type the name of the utility in a search engine such as Google to receive a list of links for that utility. A few utilities have common names, so you might have to include additional search terms, such as Windows XP. When you run across an executable that no one has documented, you need to wonder about that file. It could simply be an executable that Windows uses internally, but also consider alternatives such as a virus, adware, or spyware.

Microsoft isn't the only company that hides utilities on your hard drive. After you install a new application, take time to look through the application directory. Complex applications normally include multiple application files, any of which could be a useful utility. As with any executable file, proceed with caution because you don't know what effect that application will have on your system. The vendor documentation often contains useful information about the application. The reason you need to search the application folder is that the help file entries for these utilities are normally difficult to find when you just hunt through the help file.

TIP   Most command line utilities support the /? or /Help command line switch. The help you receive tells you about the command line switches the utility supports along with a limited amount of utility information. In some cases, the help provides enough information for you to work with the utility, but often it doesn't. Consider the utility-provided help as a good starting point—when the utility help looks interesting, spend more time learning about the utility before you use it.

Once you know more about the utilities on your hard drive, you might want to spend some time online. Magazines and Web sites often provide reviews of deserving third party shareware utilities that can make life a lot easier for you. In addition, you can visit any of the major shareware sites online. Many of these sites include a voting system and room for user comments so you can learn more about the utilities. Appendix A describes a number of third party utilities that you might want to try—these utilities are in addition to those that already appear in the book.

Some Utilities Don't Work

Not every utility you run across is going to be the best deal—in fact, most of them won't work as you thought they would. The utility might not do anything at all or it might provide disappointing results. In most cases, the author of the utility had all of the right intentions and the utility does work as expected for some people, but you aren't one of them. Researching a utility is important to ensure you know how the tool works before you really need it.

Using a test system, one that you don't care about, is always a good idea when trying a new utility, but not everyone has this luxury. When you must test a new utility on your personal system, make sure you create a backup first (see the "Performing Backups" section for details). In fact, it's usually a good idea to create a restore point as well (see the "Rolling Back Bad Installations" section of the chapter for details), just to ensure you can get back to a known good state with your machine.

Set aside time for testing the utilities. You'll normally want to place the utilities in a separate folder. When the folder contains four or five candidates, it's time to test them. As you test each utility, decide whether you can use it or not. Uninstall and erase any utilities you can't use. Otherwise, the utilities that are supposed to help optimize your system will end up clogging the hard drive.

On those occasions when you find a utility that doesn't do anything at all, try to contact the author to ensure you're using the utility correctly. In some cases, you'll find that the author has already created a newer version that overcomes deficiencies in the older version you obtained. Sometimes you'll find out that the author simply didn't design the utility for your machine configuration. Rarely will you find that the author doesn't care about the application and won't discuss it at all. The idea is to provide the author with feedback, which often leads to newer and better versions. Make sure you take time to tell the author when they are doing a good job too—everyone likes to hear good news about the program they put together (even Microsoft).

Using DriverQuery

DriverQuery is a simple utility for learning more about your drivers without having to research them through multiple applets on your machine. This utility lists the drivers on your machine or a remote system. You can discover detailed information about the driver, such as whether Microsoft signed the driver. (Signing is a verification process where Microsoft tests the driver flaws—those drivers that pass the rigorous test are less likely to cause problems on your system.)

The easiest way to use this utility is to type **DriverQuery** and press Enter at the command prompt. You'll see a list of the drivers on your system using the TABLE format. As with most Windows command line utilities, you can augment the output using command line switches. For example, you can change the output format to make it suitable for use with a database. DriverQuery provides the following command line switches.

/S *System* This switch lets you access the drivers on another machine. Simply provide the name of the remote system. In some cases, you'll need to include the /U and /P command line switches with this one to obtain access to the remote machine.

/U *[Domain\]User Name* Use this switch to provide a user name when accessing a remote system. When working on a network with a domain controller, you also need to provide the domain name as part of the switch to ensure the server recognizes the user name. Always use this switch after the /S switch.

/P *Password* Use this switch to provide a password for access to the remote system. DriverQuery will prompt you for a password when you don't include one and the remote system requests it. Always use this switch after the /U switch.

/FO *Format* This switch lets you alter the output format of the data that DriverQuery provides. The standard TABLE format is suitable for viewing. Use the LIST format when you want to group driver entries separately so that you can treat each one individually, rather than as part of a table. The Comma Separated Value (CSV) format is especially helpful when you want to place the output in a database.

/NH   Use this switch to remove the header from the output. You can only use this option with the TABLE and CSV formats. This feature makes it easier to create output that a database will readily accept.

/V   This switch provides additional information that includes a description, starting mode (manual, automatic, or disabled), current state (such as running or stopped), status, the amount of memory the driver uses, and the driver's installation location (including executable filename). The additional information also tells whether the driver will accept a stop or pause command, which is required when you want to see how the system will work without a particular driver.

/SI   This is a special switch for versions of Windows that support signed drivers. It provides additional information that tells whether Microsoft has signed the driver. You can use this switch to locate possible sources of system instability.

Using OpenFiles

The OpenFiles utility helps you monitor and control open files on a system (either shared or locally used). You can discover which files someone has opened and optionally disconnect them when necessary. The OpenFiles utility also works for remote connections, so you could determine which files you have opened on a server, as an example.

The shared usage feature is especially important. Windows doesn't provide the easiest methods for tracking open files that someone else might be using on your system. On a peer-to-peer network, it's important to know whether someone else has files opened before you shut the machine down. In addition, files opened by someone else use resources on your machine, so you need to know who is using which resources to maintain control over system performance.

When you use OpenFiles by itself, the utility will report the status of any locally shared connections. OpenFiles also supports three subcommands: /Disconnect (removes a shared file connection), /Query (requests information about local or remote connections), and /Local (works with local file resources). The following sections discuss each of the subcommands.

WORKING WITH OPENFILES /DISCONNECT

The OpenFiles /Disconnect subcommand lets you disconnect any shared file resource from any machine to which you have access. You can use this feature to release file connections for any number of reasons. For example, a user might have experienced a system crash, so releasing a file connection will let the user open the file again after bringing the machine back online. You could also use this feature to sever a connection between unauthorized applications and a file. The OpenFiles /Disconnect subcommand includes the following command line switches.

/S *System*   This switch lets you access the shared file information on another machine. Simply provide the name of the remote system. In some cases, you'll need to include the /U and /P command line switches with this one to obtain access to the remote machine.

/U *[Domain\]User Name*   Use this switch to provide a user name when accessing a remote system. When working on a network with a domain controller, you also need to provide the domain name as part of the switch to ensure the server recognizes the user name. Always use this switch after the /S switch.

/P `Password`   Use this switch to provide a password for access to remote system. OpenFiles will prompt you for a password when you don't include one and the remote system requests it. Always use this switch after the /U switch.

/ID `Open File Identifier`   Use this switch to close individual files based on their identifier. You can obtain the open file identifier using the OpenFile /Query subcommand. Provide either a numeric identifier for single files or use the asterisk (*) to indicate that you want to close all of the files.

/A `User Name`   Use this switch to close files based on a particular user name (the connections accessed by value). Note that this switch closes all of the files on that machine opened by a particular user. You can also use the asterisk (*) to indicate that you want to close all files opened by every shared connection user.

/O `Open Mode`   Use this switch to close files based on their open mode—the method used to interact with the file. The valid values include Read, Write, and Read/Write. You can also use the asterisk (*) to indicate that you want to close all shared connection files no matter which mode is used.

/OP `Open Filename`   Use this switch to close a file based on its filename. The filename can include a path so that you can specify a particular file when the same file exists in more than one location.

You can combine command line switches to obtain specific results. For example, you could combine the /OP and /A switches to close a file opened by a particular user, rather than all of the users. As another example, when you need exclusive write privileges for a file, you could combine the /OP and /O switches to close all copies of a file opened for either write or read/write access, but not those that are opened for read-only access.

WORKING WITH OPENFILES /QUERY

The OpenFiles /Query subcommand helps you obtain information about shared connections on another machine. You could use this switch for a number of tasks. For example, you might be surprised to learn how many connections you have opened on a server. Each one of these connections requires memory, hard drive, processing cycle, and network bandwidth resources, so keeping the connections to a minimum is a good way to optimize resource usage on your system. It's also possible to discover connections you didn't know about (such as those created by viruses, adware, and spyware) using this technique. The OpenFiles /Query subcommand uses the following command line switches.

/S `System`   This switch lets you access the shared file information on another machine. Simply provide the name of the remote system. In some cases, you'll need to include the /U and /P command line switches with this one to obtain access to the remote machine.

/U `[Domain\]User Name`   Use this switch to provide a user name when accessing a remote system. When working on a network with a domain controller, you also need to provide the domain name as part of the switch to ensure the server recognizes the user name. Always use this switch after the /S switch.

/P *Password*   Use this switch to provide a password for access to remote system. OpenFiles will prompt you for a password when you don't include one and the remote system requests it. Always use this switch after the /U switch.

/FO *Format*   This switch lets you alter the output format of the data that OpenFiles provides. The standard TABLE format is suitable for viewing. Use the LIST format when you want to group driver entries separately so that you can treat each one individually, rather than as part of a table. The Comma Separated Value (CSV) format is especially helpful when you want to place the output in a database.

/NH   Use this switch to remove the header from the output. You can only use this option with the TABLE and CSV formats. This feature makes it easier to create output that a database will readily accept.

/V   This switch provides additional information that includes the host name (the name of the server), number of locks on the file (a lock prevents someone else from using the file for a particular task), and open mode (read, read/write, or write).

WORKING WITH OPENFILES /LOCAL

Normally, your system doesn't track local files—those that you have opened—in a way that Open-Files can use. The options for this subcommand let you add support for this feature to the system. However, adding this support does affect performance negatively, so you should use this feature only when you suspect something is going wrong with the local system. For example, you could use it to monitor file use by local applications when you suspect virus, adware, or spyware activity (or simply an application that isn't performing as anticipated). The OpenFiles /Local subcommand provides the following command line switches. (Note that there isn't any slash in front of the switch.)

On   Turns on support for local file tracking.

Off   Turns off support for local file tracking.

Using Net

The Net utility provides a lot of network-related functions—some of which you can use for optimization. For example, the Net Time subcommand it helpful when you want to synchronize the clocks on your system, but it really isn't a performance tool. You never use the Net utility by itself; you always choose from one of the subcommands that include Accounts, Computer, Config, Continue, File, Group, Help, HelpMsg, LocalGroup, Name, Pause, Print, Send, Session, Share, Start, Statistics, Stop, Time, Use, User, and View.

TIP   You can configure many of the settings provided with the Net utility using the Local Security Policy console found in the Administrative Tools folder of the Control Panel. Other settings appear as part of the Local Users and Groups folder of the Computer Management console. The advantage of the Net utility is that you can configure these settings using one utility. In addition, you can use a script or batch file to perform the configuration.

Whenever you want to find out more about this utility, use the subcommand name followed by the /? command line switch. For example, if you want to learn more about the Time subcommand, you type **Net Time /?** and press Enter. The Net utility will tell you more about the Time subcommand. The following sections describe the optimization subcommands. I didn't include the Net File subcommand because you can perform the same task better with the OpenFiles utility (see the "Using OpenFiles" section for details).

WARNING   Some of the Net subcommands could have dangerous side effects. For example, the Net Send subcommand lets you transmit messages to one or more of the users on a network. However, to use this feature, you must run the Messenger service, which has known virus vulnerabilities. Make sure you understand how the Net subcommands work before you use them. All of the Net subcommands listed in the sections that follow are safe when used for their intended purpose.

WORKING WITH *NET ACCOUNTS*

The Net Accounts subcommand lets you configure the essential account parameters for your system. When you type this subcommand by itself, you see the current system configuration. Most of the arguments for this command are security related. For example, you can use the /MINPWAGE switch to set the minimum number of days between password changes.

One switch, /FORCELOGOFF, can help you maintain control over resource usage on your system by ensuring someone accessing your system has to log off after a specific time interval has passed. To use this switch, provide the number of minutes that you want to force a user to log off after their time has expired. For example, if you wanted to force a user to log off 15 minutes after their time expired, you would type **Net Accounts /FORCELOGOFF:15** and press Enter.

This switch only affects the forced logoff time. You must also configure the user account with specific logon hours using the Local Users or Groups folder of the Computer Management console.

WORKING WITH *NET CONTINUE, NET PAUSE, NET START,* AND *NET STOP*

The Net Continue, Net Pause, Net Start, and Net Stop subcommands all work with Windows services. You can start, stop, pause, or continue service operation from the command line. Using Net Start by itself lists the services running on your system. It's also possible to perform these tasks using the Services console located in the Administrative Tools folder of the Control Panel. The main advantage of using these subcommands is that you can script the action or use a batch file. For example, you could use Net Start to create a file containing all of the running services, use a script to check the file for services that you don't want to run, and then stop these services using the Net Stop command. The result is a performance boost for your system, along with better resource usage.

WORKING WITH *NET HELPMSG*

The Net HelpMsg subcommand provides a human readable message for an error number. These network error numbers pop up all over the place, including the event log and in messages that Windows displays on screen. Remembering that this subcommand is available can save you significant time trying to locate the error number through another source. Even though the text isn't always the most descriptive, it at least gives you a starting point for solving a problem. To use this subcommand, type **Net HelpMsg**, the error message number, and then press Enter at the command prompt.

WORKING WITH *NET PRINT*

The `Net Print` subcommand lets you manage network print jobs. You can use it to temporarily place a print job on hold to free resources for another need, or you can delete a print job submitted to the server in error. To use this command, you must provide a fully qualified printer resource name. For example, when the server name is My_Server and the printer network name is MyPrinter, you would type **Net Print \\My_Server\MyPrinter**, along with any command line switches desired. When you use this subcommand without any additional command line switches, you'll receive a list of print jobs for that printer. When you do use one of the command line switches, you must also provide a job number (obtained from the list of print jobs). Here are the command line switches for this subcommand.

/HOLD Tells the server to pause the print job to free resources for some other work. You can also place lower priority jobs on hold until high priority jobs complete.

/RELEASE Tells the server to continue printing a job that you previously placed on hold.

/DELETE Tells the server to remove a print job from the print queue. The print job will stop, even when the printer has already started printing it.

WORKING WITH *NET STATISTICS*

The `Net Statistics` subcommand helps you determine network health. You can monitor the number of bytes sent or received, along with the error counts for various statistics. For example, when you begin seeing network errors, it's an indication that you're having connectivity or other problems. Windows doesn't make you aware of these errors—it fixes them in the background as long as it can. Consequently, you can experience a sudden network card or other failure even though the network provides statistics that show the slow degradation of the component. Monitoring these statistics is one of the few ways that you can ensure good network health.

You can monitor every network connection individually. For example, when you want to discover how your machine performs as a workstation, you type **Net Statistics Workstation** and press Enter. Likewise, you can monitor server connections. Each of these statistics tells you how your machine is doing in that area.

Using FSUtil

The FSUtil utility helps you manage the disk subsystem for your machine. You never use this command by itself. Instead, you supply a subcommand to perform a particular task with the utility. The subcommands include `Behavior`, `Dirty`, `File`, `FSInfo`, `HardLink`, `ObjectID`, `Quota`, `ReparsePoint`, `Sparse`, `USN`, and `Volume`.

Not all of the subcommands are useful for optimization purposes. For example, although the `HardLink` subcommand is very useful for creating multiple entries for a single file on the file system, it's unlikely that you'll use this feature as an optimization option because it doesn't improve system performance, make the system easier to use, or enhance reliability. In addition, it's easier to perform a few of the tasks using GUI utilities and you're unlikely to script these options. For example, although you can set user quotas using the `Quota` subcommand, it's easier to perform this task using the Windows Explorer features (see the "Setting Quotas" section of Chapter 9 for details). The following sections describe the FSUtil subcommands that you'll find useful for optimization purposes.

TIP   The Internet abounds with hard drive tuning utilities that can tell you everything from the hard drive's performance figures to the current hard drive health. These utilities usually base the hard drive health information on Self-Monitoring and Reporting Technology (SMART)—some drives have this feature, but others don't. The utility will tell you when the SMART information is available. One of the better monitoring utilities available is HD Tune. This utility provides a number of hard drive performance statistics and complete SMART monitoring. By checking this information regularly, you can reduce the possibility of unexpected hard drive failure. You can download HD Tune from http://www.majorgeeks.com/download4130.html.

WORKING WITH *FSUTIL DIRTY*

The FSUtil Dirty subcommand lets you set the dirty bit for a hard drive. The dirty bit tells Windows whether to perform a ChkDsk command during the next boot cycle on the drive (see the "Using ChkDsk" section for details). Windows checks all drives with the dirty bit set.

To check the status of the dirty bit on a drive, use the FSUtil Dirty Query subcommand with the letter of the drive you want to check. For example, when you want to check the C drive, you type **FSUtil Dirty Query C:** at the command prompt and press Enter. FSUtil will tell you whether the drive is dirty. Likewise, to set the dirty bit, use the FSUtil Dirty Set command. For example, to set the C drive up for a check, type **FSUtil Dirty Set C:** at the command prompt and press Enter.

WORKING WITH *FSUTIL FSINFO*

The FSUtil FSInfo subcommand displays statistics about the file system. These statistics can tell you everything from which drives the system recognizes to the amount of data each drive has processed since the last boot. By analyzing these statistics, you can determine when the system is operating normally and detect any abnormal drive behavior. Abnormal drive behavior could mean anything from a virus infection to a failing hard drive, but it always indicates a need to check further. The FSUtil FSInfo subcommand supports the following statistical outputs.

Drives   This option displays a list of drives that the system officially recognizes. It doesn't mean that other drives aren't available; it does mean that these drives aren't accessible. When you don't see a drive that you think you should, make sure the drive is mounted, is working properly, and has any required drive mapping.

DriveType *Drive Letter*   This option displays information about a particular drive, so you need to include a drive letter with it. It tells you about the drive connection. For example, a local hard drive is a fixed drive, while a mapped drive on another machine is a remote or network drive.

VolumeInfo *Drive Letter*   This option displays all of the volume information for a particular drive, so you need to include a drive letter with it. For example, you'll discover the volume name, how the drive is formatted, and the volume characteristics (such as whether it preserves the case of filenames).

NTFSInfo *Drive Letter*   This option displays the NTFS information for a particular drive, so you need to include a drive letter with it. When you attempt to use this option on a drive formatted with another file system, FSUtil displays an error. You also can't use this option on a remote drive. The output includes several important statistics, including the NTFS version number. The reason the version number is so important is that you can discover more about NTFS features when you know the version number. Newer versions support better features and a higher level of optimization than older versions do. You can also determine the size of each cluster. This statistic is important because it tells you how much space a file takes on the hard drive. A 1-byte file doesn't consume just 1 byte—it consumes an entire cluster. For a standard drive, that means a 1-byte file actually consumes 4,096 bytes. You can use the Disk Management folder of the Computer Management console found in the Administrative Tools folder of the Control Panel to create partitions with smaller clusters in some cases, which will optimize the hard drive for use with small files.

Statistics *Drive Letter* This option displays the usage statistics for a particular drive, so you need to include a drive letter with it. When you attempt to use this option on a drive formatted with another file system, FSUtil displays an error. You also can't use this option on a remote drive. The usage statistics include how many bitmaps the drive wrote and how many times a user read files from the drive. By monitoring these statistics, you can create a pattern for the drive. When a drive begins to deviate from this pattern, you can check for potential errors.

Using SystemInfo and WinMSD

The SystemInfo and WinMSD utilities perform precisely the same task. The SystemInfo utility works at the command line so you can send data you want to a file or view it from a remote location. The WinMSD utility is GUI based, which makes working with it a lot easier. Because both utilities are essentially the same, this section describes the features provided with WinMSD.

To start WinMSD, select the Start ➢ Run command, type WinMSD in the Open field, and click OK. You'll see a summary window similar to the one shown in Figure 8.9. The left pane contains a list of information areas and the right pane contains details about the selected area.

WinMSD provides exceptionally detailed configuration information, so you can use it for various support tasks, as well as discovering new areas for optimizing your system. The File ➢ Save command lets you save the current configuration information to disk for later analysis or for comparison purposes. Use the File ➢ Open command to open a saved configuration information file.

FIGURE 8.9
Use WinMSD to learn more about your system's configuration.

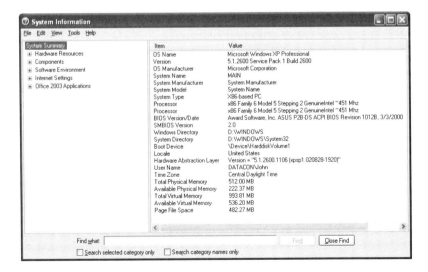

Some areas are better places than others to search for potential optimizations. For example, the `Software Environment\Running Tasks` folder contains a wealth of information about the applications running on your machine. Unlike many other lists you'll find, this one is complete (although it doesn't list all of the services running in the SvcHost application).

It's interesting to note that WinMSD also displays information about your Microsoft Office setup. Like all other areas of WinMSD, you can use this information to find potential sources of optimization. You might find that an Office application has features you don't want installed or that the setup is less than optimal for ensuring you can get work done quickly. You can use WinMSD to compare the Office setup on one machine with the setup on another machine to reduce setup time and ensure every machine has a similar setup when used for the same task.

One of the most important reasons to use WinMSD, however, is that it provides access to other system diagnostics from the Tools menu. For example, when you suspect that your sound system is less than optimal, you can select the Tools ➢ DirectX Diagnostic Tool option to get help. Many of these utilities appear in other sections of the book, so they aren't discussed in this section.

Working with the Windows PowerToys

PowerToys are special applications created by Microsoft but not supported by Microsoft (at least officially), nor are they part of Windows XP. You use a PowerToy to augment Windows XP in some way or perform tasks that Windows XP doesn't normally support. You can download any of the Power-Toys at `http://www.microsoft.com/windowsxp/downloads/powertoys/xppowertoys.mspx` or `http://www.microsoft.com/windowsxp/downloads/powertoys/create_powertoy.mspx`. However, this chapter discusses only one of the PowerToys, TweakUI. The other PowerToys are interesting and useful, but TweakUI is special because it can help you optimize your computer.

TIP Windows XP isn't the only version of Windows that has PowerToys, nor is it the only Microsoft product with this feature. You can get an overview of many of the PowerToy add-ins that Microsoft offers at `http://www.microsoft.com/windowsxp/downloads/powertoys/default.mspx`.

When a PowerToy Becomes a Useless Toy

The various PowerToys are indeed powerful and they all look so interesting that you might be tempted to install them all. The PowerToys are indeed all useful, but not everyone needs every PowerToy. As with any utility or add-on, make sure you can actually use the PowerToy before you download and install it. Fortunately, you can download the PowerToys individually and avoid the temptation to install PowerToys you don't need.

PowerToys are also easy to misuse. A PowerToy does perform tasks that Microsoft felt most users either wouldn't need to perform or shouldn't perform because the modification could result in an unstable system. Consequently, you should approach PowerToys with some amount of caution and ensure you understand the PowerToy before you use it. PowerToys that help you wreak havoc on your system are useless because they're working counter to their intended design.

WARNING   When installing PowerToys on a system with multiple users, make sure you make them available only to the administrator or the person the administrator designates. Keep Power-Toys out the hands of novices to ensure the machine you use today will still function tomorrow. Obviously, PowerToys in the right hands can make a big difference in system optimization by making the system friendlier, faster, or more reliable, but a PowerToy in the wrong hands is simply dangerous.

Using TweakUI

Of all the PowerToys that Microsoft created, TweakUI is the most powerful and the most needed. This simple tool can help you clean up many Windows XP annoyances without having to edit the registry manually. All of the changes you make with TweakUI affect the registry in some way, so you'll want to be sure to create a backup of your system before you use it. This section assumes that you've downloaded and installed TweakUI from the Microsoft PowerToys Web site.

When you first open TweakUI, you'll see a list of Windows areas that you can modify, as shown in Figure 8.10. Not all of these areas provide a substantial optimization change, and some of them are more a matter of personal taste because they really don't optimize your system. In fact, a few of the settings can actually reduce the effectiveness of your system in some respects. For example, Figure 8.10 shows the Shortcuts category. Notice that you can set a shortcut so its icon looks just like the one for a regular file. Because a shortcut now looks like a file, some people will treat it as such with potentially negative consequences. A user could copy a shortcut to a network location believing it's the actual file—anyone attempting to open the shortcut masquerading as a file will be disappointed.

Some of the settings that TweakUI provides don't work consistently, so you have to be aware of potential problems with using them. For example, look in the General\Focus folder and you'll see a Prevent Application from Stealing Focus setting. Theoretically, when you check this option, Windows prevents applications from simply popping up without warning. Instead, the application is supposed to flash its icon on the Taskbar a specific number of times. The setting works with some applications, but others ignore it and pop up anyway. Interestingly enough, Outlook Express is one of the applications that appears to ignore this setting in some cases. When you send a message and the ISP times out, Windows will display a dialog box asking if you want to continue waiting. If you happen to be typing at the time, you could end up waiting, canceling, or even not seeing the dialog box for that matter, without realizing it.

TweakUI does have a number of interesting settings. Look at the Taskbar folder and you'll see an Enable Balloon Tips option. Clear this option to get rid of the annoying balloon tips that Windows XP delights in displaying at the most inopportune times. Don't confuse this option with tooltips that provide added information about a button or other control on a form. A balloon tip displays Windows XP messages such as the need to clean up the unused icons in the Notification Area. The messages are nice, but they tend to appear right in the middle of working on your latest spreadsheet or word-processed document.

One of the features that really make TweakUI a great optimization tool is found in the My Computer\Special Folders folder shown in Figure 8.11. Normally, you don't have any control over where Windows stores data. This tool lets you change the storage locations so they meet your particular needs. Note that the changes you make affect only the currently logged in user—not all the users of the machine.

WARNING   Exercise care when you change the default location of folders on your machine. Some changes, such as changing the location of My Documents, could cause applications to behave oddly or not perform certain tasks properly because they won't be able to find the previous location of information on the system. To ensure that applications continue to work as anticipated, change the location using TweakUI, and then use Windows Explorer to move the data from the old location on the hard drive to the new location.

FIGURE 8.10
Use TweakUI to modify several categories of Windows settings.

FIGURE 8.11
Modify the location of special data on your system so you can find it when needed.

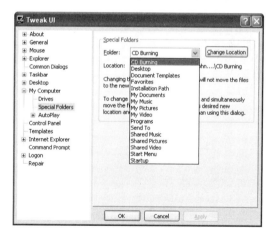

Some people don't use the Document Templates feature of Windows XP because they don't know it exists or the templates provided don't offer anything the user wants. The `Templates` folder contains a list of existing Document Templates—the ones that Microsoft decided that you need—as shown in Figure 8.12.

This list contains the items you see on the New menu when you right-click an open area in Windows Explorer. You can customize these settings in three ways.

1. Clear the check next to a template. This removes the template from the New menu, but doesn't remove it from the list in the registry. For example, you might not need to create a Briefcase now, but you could need it later, so clearing the check next to this entry makes sense.

2. Add a new template to the list by clicking Create. TweakUI will display an Open Template dialog box. Locate a file that contains the template you want to use. TweakUI will make the required registry entries and copy the file to the `\Documents and Settings\All Users\Templates` folder so it's accessible, even if you remove the original file.

3. Remove an entry you no longer need by highlighting it and clicking Delete. For example, Figure 8.12 shows an entry named CPdfSvr Document that an application left behind after installation. This entry represents yet another one of the application crumbs you need to consider (see the "Discovering Application Uninstall Remains" section of Chapter 4 for additional information).

Internet Explorer includes a very useful feature that you can't access without TweakUI (or a good knowledge of the registry). Select the `Internet Explorer\Search` folder and you'll see a place where you can define search prefixes. For example, when I want to find the meaning of an acronym online, I don't select a link from my Favorites folder. Instead, I type `af` and the acronym in the Internet Explorer Address field and press Enter—`af` is a search prefix I defined using TweakUI.

FIGURE 8.12
Create a list of document templates that you can really use.

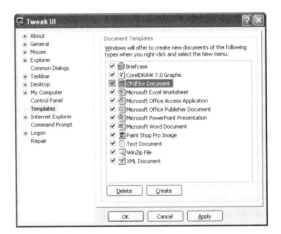

To add a search prefix of your own, you need to know something about the site you want to access. For example, Acronym Finder, the site I use to locate acronyms, relies on `http://www.acronym-finder.com/af-query.asp?String=exact&Acronym=%s` as the URL for locating an acronym. Internet Explorer replaces the `%s` with the acronym I provide in the Address field. Once you know the URL you need, click Create, type a prefix in the Prefix field, and the URL in the URL field. Remember to include the `%s` instead of a specific search term. Using these search prefixes makes you a lot more efficient and faster when you need to locate information in a hurry.

The final essential TweakUI feature appears in the `Repair` folder shown in Figure 8.13. All of the entries shown in Figure 8.13 tend to become corrupted as the Windows XP installation gets older. These entries let you fix the required files with a minimum of effort. However, what the dialog box doesn't make apparent is that repairing the file often reduces it in size—sometimes substantially. Therefore, not only are you repairing the file, but you're also cleaning it.

FIGURE 8.13

Repair Windows XP files as needed to ensure the operating system remains reliable.

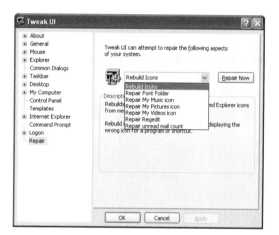

Knowing that Updates Change Settings

Part of keeping Windows clean is ensuring you apply updates as needed. An update can repair errors in the operating system; remove the threat of a virus, adware, or spyware attack; or make Windows more efficient. Sometimes an update will include new operating system features that you can use to create a better working environment. The point is that updates have some positive reason for existing, and you should carefully install them after a full backup of your system. It's also a very good idea to create a restore point in case Microsoft makes the update difficult or impossible to remove from your system.

Although updates are an important part of the cleaning cycle for your system, they also present a few challenges that you need to consider. The reason that you want to back up your system is that an update can have unexpected or undesirable effects. Sometimes an effect is subtle—an update could prevent you from running a particular utility or it might cause an odd application error to occur. In some cases, such as with Windows XP SP2, the effects aren't subtle at all. Microsoft has made it quite plain that Windows XP SP2 is going to break applications that don't handle security correctly.

Whenever you experience a problem due to an update, uninstall the update if possible or use the restore point to restore the system to a known good state. For this reason, test one update at a time. Don't leave the update off your system permanently. Instead, locate workarounds for the problems the update causes. In many cases, contacting Microsoft will help because other customers have likely complained about the same problem and Microsoft may have already created a fix for it. Once you have the workarounds, reinstall the update and make the required corrections. Generally, you benefit more from taking this approach than if you ignore the update completely.

Updates present another problem besides changing system settings and causing compatibility problems. In many cases, you'll also find that an update removes some of the optimizations you performed. Some people will assume that an update has slowed their machine, when, in fact, the update merely removed optimizations that you'll need to restore. One common problem is that an update will restart services that you know you don't need. Consequently, after you install an update, check the Services applet to ensure that the update hasn't restarted services you don't want.

It also pays to check Task Manager to ensure you don't see any new applications running. Sometimes, an update will simply assume that you want to run a new feature it includes, whether you want to run it or not. Monitoring Task Manager is a good way to keep track of your system before and after an update.

NOTE Some people have had trouble with the drivers they download from Windows Update. Theoretically, these drivers should be less troublesome than the ones you obtain from the vendor because Microsoft has spent additional time checking them. In addition, because the drivers are vendor specific, you should also obtain additional functionality. Unfortunately, these drivers aren't always compatible with the current system. The bottom line is that you might be giving up some system reliability and stability to get optimal performance and the latest features from an updated driver.

Using and Cleaning the Event Log

Windows maintains several event logs that tell you about system status, application, or security problems. In addition, applications can create their own specialized event logs. These specialized events logs normally describe events for a specific application or operating system feature such as a device driver. You view the event log using the Event Viewer console located in the Administrative Tools folder of the Control Panel. Figure 8.14 shows a typical example of the Event Viewer with the System event log highlighted. The following sections describe how to work with the standard Windows event logs (System, Application, and Security) from an optimization perspective.

TIP Sometimes an application will leave its special log in place after you uninstall it. Fortunately, you can remove the log manually by removing its subkey from the `HKEY_LOCAL_MACHINE\` `SYSTEM\ControlSet001\Services\Eventlog` key in the registry. Chapter 6 tells you more about working with the registry. After you remove the registry key and verify that the log no longer exists in the Event Viewer, remove the associated file from the `\WINDOWS\system32\config` folder. The event log will have an EVT extension and a shortened version of the event log name. Never remove the System, Application, or Security event logs.

FIGURE 8.14

The event logs on your system help you discover problems such as errant applications.

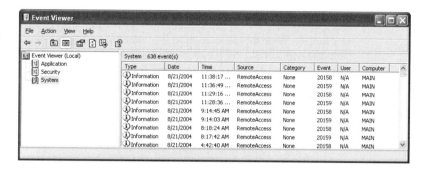

Viewing Event Log Entries

The event logs support several kinds of entries. From an optimization perspective, you only need to think about the information, warning, and error entries. The following list describes each entry type and what it means to you from an optimization perspective.

Information   Information entries tell you that Windows or an application performed a task successfully or that an application or service has had a change of status. For example, every time you dial the Internet with a dial-up connection, the Remote Access service makes an entry in the System event log. Unless you need to monitor the system for specific events, try to reduce the number of Information messages as much as possible. Most applications provide some method for reducing or eliminating the event log entries.

Warning   Warning entries tell you that a noncritical error event occurred on the system. It pays to spend time fixing as many of these errors as possible. You eliminate them from the event log by removing the cause of the problem. However, in some cases, the problem is outside your control or unlikely to occur again. A momentary glitch on the network could cause the system to lose contact with the server during a critical operation. Later, an informational message will tell you that the system restored contact, so there's no need for additional concern.

Error   Error messages tell you that your system has some type of instability or that a critical error event occurred. Always fix the source of error entries as quickly as possible. It's quite possible to set a system up so it doesn't generate any error entries. Strive for a non-error status because error entries represent the worst of optimization problems.

TIP   You can remove the excess event log entries for a dial-up connection by right-clicking My Network Places and choosing the Properties option from the context menu. In the Network Connection window, right-click the dial-up connection and choose Properties. You'll see a Properties dialog box for that connection. Select the Advanced tab and Settings. In the Advanced Settings dialog box, select the Security Logging tab. Clear the Log Dropped Packets and Log Successful Connections options. Click OK twice to close the Advanced Settings and Connection Properties dialog box.

One of the main problems with the event log is that many people tend to ignore it. Get into the habit of reviewing the event log regularly—make it part of your daily regimen if necessary. For example, you could review the log each morning after booting the system. If no errors or warnings occur, review the informational messages and remove the log entries (see the "Removing Old Event Log Entries" section of the chapter for details). By reviewing the log entries daily and removing them immediately, you optimize the system in two ways. First, the system will suffer fewer reliability problems, which makes you more productive. Second, the event logs will consume less space on the hard drive—freeing the space for your needs.

Reviewing the event logs daily is important for another reason. Some event log entries don't make sense unless you review them immediately—you must review them in the current environmental context. Figure 8.15 shows an error entry that demonstrates this problem. The error you see occurs when a CD has a media flaw. Unless you review the event log immediately, you could remove the CD and not know which one has experienced the media flaw. At some point, the CD could fail to work and you would have to recover the data it contains from another source.

A final way to view the event log from an optimization and cleaning perspective is as a check for the changes you make. Sometimes a change can have unexpected results, and the event log is one source of information for these results. For example, stopping the Windows Time service can allow the client machine time to get out of sync with its server. Consequently, some time-related events might not occur at the right time or at all and cause network problems. Windows will record all of these network error events for you in the event log. Even though having the right time might not be a very big deal, the related network problems can be. Therefore, you need to consider whether the network errors are significant enough that you need to turn the Windows Time service back on to keep everyone on the same timeline. Obviously, turning the Windows Time service back on will consume both memory and processing cycles, so you have to trade local optimization for the health of the network as whole.

FIGURE 8.15
Some event log entries require that you view them immediately and handle the problem in context.

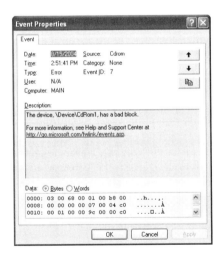

Setting the Event Log Options

Microsoft believes in huge event logs. Even when an event log has one entry, it consumes all of the hard drive space that you set aside for it. When you review the event logs daily, there isn't any reason to maintain such a huge log size, so you can optimize the event log to use space efficiently. In addition, you can set the event logs to display just the information you want to see.

To change the event log options, right-click the event log entry and choose Properties from the context menu. You'll see an event log Properties dialog box like the one shown in Figure 8.16. Note that all event logs have the same settings—only the names are different.

This Properties dialog box contains the settings that I normally use for my systems. The event log size is only 64KB, rather than the 512KB that Microsoft sets as a default. In addition, the event log only holds entries for a maximum of 7 days. If you haven't reviewed an entry within 7 days, chances are that you won't be able to do anything about it. You should also notice a few of the other fields in this list. First, the Log Name field tells you the location of the event log so that you can remove old logs from the system (never remove the System, Application, or Security logs). Second, you can click Clear Log to remove all of the entries from the event log.

The Filter tab is also important for optimization. Select this tab and you'll notice that you can remove the information messages from view by clearing the Information option. The filter doesn't remove the entries from the log; it simply removes them from view. However, removing the information entries from view lets you concentrate on the essential warning and error log entries. You can also temporarily filter the log by other entries including the user and computer names. Never retain these entries because they can hide important entries from view.

FIGURE 8.16

Modify the event log options to ensure you can work with the event log quickly.

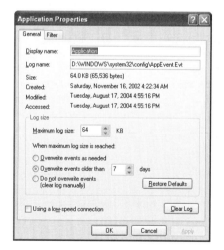

Removing Old Event Log Entries

Always remove old event log entries after you finish fixing the problems that created them. To remove the log entries for a particular event log, right-click the log entry in Event Viewer and choose Clear All Events from the context menu. Event Viewer will display a message box that asks whether you want to save the event log before you erase it. Unless you have a good reason for saving the event log, click No.

WARNING You can't remove just one or two of the event log entries. Clearing the event log removes all entries. In addition, once you clear the event log, you can't retrieve the entries (there isn't any undo feature).

Let's Start Cleaning

This chapter has covered a lot of ground. All of the topics tell you something about maintaining your system in its clean and optimized state. You probably won't use every technique in this chapter, but it's a good idea to peruse and at least try the techniques. Some of the techniques are mandatory, such a creating a backup of your system, but others are suggestions, such as learning about the utilities that Microsoft provides.

Unlike many areas of the book, you won't perform the tasks in this chapter just once or even once a year. Some tasks require constant use or your system will fall back into a state of disrepair. Because many people put things off that don't appear on their task list or other schedule, take time now to schedule the tasks that you consider important. For example, make sure you schedule time to perform a backup of your system regularly. Even if you only back your system up once a week, you'll lose less data during your next system meltdown.

Chapter 9 discusses a topic that many network administrators fear—controlling the user. It's a tough job, but someone has to do it and that someone could be you. However, this chapter isn't just for network administrators. Even single users can benefit from this chapter because sometimes it's not possible to know how you're using resources until you monitor your own activities. Sure, it takes discipline, but you wouldn't be reading this book unless you recognized that there's a problem with your current system setup. Chapter 9 provides tools you can use to help discover just where user-related problems lie, even those you create on your own system.

Chapter 9

Controlling the User

Some people think that time is the main enemy in keeping a system clean—the more time spent computing, the dirtier the system gets. While this is true to a point, the real problem is multiple users. Any time you let more than one person use a machine, the problem of keeping it clean is exponentially more difficult. That's because all of these people look at the machine as personal property that they can use to their benefit. Some users will go so far as to hoard resources so they don't run out as the result of that person on second shift grabbing all of the hard drive space. You can run into a number of other multi-user scenarios—each with their own special problems. The problem for you is to keep the system clean once you spend the time required to optimize it.

Any plans you have for keeping a system clean after you work so hard to optimize it must involve the user. Without the user's help, the system will quickly revert to its pre-optimized state or might even become worse than before (some users hate anything that looks remotely clean). You might even find that users can thwart your efforts to clean up their mess—"Hey, don't touch my garbage. I have it organized." On the other hand, you might be quite surprised to learn that some users are quite proactive in helping you keep their system clean once they understand the benefits. Sometimes the user is you and all you really want is a good guide to live by. The point is you need the user on your side whether that means using good psychology or dragging them kicking and screaming.

Fortunately, you have three tools you can use to control users in either the single or multiple user environments. These tools don't magically keep the system clean, but they do make you aware of usage problems and can act as a means of pointing out problems to the user. Removing excess user settings helps you create an environment where the user can work without the encumbering effects of too many features. As the number of settings increases again, you can point the problem out to the user and hopefully work through a reasonable level of configuration. Auditing the user helps you monitor activities that could lead to system optimization problems. Of course, you can even monitor your own activities to help rid yourself of any bad habits. Using quotas provides a maximum level of resource usage for the hard drive—the main problem when working with multiple users. However, even single users can run into problems with hard drive space and setting quotas can help them overcome this problem by alerting them to a low disk condition before it becomes a problem.

Multiple Users Means More Garbage

You or your organization could face a number of multi-user scenarios, each of which can result in less than optimal machine configuration. In all cases, one of the major sources of problems is the garbage that every user collects on the system. An average user might collect 100MB of garbage in a week. Now, multiply that number by the number of users on the machine. When a system has two users, expect 200MB of garbage each week, even though each user has less time to use the system than a single user would. Of course, at some point, as you add more users the amount of garbage per user goes down, but the overall amount of garbage continues to increase.

The amount of garbage the system collects and the level of user help you can expect depend on the multi-user situation. In some cases, you might be better off monitoring the situation yourself and performing any required cleaning at the end of the day before you shut the system down. For example, a public computer, such as one found in a library, is unlikely to receive any help from the user, even though it's in the user's best interest to clean up after the session to avoid problems such as identity theft (a fact you might want to point out with a sign near the computer). Consequently, you'll want to check the public system at the end of each day to clean the garbage left on it by the users. This act also helps you look for problems, such as viruses, adware, and spyware the user might have downloaded during the day.

In many other cases, you can and should expect help from the user. For example, in a networked environment, where everyone is working for the same company, you should be able to expect some level of support from the user. Generally, you won't be able to get full user support in a networked environment because many users won't have the skill required to perform the maintenance. However, a combination of automated maintenance using Task Scheduler or other scheduling software and user training will help reduce the work you have to do. Even though you still need to check machines regularly for viruses, adware, and spyware, the networked environment should include safeguards that reduce the number of these checks.

Even home systems are multi-user systems. In some respects, because this is your home system, you should be able to increase security and reduce the amount of garbage the user generates. You need to decide issues such as whether it's more important to visit every Web site on the Internet or set security tightly so that you can't access some Web sites at all, but your system is less likely to download a virus as well. However, home systems face certain problems that the corporate environment doesn't face. For example, running games on a corporate system isn't a concern, but it is with your home system. As more games move to using online resources, the need to balance security with the needs of the game becomes more difficult.

Home office and small office systems are the systems that should have the best control over garbage but seldom do. The problem is one of knowledge and tenacity. It's important to categorize the kinds of work you need to perform in order to maintain your business and then set security, auditing, quotas, and automation to meet that specific requirement. Once you have these issues worked out, it's a matter of learning to say no—no, we decided that the activity isn't allowed and there isn't any reason to change that decision.

Actively Soliciting the User's Help

Getting the user's help in maintaining the system can be easy or hard depending on the user's personality (work habits) and the way in which you approach the topic. In many cases, the wrong approach can make the user completely unresponsive, even if that user would normally be willing to help keep the system clean. Most of us aren't qualified as psychologists, so the precise reason that someone works in a particular way might seem elusive and difficult to understand. The issue is that the person works in that way, and you need to think about tactful ways of working with that user to obtain the overall goal of maintaining system cleanliness—sometimes despite the user's normal work habits. The object isn't to change the user's way of doing things to the method you use—that approach seldom works. Instead, work with the user to modify their way of performing that task so it achieves the correct goals.

In a single user scenario, you can often instill a level of pride in keeping a system clean by allowing that user ownership of the state of the machine. The machine is their personal work environment and it must stay clean to ensure the person can work with the least difficulty. You don't have to maintain a sterile or hospital clean environment—most of us have some amount of dirt in our homes and the Windows environment is unlikely to be different. The idea is to help the users help themselves by demonstrating the need to clean up after themselves.

MULTI-USER WORKSTATION SETUP TIPS

Many offices rely on multi-user workstation setups. One user has possession of the computer during the day and another by night. Several users might share the same computer because one user won't use it for an entire day. A manager might need access to an employee computer because the one in their office is too far away. The reasons could go on forever, but multi-user workstations are common. The following tips help you set up a multi-user workstation in the most convenient way.

Create a Default User Setup   The `\Documents and Settings\Default User` folder contains a complete set of empty folders. Every user you create for a local machine will use this set of folders as a starting point. The user will only receive input from this folder during the creation phase. Don't confuse this set of folders with the `All Users` folder.

Use the *All Users* Folder   The `All Users` folder (`\Documents and Settings\All Users`) should hold all common elements. For example, if everyone needs access to the word processor, you'll want to place the icons for it in this folder, rather than duplicate those icons for every user. However, if you had a situation where most, but not all, users required access to an application, you'd place it in the default user setup. This would allow you to remove the icons from those users who didn't need them.

Implement Start Menu Security   You might have a machine where all employees need access to some icons, but guest users shouldn't have access. Assigning security to those icons allows you to place them in the `All Users` folder, but still restrict access. Icons normally inherit rights from their parent, so you need to click Advanced on the Security tab of the Object Properties dialog box. Clear the Inherit option, then click OK before you begin setting a new security policy. Note that everyone can still see the icon, but only those with the required permissions can use it.

Create Common Desktop Elements as Needed   Everyone might work on the same project together, so placing the folder for that project in the `\Documents and Settings\All Users\Desktop` folder makes sense. This way you can ensure that everyone will use the same folder and that the system changes all of the data at the same time.

Set Security Intelligently   Always assume the user will disregard or blatantly break security rules. For example, it's safe to assume the user will fail to log out when leaving the area. You can set the screen saver to log out the user automatically and return to the login screen. This forces the user to log back into the system and protects it from prying eyes.

Multi-user scenarios and networked environments can prove very frustrating in some cases. The problem, in many cases, is how management feels about the services a network administrator provides and whether the users are in any way cooperative. It's possible that you'll try to provide a great level of support and present the user with a clean machine, only to have them laugh in your face when you try to invoke any sort of optimization procedure. Most companies are very conscious of costs today, so making a plea to management based on the cost of having you clean the users systems each month or so (when they fail due to accumulated grime) can work very well. You'll also gain points by mentioning the costs of user downtime and loss of productivity while they wait for you to repair their system. It's also possible to provide incentives to users who keep their machines in great shape—try to get management to allow you to take them out to lunch or provide other rewards based on great machine care. The worst-case scenario is that you won't get any help, but will have great job security because users will continue to have machines that don't work well simply because they're dirty. I hope that you find this is the exception rather than the rule.

Sometimes soliciting the user's help means providing aids to the user. The user might want to help, but doesn't remember to perform the required task or simply doesn't grasp the training the first time around. The following tips can prove helpful when you don't use them to excess.

Add a Daily Tip to the User's Machine   Many applications include a tip of the day now because this particular means of repetitious training has proven useful. It's a short, one or two paragraphs, bit of information that the user can read and absorb quickly. Make sure the tip of the day tells the reader what the tip affects, why the tip is important, and how to perform the task in the shortest space possible. Tips that don't include these three pieces of information are still helpful, but less effective.

Provide a Checklist   The simple act of providing the user with a checklist can often elicit better behavior because the user must think about the steps to take before submitting work or moving on to the next task. Don't make the checklist another cumbersome item for the user—make it informational instead. Have you ever seen the checklists on the envelopes for bills? They're short and helpful. You should follow this short and simple example.

Automate the Help   Many applications provide automation that you can use to your benefit. Create a script that runs whenever the user shuts down the application or closes a document. You can augment the reminders the script provides with physical checks to ensure the user gets the job done. When you notice a user is experiencing difficulty with the script (through some form of monitoring), schedule training time to ensure the user understands how to perform the task properly.

Use Wizards to Simplify Tasks   Whenever possible, provide scripts or full-fledged wizards to guide users through a task. Keep wizard questions short and to the point. Don't give the user any more choices than necessary to perform the task. The goal is to create an environment where even unskilled users can perform complex tasks by simplifying the task to the point that anyone can understand. Purposely set policies for using various cleanup utilities and then use those policies to construct the wizard. In short, even though a series of utilities for cleaning a system offer many complex options, decide for the user that some of those options are unavailable—provide access to the options that meet company policy.

Schedule Specific Cleanup Time   Set aside a few minutes each week to perform cleanup tasks. Make sure the time is specific and unchanging. Ensure you create this time as part of a company policy and get management to back it up. This particular tip is easier to implement in smaller companies where the amount of red tape is less, but it can work in larger companies too. Select a time that management is likely to agree with, such as the final 15 minutes before end of work on Friday, when employees are less productive.

Removing Excess Personal Settings and Data

Every system you own has personal settings and data on it. You can count on this additional data because everyone generates it. Personal settings and data range from small notes created in Notepad to full-fledged applications the user has brought from home. Personal settings and data can reflect a user's business practices, hobbies, personal life, or anything else you can think of. Because they're personal, the user has a stake in them and you'll find it very difficult to get the user to part with them. Even when you're the user with the personal settings and data, it can be very difficult to locate the excesses and remove them to optimize the system.

It's important to understand that personal settings and data are part of the normal optimized computer environment. Without personal settings and data, most users become inefficient and less effective. Consequently, you need to determine when personal settings and data are excessive and locate the source of that excess, rather than attempt to remove it all. The following sections consider these and other questions.

Defining Excess Personal Settings and Data

Personal settings become excessive when they reduce the efficiency of the user to the point that the user is getting less work done than with the default or standard (dictated by company policy) application settings. Likewise, personal data becomes excessive when it reduces system efficiency to the point where the user spends more time managing the data than accomplishing useful work. When either of these events occur, it's time to look at the user's system, settings, and data to locate and remove the excesses so that the user becomes productive again. The goal is to define the excesses so that you can remove them without removing the useful settings and data that add to user productivity.

NOTE Although these definitions might seem suited to a business, they work fine in other scenarios too. For example, you might be a gamer who has downloaded one too many extra scenarios for your gaming setup. Managing the extra scenario (along with the others you have) becomes so time consuming that you find you no longer play the game—you instead spend all of your time working with scenarios. Where's the fun in playing in that kind of environment? The scenarios have become excessive and you need to reduce them to a manageable level—putting the fun back into playing the game.

Of course, the first task is to realize that your environment has become less than optimal. The problem is measuring productivity in such a way that you can account for daily variances, yet see overall trends. When you detect a loss of productivity, then it's time to change the environment in which you work to regain what you lost. It's also a cycle—productivity changes over time to reflect these cycles of cleaning and getting dirty. Productivity also changes to reflect you personally—experience usually increases productivity while boredom decreases it.

TIP Set aside personal productivity measures as a way to monitor your own system excesses. As an example from my personal productivity measures, when I work on a book, I look at my daily output in pages. When I'm working with a consulting client, I look at the number of problems solved or the lines of code written. Because email is a major part of what I do, I set 3 hours aside for it each day—when that number goes up, I start looking for ways to reduce it. I also measure the number of hours I want to work in my office each week. Reductions in this number sometimes reflect a loss of efficiency in my working environment—the environment is less inviting, so I want to work less. Everyone can create a personal measure of productivity and use it to measure the level of optimization in the computer environment. Just remember that statistics are a tool and daily variances are normal.

Once you discover a personal productivity index and determine that you have lost some level of productivity, it's time to discover the source of that loss. For example, even the best email organization techniques (see the "Organizing and Categorizing Your Email" section of Chapter 5 for details) can't keep data overload at bay forever. At some point, you need to archive old email to ensure you can manage the remaining data efficiently and get work accomplished. When your email time exceeds a certain level each day (and that level depends on what you're trying to accomplish), you need to look at ways of reducing it. Of course, this means not getting lost in the computer environment and looking at the starting and ending times for your email management each day. Again, this number isn't absolute. If you receive more newsletters on Monday, set aside more time for email on Monday. Likewise, a Thursday free of email should mean less time spent working with email on that day.

Notice that this discussion is looking at specific activities and the productivity for that activity. By placing an emphasis on activities, you can reduce the number of areas you have to consider for personal settings and data. For example, if you notice that you're just as productive now as usual in email, but less productive in word processing, it could mean that you packed your word processing application with add-ons or that it has inefficient settings. Perhaps your system as a whole is just fine—only this one area needs work.

WARNING   One of the biggest traps you can fall into when working through the advice in this section is letting personal management become a time sink. It's not important to keep precise written records. Don't become obsessed with the strategies in this section either—they're general guidelines you can use to observe problems before they become so severe that someone else points them out.

Creating a Personal Data Archive

Chapter 5 discusses data archiving techniques, but it tends to focus on archives for a company, small office, or other environment as a whole. Even a one-person shop has a need for archives that reflect the final state of a task—be it a game competition, a book, or a business deal. However, you should keep personal data—the notes and other interim information—separate from your final archive unless you need to include the data as part of the project. This separate personal data archive is something you should maintain on your own. Some people maintain this personal data on their machine until it becomes an optimization problem. The best policy is to archive the personal data on CD or other easy-to-use media until you know you no longer need it and then dispose of it. Remove the personal data from your system when you no longer need it.

The question of personal versus project data begs two questions. First, you need to consider whether the data is actually personal or whether it's part of the project and should be included with the task archive. Second, you must consider whether to archive the data at all—in some cases, you don't need personal data after the fact and it could create a confusing mess when you need to work on the project again later.

You can answer the first question by determining whether the data contributes to the project in a material way. For example, the personal data might include computations you used to create a result for the task. The computations aren't needed as part of the task, but because they contribute to the task, you should store them with the task data. By storing the computations, you can answer the question of how you derived the task data later. On the other hand, a note telling you to call Fred (including his number) might not be useful as task data. You can create a personal archive that includes the note when you think you'll need it later.

Now you can answer the second question. When data appears as part of the general company information, you generally don't need to store it in your personal data archive as well. For example, looking again at the call Fred note, you'd save the note when Fred doesn't appear in your list of names and addresses (and you don't intend to include it there because your chances of calling Fred again are small). However, when Fred does appear in a local resource, get rid of the note to avoid calling Fred later with an old number (and wasting time finding the new one).

Use the techniques in Chapter 5 to create your personal archive. However, instead of looking for long-term storage techniques that might not work very well for the data you want to store, look instead at convenience. Many systems today come with a CD burner that you can use to create the archive. When your system doesn't have a CD burner, consider using floppy disks or other convenient means for creating the archive. The point is to get the data off your hard drive and into an archive for future use.

Removing Personal Applications

Home users have an advantage over everyone else—all of their applications are personal. All you ever need consider is whether the applications are useful or not—keep those that are and remove those that aren't. However, other business users have to consider the problem of personal applications and discover how they happened to get on the company machine. Without a doubt, personal applications cause all kinds of problems in the business environment and the larger the business, the bigger those problems are. In fact, network administrators often complain that personal applications create the following problems.

◆ Reduced user productivity from using the nonstandard application (the application often becomes a toy, rather than a tool)

◆ Increased support costs when the nonstandard application creates compatibility problems

◆ Increased training costs when a user asks questions about the nonstandard application

◆ Increased chance of virus, adware, and spyware infection from using the nonstandard application

◆ Impaired system reliability due to the problems caused by unpatched personal applications

◆ Increased chance of application or other audits when vendors and other organizations learn about the existence of the nonstandard application in the business environment

◆ Reduced other user productivity when they discover the nonstandard application (George has WonderTool, why can't I?)

You might think from this list that every personal application is to blame for all the woes that users experience with computers. The fact is that not every personal application is ill conceived, unpatched, and generally bad for the business environment, but every personal application used without permission is a potential source of problems. A good way to handle this problem is to provide a standardized method for incorporating personal applications into the business environment (see the "Developing Standards from Personal Settings and Data" section of the chapter for details). You should have an equally strong policy against adding personal applications to a system without permission.

WARNING   Users who bring applications from home present a very real threat to your organization. Most software licensing agreements specify usage requirements that don't allow a user to use the application at home and at work. When organizations such as the Business Software Alliance (BSA) (`http://www.bsa.org/`) learn of these indiscretions, they can hold your organization responsible. Consequently, you'll want to create a company policy that prohibits users from bringing applications from home unless they can use the application within the licensing requirements and you have some way to verify this use.

When you do discover an unauthorized personal application on a system, it's important to remove it as quickly as possible to keep problems at bay. However, you shouldn't simply remove the application without discussing the problem with the user. Otherwise, the user is likely to install the application behind your back and an ongoing war of wills will ensue. Sometimes the war happens anyway, but you have better things to do with your time, so avoiding these turf wars is always the best policy. With this goal in mind, use the following steps to remove the unwanted application.

1. When your company has a policy in place for using personal applications, work with the user to obtain the required authorization. This step avoids the war of wills by letting the user keep the personal application under supervision. You might also gain use of a new application for company use.

2. Explain company policy with the user and discuss why you remove unauthorized applications from systems. When your company has sanctions described in the personal application use policy, consider invoking one or more of them on the second and successive use of an unauthorized personal application.

3. Provide the user with a chance to remove any data created by the application and save any settings. Assist the user in archiving the data and settings if necessary—this step produces a level of goodwill between user and you.

4. Remove the application from the system using the Add/Remove Programs applet in the Control Panel. Use the techniques in Chapter 4 to remove any application crumbs. This step reduces the chance the application will continue to cause problems.

5. Record the offense in the user's record. Otherwise, anyone working with you won't know about the unauthorized personal application and won't be looking for the problems it can cause during subsequent machine errors. In addition, this step ensures the user can't claim ignorance of company policy later—keeping unauthorized applications off systems is essential.

Developing Standards from Personal Settings and Data

No matter how nicely you ask, how long you stomp your feet, and how many times you remove unauthorized applications from systems, users will continue to bring applications from home. Yelling is ineffective, in many cases, as are sanctions. Having any users in an organization at all means dealing with multiple personalities, some of whom will insist on using their personal applications. Consequently, you can fight a losing war against a tide of users who use unauthorized applications, in part, because you don't allow them, or you can find a productive way to work through the situation.

Even if you manage to keep the unauthorized applications under control, users are going to find ways to configure their applications in ways that are definitely outside of company policy. Configuration changes are a little easier to manage because the application is still company purchased and managed, but they still present problems. Again, you can choose to fight the problem or you can find a positive way to handle the problem.

In both cases, the problem comes down to one of wills. You have tested specific applications with certain settings and concluded that they work best to meet an average user's need. The user disagrees by using applications and settings that you either haven't tested or decided don't meet average needs. The solution is to acknowledge that each user is unique and that this user could work better with alternative applications or settings. In fact, companies often find new solutions to problems by going out on a limb and letting a user try something new.

As with everything else in this book, you can optimize the results of this action and can even keep the system optimized with a little work. The following steps can help you create an effective testing strategy for the new settings or applications.

1. Ask the user to define why they like the new settings or application. Answers such as "It's what I'm used to" probably won't provide enough of a reason to perform any testing. The user can learn the company application in this case.

2. Consider licensing issues for the new settings or application. You don't want to create an environment where a third party could hold the company responsible to dubious user choices.

3. Consider system use issues. For example, you need to decide whether the application will use too many system resources.

4. Determine whether the new settings or application will do what the user says they will. To complete this task, you must define a test environment with goals that define what the settings or application are supposed to accomplish. For example, you can measure the user's productivity using the new settings or application as compared to productivity using the standard company settings or application.

5. Decide whether the cost benefit to the company is worth the expense of using the new settings or application. Make sure the user understands that the company will monitor settings and application use and can terminate that use at any time. In addition, ensure the user knows that the company won't provide support of any kind for the new settings or application.

These steps provide a generic framework. Make sure you take time to personalize them to meet the needs of your company. Write the result as a company policy and ensure users know this policy is in place. Such a policy can encourage users to try new things and give you an edge that the competition doesn't have. More importantly, this approach avoids the battle of minds that often occurs within companies. You're giving the user the opportunity to prove the settings or application works within a fair environment—that's more than many companies do today.

Something interesting can happen in this environment. Companies sometimes find that new settings or an application introduced by one user also work great for other users in the organization. In fact, the benefits can become so great that the company may switch to the new settings or application and realize a substantial cost savings. The best part is that the user has performed much of the preliminary testing and setup for you. The user has taken a risk that most network administrators can't take today.

Auditing User Actions

Auditing is one of two tools that Windows provides for checking the results of changes you make to the system when implemented by the user. (Quotas are the second tool and you can learn about them in the "Setting Quotas" section of the chapter.) You can also use auditing to locate new places for optimizing a system or discover user habits so you can provide customized user assistance in the form of special settings or training. Of course, you can use audits for a number of other purposes, most of which you won't find this chapter. For example, you could use auditing to discover whether an employee is using the Internet incorrectly, conspiring with a competitor, or creating a security breach. All of these uses are legitimate, but they don't really optimize your system.

Of course, auditing, by its very nature, is invasive and most users will resent your use of it. Consequently, this section discusses ways to make auditing a little more palatable. You don't have a choice about using auditing, in some cases, because there isn't any other good way to discover the information you need. For example, it's impossible to discover a user's habits without auditing. However, you don't have to make auditing permanent—in fact, less permanent is better. Finally, this section shows how to create an audit and process the results.

TIP   Don't assume that auditing is always going to involve someone else. In some cases, you can use auditing as a means of discovering your own habits and refining how you work. Auditing reveals hidden traits, in many cases—things you do without really thinking about them. By auditing your own work, you gain a better perspective of how you use your machine and reveal new ways to optimize it to the way you work.

Avoiding a Big Brother Reputation

People don't want you to spy on them. In fact, throughout history, some of the worst reactions people have had to any kind of intervention have spying at their core. Consequently, you need to consider whether to use auditing at all. Auditing is your option of last resort for optimizing a system—it's the option to use when all other types of optimization procedures fail. For example, you can try to use surveys or other forms of user questioning to obtain information in many cases. Auditing only becomes an option when it's apparent that users don't understand a process very well—at least from an optimization perspective.

Two schools of thought exist on this topic. Some people use auditing covertly—stating that covert auditing produces the best results because the user acts naturally and is more likely to perform tasks using the same process as normal. It's true that covert auditing does produce natural results and you might want to use it briefly to determine whether settings changes have optimized the system in the way you anticipated. The backlash from this form of auditing can be severe, however, so you don't want to use it for every task. Users have the right to know that you're auditing them for optimization purposes.

Other people view covert auditing as unethical and insist that the user must know about any form of auditing. Letting the users know is a very good policy because there isn't any chance of backlash—users can't say later that they didn't know you were auditing their actions. This is the best form of auditing to use when you intend to monitor usage habits or perform long-term auditing. Unfortunately, because the user is aware that you are monitoring them, you can't count on seeing completely natural behavior, at least for the first week or two. Most users tend to forget about the monitoring after a while and their behavior returns mostly to normal, so you get good results without the intrigue.

Once you decide to audit a user and determine whether you want to inform the user about the activity, you need to decide how long to monitor the user and what to audit. The "Deciding between Permanent and Temporary Audits" section of the chapter answers the first question, while the "Creating a Security Audit" and "Creating a Drive, Folder, Application, or File Audit" sections answer the second. The point is that you need to decide how to proceed and create an auditing plan. When the user knows about the auditing, you should also let them know about the auditing plan when revealing this information won't upset the purpose of the auditing. Keeping the users informed reduces any cry of foul later because you informed the users from the outset.

As a final hedge against users seeing you as Big Brother, make sure you maintain records of all of your auditing activity. Ensure you maintain accurate records and have them verified by a third party. The goal is to collect data for use in optimizing a system, not create an environment complete with conspiracy theories. Make these records available to users as needed. Of course, make sure you also follow privacy policies for your company—no one should typically see anything but their own auditing record.

Deciding between Permanent and Temporary Audits

At some point, you need to decide how long to audit the system. The problem is that most people have no idea of how long an interval to use because there are few absolutes when collecting this kind of data. Here are a few items to consider when choosing an audit interval.

User Comfort and Privacy   User discomfort is directly proportional to the length of the audit you choose. It's true that users will eventually get used to having the auditing software in place so you can collect accurate data, but the fact remains that auditing is a comfort problem and leads to decreased user productivity. It's important to remember that part of the optimization process is making the environment user friendly to increase productivity, so auditing runs counter to optimizing the system. In addition, with all of the privacy issues discussed in the trade press today, you could also factor privacy problems when collecting the data for extended times.

Data Accuracy   Unfortunately, short auditing times tend to cause a number of data accuracy problems. You get better data when you collect it for an extended time and filter out extremes of user behavior. It's also a good idea to let the user get over the initial shock of auditing before you collect real data to use in optimization. If you don't get good data, the auditing effort is wasted and you'll need to perform the task again.

System Optimization   The act of auditing a system uses system resources such as hard drive space to store the data and processing cycles to examine user activities. Although the resource use isn't very high, it still saps the system of resources it needs to perform tasks for the user. Although auditing is an important means of collecting user data for problems that aren't well defined, it still means that the system is running in a less than optimal state and you need to remove the performance impediment as soon as possible.

NOTE   Always is a very long time, so you need to decide on a definition for the term *permanent*. Many companies define this interval as more than three months. However, nothing stops you from defining an alternative interval or even using different terms than those found in this section. You might want to use terms such as short-term, long-term, and permanent to define three intervals. The idea is that you need to determine how long monitoring will occur at the outset and provide a means for stopping monitoring when the time comes.

Deciding between a temporary and a permanent audit is a matter of the goals you have in mind. Generally, the more complex the data you want to collect, the longer you need to collect the information. A user who is aware of the audit will also require additional time so you have enough data to filter for extremes in user behavior—you need to be able to see trends in usage. Finally, you need to reduce the length of the audit when the user's system is less robust. A user who has a system that is already critically short on memory and processing cycles won't appreciate you adding to the problem with the auditing software.

Systems also get old enough that an audit is no longer useful. When a system is memory constrained, has an older overworked drive system, or a processor that's already woefully inadequate for the tasks that the user must perform, consider replacing the system instead of auditing. Even the best optimization techniques won't resurrect a system that is past its prime.

Creating a Security Audit

Windows provides several places for auditing the user. A unique place to gather this information is in the Local Security Policy console found in the Administrative Tools folder of the Control Panel. As shown in Figure 9.1, this console actually contains an Audit Policy folder you can use to set security-related auditing policies. Not all of these policies will help with optimization tasks, but some, such as Audit Directory Service Access and Audit Object Access, can definitely help.

To use this auditing feature, double-click an entry you want to audit and you'll see the Properties dialog box shown in Figure 9.2. Notice that you can audit successful and failed accesses. The failed access option is especially helpful because it can help you understand how often the user requests an object and doesn't have that request fulfilled. This setting can point out the need to provide additional access or simply that the object isn't available for other reasons, such as lack of memory.

It turns out that not all of the security audits appear in the Audit Policy folder. Look in the Security Options folder and you'll find other audit entries as shown in Figure 9.3. The only option that's interesting, in this case, is Audit: Audit the Access of Global System Objects. Unlike other audits, you can only enable or disable this feature. It helps you understand the security picture better and gain security statistics that can help you optimize the user environment. In some cases, you'll find that you can restrict security further. In other cases, though, you'll find that security is set too tightly to allow the user to perform all required tasks.

FIGURE 9.1
Use the Audit Policy folder of the Local Security Policy console to set security auditing options.

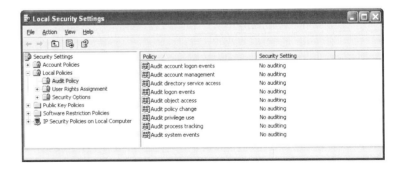

FIGURE 9.2
Track object access to determine how the user works with objects on the system.

FIGURE 9.3
Look for audits in locations other than the obvious—Microsoft hides them everywhere.

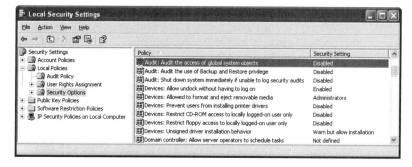

Security audits might seem a little like cloak and dagger for optimizing the system, but security deficiencies are a real problem. Without the proper security setup, the user doesn't have the required access to the system and applications end up working less reliably than they could. In addition, because Windows tries every security access multiple times, the system can slow to a crawl simply since Windows is performing the same task multiple times before giving up. The user could also end up viewing the security problem as a reliability problem—the application doesn't appear to work correctly. The issue might not be the application—it could be that security is hampering the application from working.

TIP Because Windows XP SP2 places such a strong emphasis on security, you might find that a security audit is precisely what you need to work out application problems after you install this update. You are almost certain to run into security issues after you install Windows XP SP2 and some subtle problems will require auditing to resolve.

Creating a Drive, Folder, Application, or File Audit

Windows provides a means for auditing all drive, folder, application, and file activities on your system. For example, if you want to know every time a user successfully deletes a file, you can create an audit entry for it. These audits track user activity, rather than the performance of tasks as a security audit will. The difference is subtle, but important. A user can delete a file (an activity) without accomplishing any work (a task). The security audit tells you that the user has requested access to something as a precursor to performing work, but these audits tell you that the user looked at a drive for something. Consequently, the audits described in this section actually work better for performing many optimization tasks. Here are ways to use the various audit levels.

Drive   Use this option to track activity on network drives. You might find the user needs additional local drive support to reduce network bandwidth usage or that the user requires additional space on a network drive for personal storage. Drive auditing also helps you determine how often to clean the network drive and whether the user has accessed specific files on the network drive for a given time. You can use the statistics you gather as a way of determining which files to archive.

Folder   Use this option to track individual file access for group projects. You can also use this technique to detect applications that require a lot of background access to the folder. For example, you might find that a browser is accessing a folder more often than you thought and use this information to change settings to improve reliability.

Application   Use this option to detect how often a user actually uses an application. In some cases, you can build a case for removing an application from a system because the user never actually uses it. However, in other cases, you might find that the user actually needs a more robust application because the user relies heavily on the existing application. For example, you might find that the user relies heavily on a graphics application, but wastes a lot of time and resources because the vendor didn't design the current application to create the kinds of images the user needs.

File   Use this option to determine the best placement for a file. Sometimes a user works with a file so often that it's better to move it from the network to a local drive to improve network performance. You can also use this kind of auditing to determine when to archive older files.

Before you can set auditing for a file system object, you must set up the system to perform the required audit. Open the Local Security Policy console located in the Administrative Tools folder of the Control Panel. Select the `Audit Policy` folder and double-click the Audit Object Access entry. Select Success, Failure, or both. Click OK. The system will now record the audits you set up. If you don't perform this step, Windows XP will display an ambiguous message box when you set up auditing telling you that the system isn't set up correctly.

You can enable auditing in a number of ways, but the easiest method is to right-click a drive, folder, application, or file in Windows Explorer, and choose Properties from the context menu. Select the Security tab in the Drive Properties dialog box, and then click Advanced. You'll see an Advanced Security Settings dialog box. Select Auditing and you'll see a dialog box similar to the one shown in Figure 9.4.

To add a new entry, click Add. You'll see a Select User or Group dialog box. Click Advanced, then Find, to display a list of local user and group names. Select a user or group from the list, then click OK. You'll see an Auditing Entry dialog box like the one shown in Figure 9.5. Select the tasks you want to monitor. Choose Success, Failure, or both, and then click OK. Windows XP will add the new auditing entry to the drive, folder, application, or file. The audit will remain in place until you remove it.

As you can see from the Auditing Entry dialog box in Figure 9.5, you can monitor users for success, failure, or both success and failure in performing certain tasks. For example, when working with an application, you'll want to audit the Traverse Folder/Execute File task for success or failure. Windows XP helps you monitor everything from taking full control of the drive to deleting files to simply changing the file attributes.

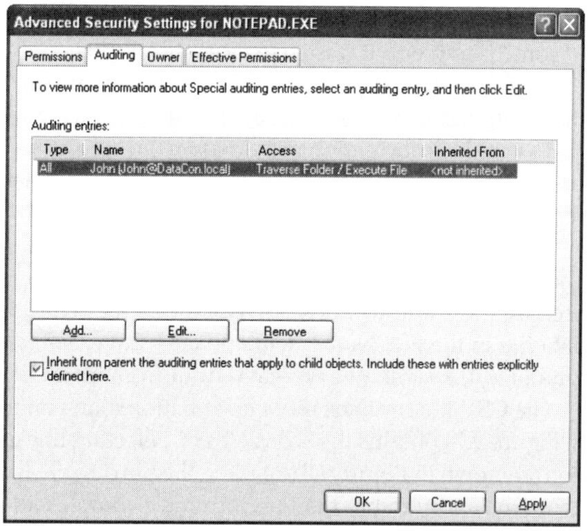

FIGURE 9.4

The Auditing tab allows you to observe user activity on your local hard drive.

You can modify any Auditing tab entry by clicking Edit. Windows XP will show you the Auditing Entry dialog box shown in Figure 9.5. Simply check or clear options as needed to meet the new auditing need.

Likewise, you can remove auditing entries you don't need any longer by highlighting an entry and clicking Remove on the Auditing tab. Windows XP simply removes the entry—it doesn't provide any warning, so exercise care when using this option. If you remove an entry accidentally, you can click Add to create it again.

FIGURE 9.5

Select the tasks you want to audit and decide whether you want to audit success or failure.

Processing the Audit Results Manually

At some point, you'll want to process the audits you've performed. You won't find a statistic for security or file system object audits. These entries appear in the Security folder of the Event Viewer as shown in Figure 9.6. Of course, they aren't much good to you in there.

To use the information provided by the security or file system objects audits in a meaningful way, you need to export the data to a database, spreadsheet, or other analysis program. Right-click the Security folder and choose Save Log File As from the context menu. Select the Text (Tab Delimited) or CSV (Comma Delimited) option from the Save as Type field of the Save "Security" As dialog box. The Command Separated Value (CSV) option works especially well for spreadsheets and databases because these applications often include special import features for this file type. Type a name for the data file in the File Name field and click Save. You can now import the data into your analysis program. Figure 9.7 shows typical output from an audit when displayed in Microsoft Excel.

The CSV file contains more information than you might think initially. Notice that the selected line in Figure 9.7 contains the word Object. Selecting this entry usually displays a wealth of object information as shown in Figure 9.8. Reading the file directly like this is good when you need quick information about the audit, rather than performing a complex analysis of the information.

Notice that besides the information you would expect, such as the application name, the data also includes the Process ID or PID. It's relatively easy to locate these values as part of the Process counter in System Monitor (see the "Using System Monitor" section of Chapter 7 for details). You can also use the PID with various command line utilities, such as the TaskList utility described in the "Using the TaskList Utility" section of Chapter 7. You can combine this information with statistics you obtain with various other sources to build a complete picture of system activity.

The output shown in Figure 9.7 still isn't very easy to read, but you can correct that problem by importing the file and creating custom filters to interpret it, rather than opening the file directly. For example, when using Excel, you can rely on the Data ➤ Import External Data ➤ Import Data command to import the data in an easier to read format. Figure 9.9 shows a standard import of the CSV data. You would use this technique when you want to create a permanent data store for analysis.

FIGURE 9.6
Windows saves security audits in the Security event log, rather than in a statistical file.

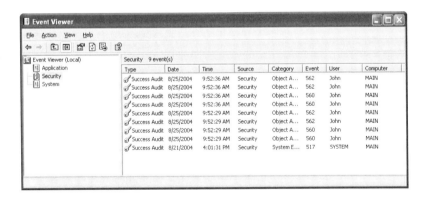

FIGURE 9.7

Import the results of an audit into an analysis application to discover optimization ideas.

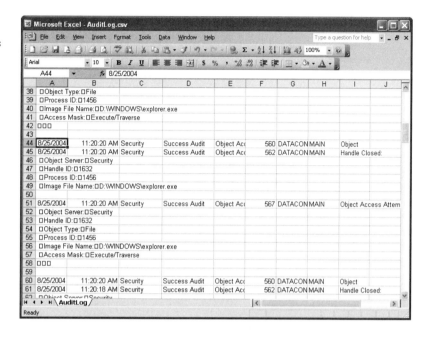

FIGURE 9.8

Use the object statistics in the audit to create a link to System Monitor output.

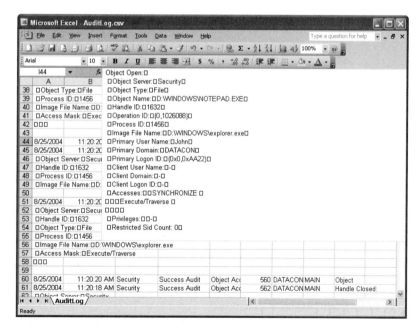

FIGURE 9.9
The imported CSV file
is formatted and easier
to use for long-term
analysis.

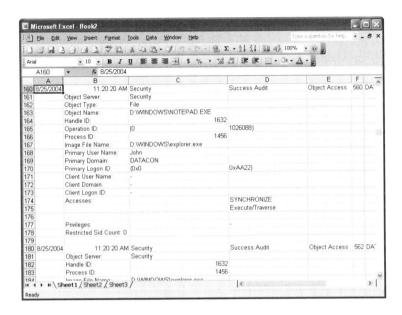

Using Automation to Process the Audit Results

Processing the audit logs manually is one option, but not the only option. A number of event log analysis tools are available, some of which specialize in the Security event log used for auditing. Most of these products cater to large companies and include complex features. One such product is LogCaster from RippleTech. You can download a 15-day trial version of this product at http://www.rippletech.com/downloads/logcaster/index.asp. This company requires that you fill out a registration form to obtain the trial version of the product. Another product to check out is Monitor-Magic at http://www.advtoolware.com/t4e/monitor/monitor_default.asp. This product features a more complete set of services, but doesn't provide a free download.

The solution described in this section is WELAMT Software's EventReader. You can learn about the company at http://www.windows-event-log.com/company.htm and download a 30-day trial version of the product at http://www.windows-event-log.com/eventrd/index.htm. This shareware product lets you test using a third party product to monitor the event logs, especially the audits. It isn't quite as functional as the other offerings described in this section, but most small businesses and many medium-sized businesses could use this option without any problem.

NOTE You must have an Open Database Connectivity (ODBC)–compliant database such as Microsoft Access or Microsoft SQL Server to use with EventReader. Theoretically, the product will work with other ODBC data sources, but the product command structure favors these two options.

Begin working with EventReader by opening the Event Reader utility using the Start ➢ Programs ➢ Event Reader ➢ EventReader command. The first problem is creating a data source to use. If you select the sample Microsoft Access database during installation, you're ready to go. In fact, this is the best option to select for experimenting with the product because it offers a wealth of forms and reports you can use to see how to manipulate the data. Otherwise, you need to use the ODBC Data Source ➢ Create New command to create an ODBC data source to use with the product. Once you create the new data source, use the ODBC Data Source ➢ Create Tables command to create the tables required to store the event log information in the database. After you create the data source, you'll notice that many of the previously disabled menu commands are available for use.

At this point, you can collect data for the database using a number of techniques. For example, you can set up the application to work with live logs and collect the data in real time. In fact, you can collect data from multiple machines. For the purposes of this section, I'll assume that you've collected the audit data you want to use and saved it as an EVT file (see the "Processing the Audit Results Manually" section for details on saving an event log to disk). Use the following steps to import this data into the database you selected.

1. Choose the Event Logs Gathering ➢ Read from Archive File command. You'll see the Settings for Reading Event Log from Archive File dialog box shown in Figure 9.10.

2. Click Select to choose the database you want to use from the Select ODBC Data Source dialog box.

3. Click Verify to ensure you can access the database. Event Reader will display a success message when the connection is valid.

4. Select the Archive tab. Type the name and path of the archive file you want to use in the Archive File to Read field. You can also click on the ellipsis (...) button that appears below the Archive File to Read field and select the archive file using the Open Event Log Archive dialog box.

5. Choose an event log option. Because we're working with a Security event log containing audit information, choose that option.

6. Click OK. It will appear that nothing has happened, but Event Reader will read the log file into the database.

This section assumes that you used the sample database to store the information. Use the Start ➢ Programs ➢ Event Reader ➢ Sample Database command to display the database on screen, as shown in Figure 9.11. Notice that this isn't the standard Microsoft Access interface—the vendor supplies this custom interface for working with the information in the database. When you create a custom database, the product doesn't create this special interface for you—it's up to you to create an interface for working with the data.

FIGURE 9.10

Choose a data source, test it, and then import the data using this dialog box.

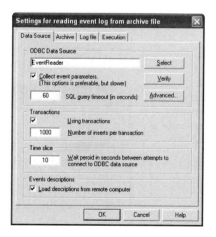

The two main display options are to view all of the events or to use a custom event view from one of the sections. Figure 9.10 shows the auditing selections. Generally, when you want to use the event logs for optimization purposes, you'll need to create a custom filter. Fortunately, the sample database provides a fast method for performing this task. Select the View All Events button for the Security log. You'll see a list of all of the security events. Click Objects and you'll see a list of objects within the Security log as shown in Figure 9.12.

To choose an object, highlight it and click Filter. You'll see a list of object events, an application, in this case, that you can work with for optimizing the system as shown in Figure 9.13. Of course, there are other means of filtering the data. The options you choose depend on what kind of information you audited and how you want to use it to optimize the system. The goal is to use filtering to locate the information you want quickly because auditing produces many entries quickly. Close the view of all the entries by clicking the close box in the upper right corner of the window—EventReader doesn't provide a special button for the task.

FIGURE 9.11

The sample database includes a wealth of reports and views you can use to work with audits.

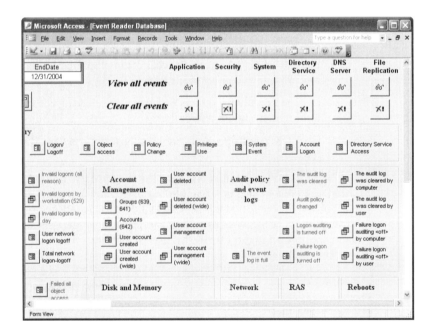

FIGURE 9.12

Select an object or other means of filtering the data so you can locate optimization information faster.

EventReader also provides access to many predefined reports. You access these reports by clicking Reports on the main form. Figure 9.14 shows some of the reports you can select. Generally, the reports aren't quite as helpful as the rest of the features EventReader provides for working with the event logs, from an optimization perspective, because they don't provide filtering. However, you can still use them to generate an overview of the event log entries and they provide a great resource for creating custom reports of your own. Think of these reports as a jumping off point for creating reports that will help you optimize systems quickly.

FIGURE 9.13

The filtered output is a lot easier to manage and review for usage patterns.

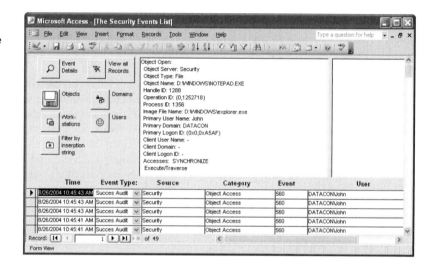

FIGURE 9.14

Select reports for gaining access to general information in the event logs.

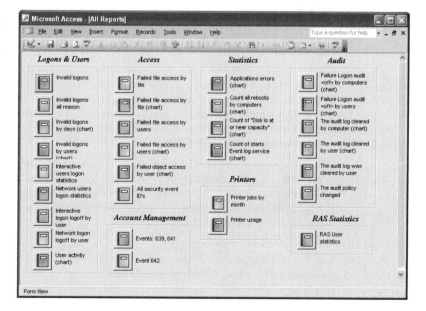

Setting Quotas

The term *quota* appears in many contexts. Many people view it as a means of measuring productivity. A worker must meet a certain quota or the boss isn't very happy. In this case, a quota is a measure of hard drive use. When you use up your quota, then the drive won't accept any more entries in some cases. Just how Windows reacts to a quota depends on how someone sets it up.

Of course, the most obvious use of quotas is on large networked systems where the network administrator doesn't want to add more hard drive space every day. For many network administrators, setting quotas is the first choice when trying to keep user hard drive usage under control. The idea is that a user is going to be obstinate, not clean their system, and generally give the network administrator a hard time. The network administrator assumes all this on the user's first day of work and never bothers to change that opinion during the entire course of the user's employ. Believe it or not, users can feel the negative vibes within 2 seconds of hitting the network administrator's office (that derogatory sign on the desk doesn't help). This is perhaps the worst possible way to use quotas and the reason that most users approach quotas with all the joy of a rainy day.

It's possible to use quotas in a positive way on any system. When used as a self-monitoring system, quotas can help anyone keep their hard drive clean. The idea is to let the system alert you to the loss of available hard drive space. You can then clean the drive to regain the lost space and go back to working on tasks. When used as a drive management technique, rather than a bludgeon, quotas can produce very positive results even if the only user on your system is you.

Saving Space for the System

A problem with many quota setups, and the reason they fail to produce the desired results, is that the person setting up the quota system doesn't leave enough space for the system. One of the biggest mistakes you can make is to attempt to obtain system usage of the hard drive when you have just cleaned it. The hard drive won't remain in a clean state because as you generate more data and perform more tasks, the system use of the hard drive also increases. You normally need to provide enough space for the system so it can continue to run after you use it for a while. Consider the clean state as the minimum you can set aside, but don't use it as the actual estimate of system drive usage.

The problem is to figure out how much drive space to set aside for the system once it gets dirty. In fact, you have to consider what you mean by the term *system* in this case—do you mean just Windows or everything that the user doesn't maintain? It's not an easy question, but you can usually come up with something that works for your particular needs. Most organizations will set up a system value that includes installed applications and other features that the user doesn't maintain simply to make the calculation easier. With this in mind, you should include the following folders in your estimate of system drive space needs.

\Windows   This folder contains most of the files that actually belong to Windows, but not the applications that Microsoft supplies with Windows. For example, when you install the Windows games, they appear in the \Program Files folder. In most cases, the \Windows folder also contains entries from applications, such as installation log files. The presence of these extra files is the reason that most people include all applications as the system disk usage value.

\Program Files   This folder contains all of the applications you install on the machine. Make sure you include all permanent applications in your calculation. Problems can occur when you have one or more programs installed for evaluation purposes and plan to remove them soon. Don't include temporary applications in your calculation when you truly intend to remove them soon after you perform your system survey.

\Documents and Settings   This folder contains all of the user data and settings. You want to consider the settings because the user normally won't change them directly, but you don't want to consider user data. Consequently, you'll want to remove the \Documents and Settings*User Name*\My Documents and \Documents and Settings*User Name*\Application Data folders from your calculation because they contain user data and are generally accounted for in the quota you create for the user.

\Inetpub   This folder appears on systems that contain a Web server—it contains all of the Web pages and other files the Web server presents to requesters. It's unusual to see this folder on an individual user's machine. When you see this folder, make sure you count it in the calculation and consider looking into why this folder appears on a user machine.

Pagefile.sys   This file contains the paging file. It always appears in the root directory of the machine and matches any paging file you create in size. Make sure you change the paging file size to an optimum setting before you account for this file in your calculation. The "Choosing a Paging File Size" section of Chapter 3 tells you how to size the paging file.

Other Application Folders   Most modern applications place their application and settings files in the \Program Files folder. However, some older applications still place their entries in the root directory. You need to account for these applications in your calculation by adding up the individual folder values.

To get numbers for each of these folders, right-click the folder in Windows Explorer and choose Properties. After a few seconds, the General tab of the Properties dialog box will show you the number of bytes for that folder as shown in Figure 9.15. Notice that there's a Size and a Size on Disk field. Use the value in the Size on Disk field for your calculation. The reason you use this number is that it considers any file compression and tells you the true size of small files (should you include any in your calculation).

You won't usually perform a survey of system disk space requirements just once. Most systems change often enough that you'll need to perform this task regularly—once or twice a year—to ensure you set reasonable quotas that consider system requirements. Making notes about how you perform this audit can help because you can refine your auditing processing over time and perform it more quickly. Using notes also ensures that you can add a level of consistency to the way you perform the audit so quotas on one machine are very much like quotas on every other machine.

FIGURE 9.15
Use Windows Explorer to determine the amount of space used by the files in a folder.

Setting Reasonable Quotas

At some point, you need to decide how much drive space to give to each user on a machine, even if only one user will need that drive space. You determine the total drive space by right-clicking the drive and choosing Properties from the context menu. The Capacity field on the General tab of the drive Properties dialog box tells you the total space on the drive. The "Saving Space for the System" section of the chapter tells you how to calculate the amount of system space to subtract from this value. The rest of the drive is open to users for data.

However, you can't assign all that space to the user because you need to reserve some space for changes in system status and to perform maintenance. For example, the Disk Defragmenter utility doesn't work well until you have at least 10 percent of the drive space left. A larger amount of drive space works better though, so you need to decide just how much drive space to keep in reserve for disk maintenance needs. In short, when you have a 10GB drive, 1GB is the minimum you should set aside for maintenance. When the system requires another 4GB of that space, the drive has 5GB left for user needs. When working with a single user machine, you'll want to reserve a little of that remainder to ensure the user has time to clean the drive—another 10 percent works well, so you'd set the quota for the single user drive at 4.5GB.

Problems occur when you start working with multi-user machines. For one thing, both users are eyeing each other suspiciously, in many cases—they're certain that you favored one user over the other. When both users perform precisely the same work, you can simply divide the space in half. Using the previous example as a starting point, each user would receive 2.25GB of hard drive space.

When the two users perform different tasks, you need to consider the tasks that each user performs. Someone performing development will almost certainly generate more data than someone performing word-processing. You could use the contents of their data folders as a starting point, but you might not have a good data sample to use. In this case, you could have each user provide sample documents you can use for comparison purposes and set up the quota for each user based on that information. You could also create a company policy of standardized quotas based on empirical data.

Creating the Quotas

Once you decide how to set the quotas for each user on a machine, you need to configure the drive. You can enable drive quotas under Windows XP in a number of ways, but one way is easier than all the rest. Open a copy of Windows Explorer, right-click the drive you want to modify, choose Properties from the context menu, and then select the Quota tab. You'll see a display similar to the one shown in Figure 9.16. The first step in using drive quotas is to check the Enable Quota Management option as shown in the figure.

You'll want to decide if new users should have an automatic quota set on their accounts, or if you want to set the limit as necessary. You can also choose to log any excessive use of disk space. The log can contain just the users who exceed their limit, or you can include those who reach the warning level as well.

Enabling quotas and setting a default limit isn't enough to ensure good resource management. You also need to review the users who have a quota. To do that, click Quota Entries. You'll see a Quota Entries dialog box like the one in Figure 9.17 that contains a list of users who have a quota for this drive. The list indicates their warning level and quota limit. You'll also see how much space the user has already used and learn if they've exceeded their limit.

To add a new user to the list, click New Quota Entry. You'll see a Select Users dialog box. Type a user's name or locate it using the Advanced button. Click OK and you'll see a New Quota Entry dialog box like the one shown in Figure 9.18. Select a quota limit and warning level for the new user and click OK. Make sure you set the warning level to keep the reserve level you provided in mind. The "Setting Reasonable Quotas" section described an example where the user actually has 5GB of drive space available, but you want them to start cleaning the drive when they reach the 4.5GB level. As shown in Figure 9.18, you'd change the Set Warning Level To value at 4.5GB, but the Limit Disk Space To value at 5GB to achieve this goal. After you click OK, the user's name will appear in the Quota Entries list.

FIGURE 9.16

Use the Quota tab to control user access to drive resources.

FIGURE 9.17

The Quota Entries dialog box tells you how much space each user has used on the drive.

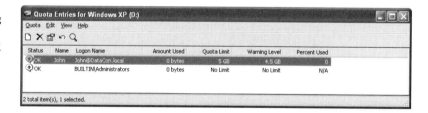

FIGURE 9.18

Set the maximum and minimum quota values to account for your calculations.

Let's Start Cleaning

This chapter discusses controlling the user as a form of maintaining a useful system state. The user could be anyone—the user could include a group of people using the computer or a single user that you manage as part of a network. The user could even be you. The term *user* means someone who uses the computer for any purpose from playing games to creating business reports. A user need not even produce a useful or permanent result—perhaps the user is surfing the Internet performing research. The point is that every user creates garbage that you must control to maintain a system in an optimized state.

Although this chapter provides you with a number of creative ways of controlling the user, you have to decide how to implement the tips on your system. It's important to consider concepts such as the user's perception of the helpful aids that you provide. A user could view the auditing provided to help discover bad usage habits as a kind of "Big Brother" approach—spying, if you will. Consequently, you not only need to profile the kinds of help you want to provide and the way you want to provide them, but also the method you plan to use to present the techniques to the user. In most cases, you'll want to create a written plan so that you can maintain a focus on the goals of the process. The time to put such a plan together is now, before you begin implementing the tips in this chapter.

Users and the applications they use aren't the only source of dirt on a system. In fact, the number of outside dirt sources increases each day. Some experts now worry that the outside sources of dirt could soon outnumber the internal sources. Keeping this outside dirt at bay is the topic of Chapter 10. Unlike Chapter 9, where you need to control the amount of dirt a user creates, Chapter 10 is all about placing obstacles in the way of incoming dirt because you don't need any of it on your system. Of course, it's equally important to realize that you can't keep all sources of outside dirt at bay, so this chapter also discusses what you can do to clean up outside dirt that does get into your system.

Chapter 10

Guarding against Outside Dirt: Keeping Adware, Spyware, and Nuisances at Bay

Optimization problems don't just occur on the inside of your machine—they can occur on the outside of your machine as well. Even the best optimization plan won't keep your machine clean when outside sources conspire to add all kinds of trash. Given the Internet environment today, it pays to have a strong policy toward security optimization, but you need to keep other problems in check, too. Even though spyware, adware, and viruses are all bad, companies that use cookies as a method for assaulting your privacy are just as bad. Even downloads that theoretically save you time and effort aren't much good when you don't want them on your system—yet unwanted downloads occur all the time. This chapter considers various techniques for keeping your machine clean, even when you have to leave the security of your network for the Internet.

Fortunately, you don't have to perform all the work required to keep your system free of outside dirt on your own. Many utilities exist for preventing spyware, adware, and virus infestations in the first place. You can also locate utilities that help you detect and remove these applications once they do find a home on your system. The idea is that you can use these professional tools to make your job easier. Although this chapter only samples some of the more interesting tools, you should be able to locate a tool for any need.

You don't always need to install a tool to improve the application environment. Many people use the default security settings for their application, which normally means the system is wide open to attack. By changing your application settings to provide better security, you can keep attackers at bay. Fortunately, you also have means for allowing those you trust increased privileges in most cases. The idea is to create an environment that is hostile to attackers and friendly to helpful Web sites. This chapter provides ideas that you can use with any application (it concentrates on Internet Explorer and Windows, but the principles work for any application on your system).

Sources of Outside Dirt and Grime

Outside dirt doesn't come in just one form—you have multiple forms to consider when protecting your system. Each source is trying to make your life difficult by adding dirt to your system and increasing your workload. However, each source adds dirt in a different way and for a different reason. Here's a quick overview of the sources of dirt described in this section.

Adware and Spyware Adware and spyware create problems in several ways. They add to the clutter on your hard drive because you might have an application that you don't know about installed on the system. Both use up system resources such as memory, network bandwidth, and processing cycles because both kinds of applications run continuously. In both cases, you lose the battle to maintain privacy because both application types monitor your activities and report them to someone else. In short, adware and spyware break every optimization rule in the book and offer you nothing in exchange.

Viruses Viruses are the worst form of outside dirt because they not only use your resources and infringe on your privacy, they also damage your system and could cause you to lose access to resources you need such as your Internet connection. You never receive any benefit from viruses and always have to clean up the mess they create. In general, viruses present the worst face of computing because someone who should know better normally writes them.

Trojan Horses A Trojan horse, as the name implies, is something that looks good, but really contains something bad. For example, you could click on an URL that looks like it goes to your bank, but end up downloading an application that redirects your dial-up Internet connection (if you have one) to some expensive location offshore. Unlike viruses, Trojan horse programs normally don't replicate because the developer needs a direct connection to the computer in order to obtain some benefit, such as your bank account information. You can learn more about the differences between viruses and Trojan horse programs at `http://service1.symantec.com/SUPPORT/ nav.nsf/docid/1999041209131106`. Always use a third party product to remove Trojan horses from your system.

Worms Worms are a special kind of virus that focuses on replicating, rather than infecting a system with a special application. In many cases, a worm increases its use of resources, such as memory or network bandwidth, until the host system crashes or experiences some other fatal result, such as the loss of data. Worms travel through files, but they don't need a specific file. For example, some worms travel through Excel documents—it doesn't matter which Excel document. Most worms will try to infect as many files as possible, so getting rid of one damaged file isn't enough— you must get rid of them all. In addition, worms travel between machines using any conduit available, including the Internet and your Local Area Network (LAN). In short, worms become very visible, quite quickly, but their behavior makes cleanup especially difficult. Always remove worms using a third party product, rather than attempt to remove them by hand.

Unwanted Downloads Unwanted downloads aren't necessarily bad. In fact, you can get something from them. For example, an application update is unwanted when you need the Internet connection to perform research, but characteristically, it's something you'll want at some point. Sometimes an unwanted download is a mistake—you click a link that you think leads to a great Web site, but you get a file instead. In other cases, the intent is malicious—the Web site designer creates the link in such a way that you download the file without really knowing it. No matter what kind of unwanted download you experience, the result is the same—your system uses network bandwidth, processing cycles, memory, and hard drive space for purposes other than what you want.

Known Sources of Dirt   Known sources of dirt include a number of items such as cookies, cached data, and automated form settings. You always know about these sources of data but might not choose to do anything about them. In some cases, it's not a matter of choice, but rather of knowing how to get rid of them. All known sources of dirt use some system resources, but not as much as other outside dirt, and because you know about them, are usually innocuous.

Unwanted Features   Many applications today include features that require an Internet connection for use. Because the feature works in the background, without your knowledge, it can cause problems with your system. For example, an automatic update feature might sound nice for your word processor, but using it means that you lose the ability to decide which updates to install. Generally, unwanted features cause mild system problems and use resources when you don't want to provide them. They're more a nuisance than a major problem, but it's best to discover how to turn them off so you have full use of your system.

Understanding Adware and Spyware

You acquire adware and spyware in a number of ways, but the most common way is to visit a Web site. Clicking a link or using a service that includes scripting or other executable content lets the Web site download the adware or spyware to your machine. In most cases, the adware or spyware appears as an application on your machine and executes every time you start your machine. Consequently, you can normally open Task Manager (right-click the Taskbar and choose Task Manager from the context menu) and see the adware or spyware as an entry on the Processes tab. The only way you can detect adware or spyware, in many cases, is to track down each of the applications on the list and determine whether you know about it. Having a list of known applications written down is extremely helpful. The "Using Task Manager" section of Chapter 7 tells you how to track down your applications and it also provides a list of common applications.

Knowing which entries are in the processes list won't remove the adware or spyware, but it's a good start. When working with adware, always check the Add or Remove Programs applet for an entry for that application. When you find one, you can use the standard technique to remove the application from your system. Applications that don't use the normal installation techniques require stronger measures, which include a trip to the registry. The "Running Applications Automatically" section of Chapter 6 describes how developers make applications run automatically when you log into Windows. Use the instructions in that section to remove the entry that tells the adware or spyware to run when you start your system. Once you stop the adware or spyware from running, remove the software from your system. Sometimes, this means manually removing the folder from your system. Use the registry entries to determine the location of the folder on your system.

A few pieces of adware or spyware install themselves as an add-in for your browser, which means you'll need to look in the HKEY_LOCAL_MACHINE\SOFTWARE\Microsoft\Internet Explorer\ Extensions key of the registry to find it. The extensions use a Globally Unique Identifier (GUID), as shown in Figure 10.1. Of course, your GUID will differ from the one shown because I'm using the Sun Java Console as an example. Every add-in has a unique GUID.

Within the entry, you'll find a CLSID (Class Identifier) entry that has another GUID. Again, your GUID will differ from the one shown. Double-click this entry and press Ctrl+C to copy the GUID to the clipboard. Click Cancel to close the Edit String dialog box. Place your cursor at the top of the registry (My Computer) and choose the Edit ➤ Find command to display the Find dialog box. Press Ctrl+V to paste the GUID into the Find What field and click Find Next to search for this GUID in the registry. You'll locate the component entry. Within the component entry is an InprocServer32 key that contains the location of the component, as shown in Figure 10.2.

In this case, the component is located at %SystemRoot%\System32\SHDOCVW.DLL. The %SystemRoot% entry is an expansion string for your Windows folder. For example, when your Windows installation is at C:\Windows, the registry expands %SystemRoot% to C:\Windows. To remove the component, in this case, you would open a command prompt at C:\Windows\System32. At the command line, type **RegSvr32 -u SHDOCVW.DLL** and press Enter. Windows will remove all of the registry entries for this component from the system. At this point, move the DLL to another folder for a while to ensure you really don't need it (a week or two) and then delete it. Of course, when working with adware or spyware, you substitute the name of the adware or spyware DLL for SHDOCVW.DLL. Don't remove this particular DLL—it belongs to the Sun Java Console.

FIGURE 10.1

Internet Explorer and other Windows browsers normally rely on GUIDs to help you locate add-ins.

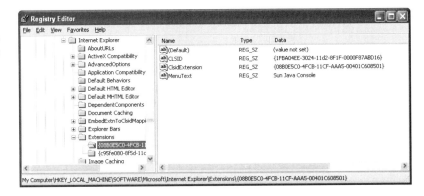

FIGURE 10.2

Find the location of the component that you want to remove from your system.

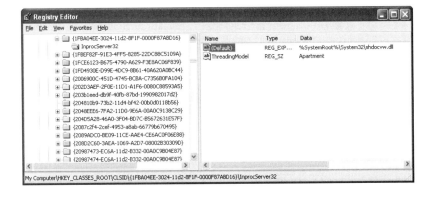

NOTE   If you find that you removed by mistake a DLL that you need, move the DLL back into the original folder. Open a command prompt in that folder. At the command line, type**RegSvr32** *Name of DLL* and press Enter. Notice that you don't use the −u (uninstall) command line switch in this case.

UNDERSTANDING THE DIFFERENCES BETWEEN ADWARE AND SPYWARE

Some people simply lump adware and spyware together. The two technologies do have one thing in common; they both install unwanted software on your system that can report your activities to a central location. The essential goal is the same in both cases—learning more about you and your computer habits. However, at this point, the similarities between adware and spyware end.

Adware products always installs after asking your permission, so you know about the presence of adware on your machine. (Some industry observers say that adware information purposely leaves out information you need to make a good decision—hopefully, adware vendors will correct this problem in the future.) In addition, you normally receive adware in exchange for a service or other feature of a Web site. Because adware's purported reason to exist is to sell you products, you'll receive constant reminders about the adware installation on your machine through the advertisements it displays. Finally, adware is normally easy to uninstall using standard techniques you use for any application. Of course, when you uninstall the adware, you also lose access to any Web site functionality that the adware supports.

Spyware products, as the name suggests, are covert. The makers of this kind of application hope to slip in under your radar so they can observe you quietly. The spyware developer hopes you won't notice the intrusion and usually has something more personal than your buying habits in mind. For example, spyware is one technique people use to steal your identity. They gain information about you as you type passwords, account numbers, and other valuable information. Needless to say, spyware usually makes it quite hard for you to remove the software and often stores multiple copies of itself on your machine.

Understanding Viruses

Viruses are worse than adware or spyware, but many of the same principles described in the "Understanding Adware and Spyware" section of the chapter apply. In addition to clicking a link or using a service, however, a virus can spread by other means. For example, opening an email or viewing a picture can let a virus gain access to your system. The point is that visiting Web sites you don't know and opening email when you don't know the recipient are dangerous—avoid these activities whenever possible.

In some cases, you don't have to do anything to get a virus infection. The virus can obtain access to your system through a security hole, so keeping your system patched is essential. The "Using the Four Security Zones in Internet Explorer" section of the chapter provides additional information on techniques you can use to reduce your exposure.

You should also install virus-scanning software on your system. The virus-scanning software looks for viruses in the messages and files you download. In addition to a good virus scanner, make sure you use a firewall—a special piece of software that helps to prevent unauthorized system access. The firewall ensures that another system can't sneak in through the back door. Windows XP includes a firewall that works for personal use, but it's better to get a reliable third party firewall for your system.

TIP The Forum of Incident Response and Security Teams (FIRST) has an interesting list of resources for ensuring your system remains virus free at `http://www.first.org/docs/guides/`. This list of links includes performing tasks such as hardening your system against attack and best practices for many Internet technologies. You should also check out the SysAdmin, Audit, Network, Security (SANS) Institute of top 20 vulnerabilities for your system at `http://www.sans.org/top20/`. This organization provides specific information about threats to your system and techniques for resolving those threats.

Before you assume that you have a virus on your system, check out a reliable resource. Some people spread hoaxes either because someone has fooled them or because they're trying to scare you. Always check for viruses using a reliable resource. Here are some resources you can use to verify that you really do have a virus on your machine.

◆ HOAXBUSTERS (`http://hoaxbusters.ciac.org/`)

◆ Stiller Research (`http://www.stiller.com/`)

◆ Urban Legends Reference Pages (`http://www.snopes.com/`)

◆ VMyths.com (`http://www.vmyths.com/`)

The Stiller Research site is especially interesting because it provides typical infection scenarios, as well as information about various myths and hoaxes. The Urban Legends Reference Pages site covers a lot more than computer viruses. You can find entries debunking a vast number of myths in all kinds of categories. If you're new to computing, the VMyths.com site is especially important because it tells you how to spot a myth and reduce the amount of time you spend sweating things that don't exist.

Unlike other kinds of dirt, it's usually very difficult to remove viruses from your system. Because every virus is different, you need to follow specific instructions for removing that virus. Consequently, this section doesn't provide virus removal instructions. However, many Web sites do provide good virus removal instructions. Your virus scanner should also provide some means of removing viruses, but sometimes you still need to rely on manual instructions to remove the entire virus. Here are some places you should check for your virus—normally you'll need to search the site for the information you require.

◆ Microsoft Knowledge Base (`http://support.microsoft.com/default.aspx?scid=fh;EN-US;KBHOWTO`)

◆ Symantec Anti-Virus Center (`http://www.symantec.com/avcenter/`)

◆ University of Michigan Virus Busters (`http://virusbusters.itcs.umich.edu/`)

◆ U.S. DOE (Department of Energy) CIAC (Computer Incident Advisor Capability) (`http://www.ciac.org/ciac/`)

Defining Unwanted Downloads

Any time you receive downloaded information you didn't request, it's unwanted. The fact that the download does something good is immaterial—the fact that you received the download unasked is the only important issue. Generally, it's a bad idea to let any software decide that you require a download. Sometimes you don't have a choice in the matter once you take certain steps. For example, adware, spyware, and viruses all download unbidden (or at least under coerced conditions) and you can do little about it once you click the link, use the service, open the email, or leave open a security hole that triggers the download.

Unwanted downloads come in a number of other forms too. You might simply click a link that you thought led to another site only to discover it actually downloads a file. All you need to do, in this case, is click Cancel on the download dialog box and the download ends. Not all unwanted downloads are automatic or performed without your permission—you simply have to take control as needed.

It's also possible to cause problems for yourself by not configuring your software properly. You always have a choice about configuring your software, so use it to keep your system clean and optimized. For example, Windows XP has an automatic update feature. You access it by right-clicking My Computer and choosing Properties from the context menu. The automatic update feature appears on the Automatic Updates tab shown in Figure 10.3.

FIGURE 10.3

Use automatic updates with extreme care because they often backfire.

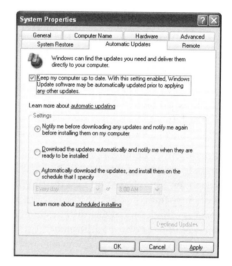

WARNING   Windows XP Service Pack 2 (SP2) displays a dialog box that insists you should turn automatic updates on. Don't turn automatic updates on unless you truly understand what using this feature means. Always use Windows Update to scan your system for changes and install only those changes you actually need. Test every change individually on a single machine before you install it on any other machine you might have. Exercise extreme care in using automatic updates because you never know when an update or patch will cause your system to malfunction.

If you must use automatic updates, the only safe option is the one shown selected in Figure 10.3—the first option tells Windows that you want notification before it downloads any updates and require notification again before it installs anything. Even though this option means more work on your part, you remain informed about changes to your system and can reject changes you don't want. Microsoft prefers that you blindly download everything they have to offer because this choice saves them time and effort at the expense of time and effort on your part fixing their mistakes. Patches and updates do fail to perform as advertised. Some people are so leery of Microsoft's patches and updates that they let other people test them for a long time before downloading them. In general, using the Windows automatic update feature causes these problems.

Loss of Patch and Update Control When you decide to let Windows take control of the update and patch process, you leave an important source of control out of the loop—you. For example, when you read about a patch, you might find out that it doesn't work well with systems that have a certain kind of hardware. If you have this hardware, you can decide not to download the patch so it doesn't cause problems. However, when you use the automatic update feature, Windows downloads and installs everything, regardless of any warnings about the patch. Consequently, you could end up with hardware that doesn't work or a Windows installation that won't boot at all.

Downloads at Inappropriate Times You're in the middle of a game and Windows decides it's time to start downloading patches. Which process do you think will get the network bandwidth needed to finish the task? Gamers, among others, have decided that the automatic update feature will always choose the worst possible moment to begin a download. Unless you want your fun or work time disrupted by a download you don't want, you have to take control over the download process.

System Stability Problems Because the automatic update feature performs its task at less than optimal times, you don't always get a good update or patch installation. This issue can lead to system stability problems. Installing patches and updates when the machine is set aside specifically for that task (no other applications running) means you have a better chance for getting a good installation. Consequently, you'll experience fewer stability and reliability problems.

Waiting for other people to test patches and updates is an open invitation to virus infection. In addition, the patch or update usually fixes errors that could cause your system to run in a less that optimal manner. Therefore, you face the dilemma of determining whether the cure (the patch or update) is worse than the disease (the error in Microsoft's code). A better choice is to check Windows Update once a month for patches and updates. Read about the patch or update using the material that Microsoft provides. Look for additional information about the patch or update online on sources such as Windows 2000 News (`http://www.w2knews.com/`) or Windows XP News (`http://www.winxp-news.com/`). When you decide a patch or update will do something good for your machine download just one patch to a single machine and then test it for a while. If the patch works on that one machine, install it on any other machines you own. Keep following this process until you download every patch or update that Microsoft provides (or until you determine that you don't want to download that patch or update).

The problem of automatic updates is far greater than you might think. All Microsoft products include some type of automation now and other vendors are following suit. For example, download Adobe Reader to your system and you'll get constant requests to update your product unless you use the Edit ➤ Preferences command to display the Preferences dialog box shown in Figure 10.4. Select the Updates tab and choose Manually in the Check for Updates field. Automatic updates assume that you're too lazy to take care of the products that you own. It's better to take charge of your system to ensure it stays clean and operates in the manner that you want.

FIGURE 10.4

Many vendors are following Microsoft's lead and including automatic updates in their products.

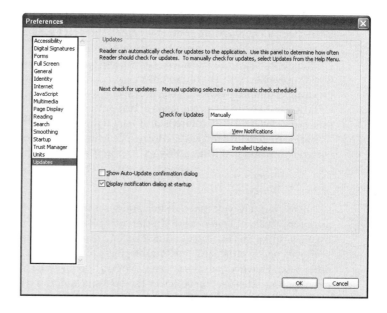

TIP   Most applications that provide an update feature also let you choose to update the product manually with an entry on the Help menu. For example, to update Microsoft Office, select the Help ➢ Check for Updates command. After some time passes, the product normally displays a list of updates for your product and you choose the updates you want to download. In general, you can also locate a source of updates for most products online. For example, when working with Microsoft Office, you can go to the Office site at `http://office.microsoft.com/en-us/default.aspx` and click Check for Updates.

Defending against Known Sources of Dirt

The "Taking Out the Internet Explorer Trash" section of Chapter 3 describes a number of outside dirt horrors including cookies, automatic form entries, and cached data. You know about these sources of dirt and understand how to clean them from your system (at least, when you remember to). However, cleaning up after Web sites every time you use a browser probably isn't a top priority—you have better things to do with your time. In short, keeping the dirt out is a better way to deal with the problem.

Known forms of outside dirt come in other packages as well. Some vendors think that you want to update every application on your system all the time, so every visit to the Internet also means visits to several Web sites that you don't know or care about to ensure your application is updated. The "Defining Unwanted Downloads" section of the chapter describes some ways around this problem, but you have other techniques at your disposal.

DEFEATING INTERNET DIRT SOURCES

In all cases, a known source of dirt is something you have heard about. The browser has likely told you that it's downloading cookies—the application ensures you know that the updates are available. Nothing is hidden or unexpected, you simply have chosen not to do anything about the problem or don't know that there's a solution. A proactive approach always works best, even if it requires a few precious minutes of work on your part when it's least convenient.

First, you need to know the signs of bad data. Many applications provide you with cues. For example, look at the Internet Explorer status bar (at the bottom of the windows). When you see an icon that includes an eye with a red circle with a minus sign in it, as shown in the following illustration, double-click the icon and you'll see a Privacy Report dialog box.

This report tells you that the site contains a source of cookies from a site that doesn't have a Platform for Privacy Preferences (P3P) statement in place, as shown in Figure 10.5. You normally can't trust a site like this to protect your security. The odd thing is that these cookies come from advertisements on a Web site that you might trust—the two sites aren't the same so you have to treat them differently. However, unless you set a specific policy that tells Internet Explorer to handle them differently, both sites use the policy of the host site and you receive the cookies from the advertiser.

To see the advertiser privacy policy, highlight an URL you don't recognize and click Summary. Internet Explorer will display the Privacy Policy dialog box shown in Figure 10.6. This dialog box might not contain any information at all, but it does let you determine whether to let the advertiser download cookies to your computer. In almost every case, you want to set this value to Never Allow This Site to Use Cookies because the advertiser will track you as you move between Web sites otherwise.

You also want to restrict access to your system. The "Using the Four Security Zones in Internet Explorer" section of the chapter discusses security settings you can use to keep outside dirt at bay. However, you can also control cookies directly too. To reduce the chance that cookies you don't want will appear on your system, click Settings in the Privacy Report dialog box shown in Figure 10.5. You can also access these settings using the Tools ➢ Internet Options command in Internet Explorer and selecting the Privacy tab. In both cases, you'll see the Internet Options dialog box shown in Figure 10.7.

FIGURE 10.5
Web sites that lack a privacy policy normally don't protect your personal information.

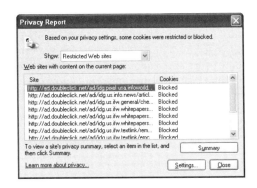

FIGURE 10.6

Avoid sources of extra cookies by setting a policy against them.

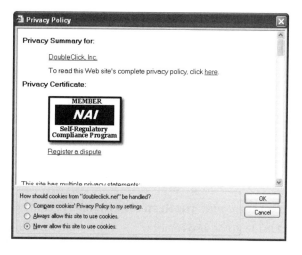

FIGURE 10.7

Set privacy settings to high to reduce the chance of getting cookies you don't want.

The High setting shown in Figure 10.7 blocks all cookies except those that follow all the rules. The next setting blocks all cookies—a setting that won't work, in most cases, because many Web sites have legitimate reasons for using cookies. For example, you'll find it very tough to buy products online without enabling cookies because the vendor uses a cookie to track your purchases. In this case, the cookies actually work to your benefit because all of the purchasing information remains on your machine until you check out. Your privacy remains intact should you decide not to make the purchase after all.

AVOIDING LOCALIZED SOURCES OF DIRT

It's easy to build up dirt from localized sources too. You can generate some of this extra load on your system quite easily. For example, many people keep rough notes as they work. Unfortunately, the rough notes never go away. Removing the rough notes is an essential part of keeping your system clean. (Rough notes can come from more than one source—if necessary, archive those rough notes that come from your boss or client to ensure you have them later.)

Other people can also provide you with a wealth of unneeded material on your system. For example, all those emails that tell you about company events, like the picnic that happened last year, should get removed the instant you no longer need them. All of those small emails build up rather quickly.

Despite strongly worded rules and regulations, most people also have an accumulation of neat games and cute cards, along with jokes and other materials that tend to clog up the system. Yes, it's important to customize your system and feel comfortable with it, but, at some point, you have to tell yourself that you no longer need these materials or archive them somewhere like a CD. In fact, a happy CD can bring sunshine to an otherwise gloomy day and it tends to keep your system clean so you can perform work when you don't need cheering up.

Understanding the Need for Physical Cleanliness

Outside grime also comes in the form of physical dirt. All those fans in your PC suck in dirt like a vacuum—in fact, the PC might do a better job. A PC needs good airflow to stay cool. Some of the components in your PC run so hot you could fry an egg on them. Of course, this begs the question of what a hot PC has to do with optimization. The fact is that as your PC runs hotter when you don't clean it, it can run into a wealth of reliability and stability problems. The mysterious reboot you suffered last week might have a lot less to do with not having enough memory and more to do with the memory chips that are running too hot. In fact, in one well-known case, a dirty dust-encrusted monitor was the cause of a machine rebooting almost daily. It turned out that the user kept pointing to things on the monitor where the dust had built up a strong static charge from the electrons hitting the front of the monitor screen. The user received the static charge that they then released into the keyboard—rebooting the machine. Yes, it really did happen.

The best thing you can do for your PC is open it up once every three months (shut Windows down and turn the system off first), inspect the inside for any damage, and then blow out the dust with compressed air. Make sure you use the cans of compressed air specifically designed for computer use. You can get it at places like Staples or any other office supply company for that matter. Most computers stores also sell compressed air. While you're at it, clean the outside of the case and make sure you double-check any air holes or filters. Clean the fan blades completely, especially those on the inside of the machine attached to the processor and display adapter.

Some people might not feel ambitious, are worried about damaging the inside of their machine, or their warranty prevents them from opening the machine. In this case, turn the system off. Use a vacuum cleaner to remove the dirt from the outside of the case. Make sure you keep the vacuum as far as possible from the computer to avoid any problems that the magnetic field of the motor might cause, such as erasing your data. A vacuum specifically designed for computer use works best. Again, make sure you get all of the air holes including those on the back of the machine. Work carefully to avoid causing problems by stressing the cables.

Now that you have a nice clean system unit, clean your mouse, monitor, and keyboard as well. To clean the mouse, wipe the outside with a lint free cloth. Remove the ball, if there is one, and clean it with mild soap and water. Don't put the ball back into the mouse until it has dried thoroughly. Blow any dust out of the mouse using compressed air. Use static free wipes for your monitor. Many office supply companies sell special wipes for the monitor that keep dust at bay. All you need to do with the keyboard is blow the dust that has accumulated out of the keys. Again, use care to ensure you don't dislodge any of the keys.

Determining When a Feature Is Unwanted

Most applications have unwanted features. However, when that feature also adds to the collection of garbage on your system, it's time to mark it unwanted and try to get rid of it. One such feature is automatic updates, which the "Defining Unwanted Downloads" section of the chapter discusses. However, applications include other unwanted features that make them difficult or time consuming to use, and definite attractors of unwanted hard drive content.

One such feature is application help that looks for updated content online. This might sound like a good feature and it normally is, but only so long as you're aware that the feature is in use. For example, most Office 2003 products include a feature that lets you share hardware and usage information with Microsoft. In exchange, you receive help file updates and hopefully improved support. The catch is that this option not only uses extra hard drive space, but it also runs applications on your system that use processing cycles, memory, and network bandwidth. Fortunately, you have to turn this option on either during installation or manually using the Help ➤ Customer Feedback Options command. Figure 10.8 shows the Services Options dialog box you'll use to change this setting.

FIGURE 10.8

Sharing your hardware and usage information with Microsoft could mean better product support.

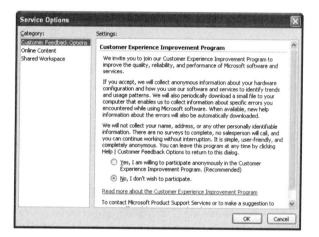

WARNING   You should consider the automatic help update feature carefully, especially when it includes information exchange as the Office 2003 option does. Most vendors will protect your privacy and many, including Microsoft, won't collect any personally identifying information. However, the risks of abuse are relatively high because you have no way of verifying how much or knowing what type of information the vendor collects about your system.

Online content is another dirt attractor. Many applications now provide the online content for a number of purposes. For one thing, the vendor can keep providing new content for the application long after its published—that's the good part. The bad part is that some vendors use online content as a means for tracking your activity. It's possible to derive marketing information based on the selections you make. In addition, the online content doesn't go away when you finish using it. Removing the content manually usually requires in-depth knowledge of the product. Sometimes people download online content with no intent of even using it because they're curious as to what it looks like. Using Office 2003 as an example again, choose the Help ➤ Customer Feedback Options command to display the Service Options dialog box. Select the Online Content category and you'll see the options shown in Figure 10.9.

These three examples tell you that most vendors are considering ways of providing you with a better deal in exchange for some information. This personal information is important to the vendor because it helps the vendor create products that suit your needs better. In a perfect world, this information should result in smaller products that perform better. In the real world, it often results in bloated products that require you to buy new hardware. The important consideration is determining whether you actually need the feature the application offers. When there's doubt, try the feature out and then remove it if you find that you don't need it.

FIGURE 10.9
Online content augments the features of your application, but at relatively high price.

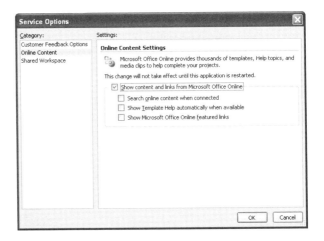

Discovering Nasty Intruders

Somewhere, someone is trying to gain access to your system through adware or spyware. The problem is that they will eventually get through. Just how long it takes depends on how careful you are and the way you set up your security. Good security measures and careful use of the Internet will reduce your risk, but someone who is intent on gaining access to your machine will eventually find a way to do it. Consequently, you need a product that also searches your system and looks for these nasty intruders. Although adware will alert you to its presence, spyware is especially nasty because it hides on your system. The only way that you'll know about spyware is to scan for it. The following sections describe several products that can help you find these intruders.

TIP Some Web sites don't provide an actual download you can use to scan your system—they provide a link you use to scan your system while online. For example, SpyBouncer (`http://www.spybouncer.com/spyaff.asp`) provides this feature. In general, these sites are a little risky because you have to trust an online connection to perform the scan. Look for reviews from independent Web sites before you use this kind of scanner. In addition, make sure you only give the site enough rights to perform the scan. The advantage of using this kind of scan is that you don't have to clutter your system with additional utilities.

OVERCOMING PROBLEMS WITH WINDOWS XP SP2

Microsoft made security the main goal of Windows XP Service Pack 2 (SP2). This sidebar discusses some of the security optimization issues you'll face. Don't get the idea as you read this sidebar that you shouldn't install Windows XP SP2. This update provides great security optimization for your system and you should consider it essential. However, it's also important to realize that the update isn't perfect, so you should test it on a machine that doesn't contain critical data first, tweak the settings as needed for your organization, and then move it to the other machines you own. Make sure you search Google for articles that relate to your specific needs as well—more SP2 problems appear daily so I can't discuss them all here.

If you only have one machine, then it's important to have a good backup that you've tested before you install Windows XP SP2. (Generally, you should exercise extreme care installing Windows XP SP2 if you only have one machine because the problems it causes could put that machine out of action.) Check out the ComputerWorld article at `http://www.computerworld.com/softwaretopics/os/windows/story/0,10801,95390,00.html` for an overview of some of the important Windows XP SP2 features.

In many areas, Microsoft succeeded making security airtight—well, at least for the moment. For example, after I installed Windows XP SP2, I found I could no longer make backups on my network. The problem was that Windows XP SP2 turns on the firewall for local drives as well as Internet connections and I hadn't configured the firewall to allow a backup to take place. You can read more about the success of the firewall at `http://searchwin2000.techtarget.com/originalContent/0,289142,sid1_gci967408,00.html?track=NL-118&ad=489731` and `http://searchwin2000.techtarget.com/tip/0,289483,sid1_gci1000900,00.html?track=NL-118&ad=489731`.

Unfortunately, the update is less than perfect. Security experts warn that even though Windows XP SP2 is better, it still has a long way to go. For example, the article at `http://zdnet.com.com/2100-1105_2-5315063.html` points out that Windows XP SP2 has serious security deficiencies. The ComputerWorld article at `http://www.computerworld.com/softwaretopics/os/story/0,10801,74564,00.html` points out that Windows XP SP2 actually interferes with some of the software you need to secure your network completely. You'll even encounter potential new spoofing attacks based on new Windows XP SP2 features (see `http://searchwin2000.techtarget.com/columnItem/0,294698,sid1_gci1002781,00.html?track=NL-118&ad=490426`).

Like many things in life, Windows XP SP2 is a combination of pros and cons when it comes to optimization. Yes, you'll receive extra security, but you'll pay for it with broken applications and the need to tweak your machine after you install it. The article at `http://searchwindowssecurity.techtarget.com/tip/0,289483,sid45_gci1002258,00.html?track=NL-122&ad=489804` gets it right by saying there are pros and cons you need to consider (you may need to register to read the article). You can find an excellent list of Windows XP SP2 links at `http://searchwindowssecurity.techtarget.com/featured-Topic/0,290042,sid45_gci999352,00.html?track=NL-122&ad=489804`.

Using PestPatrol

PestPatrol (`http://majorgeeks.com/download1187.html`) consists of a number of programs, each of which checks a specific area of your system. For example, the CookiePatrol Log Viewer shows which cookies on your system could contain spyware data. Installing this product was an unusual experience. The first thing it did after installation was obtain an update from the PestPatrol Web site. This act fills me with some hope that the vendor is very serious about keeping up with the latest crud that can infect a system.

After you get PestPatrol started, you'll want to enable two of the features it provides. Right-click the PestPatrol icon in the Notification Area of the Taskbar and you'll see a context menu containing several entries. Turn on cookie monitoring using the CookiePatrol ➤ Start Cookie Patrol option, and then turn on memory checking by using the MemCheck ➤ Start MemCheck option.

PestPatrol is mainly concerned with protecting your system from various threats including adware, spyware, and viruses. In addition to automatic scanning, you can perform manual scanning of your hard drive for specific threats (a very long list included on the options tab of the product). PestPatrol also scans your registry and other areas of the system.

This program seems to be extremely thorough if all you want is adware, spyware, and virus protection. However, it doesn't provide the firewall and threat support provided by other applications. In addition, during testing, PestPatrol registered a false positive on a known clean system—a check of the affected registry key turned out to point to another application. However, other applications of this sort also register false positives, which is why you always want to check them out before deleting something you might need. The final oddity is that the program didn't appear in the Add or Remove Programs applet—I needed to use a special uninstall program located in the PestPatrol folder.

Using SmartFix

SmartFix (`http://www.majorgeeks.com/download4054.html`) doesn't appear to do anything when you start the application. That's because it places an icon in the Notification Area of the Taskbar and gets right to work. To see an overview of what SmartFix does, click on the icon in the Notification Area. The wealth of features this product provides is overwhelming. You get everything from a firewall to virus protection. The application will change settings on your system to make it more secure and even defragment your drive.

However, the protection doesn't stop with automatic features. You can also perform a wealth of manual tasks. For example, with a simple selection of an option on the menu, you can get information about the latest security alerts—SmartFix retrieves them for you from the Internet. When you want to learn more about a particular virus, simply click its entry and SmartFix will display more information about it. You can also discover the most prevalent threats. SmartFix even tells you how well the virus is doing so you have some idea of how easy it's going to be to catch.

Many of the features of this application aren't enabled when you first install it. For example, you must specifically enable the pop-up advertisement blocker and you don't get adware protection unless you specifically request it. You can even enable a laptop friendly energy-saving mode. This product really hits the spot when optimizing your system for performance is a concern.

The biggest downside to this product is that it doesn't contain much of a user interface. You really don't know much about what it does. Yes, the settings are all there, but you have no idea whether SmartFix has located any adware or spyware today. The spartan approach this application will work for anyone who wants the tasks done with a minimum of system interruption (sounds optimized for performance to me), but many users will want to have a warm fuzzy feeling that this application is actually doing something now. You do receive messages from SmartFix when it does detect a problem, so the lack of a resource consuming user interface should have a minimal impact.

Using SpyBot Search and Destroy

SpyBot Search and Destroy (`http://www.tucows.com/preview/310138.html`) provides a nice interface and is extremely user friendly. The program includes a tutorial you can use to learn more about set up and searching your drive for potential problems. In addition, this is one of the few applications that I've downloaded that has special settings to assist blind users.

When you run the application, it quietly checks your system for known spybots. You can set the program to run automatically when you start Windows. The program will also automatically update itself should you decide to do that. The feature I liked best about the automation is that you can set SpyBot Search and Destroy to change its priority. The priority determines how much time Windows gives the application to run, which means you ultimately control some of the resources that SpyBot Search and Destroy uses.

The interesting feature of this application is that it doesn't just look for spyware and stop. SpyBot Search and Destroy also pointed out registry settings that could cause problems and included known holes in Microsoft's product in the list of things to fix. It even provides a link where you can learn more about the security hole, but not necessarily obtain a fix. This list is nice because it gives you something to look for in future Microsoft updates and patches if you are already up-to-date (and encourages you to update if you aren't).

This program won't provide everything you need to protect your system, but it does provide outstanding support for ridding your system of spyware. When you combine this application with a program that provides virus protection and a firewall, you have protection from the vast majority of online threats.

Setting Applications to Deter Outsiders

Many applications today provide features that help you deter outside sources of dirt. These features won't prevent the dirt, but they at least slow it down. In some cases, with careful use, you can slow the dirt down enough that cleanup is almost trivial. All you need to do is learn about the secrets that your application is hiding. For example, most people don't realize that Internet Explorer supports four security zones that you can use to keep a lot of outside dirt at bay and that these security zones work extremely well when set correctly. The following sections provide you with details of a number of techniques you can use to deter outsiders who want to make your machine dirty.

Adopting a Positive Attitude

It might sound corny, but a positive attitude helps a lot in finding ways to use application features to your benefit. For example, you might discover that you seldom view the pictures on Web sites you visit—they're mainly company logos and extraneous materials you'll never use anyway. You can set your browser to download the text and not the pictures, in most cases, with a simple configuration change. This simple change reduces the risk of getting a virus because you won't download pictures with potentially nasty content and also decreases the time to download the page because graphics are much more time intensive than text.

The vendor might not have had security or optimization in mind when adding the picture feature, but by looking at the browser in a new way, you could discover this use of the setting. The best part is that you really haven't lost anything. When you decide that you want to view a picture, all you need to do is right-click it and choose Show Picture from the context menu.

When working with Internet Explorer, you can change the picture setting by choosing the Tools ➤ Internet Options command. Select the Advanced tab of the Internet Options dialog box. Clear the Show Pictures option and click OK.

In many cases, you'll begin to see other uses for application features once you use the application for a while. These other users often translate into an optimized environment that drags in less dirt from other locations. To make this work, however, you need to keep follow these steps:

1. Explore the application as time permits to discover all of the settings the vendor provides.

2. Look for new uses for the settings you discover by learning precisely how the setting affects your system.

3. Experiment with the changes you find to determine whether the change has a positive long-term effect.

Using the Four Security Zones in Internet Explorer

Internet Explorer has the potential to provide good security, but most people don't realize it. Unfortunately, Microsoft isn't particularly good at advertising the security features because they have a particular agenda in mind for them. The four security zones are supposed to relate to your location—whether you're using local or remote resources. However, the four security zones are more a matter of your level of trust for a particular URL, not its location. Here are the four security zones and my decidedly non-Microsoft view of using them.

Local Intranet You trust these sites the most, so you give them the maximum freedom. Sites that have this level of trust have full scripting and ActiveX support, along with full Java capability. It's very likely that you'll add this site to the list of places that you always accept cookies from as well. Of course, you still have to exercise care because you don't know whether a virus or other application has thwarted security on the remote machine. The idea is that you trust these machines the most—no matter where they might appear. Never give this level of access to any Web site that you don't control directly. However, you might give this level of access to your home page because you do control it or a corporate page because you know the people who control it.

Trusted Sites This level of trust means that the site isn't under your direct control, but you have worked with the vendor long enough to know that it won't do anything to your system. A trusted site will probably enjoy scripting support, along with some forms of signed ActiveX support and high permission Java support. In many cases, you'll also accept cookies from the vendor. Never give any site that has banner ads this level of support. The mixed content on those pages means that you can't trust the vendor completely because the vendor doesn't have full control of the Web site. However, you might give this level of access to an online news site or to an online store that doesn't run banner ads. Normally, it's a good idea to work with a store at least one year before you allow this level of access—two or more years is better.

Internet You'll use this general level of trust for all Internet sites that you neither trust nor distrust. Every Web site gets this level of trust unless you specifically configure it for another setting. Because you can't trust these sites, they don't enjoy any scripting support, they can't run ActiveX controls, you don't allow any form of Java, and you might even disable some special features such as using META REFRESH and displaying mixed content. In short, the site will display, but it might not work completely because you don't trust it.

Restricted Sites This level of mistrust means that you have seen evidence that disreputable people run the site and you would rather not display it at all. Even though the text on the site will display, the security settings ensure that nothing else will. This site doesn't have any rights at all.

To define the security zones for your machines, select the Tools ➢ Internet Options command. Select the Security tab and you'll see the four security zones, as shown in Figure 10.10. To work with a site, begin by choosing the zone for that site.

FIGURE 10.10

Use security zones to control how your browser interacts with Web sites.

TIP   One of the Windows XP SP2 problems you'll eventually encounter is an almost absurd lock-down on anything from the Internet. Fortunately, you can test your plug-ins for potential problems using a new toolkit that Microsoft provides. Learn more about it at `http://searchwin2000 .techtarget.com/originalContent/0,289142,sid1_gci1002587,00.html?track= NL-118&ad=490426`. You can download the kit at `http://www.microsoft.com/downloads/ details.aspx?FamilyId=9300BECF-2DEE-4772-ADD9-AD0EAF89C4A7`.

CUSTOMIZING SITE SECURITY SETTINGS

Internet Explorer provides default settings for each zone. In general, these settings are far too optimistic for today's Internet. For example, the default settings allow scripts to run on Web sites you don't know. Letting a script run on a site you don't know is like inviting a crook into your home. When the crook robs you, the police are going to have a very hard time understanding why you let the person into your home in the first place. A better approach is to assume that every site is out to get you until you know otherwise. In short, you need to customize the security settings on your machine to hinder bad behavior proactively.

To customize your security settings, choose one of the zones shown in Figure 10.10 and click Custom Level. You'll see a Security Settings dialog box like the one shown in Figure 10.11. Notice that each of the settings tells you what will happen when you enable it and provides an option for prompting you. A prompt means that the browser will ask you before it uses an ActiveX control, executes a Java applet, or runs a script. In some cases, prompting is a good idea because you can decide whether to trust the site when you arrive. Unfortunately, setting everything to prompt isn't a good idea because you can quickly tire of clicking yes or no for each prompt and make mistakes. (Imagine having to click through 40 or 50 script prompts per Web page and you can see why it's better to have a good policy in mind and follow through with it.)

FIGURE 10.11
Security settings let
you disable, enable, or
prompt for an action.

Many of the setting choices appear in the introduction to this section, but a few require special consideration. For example, in the Microsoft VM section, the Java Permissions option only affects the Microsoft version of Java. When you install a version of Java from another vendor such as Sun, you need to use any features that the third party vendor provides to secure Java.

The remaining special settings appear in the Miscellaneous section. Of special interest is the Access Data Sources Across Domains setting. Always disable this setting except in the Local Intranet zone because it lets the current page access information from another Web site. The other Web site could contain anything—including a virus or spyware. The Allow META REFRESH setting is also somewhat dangerous because it allows a Web page that you want to visit to redirect you to another location without your permission. While you can allow this setting for the Local Intranet and Trusted Sites zones, you shouldn't allow just any Web page to redirect your browser to another location.

Some of the settings depend on the Web sites you visit. For example, the Display Mixed Content setting might be OK for the Local Intranet zone assuming that the two or more sites providing content for the page are all trustworthy. Mixed content creates one page from the content provided by multiple sites, so it complicates matters and you might not want to allow it at all. Fortunately, whenever you want to learn more about a setting, you can click the question mark in the upper right corner of the Security Settings dialog box and point to the item. Internet Explorer will display the information you need.

ADDING SITES TO A SPECIFIC ZONE

Once you've decided on the security settings for each zone, you need to add Web sites to them. The sites don't do anything by themselves. Generally, to add a Web site to a zone, click Sites in the Security Settings dialog box shown in Figure 10.10. Except for the Local Intranet zone, you'll see a sites dialog box similar to the one shown in Figure 10.12. When working with the Local Intranet zone, display the Local Intranet dialog box first, and then click Advanced to display the dialog box shown in Figure 10.12.

Type the full URL for the Web site you want to add to the zone. Use enough of the Web site URL to ensure you control security. For example, many personal Web sites exist as special folders on a main Web site. You would type the main Web site plus the personal folder (such as `http://www.main.com/personal_site`). After you type the URL, click Add to add the Web site to the list. If you ever choose to remove the Web site from a particular zone, highlight the site in the list and click Remove. Click OK to close the site's dialog box.

FIGURE 10.12
Add Web sites to each of
the zones as needed to
ensure each zone has
proper security.

Optimizing Outlook Express Usage

Outlook Express can be a good friend or your worst nightmare when it comes to optimizing your system. Two settings can make a big difference when using this application. The first one adjusts the security settings used to download email. Choose the Tools ➤ Options command to display the Options dialog box. Select the Security tab and you'll see options similar to those shown in Figure 10.13.

All of these settings are important, but depending on your needs, you might not use them all. For example, not everyone needs to restrict access to file attachments sent with email and this setting could reduce your efficiency in some cases. In addition, the most secure email requires the use of digital signatures and the like, but there's one setting change everyone should make. Notice the option to choose an Internet Explorer security zone to use with Outlook Express at the top of the dialog box in Figure 10.13. Selecting the Restricted Zone can add a measure of security to Outlook Express by denying access to just about everything.

FIGURE 10.13
Set strict security mea-
sures with Outlook Ex-
press to protect your
system.

To see the second setting, select the View ➢ Layout command. Clear the Show Preview Pane option. This option can cause significant problems because it displays the content of messages when you select them. Some viruses rely on this feature to begin executing. The second you click on one of the message headers, the virus starts its work. Consequently, you get better security leaving the Preview Pane off or at least leaving it off when you download new messages.

Turning off the Preview Pane gives you another option for examining messages. Whenever you receive a message from someone you don't know, determine whether you want to view it at all. Sometimes it's better to simply delete the message than open yourself to virus attack. When you think the message might be legitimate, right-click it and choose properties. Select the Details tab and click Message Source. You'll see a Message Source window similar to the one shown in Figure 10.14.

At the top of the window, you'll see the message heading information. You can review this information to determine the sender's email address, when legitimate. Spoofed (false) email addresses sometimes contain odd phrases or combinations of letters and numbers that a real person wouldn't use. After the header, you can read the content of the message safely. No, it won't have any formatting, but you can see what the message is about and whether you want to explore it further. Beware when the message contains content that you can't read or no message at all. Content that looks like odd combinations of letters, numbers, and special symbols is often executable code that you don't want to open. A message without any content often contains trickery as part of the header. Neither option is good and you're better off removing the message than letting it stay on your system.

FIGURE 10.14
View the raw message to ensure it's from someone you trust.

Creating Security Buffers

One of the topics of this chapter is creating security buffers as a means of protecting your system. Each buffer by itself isn't very strong, but it adds to the strength of the entire system. By creating multiple buffers, you delay encroachments and deter attempts to steal your data or clutter your system. In short, you optimize your system in such a way that it's easy to use, remains reliable and stable, and still keeps the bad guy out most of the time. It's important to remember that no matter what you do, the bad guy can gain access to your system given enough time, opportunity, and reason. Here's the way you should view the security buffers on your system.

Firewall A firewall is your first line of defense. This software keeps outsiders from probing your system in the first place. When some types of viruses look for machines to infest, the first thing they do is look for a way onto your machine through the Internet. You use a firewall to prevent unauthorized accesses to your machine.

Virus Scanner A virus scanner is a piece of software that looks for nasty additions to email and files you download. Some virus scanners also work with your browser. The intent is to keep your system secure by removing the threat of software that does make it onto your machine.

Windows and Application Patches and Updates Nothing you do will prevent someone from accessing your system if you don't keep it patched and updated. You can't patch just one application either—any application that has any contact with the system at all requires the most recent patches and updates to perform optimally and keep the system safe. Apply patches and updates wisely—ensure you know what the patch or update will do before you apply it so you can anticipate problems. Finally, when an application gets too old to patch or update, consider replacing it so that you can continue to receive performance and security gains.

Internet Application Settings Good browser and other Internet application settings can prevent certain kinds of virus-laden software from downloading including infected pictures, ActiveX components, Java applets, and scripts. These settings also reduce the stress on your system by preserving resources. Even if a script, ActiveX component, or Java applet is legitimate, it still uses resources that you could need for other purposes.

Desktop Application Settings Even though viruses seldom enter through desktop applications, the value-added features that many applications provide do provide a virus with a foothold. Using online content, automated updates, and help updates carefully can help keep your system safe. In addition, all of these features require additional resources that take away from the central use of the desktop application. Consequently, you get a performance and ease-of-use bonus while keeping your system safe by using these extra features with care.

Application Usage Habits Always consider the result of an act before you do it. For example, leaving the Preview Pane intact when you view an email from someone you don't know can start a virus. Leaving the default Internet Explorer settings intact when you view a Web site you don't know could allow a script to download spyware to your system. Everything you do affects your system, so you need to modify your usage habits to ensure your system works optimally and remains safe.

Vigilance When someone is determined to access your system, they're going to do it. All anyone needs is the right tools and a lot of time. Of course, they also need a good reason to spend all that time accessing your system. By keeping your system patched, using a firewall and virus scanner, and relying on good usage habits, you deny someone the normal casual means of attacking your system. This means they'd need a very specific reason to attack you and most attackers simply don't have the time. Even so, you need to watch your system for changes you hadn't anticipated. Vigilance is the best weapon you have for keeping other people out of your system.

Let's Start Cleaning

This chapter concentrates on keeping the dirt that exists outside your computer from getting into the machine. The many forms of outside dirt mean that you have to be proactive in protecting your system. It's important for everything from keeping your machine updated to ensuring you configure the software properly. Good security is also important because security can keep some types of outside dirt at bay. Of course, it's equally important to know what you have stored on your system so that you notice any changes made by an application you don't know. It also pays to have a healthy dose of suspicion. Any source of information that you don't know is suspect and you can't trust it on your system.

It's time for you to get started keeping outside dirt at bay. Make sure you create a list of things to do based on the content of this chapter or you'll miss that one important modification you really need to perform. Begin by updating Windows and your applications with the latest updates and patches. Don't install everything—just those updates and patches that you actually need (I can't make that determination because every system is different). After you get your software updated, change any settings required to improve security and give you better control over the download process. Finally, make changes in how you use the software. Don't trust the software to make decisions for you—take charge and track the tasks the software performs.

Chapter 11 seems to run counter to the instructions in this chapter of maintaining control over your system, but it really doesn't. Once you understand a process and know precisely how you want it performed, you can automate it. The difference is that you've made the decision on what to do and how to do it—you haven't left the choice up to a vendor who doesn't even know you. Chapter 11 demonstrates various techniques for automating tasks using your methods and settings so that you still maintain control of the system, but have to perform less work to keep it clean.

Chapter 11

Automating Cleanup Tasks

Automation can help you perform tasks faster, but it's only useful when you fully understand the task you're performing. All of the manual steps discussed in other chapters of this book help you understand what Windows and other utilities can do for you in optimizing your system in a specific way. Now that you know what those utilities do and have experimented to find the best ways to use those utilities with your system, it's time to look at ways to make the task faster and easier by using automation.

The batch file is the basic form of automation for many people. A batch file simply tells the system to perform one task after another without your intervention. It ensures that you run all of the required maintenance in a given order without having to think through the process every time. Operating systems have relied on batch files for a very long time, so they're stable technology that you'll use on many systems.

You might think that the main reason to use automation is speed or reducing your workload, but the reality is that automation ensures consistency. The Task Scheduler and AT utility can help you ensure that you run maintenance every time you need to without having to think too often about performing it. It's all too easy to get caught up in work and only discover at the end of the day that you haven't performed your required maintenance. After a few weeks or months, your system is back to its former state and you begin wondering where all of that optimization went. Consequently, many of the sections in this chapter not only focus on automating a task, but helping you to perform that task consistently as well.

Another reason to use automation is to help other people. It's sort of like cloning yourself so you can be in multiple places at the same time. Scripting is a form of automation that helps you create an environment where you can optimize more than one machine at a time. Although this might seem like something that only a corporate administrator would use, individuals can use it as well. Scripting also adds flexibility to the optimization process. Instead of simply telling the system to perform a task, you can check for environmental conditions that could preclude running a utility.

Creative Uses for Batch Files

Batch files are essentially a list of things to do. Yes, they have special commands you can use to make them act like low-powered scripts, but the essential part of a batch file is a list of tasks to perform. All you do is create a text file that contains one command after the other—each command appearing on a different line of the batch file. The file itself includes a BAT extension so that Windows treats it as a batch file. Here's a simple example of a batch file.

```
Echo Off

REM Copy the directory to a file.
Dir /Q /4 >> TempDir.TXT

REM Copy the file to the printer.
Copy TempDir.TXT LPT1:

REM Erase the temporary files.
Erase TempDir.TXT

Echo On
```

This batch file copies the current directory to a file and then prints it out. Afterward, the batch file automatically cleans up after itself to remove the temporary file the Dir command creates. The file begins by turning echo, or the display of messages, off so the user won't see any of these messages as the batch file runs.

TIP When working with Notepad, make sure you set the Save As Type field in the Save As dialog box to All Files. Otherwise, Notepad will add a TXT extension after the BAT extension, making the file look like a text file.

Each line that begins with REM is a remark—the batch file processor won't execute any remarks. You use remarks to describe the tasks the batch file performs. Using remarks documents that batch file and makes it easier to remember why you created it later.

In this case, the Dir command outputs the current directory in a form that includes the name of the person who owns each file. You could use this technique to help discover who owns each file on a networked drive to help in a cleanup effort. The /4 switch tells the Dir command to use 4-digit years. The Copy command sends the file to the printer, which has the special device name LPT1:. Accessing the printer this way is like using any other device. For example, the first hard drive on your system is C:, which is a special way of identifying that drive. Erasing the file after it's printed comes next. Finally, the batch file turns echo back on so that the user can see any messages.

TIP You might wonder why an old technology like batch files appears in a modern book. The fact of the matter is that most people have two options: scripts and batch files for automating tasks. Many people don't trust scripts because they can contain viruses, so batch files make a good alternative. You can learn how to remove Windows Script Host (WSH), the source of scripting capability in Windows XP, at `http://securityresponse.symantec.com/avcenter/venc/data/win.script.hosting.html` should you decide to optimize your system to use batch files. In addition to reducing the chance of virus infection, the learning curve for batch files is extremely small—they're fast and easy to construct. As with every optimization, you have to give something up to use batch files—they aren't as flexible as scripts and they do rely on a command line interface.

Controlling Execution Using *If*

Sometimes you want to control batch file execution. For example, you might want to know that the previous task succeeded before you begin the next task. In some cases, you'll look for a specific file or act on user input to the batch file. You can also verify that the user provided a certain input string. The point is that you can exercise some control over how the batch files reacts to system and environmental conditions. Batch files don't provide extensive decision-making support, but you can use these three forms of the If statement to increase the flexibility of your batch files.

- If [Not] ErrorLevel *number command*

- If [Not] *string1==string2 command*

- If [Not] Exist *filename command*

In all three cases, you can add the word Not to perform the reverse of the check. For example, you can perform a task when a given file doesn't exist, rather than when it does exist. By combining both versions of the If statement, you can create the equivalent of an If...Else statement found in most programming languages. Listing 11.1 shows examples of the various If statement forms at work.

LISTING 11.1:   Using the *If* Statement in Batch Files

```
Echo Off

REM Verify the user has provided an action.
If %1Err==Err GoTo ProcessError

REM Simulate an error when the file doesn't exist.
Copy MyFile.TXT MyFile2.TXT
If Not ErrorLevel 1 Goto CheckFile
    Echo The File doesn't exist so the batch file can't copy it.

REM Check for a specific file and process it when it does exist.
:CheckFile
If Exist MyFile.TXT Goto ProcessFile

REM If the file doesn't exist then create it. Display a message with
REM instructions and then let the user type the text.
Echo Type some text for the test file. Press Ctrl+Z when you finish.
Pause
Copy CON MyFile.TXT

REM This is a label for processing the file.
:ProcessFile

REM Determine whether the user wants to display the file.
If Not %1==display Goto Process2
```

```
        Echo MyFile.TXT Contains:
        Type MyFile.TXT
        Goto TheEnd

    REM Determine whether the user wants to delete the file.
    :Process2
    If Not %1==delete Goto ProcessError
        Erase MyFile.TXT
        Echo Deleted MyFile.TXT
        Goto TheEnd

    REM The user didn't define a processing action.
    :ProcessError
    Echo You didn't tell the batch file what to do!
    Echo Type UseIf Display to display the file or
    Echo UseIf Delete to delete the file.

    :TheEnd
    Echo On
```

The first line of this example demonstrates a principle that you should always use in batch files that you expect someone else will use—check for errors within the limits of the batch file to do so. In this case, the batch file expects the user to provide an input value of delete or display. When the user doesn't provide any input value, then the first input value, %1, is blank so the string Err equals Err and the code goes to a label named ProcessError. Batch files can work with up to nine input values at a time using %1 through %9 as variables. The Goto statement always tells the code to go to a label within the batch file. You define a label by preceding the label name with a colon such as :ProcessError.

The next segment of code attempts to copy a temporary file to another file. The operation results in an error that you can trap using the ErrorLevel statement when the file doesn't exit. An error level is a special number that a command line utility returns when it experiences an error. The command line utility defines the error level numbers it returns, but generally, this value is 1 for an error and 0 for success. Make sure you check the command line utility documentation for special values. When the ErrorLevel value matches the value you provide, then the If statement executes the command. In this case, because the code uses the Not clause, the reverse is true, the If statement only executes the Goto command when the error level is not 1. Notice that, in this case, the code uses the Echo command to display an error message to the user—Echo works not only for turning messages on or off, but for displaying custom messages to the user that the Echo setting doesn't hide.

Once the code performs these initial steps, it determines whether the MyFile.TXT file does exist using the Exit clause of the If statement. When the file exists, the code immediately begins processing it. Otherwise, the code displays a message prompting the user to type information for such a file. Notice the Pause command, which pauses the batch file execution until the user presses a key. The Copy command sends whatever the user types at the console (CON) to the MyFile.TXT file until it detects an end of file character, which the user creates by pressing Ctrl+Z.

NOTE   The console, in this case, is the command line prompt and not the special applications located in the Administrative Tools folder of the Control Panel. Windows uses the term *console* to mean a number of things, so it's important to understand what console means in a particular context.

Now that you know the file exists, the batch file can process it. This batch file provides two options: displaying the file and deleting it. The problem with batch files is that they use case-sensitive string comparisons—the word `delete` is different from the word `Delete` so error trapping can cause false problems. Some developers resolve this problem by using single character command line switches for batch files. That way, all you need to do is perform two checks, one for uppercase and another for lowercase. The example uses a full word for the purpose of demonstration. To see how this works, type `Delete` at the command line instead of `delete`—the code will display a failure message. When the user does type `delete`, the batch file erases the file and displays a success message. Likewise, when the user types `display`, the code sends the content of `MyFile.TXT` to the display. In both cases, the code goes to `TheEnd` where the batch file turns echo back on.

Giving the User Options Using *Choice*

The `Choice` command lets you add interactive processing to batch files. Whether you use this option depends on the kind of automation you want to add to your processing tasks. Most of the automation you create for optimization tasks won't require any kind of interactivity because you already know how you want the task performed based on experience you obtained performing the task manually. However, sometimes you do need to add some interactivity. For example, you might run the command one way on Friday and a different way the rest of the week. The `Choice` command can also help you add safeguards that ensure the user understands the ramifications of performing a certain task before they actually do it. The `Choice` command provides the following optional arguments.

Text   Provides text that the `Choice` command displays to explain the choice to the user. This is the same as combining the `Choice` and `Echo` commands, but only requires one line of code.

`/C:Keys`   Defines the single character response the user can type. The default values are Y (for yes) and N (for no). The valid input values appear within brackets. For example, when you use `/C:ABC`, the `Choice` command displays them as [A,B,C] on the command line. You can override this option using the /N switch—the keys remain, but `Choice` doesn't display them.

`/N`   Tells `Choice` not to display the valid keys at the command prompt.

`/S`   Makes the inputs case sensitive—normally `Choice` treats uppercase and lowercase letters the same. Using case-sensitive input doubles the number of letter choices, but can also create user confusion.

`/T:Character,Number of Seconds`   Provides an automatic selection feature. `Choice` automatically types the character for the user after the number of seconds elapses. The number of seconds can range from 0 to 99, where a value of 0 makes the choice automatically without pausing for user input.

When you use `Choice` by itself, it displays a simple [Y,N] prompt that doesn't accomplish much unless you also provide an `Echo` command to describe what the user should say yes or no to. Normally, you'll combine the `Choice` command with one or more arguments. Listing 11.2 shows a simple example of the `Choice` command at work.

LISTING 11.2:   Using the *Choice* Command

```
Echo Off

REM Keep repeating until the user enters E.
:Repeat

REM Display the choices.
Choice /C:DCE /N /T:E,10 Choose an option (D)isplay, (C)opy, or (E)nd.

REM Act on the user choice.
If ErrorLevel 3 Goto End
If ErrorLevel 2 Goto Copy
If ErrorLevel 1 Goto Display

REM Copy the file.
:Copy
Echo You chose to copy the file.
Goto Repeat

REM Display the file.
:Display
Echo You chose to display the file.
Goto Repeat

REM End the batch processing.
:End
Echo Goodbye
Echo On
```

The code begins by creating a repeat label so the batch file continues working until the user specifically stops it. Next, the code uses the Choice command to display the choices to the user. The /C switch tells Choice that the valid options are D, C, or E instead of the default Y or N. Because the text specifically defines the characters that the batch file expects, the batch file uses the /N switch to suppress displaying the valid key choices on the command line. The /T command line switch tells Choice to automatically choose E after 10 seconds.

Although this batch file doesn't actually do anything with a file, it shows how you'd set up the batch file to process the user choice. Notice that the batch file uses the ErrorLevel clause of the If statement to detect the user choice. The ErrorLevel clause detects every choice lower than the user selection, so you must place the values in reverse order, as shown. In addition, you must specifically set the batch file to go to another location because it will process all other statements after the current error level.

The processing code simply displays a string telling you what choice the user made. Normally, you'd add tasks that the batch file should perform based on the user's selection. Notice that the copy and display selections tell the batch file to go back to the `Repeat` label. This is the most common technique for creating a menu loop in a batch file. The batch file ends by telling the user goodbye and turning echo back on.

Executing a Command Multiple Times Using *For*

You might want to process all of a particular kind of file in a directory without knowing the precise filenames. In some cases, you can simply use a wildcard character to work with the file. For example, `Dir *.DOC` displays all files with a DOC file extension, while `Dir C*.*` displays all files beginning with the letter C regardless of file extension. You can also use `Dir *.?LL` to display all files that have a single letter before the letters "LL" in their file extension. For example, this command would display all uncompressed DLL files and compressed DLL (_LL extension) cabinet files in a directory. The asterisk (*) represents all characters of any length, while the question mark (?) represents any single character.

Unfortunately, using wildcard characters won't always work. Sometimes you need to know the name of the file. A command line utility might not support wildcard characters or the file argument doesn't easily fit within the wildcard method of description. That's where the `For` statement comes into play for batch files. This command takes the form:

```
FOR %%variable IN (set) DO command [command-parameters]
```

You can also use this command at the command prompt to process files manually. Instead of using one percent (%) symbols, you use two in front of the variable. Here's a sample of how you can use this command in a batch file.

```
Echo Off
For %%F In (*.BAT *.TXT) Do Dir %%F /B
Echo On
```

In this case, the `For` command processes all of the files that have a BAT or TXT extension in the current directory. The command processes the files in the order in which they appear in the directory and you have no guarantee what the order is. The `%%F` variable contains the name of an individual file. The `Dir` command is called once for each file with the `%%F` variable as an input. In this case, the command outputs the filenames using the bare format, so you could use this batch file to create a text file containing a list of files that match the criteria. Additional processing could archive the files or do anything else that you might like.

Using the Task Scheduler

The Task Scheduler is one of the handier utilities provided with Windows XP. It helps you create automated jobs that will run on a predefined schedule. You can schedule work for your computer and not worry about it afterward. However, because the Task Scheduler constantly uses processing cycles, you need to determine whether you want to optimize your system for performance or use the functionality that Task Scheduler provides. There isn't a right answer—just the one that matches your optimization strategy.

You can use the Task Scheduler for a number of tasks. In fact, some people end up overusing this utility in an attempt to cut down their work. The Task Scheduler works well for repetitive tasks that rely on a single application. You can combine tasks using a batch file as well (see the "Creative Uses for Batch Files" section for details). In addition, the application or batch file must perform the same steps every time you use it because the Task Scheduler can't think. In other words, the Task Scheduler is quite useful, but it can't replace the human at the other end of the monitor.

One of the best uses for Task Scheduler is machine maintenance because this task uses the same precise set of steps every time you do it. For example, you could schedule a disk defragment every morning before you start work or make it something that you do during your lunch hour. You could combine various activities in a batch file to ensure that each task succeeds before you perform the next one. For example, once a week you could use a batch file to back up your system, clean up any temporary files, and then defragment your hard drive. The idea is to automate a task that you perform manually and know is repetitive—a task that always uses the same steps and input arguments.

WARNING   Only clean up temporary files using Task Scheduler when you know your system won't need to save any of those files. For example, you might be temped to delete all LOG files on your system, but you don't know whether some of the LOG files are in use. Manually deleting the files lets you preserve any LOG files that you need, but automation brings the chance for error and deletion of something you really wanted after all.

In some cases, Task Scheduler is actually redundant and can't perform as well as the application. For example, Outlook Express will faithfully check your email every half hour (or other selectable interval) using settings on the General tab of the Options dialog box (accessible using the Tools ➤ Options command).

TIP   Task Scheduler provides two distinct interfaces. Actually, they're separate commands, but the effect is the same. The Graphical User Interface (GUI) is the easiest way to use Task Scheduler for manual entries. Use the AT command line (character mode) utility for scripts and batch files. The "Using the AT Utility" section of the chapter tells you more about the AT command line utility.

Now that you have a better idea of what Task Scheduler is like, it's time to learn how to use it. The following sections show you how to start Task Scheduler, set its options, create new tasks, manage existing tasks, and delete tasks that you no longer need.

Starting Task Scheduler

The easiest way to learn about Task Scheduler is to start the program using Start ➤ Programs ➤ Accessories ➤ System Tools ➤ Scheduled Tasks. If the program won't start, make sure you haven't disabled the Task Scheduler service located in the Services console of the Administrative Tools folder of the Control Panel. You'll see the Scheduled Tasks window shown in Figure 11.1.

The Task Scheduler includes entries for each scheduled task when you choose the View ➤ Details command. The entries include the task name, run interval, the next run time, the time the Task Scheduler last ran the task, the last result, and the task creator. Note that the Task Scheduler (using the Scheduled Tasks window) shows all of the scheduled tasks—even those of other users on the current machine.

The essential management fields are Last Time Run and Status. These fields tell you the last time the task ran successfully and the status of the task when it doesn't run correctly. The "Setting the Task Scheduler Options" section describes the methods for managing your entries in detail.

FIGURE 11.1

The Scheduled Tasks window shows a list of tasks for your machine and provides statistics about them.

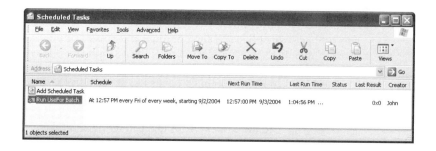

Setting the Task Scheduler Options

Once you have Task Scheduler up and running, you'll want to configure it for use or to manage tasks that you create. Although Figure 11.1 shows many menu options, the only menu you're interested in for Task Scheduler is the Advanced menu. The following list describes the menu entries.

Stop Using Task Scheduler   Select this option and Windows XP will stop the Task Scheduler service on your machine. It will also prevent the Task Scheduler service from running automatically. The menu entry will change to Start Using Task Scheduler and you'll notice that the application grays out several other options. Normally, you'll use this option only if you decide not to use Task Scheduler at all. However, you could also use it to stop Task Scheduler long enough to clean out the log file. Use the View Log option to open the log with Notepad, clear out the text, and save the file.

Pause Task Scheduler   Select this option if you want to stop the Task Scheduler temporarily. Windows XP will simply pause the Task Scheduler service. The menu entry will change to Continue Task Scheduler, so you can continue where you started. All of the other menu options remain enabled and Windows XP will automatically restart Task Scheduler the next time you boot the machine. You can use this feature if Task Scheduler wants to run a task at an inconvenient time. For example, Task Scheduler might decide to perform a disk defragment in the middle of a file download.

Notify Me of Missed Tasks   Use this option if you want Task Scheduler to remind you of missed tasks. The notice you receive lets you run the missed task. Of course, this feature can become a nuisance if you already know that you missed the task and don't want Task Scheduler to remind you.

AT Service Account   The AT command line utility can add entries to the Task Scheduler. You'll find the entries aren't the same as those created using the GUI. See the "Using the AT Utility" section of the chapter for details on how to use it. The account runs separately from the user account, a necessity if you want the AT utility to add tasks to everyone's account.

View Log   Use View Log to see the log entries for the Task Scheduler. The default is to use Notepad for viewing the log entries and this option usually works. You'll need to stop the Task Scheduler service to delete any log entries, but you can easily view them while the service is running.

As previously mentioned, the AT service account defaults to the system account. If you select the AT Service Account option, you'll see the AT Service Account Configuration dialog box. The dialog box contains two options: System Account and This Account. If you choose This Account, you'll also need to enter the name and password of the account you'd like to use. Generally, you'll never need to use this option unless you want to allow regular users access to the AT utility.

The View Log option actually opens the `SchedLgU.TXT` file found in the `\WINDOWS` folder. Figure 11.2 shows some typical log file entries. Note that this log came from a system patched with Windows XP SP2.

When you read the entries in this log, you'll find several entries for starting the `UseFor.BAT` file. In the first case, the task lacked proper permission to start the job. The second failure occurred when the job used an incorrect parameter to access the batch file. Each of these entries contains the `** ERROR **` designator at the start of the job so you can find it easily. The successful run shows two entries. The first contains the starting time, while the second contains the ending time and the exit code. An exit code of 0 indicates success.

The `[ ***** Most recent entry is above this line ***** ]` entry always tells you where the application writes the latest entry. Because Task Scheduler reuses this file, the most recent entry can appear anywhere in the file.

Some machines produce a Unicode log that looks like the one in Figure 11.3. When this problem occurs, use WordPad or another Unicode-compatible editor instead of Notepad to read the file. All patched versions of Windows XP should produce the easily readable ASCII file shown in Figure 11.2, but you might run into this problem with older versions of Windows and unpatched copies of Windows XP.

SchedLgU.Txt - Notepad

File Edit Format View Help

```
"UseFor.job" (UseFor.BAT) 9/2/2004 12:59:19 PM ** ERROR **
        The attempt to log on to the account associated with the task failed, therefore, the
task did not run.
        Verify that the task's Run-as name and password are valid and try again.
"Run UseFor Batch.job" (UseFor.BAT) 9/2/2004 1:03:08 PM ** ERROR **
        Unable to start task.
        The specific error is:
        0x80070057: The parameter is incorrect.
        Try using the Task page Browse button to locate the application.
"Run UseFor Batch.job" (UseFor.BAT) 9/2/2004 1:04:26 PM ** ERROR **
        The attempt to log on to the account associated with the task failed, therefore, the
task did not run.
        Verify that the task's Run-as name and password are valid and try again.
"Run UseFor Batch.job" (UseFor.BAT)
        Started 9/2/2004 1:04:57 PM
"Run UseFor Batch.job" (UseFor.BAT)
        Finished 9/2/2004 1:04:57 PM
        Result: The task completed with an exit code of (0).
[ ***** Most recent entry is above this line ***** ]
```

FIGURE 11.2
Typical log entries include the starting of various tasks and their status.

SchedLgU.Txt - Notepad

File Edit Search Help

```
ÿþ" I d l e T a s k "   ( T a s k I d 5 ) □ □    S t a r t e d   8 / 2 7 / 2 0 0 1   6 : 3 9 : 1
1   P M □ □ " I d l e T a s k "   ( T a s k I d 5 ) □ □        F i n i s h e d   8 / 2 7 / 2 0
0 1   6 : 3 9 : 1 3   P M □ □   R e s u l t :   T h e   t a s k   c o m p l e t e d   w i t h
a n   e x i t   c o d e   o f   ( 0 ) . □ □ " I d l e T a s k "   ( T a s k I d 1 ) □ □
S t a r t e d   8 / 2 7 / 2 0 0 1   6 : 5 0 : 2 2   P M □ □ " I d l e T a s k "   ( T a s k I d
1 ) □ □      F i n i s h e d   8 / 2 7 / 2 0 0 1   6 : 5 0 : 4 0   P M □ □   R e s u l t :
T h e   t a s k   c o m p l e t e d   w i t h   a n   e x i t   c o d e   o f   ( 0 ) . □ □ " T
a s k   S c h e d u l e r   S e r v i c e " □ □      E x i t e d   a t   8 / 2 7 / 2 0 0 1
8 : 0 8 : 2 6   P M □ □ " T a s k   S c h e d u l e r   S e r v i c e " □ □     S t a r t e d
a t   8 / 2 8 / 2 0 0 1   6 : 5 9 : 2 4   A M □ □ " T a s k   S c h e d u l e r   S e r v i c e
```

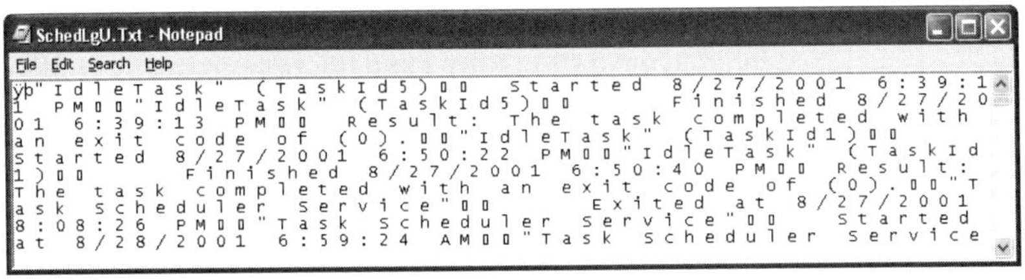

FIGURE 11.3
On some systems, you can see this messy Unicode log display.

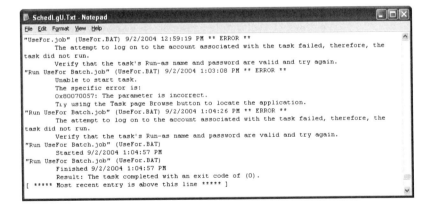

TIP   You can fix the View Log problem with Task Scheduler using a simple registry change. Locate the HKEY_LOCAL_MACHINE\SOFTWARE\Microsoft\SchedulingAgent key. This key contains a LogPath value that you can change to another extension. Instead of using SCHEDLGU.TXT, try using SCHEDLGU.DOC. You'll find that the View Log option now works as intended. If you have Word installed on your system, you'll even find this fix negates the need to shut down the service. Word will simply tell you that the file is in use by someone else and will ask if you want to make a copy. Click Yes and you'll see the existing log on screen. Because you won't make any changes to the log, this method of access is completely safe and won't interfere with normal Task Scheduler operation. Note that the key also contains values that enable you to change the default log size, the number of minutes before the Task Scheduler goes into idle mode, and the location of the tasks folder.

Creating Tasks

One of the first tasks you need to perform with Task Scheduler is creating some tasks to perform. Creating the task is easy. Right-click the Scheduled Tasks window, and then choose the New ➢ Scheduled Task option from the context menu. Type a name for your task, and you're ready to go, except, you haven't configured anything.

If you want to create a new task the easy way, double-click the Add Scheduled Task icon in the Scheduled Tasks window. You'll see the Welcome screen for the Scheduled Task Wizard. The following steps show you how to use the wizard.

1. Click Next. You'll see a list of applications on your machine. In some cases, the applications will also include version numbers so you can choose a particular version.

NOTE   The interesting thing about the application list is that it contains only the registered applications on your machine, which leaves out many obvious application choices. If you have a script, an older Windows application, or even an old DOS application you want to run, you'll need to click Browse to find it. The list also contains some choices you'll want to ignore. For example, no one would want to schedule Minesweeper to run at a given time (except as a means to remind yourself to take a break). Finally, some obvious choices are missing. For example, if you are running Windows XP and want to defragment your disk, you'll need to locate the DFRG.MSC file in the \WINDOWS\SYSTEM32 folder.

2. Highlight the application you want to run, then click Next. You could also click Browse, then use the Select Program to Schedule dialog box to choose an application. Remember that applications include batch files and scripts, so you can perform a number of tasks with a single selection. In all cases, the Scheduled Task Wizard will display a dialog box that asks for a task name and scheduling time. You can choose intervals that include daily, weekly, monthly, one-time only, when your computer starts, or when you log onto the system.

3. Type a name for the task and select a task interval. Click Next. You'll see the Start Time dialog box. The content of this dialog box varies according to the schedule you select. Figure 11.4 shows a typical example of a weekly interval. In most cases, you'll need to select a time to run the application. However, the other start time information will vary. For example, you might have to provide a list of months in which to run the application or the day of the week. Some options, such as When I Log On, don't ask for a starting time. In this case, you'll skip to step 5.

4. Select the start time information for your application. The Scheduled Task Wizard will ask for your name and password.

5. Type your name and password. When working on a single machine, all you need is your name—networked machines will require the domain name, followed by a backslash (\) and your name (as an example, MyDomain\George). Click Next. You'll see a completion dialog box. Notice the option for opening the Advanced Properties dialog box. The Advanced Properties dialog box helps you further refine your task options. In most cases, you won't need to do anything more at this point.

6. Determine whether you need to modify any advanced properties (we'll see what they are in "Modifying Tasks" section). Click Finish. The Scheduled Task Wizard will create your task.

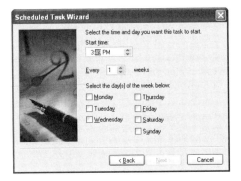

FIGURE 11.4
Select a start time for your application based on the interval you chose.

Modifying Tasks

What happens if you change your mind about a scheduled task or want to refine the schedule you create for it? That's where modifying the task comes into play. Double-click the task and you'll see a task properties dialog box.

The General tab of the task properties dialog box contains application specifics. You'll note that the Scheduled Task Wizard didn't allow you to add any command line parameters. This is where you add the parameters. Just type them into the Run field along with the application path. This dialog box also contains fields for changing the starting directory, adding some comments, and changing the username and password. Notice the Enabled option at the bottom of the dialog box. Clear this option if you want to disable the task, but want to retain the task for future use.

The Schedule tab shown in Figure 11.5 determines when the application will run. The figure doesn't show the default state of the dialog box. Notice the Show Multiple Schedules option at the bottom of the dialog box. Check this option if you want to run the application on more than one scheduled time. For example, you might want to run it once a week and once a month at given times. To add a new scheduled run time, click New. You can remove scheduled run times by selecting the entry and clicking Delete.

Figure 11.5 shows the setup for a weekly task. However, you can change the interval using entries in the Schedule Task field. In addition to the normal entries provided by the Scheduled Task Wizard, this list also includes a When Idle option. The When Idle option is a great choice for tasks that you can perform a little at a time when the user isn't doing anything else with the system. For example, the user might be reading a Web page. You set the time interval that Windows will wait before it begins the task. As soon as the user starts a new activity, the task will pause and wait for another idle period.

You'll find some differences on the Schedule tab when compared to the Scheduled Task Wizard. For example, the Schedule tab hides more items. In Figure 11.5, you'd need to click Select Months to change the month in which the application will run. You'll also see an Advanced button that displays the Advanced Schedule Options dialog box. Fields in this dialog box select the start date and end date. The Advanced Options dialog box also includes an option to repeat the task over a given interval.

Figure 11.6 shows the Settings tab. The options on this tab control task execution, rather than the application. Notice that you can set the task to delete itself automatically if you haven't scheduled it to run again. This keeps your Scheduled Tasks window from filling with old information.

This tab also contains an idle time setting. However, this time the setting affects the task, not the application. Once the application begins running, it will continue to run until it runs out of time or it completes its task. Use this option to ensure the machine isn't in a high state of activity when you start the application.

FIGURE 11.5
Task Scheduler offers
to run an application
on as many schedules
as required to meet
specific needs.

FIGURE 11.6
Use the Settings tab
to change the way the
task runs.

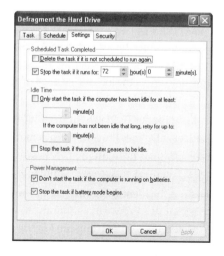

Finally, this tab contains power management options. You'll use these options with laptop machines. For example, you wouldn't want to defragment the disk while the laptop is on battery power because excessive disk use drains the battery quickly. Task Scheduler will simply wait until you connect the laptop to AC power to start the task.

Deleting and Renaming Tasks

You rename and delete tasks much the same as you do anything in Explorer. Right-click the task you want to delete or rename, then select the appropriate option on the context menu. Deleted tasks remain in the Recycle Bin until you empty it. Unlike Windows Explorer, using Shift+Delete doesn't remove the task permanently; it still ends up in the Recycle Bin.

Using the AT Utility

The AT command line utility lets you schedule tasks without using the Scheduled Tasks folder. This program is actually a leftover from early Windows NT implementations, but it serves a very useful purpose. You can use the AT utility to create tasks with scripts, rather than manually entering them using the Scheduled Tasks folder. This feature saves time when you have to configure a number of machines with the same scheduled tasks. The AT utility uses the following command line options.

```
AT [\\Computer] [[<Id>] [/DELETE] | /DELETE [/YES]]
AT [\\Computer] <Time> [/INTERACTIVE] [/EVERY:<Dates> | /NEXT:<Dates>] <Command>
```

The first form removes tasks, while the second adds them. Here's a list of arguments that the AT utility accepts.

/DELETE   Remove a job from the list. If you omit the Id parameter, AT will remove all jobs that it created from the list. This command doesn't affect other jobs created using the Scheduled Tasks folder. However, AT requests confirmation for each deleted job unless you specify the /YES switch.

/EVERY:*Dates*   Runs the job during the specified day of the week or month. Adding more than one entry will run the job on multiple days of the week or month. If you omit the date parameter, AT assumes you want to run the job monthly during the current day of the month.

/INTERACTIVE   Determines whether the user can interact with the job (and vice versa). The default setting runs the job in the background without any interaction.

/NEXT:*Dates*   Runs the job during the next occurrence of the day of the week or month. Adding multiple dates runs the job during each of the specified dates. If you omit the date parameter, AT assumes you want to run the job during the current day.

/YES   Prevents AT from asking whether it should delete each job in the list.

Computer   Defines the name of a remote computer used to run the AT utility.

Command   Defines the path of the command you want to run, including any command line switches. You must enclose the command in double quotes.

Id   Defines the identifying number of the job. The AT command begins at 1 and moves up from there.

Time   Determines the starting time of the job.

Listing Jobs Using AT

The AT utility only lists jobs that you create with it. Any jobs you create in the Scheduled Tasks folder will remain hidden. For this reason, you'll probably want to choose one method for adding tasks to your system, even though it might be inconvenient to do so. When you do decide to use both techniques to create new jobs, use the Scheduled Tasks folder to view them because it will show you both kinds of jobs. To list the jobs created using the AT utility, type **AT** at the command prompt and press Enter. Figure 11.7 shows typical output for this command.

The output is simple but useful. The Status column won't contain any information until the job runs the first time. The ID column contains the job ID—you must know this value to delete the job. The remaining columns tell you how often the job runs, what time the system runs it, and the location and name of the application.

FIGURE 11.7

The AT utility lists only the jobs you created using it, not the Scheduled Tasks folder.

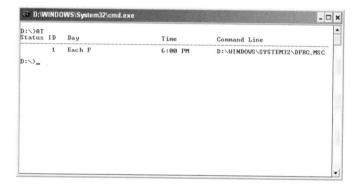

Creating a Job with AT

Creating a job with AT is relatively easy. The "Creating Tasks" section of the chapter shows how to create a defragmenter job that runs at 6~PM every Friday. You can create a similar job using the following command line.

```
AT 6pm /Every:Friday "D:\WINDOWS\SYSTEM32\DFRG.MSC"
```

You don't obtain the same level of configuration features using AT that you would using the Scheduled Tasks folder. Many of the special configuration features discussed in the "Modifying Tasks" section are unavailable. If you modify an AT task using the Scheduled Tasks window, AT won't track it any longer. The second you apply the changes AT removes the task from its list and the job becomes part of the Scheduled Tasks folder instead.

Deleting a Job with AT

Eventually, you'll want to delete a job with AT. Note that you can't modify AT jobs—you can only create and delete them. Consequently, when you want to modify an AT job, you delete the old job and create a new one with the modified settings. To delete a job, you must know its ID. When you use the /Delete command line switch without the ID, AT removes all of the jobs from the list. Fortunately, AT warns you about the consequences of your action.

To remove the job from the list, use AT, followed by the ID and the /Delete switch. The command line won't work if you place the /Delete switch first. For example, to remove the first job from the list, type **AT 1 /Delete** and press Enter. The AT utility doesn't provide any warning when removing a single job. In fact, it won't look like it has done anything at all, but you can verify that the job is removed by typing **AT** and pressing Enter.

Combining the AT Utility with Task Scheduler

The Scheduled Tasks folder tracks jobs created using both the Scheduled Tasks folder and the AT utility. AT only tracks jobs that it creates. If you type AT at the command prompt and press Enter, all you'll see are the AT jobs. Figure 11.8 shows a typical example of the same defragmenter job created using the GUI and AT. Notice that the AT job name has At plus the number of the job.

As you can see, from a Scheduled Tasks folder perspective, both jobs are the same. The only two differences are the job name and the creator name. Unless you change the default setting, the system creates all AT jobs. Any job created using the Scheduled Tasks folder will appear under the user's name.

FIGURE 11.8

AT jobs appear in the Scheduled Tasks window as "At" jobs.

Relying on Scripts

Scripts let you automate tasks with greater ease than using batch files. They represent a middle ground between using a full-fledged programming language and working with batch files from an ease of use and flexibility perspective. You can start scripts from a variety of places. Scripts permeate every part of Windows XP. For example, you'll find scripts in your browser and most likely your word processor as well. A script can make the difference between an application that works well and one that only performs simple tasks.

Scripts use a special application called the Windows Script Host (WSH) to run. WSH is an interpreter, something that reads human words and converts them into machine language the computer can understand. WSH is extremely flexible. It can run a number of languages if you install the required support. Windows XP comes with support for both JavaScript (JS files) and Visual Basic Script (VBS) built in. The VBS files usually have a Visual Basic Editor (VBE) extension in Windows XP.

NOTE You'll see several different names for JavaScript. The most popular alternative name right now is JScript. It also appears under the name of ECMAScript (http://www.ecma-international. org/publications/standards/Ecma-262.htm) because this organization is producing a standardized form of the language. The big thing is not to confuse JavaScript with Java. The two are completely different. You'll find JScript in Windows XP, but Java support has gone by the wayside due to Microsoft's legal loss to Sun. For the purposes of clarity, I'll always use JavaScript in the book.

Using CScript and WScript

Windows XP supports two methods of starting scripts. The CScript application works at the command prompt, while the WScript application works from within the graphical user environment. Both applications accomplish the same task—they provide a means for interpreting a script file you create.

```
CScript <Script Name> [<WSH Command Line Switches>] [<Script Arguments>]
WScript <Script Name> [<WSH Command Line Switches>] [<Script Arguments>]
```

CScript and WScript use the same command line. You must provide a script name as the first command line argument. Most scripts have a VBE or JS file extension, but any extension is acceptable. For example, you can still use VBS files with WSH, but the icon won't look right, in some cases, and you can't double-click it to start the execution with any version of Windows XP. The VBS extension is the right choice for older versions of Windows. The icon is yellow for VBE files and blue for JS files.

WSH provides a wealth of command line switches that you can use to modify its behavior. The following list describes the command line switches that WSH provides.

//? Displays the currently documented command line switches. The newest versions of WSH tend to reject older switches, even those of the undocumented variety.

//B Use this mode when you don't want the user to interact with the script. Batch mode suppresses all non–command line console user interface requests from the script. It also suppresses error message display (a change from previous versions).

//D Activates debugging mode so you can fix errors in a script.

//H:CScript Makes CSCRIPT.EXE the default application for running scripts. (WScript is the default engine.)

//H:WScript Makes WSCRIPT.EXE the default application for running scripts.

//I Allows full interaction with the user. Any pop-up dialog boxes will wait for user input before the script continues.

//Job:Job Name Executes a WSH job. A WSH job has a Windows Script File (WSF) extension. This file enables you to perform tasks using multiple scripting engines and multiple files. Essentially, this allows you to perform a "super batch" process. Creating WSF files is an advanced technique not discussed in this book because it isn't very useful in most cases. You can learn more about this topic at http://msdn.microsoft.com/library/en-us/script56/html/ wsAdvantagesOfWs.asp.

//Logo **and** //NoLogo   WSH normally prints out a logo message. You'd use the //NoLogo switch to prevent WSH from displaying this message.

//S   This command line switch allows you to save current command line options for a user. WSH will save the following options: //B, //I, //Logo, //Nologo, and //T:n.

//T:*Time Limit*   Limits the maximum time the script can run to the number of seconds specified. Normally, there isn't any timeout value. You'd use this switch in situations where a script might end up in a continuous loop or is unable to get the requested information for other reasons. For example, you might use this switch when requesting information on a network drive.

//X   Starts the script in the debugger. This allows you to trace the execution of the script from beginning to end.

//U   Outputs any console information using Unicode instead of pure ASCII. You use this switch on systems where you need to support languages other than English. This is a CScript-only option.

Notice that all of these command line switches start with two slashes like (//) to differentiate them from switches you may need for your script. WSH passes script arguments to your script for processing. Script arguments can be anything including command line switches of your own or values needed to calculate a result.

NOTE   Users of older versions of CScript and WScript may remember the //C and the //W switches used to switch the default scripting engines. Newer versions of CScript and WScript replace these switches with the //H switch. You'll also find the //R (reregister) and //Entrypoint switches missing from WSH because script developers no longer need the functionality. Always use the correct command line switches for the version of Windows and WSH installed on your machine.

You can work with WSH in either interactive or batch mode. Use batch mode when you need to perform tasks that don't require user input. For example, you might want to run Scan Disk every evening, but use different command line switches for it based on the day. You could use Task Scheduler to accomplish this task, but using it in conjunction with a WSH script will improve the flexibility you get when running the task.

Another kind of batch processing might be to send log files to your supervisor or perhaps set up a specific set of environment variables for a character-mode application based on the current user. On the other hand, interactive mode requires use user interaction. You'd use it for tasks such as cleaning the hard drive because you don't always know whether the user needs a particular file. Such a script could ask the user a set of general questions, and then clean excess files from the hard drive based on the user input. The cleaning process would follow company guidelines and save the user time.

TIP   Because batch processing doesn't require any form of user input, it's usually a good idea to include the //T switch with the //B switch. This combination stops the script automatically if it runs too long. In most cases, using this switch setup stops an errant script before it corrupts the Windows environment or freezes the machine. However, you can't time some tasks with ease. For example, any Web-based task is difficult to time because you can't account for problems with a slow connection. In this case, you'll need to refrain from using the //T switch or provide a worst-case scenario time interval.

The next set of command line switches to consider is //Logo and //NoLogo. There isn't any right or wrong time to use these switches, but you usually use the //Logo switch when testing a script and the //NoLogo switch afterward. The reason is simple. During the testing process, you want to know about every potential source of problems in your script environment, including an old script engine that might cause problems. On the other hand, you don't want to clutter your screen with useless text after you debug the script. Using the //NoLogo switch keeps screen clutter to a minimum.

Configuring the Host and Property Page Options

You don't have to rely exclusively on command line switches to configure WSH; you can configure two WSH options from the Windows Script Host Settings dialog box shown in Figure 11.9. Run WScript by itself and you'll see the Windows Script Host Settings dialog box.

The Stop Script After Specified Number of Seconds check box tells WSH to stop executing a script after a certain time interval has elapsed. The edit box below it contains the number of seconds to wait. Setting this option is like adding the //T command line switch to every script that you run.

The Display Logo When Script Executed in Command Console check box determines whether WSH displays WSH logo when running scripts from the DOS prompt. Normally, Windows checks this option, which is the same as adding the //Logo command line switch to every script that you run. Clearing this option tells WSH that you don't want to display the logo, which is that same as using the //NoLogo command line switch.

You can also display the Windows Script Host Settings dialog box for individual scripts. Simply right-click the script file and select Properties from the context menu. Select the Script tab to see the options. These settings only affect the individual script file; the options for WSH in general remain the same.

FIGURE 11.9
Configure WSH to meet specific needs.

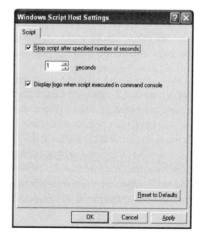

Accessing Common Windows Objects

A section of a chapter can't provide you with a complete tutorial on scripting. Some developers require months to learn everything there is to know about the scripting language and the objects the language controls. This section helps you understand the various objects that WSH supports. You won't become a guru overnight, but you could create some simple scripts. As you learn more, you'll be able to create scripts of increasing complexity. Scripting isn't hard to learn, but you need to take your time and learn it a bit at a time.

TIP Windows XP doesn't include any sample scripts. However, earlier versions of Windows do include a samples directory for scripts that you can use to learn more about the scripting process. You can still download the script samples from Microsoft's site at http://msdn.microsoft.com/ scripting/.

WSH depends on objects that Microsoft supplies as part of Windows to perform tasks such as outputting text to the display. This chapter demonstrates the latest version of WSH. Every version of Windows has similar objects, but you might not find some objects in older versions of Windows.

NOTE An object consists of three elements: properties, methods, and events. A property describes the object and determines its functionality. For example, you can say an apple is red. In this case, red is a property of the apple. However, you can also paint the apple blue. In this case, you changed the color property of the apple to another value. Methods are actions you can perform with an object. For example, looking at an apple again, you can say that it has a grow method. As the tree applies the grow method, the apple becomes larger. Events are responses to specific object actions. For example, when the apple becomes mature, it raises the "color" event to tell you that it's ripe.

Writing scripts in Windows XP means knowing the object you want to work with, the properties that object provides, and the methods you can use with that object. You don't have to know about every object. In fact, you'll find it easier to learn about one object at a time. The following sections will tell you about the main scripting object, WScript, and some of the supporting objects it contains. These sections also provide some scripting examples in both VBScript and JavaScript.

TIP The combination of WSH and a scripting engine form an interpreter that accepts a script file as input and outputs application data from the computer. Of course, WSH and its associated scripting engines are more complex than any previous interpreter. You can read about Microsoft's original vision for WSH at http://www.microsoft.com/mind/0698/cutting0698.htm. The Internet includes many useful WSH resource sites. Of the more interesting sites is the Scripting Guide for Windows site at http://www.winguides.com/scripting/. You can find books about WSH at http://ourworld.compuserve.com/homepages/Guenter_Born/WSHBazaar/USBook.htm. You'll find quite a few other resource sites throughout the sections. Make sure you check them out to get the most out of the material presented in this chapter.

USING THE WSCRIPT OBJECT

The WScript object is the main object for WSH. You'll access every other object through this one. The following list tells you about the properties that the WScript object supports.

Application   Provides you with access to a low-level interface for WScript. An interface is a pointer to a list of functions that you can call for a particular object. Only advanced programmers will need this property because WSH exposes all of the basic functions for you.

Arguments   Provides a complete list of the arguments for this script. Applications pass arguments on the command line. WSH passes the argument list as an array. You create a variable to hold the argument list, and then access the individual arguments as you would any array. The Arguments.Count property contains the total number of array elements.

FullName   Contains the full name of the scripting engine along with the fully qualified path to it. For example, if you were using CScript, you might get `C:\WINDOWS\SYSTEM32\CSCRIPT.EXE` as a return value.

Interactive   Returns true if the script is in interactive mode.

Name   Returns the friendly name for WScript. In most cases, this is Windows Script Host.

Path   Provides just the path information for the host executable. For example, if you were using CScript, you may get a return value of: `C:\WINDOWS\SYSTEM32\`.

ScriptFullName   Contains the full name and path of the script that's running.

ScriptName   Provides just the script name.

Version   Returns the WSH Version number.

Remember that all of these properties tell you about the WScript object. You can also use methods to perform tasks with the WScript object. The following list provides a brief overview of the more important methods you'll use with the WScript object. Note that most of these methods require you pass one or more parameters as input. A parameter is a piece of data the method uses to perform a task.

CreateObject(strProgID)   Create the object specified by `strProgID`. This object could be WSH specific like "WScript.Network" or application specific like "Excel.Application."

GetObject(strPathname [, strProgID])   Retrieves the requested object. `strPathname` contains the filename for the object you want to retrieve. In most cases, this is going to be a data file, but you can retrieve other kinds of objects as well. As soon as you execute this command, WSH will start the application associated with that object. For example, if you specified `C:\MyText.TXT` as the `strPathname`, then WSH may open Notepad to display it. The optional `strProgID` argument allows you to override the default processing of the object. For example, you may want to open the text file with Word instead of Notepad.

Echo(AnyArg)   Displays text in a window (WScript) or to the console screen (CScript). AnyArg can contain any type of valid output value. This can include both strings and numbers. Using Echo without any arguments displays a blank line.

GetScriptEngine(strEngineID**)** Registers an alternative script engine such as PerlScript (see the Perl and WSH Web site at http://pages.infinit.net/che/perlwsh/perlwsh0.html or the Windows Script Host Resources site at http://labmice.techtarget.com/scripting/WSH.htm for details on this alternative). strEngineID contains the identifier for the script engine that you want to retrieve. You'll need to register the engine using the GetScriptEngine.Register() method before you can actually use it. A script engine also requires you to provide a default extension.

Quit(intErrorCode**)** Exits the script prematurely. The optional intErrorCode argument returns an error code if necessary. You can test for this value using the ErrorLevel clause in batch files (see the "Creative Uses for Batch Files" section of the chapter for details).

USING THE WSCRIPT.WSHARGUMENTS OBJECT

Whenever you start a script, you have the option of passing one or more arguments to it on the command line. That's where the WshArguments object comes into play. It helps you determine the number of arguments, and then retrieve them as needed. You'll always use the WScript.Arguments property to access this object; it's not directly accessible. The following list describes the properties for this object.

Item(intIndex**)** Retrieves a specific command line argument. intIndex contains the index of the argument that you want to retrieve. The array used to hold the arguments is 0 based, so the first argument number is 0.

Count() Returns the number of command line arguments.

Length() Returns the number of command line arguments. WSH provides this property for JScript compatibility purposes.

USING THE WSCRIPT.WSHSHELL OBJECT

You'll use the WScript.WshShell object to access the Windows shell (the part of Windows that interacts with applications and creates the user interface) in a variety of ways. For example, you can use this object to read the registry or to create a new shortcut on the desktop. This is an exposed WSH object, which means you can access it directly. However, you need to access it through the WScript object like this: WScript.WshShell. The following list describes the WshShell methods.

CreateShortcut(strPathname**)** Creates a WSH shortcut object. strPathname contains the location of the shortcut, which will be the Desktop in most cases.

DeleteEnvironmentVariable(strName [, strType]**)** Deletes the environment variable specified by strName. The optional strType argument defines the type of environment variable to delete. Typical values for strType include System, User, Volatile, and Process. The default environment variable type is System.

GetEnvironmentVariable(strName [, strType]**)** Retrieves the environment variable specified by strName. Default environment variables include NUMBER_OF_PROCESSORS, OS, COMSPEC, HOMEDRIVE, HOMEPATH, PATH, PATHEXT, PROMPT, SYSTEMDRIVE, SYSTEMROOT, WINDIR, TEMP, and TMP. The optional strType argument defines the type of environment variable to delete. Typical values for strType include System, User, Volatile, and Process. The default environment variable type is System.

Popup(strText [,intSeconds] [,strTitle] [,intType]**)** Displays a message dialog box. The return value is an integer defining which button the user selected including the following values: OK (1), Cancel (2), Abort (3), Retry (4), Ignore (5), Yes (6), No (7), Close (8), and Help (9). strText contains the text that you want to display in the dialog box. intSeconds determines how long WSH displays the dialog box before it closes the dialog box and returns a value of –1. strTitle contains the title bar text. The intType argument can contain values that determine the type of dialog box you'll create. The first intType argument determines button type. You have a choice of OK (0), OK and Cancel (1), Abort, Retry, and Ignore (2), Yes, No, and Cancel (3), Yes and No (4), and Retry and Cancel (5). The second intType argument determines which icon Windows displays in the dialog box. You have a choice of the following values: Stop (16), Question (32), Exclamation (48), and Information (64). Combine the intType argument values to obtain different dialog box effects.

RegDelete(strName**)** Removes the value or key specified by strName from the registry. If strName ends in a backslash, then RegDelete removes a key. You must provide a fully qualified path to the key or value that you want to delete. In addition, strName must begin with one of these values: HKEY_CURRENT_USER, HKEY_LOCAL_MACHINE, HKEY_CLASSES_ROOT, KEY_USER, HKEY_CURRENT_CONFIG, or HKEY_DYN_DATA.

RegRead(strName**)** Reads the value or key specified by strName from the registry. If strName ends in a backslash, then RegDelete reads a key. You must provide a fully qualified path to the key or value that you want to read. In addition, strName must begin with one of these values: HKEY_CURRENT_USER, HKEY_LOCAL_MACHINE, HKEY_CLASSES_ROOT, KEY_USER, HKEY_CURRENT_CONFIG, or HKEY_DYN_DATA. RegRead can only read specific data types including REG_SZ, REG_EXPAND_SZ, REG_DWORD, REG_BINARY, and REG_MULTI_SZ. Any other data types will return an error.

RegWrite(strName, anyValue [, strType]**)** Writes the data specified by anyValue to a value or key specified by strName to the registry. If strName ends in a backslash, then RegDelete writes a key. You must provide a fully qualified path to the key or value that you want to write. In addition, strName must begin with one of these values: HKEY_CURRENT_USER, HKEY_LOCAL_MACHINE, HKEY_CLASSES_ROOT, KEY_USER, HKEY_CURRENT_CONFIG, or HKEY_DYN_DATA. RegRead can only write specific data types including REG_SZ, REG_EXPAND_SZ, REG_DWORD, and REG_BINARY. Any other data types will return an error.

Run(strCommand [, intWinType] [lWait]**)** Runs the command or application specified by strCommand. You can include command line arguments and switches with the command string. intWinType determines the type of window that the application starts in. You can force the script to wait for the application to complete by setting lWait to True; otherwise, the script begins the next line of execution immediately.

SetEnvironmentVariable(strName, strValue [, strType]**)** Sets the environment variable named strName to the value specified by strValue. The optional strType argument defines the type of environment variable to delete. Typical values for strType include System, User, Volatile, and Process. The default environment variable type is System.

USING THE WSCRIPT.WSHNETWORK OBJECT

The WshNetwork object works with network objects such as drives and printers that the client machine can access. This is an exposed WSH object, which means you can access it directly using the WScript.WshNetwork object. The following list describes properties associated with this object.

ComputerName   Returns a string containing the client computer name.

UserDomain   Returns a string containing the user's domain name.

UserName   Returns a string containing the name that the user used to log on to the network.

As with any other WSH object, the WshNetwork object uses methods to work with network resources. The following list describes the methods associated with this object.

AddPrinterConnection(strLocal, strRemote [, lUpdate] [, strUser] [, strPassword]**)**   Creates a new printer connection for the local machine. strLocal contains the local name for the printer specified by strRemote. The strRemote value must contain a locatable resource and usually uses a UNC format such as \\Remote\Printer. Setting lUpdate to true adds the new connection to the user profile, which means Windows will make the connection available each time the user boots their machine. strUser and strPassword contain optional username and password values required to log onto the remote machine and create the connection.

EnumNetworkDrives()   Returns a WshCollection object containing the list of local and remote drives currently mapped from the client machine. A WshCollection object is essentially a 0-based array of strings.

EnumPrinterConnections()   Returns a WshCollection object containing the list of local and remote printers currently mapped from the client machine. A WshCollection object is essentially a 0-based array of strings.

MapNetworkDrive(strLocal, strRemote [, lUpdate] [, strUser] [, strPassword]**)**   Creates a new drive connection for the local machine. strLocal contains the local name for the drive specified by strRemote. The strRemote value must contain a locatable resource and usually uses a UNC format such as \\Remote\Drive_C. Setting lUpdate to true adds the new connection to the user profile, which means Windows will make the connection available each time the user boots their machine. strUser and strPassword contain optional username and password values required to log onto the remote machine and create the connection.

RemoveNetworkDrive(strName [, lForce] [, lUpdate]**)**   Deletes a previous network drive mapping. If strName contains a local name, Windows only cancels that connection. If strName contains a remote name, then Windows cancels all resources associated with that remote name. Set lForce to True if you want to disconnect from a resource whether that resource is in use or not. Setting lUpdate to true will remove the connection from the user profile so that it doesn't appear the next time that the user logs onto the machine.

RemovePrinterConnection(strName [, lForce] [, lUpdate]**)**   Deletes a previous network printer connection. If strName contains a local name, Windows only cancels that connection. If strName contains a remote name, then Windows cancels all resources associated with that remote name. Set lForce to True if you want to disconnect from a resource whether that resource is in use or not. Setting lUpdate to true will remove the connection from the user profile so that it doesn't appear the next time that the user logs onto the machine.

Using Custom Scripts for Common Tasks

This section shows how to create basic scripts in both VBScript and JavaScript so you can see the differences between the two languages. You'll also see how to use some of the objects described in the "Relying on Scripts" section of the chapter. The following code shows a basic example in VBScript.

```
' Test1.VBS shows how to use functions and subprocedures
' within a WSH script.

WScript.Echo("The value returned was: " + CStr(MyFunction(1)))

function MyFunction(nSomeValue)
    WScript.Echo("Function received value of: " + CStr(nSomeValue))
    Call MySubprocedure(nSomeValue + 1)
    MyFunction = nSomeValue + 1
end function

sub MySubprocedure(nSomeValue)
    WScript.Echo("Subprocedure received value of: " + CStr(nSomeValue))
end sub
```

As you can see, the sample code uses the WScript object to send some information to the screen. I thought it important to introduce you to the idea of functions and subs, the two building blocks of VBScript. The following code shows a similar example for JavaScript.

```
// Test1.JS shows how to use functions within a WSH script.

WScript.Echo("The value returned was: " + MyFunction(1));

function MyFunction(nSomeValue)
{
    WScript.Echo("The value received was: " + nSomeValue);
    return nSomeValue + 1;
}
```

JavaScript only provides functions, so that's all this example demonstrates. It's also important to notice that VBScript requires you to convert numeric values to a string, while JavaScript performs the conversion automatically. The following sections show how to perform certain tasks using scripting.

Scripting the Command Line and System Environment

Many of your scripts will require access to the command line. The command line is where you type switches to modify the behavior of the script, as many of the utilities described in this book do. The system environment contains user, application, and operating system values, such as the user's name or the version of the operating system. The JavaScript code in Listing 11.3 retrieves information from the command line. It also retrieves information about the application environment.

LISTING 11.3: Working with the Command Line and System Environment

```
// ProgInfo.JS determines the specifics about your program and then
// displays this information on screen.

// Create some constants for display purposes (buttons and icons).
var intOK = 0;
var intOKCancel = 1;
var intAbortRetryIgnore = 2;
var intYesNoCancel = 3;
var intYesNo = 4;
var intRetryCancel = 5;
var intStop = 16;
var intQuestion = 32;
var intExclamation = 48;
var intInformation = 64;

// Create some popup return values.
var intOK = 1;
var intCancel = 2;
var intAbort = 3;
var intRetry = 4;
var intIgnore = 5;
var intYes = 6;
var intNo = 7;
var intClose = 8;
var intHelp = 9;

// Create a popup display object.
var WshShell = WScript.CreateObject("WScript.Shell");

// Create a variable for holding a popup return value.
var intReturn;

// Get the program information and display it.
WshShell.Popup("Full Name:\t" + WScript.Fullname +
        "\r\nInteractive:\t" + WScript.Interactive +
        "\r\nName:\t\t" + WScript.Name +
        "\r\nPath:\t\t" + WScript.Path +
        "\r\nScript Full Name:\t" + WScript.ScriptFullName +
        "\r\nScript Name:\t" + WScript.ScriptName +
        "\r\nVersion:\t\t" + WScript.Version,
        0,
        "Program Information Demonstration",
        intOK + intInformation);

// Ask if the user wants to display the argument list.
```

```
intReturn = WshShell.Popup("Do you want to display the argument list?",
        0,
        "Argument List Display",
        intYesNo + intQuestion);

// Determine if the user wants to display the argument list and
// display and appropriate message.
if (intReturn == intYes)

    // See if there are any arguments to display.
    DisplayArguments();
else
    WScript.Echo("Goodbye");

function DisplayArguments()
{

    // Create some variables.
    var strArguments = "Arguments:\r\n\t";    // Argument list.
    var intCount = 0;              // Loop counter.

    // See if there are any arguments, if not, display an
    // appropriate message.
    if (WScript.Arguments.Length == 0)
        WshShell.Popup("There are no arguments to display.",
            0,
            "Argument List Display",
            intOK + intInformation);

    // If there are arguments to display, then create a list
    // first and display them all at once.
    else
    {
        for (intCount = 0;
            intCount < WScript.Arguments.Length;
            intCount++)

            strArguments = strArguments +
                        WScript.Arguments.Item(intCount) + "\r\n\t";

        WshShell.Popup(strArguments,
                0,
                "Argument List Display",
                intOK + intInformation);
    }
}
```

When you run this script, you'll see a dialog box containing all of the information about the script engine. When you click OK, the program will ask if you want to display the command line arguments. If you say yes, then you'll see anything you typed at the command line. Otherwise, the script displays a Goodbye message.

You should notice a few things about this example. First, I create an object in this code. You need access to the WshShell object for many of the tasks you'll perform with scripts. The code also shows how to use the Popup() method to obtain information from the user. Finally, the code uses the Arguments object to access the command line information. Notice the object hierarchy used in this example.

Scripting the Registry

The example in Listing 11.4 shows how to use VBScript to access information in the registry. You don't want to change information unless you have to, but seeing what's available in the registry is a good way to build your knowledge of both scripting and the registry. Note that this example uses the command line argument to determine which file extension to look for in the registry. The example will use the TXT file extension when you don't supply one.

LISTING 11.4:   Working with the Registry

```
' RegRead.VBE will display the application extension information
' contained in the registry.

' Create an icon and button variable for Popup().
intOK = 0
intInformation = 64

' Create a popup display object.
set WshShell = WScript.CreateObject("WScript.Shell")

' Create variables to hold the information.
strExtension = ""    ' File extension that we're looking for.
strFileType = ""     ' Holds the main file type.
strFileOpen = ""     ' File open command.
strFilePrint = ""    ' File print command.
strDefaultIcon = ""  ' Default icon for file type.

' See if the user provided a file extension to look for.
' If not, assign strExtension a default file extension.
if (WScript.Arguments.Length > 0) then
    strExtension = WScript.Arguments.Item(0)
else
    strExtension = ".txt"
end if
```

```
' Get the file type.
strFileType = WshShell.RegRead("HKEY_CLASSES_ROOT\" +_
                 strExtension + "\")

' Use the file type to get the file open and file print
' commands, along with the default icon.
strFileOpen = WshShell.RegRead("HKEY_CLASSES_ROOT\" +_
                 strFileType +_
                 "\shell\open\command\")
strFilePrint = WshShell.RegRead("HKEY_CLASSES_ROOT\" +_
                 strFileType +_
                 "\shell\print\command\")
strDefaultIcon = WshShell.RegRead("HKEY_CLASSES_ROOT\" +_
                 strFileType +_
                 "\DefaultIcon\")

' Display the results.
WshShell.Popup "File Type:" + vbTab + vbTab + vbTab + strFileType +_
       vbCrLf + "File Open Command:" + vbTab + strFileOpen +_
       vbCrLf + "File Print Command:" + vbTab + vbTab + strFilePrint +_
       vbCrLf + "Default Icon:" + vbTab + vbTab + strDefaultIcon,_
       0,_
       "RegRead Results",_
       intOK + intInformation
```

When you run this script, it reads the command line. If you haven't supplied a value, the script will assign a default extension of .TXT. The script uses the extension to locate information in the registry such as the file open and print commands. Finally, the script uses the Popup() method to display the output.

You should notice several differences between this example and the JavaScript example we looked at previously. First, the method for creating an object requires the use of a set—you can't simply assign the object to a variable. You'll also notice that VBScript has access to all of the standard Visual Basic constants such as vbTab and vbCrLf. Finally, VBScript handles many of the method calls as subs, not as functions. You need to exercise care when working in a mixed environment.

Let's Start Cleaning

This chapter demonstrates a number of automation techniques. The important concept to remember is that one automation technique isn't better than any other automation technique—the only consideration is what works best for you. For some people, using batch files works best because they minimize the risk of virus infection. Other people will rely exclusively on Task Scheduler to ensure tasks are done on time—Task Scheduler represents the simple graphical way to automate. Still other people need the flexibility and power of scripts or a combination of all three techniques.

You might not be ready to use automation yet. The first task is to ensure you know how to perform any required maintenance manually and that you have a stable procedure to use. Automation only works well for repetitive tasks that you can define with a specific procedure. A good test is to write the steps down on paper, leave them until the next day, and read the steps again to see if you still agree that they'll work. The second task is to choose a type of automation that will work for you once you have a stable procedure. The third, and final, task is to create the automation and then test it several times before you begin relying on it.

Despite all of the safeguards discussed in this book and the care you use in accomplishing a task, mistakes happen. Using automation tends to amplify even small mistakes so they become a major problem. Chapter 12 provides some guidelines on fixing the most common mistakes people make when optimizing their machine. Chapter 12 isn't an all-inclusive troubleshooting guide—it focuses on optimization mistakes.

Chapter 12

When You Make a Mistake

Everyone makes mistakes. It doesn't matter how well you know computers, how much sleep you got last night, or how perfect your mood—you'll eventually make a mistake. The problem isn't the mistake, it's how you deal with the mistake. Because mistakes are part of working with computers, you should just assume that you're going to make some and not get upset when you do. In fact, it might be best to view mistakes as learning experiences, because that's what they are. Of course, some mistakes are harder to fix than others and some you can't fix at all, so it pays to avoid them when you can.

TIP The best thing you can do to take advantage of mistakes is create a learning experience or mistake log, depending on whether you're an optimist or a pessimist. Don't record the date of the mistake—it doesn't matter. Do record the kind of machine you were working on, the mistake, and what you did to fix it eventually. Once you have time to think about the problem for a while, write down what you think you could have done to keep that problem from happening. Now, when a mistake does occur, you can look back at your log to see if you made that mistake before. When you find the mistake in your log, at least you have some idea of how to fix it.

This chapter doesn't beat anyone over the head with the rules of working with computers. What it does provide is some ideas on how to avoid mistakes or at least optimize the learning experience when you do make a mistake. Interestingly enough, some of the hints and tips in this chapter came from my learning experience log (yes, I'm an optimist), so you can think about the source of the information as you read through the chapter. Some of the entries are common sense and a few come from the experiences of other people. In short, someone had to make a mistake to discover the information that appears in this chapter.

The chapter discusses major system areas that are most prone to error. You won't find repair information in this chapter—all of this information centers on optimizing your system. For example, the chapter discusses how to use backups to fix the operating system or file system after a bad optimization, rather than using backups to fix a crashed hard drive. You'll also discover how to fix application and Dynamic Link Library (DLL) optimizations that have gone wrong, as well as undoing temporary changes. Finally, the chapter tells you how to fix service optimizations. It would seem as if all of these areas are straightforward, but you can run into some very interesting problems. Mistakes can lead to all kinds of interesting system behavior and some mistakes actually lead to new optimizations for specific tasks. The bottom line is that you should never be afraid to make a mistake!

Fixing Operating System and Disk Problems

The fancier that Microsoft makes Windows, the easier it will be to break it. The complexity that adds flexibility and new capabilities also increases reliability problems, which means your system has a likelihood of breaking more often. Many people have adverse reactions when a system glitch occurs because they automatically assume that they have done something to cause it. While it's true that users can, and do, cause system errors, the system itself must bear some of the blame for reliability problems. Device drivers that work most of the time and applications that generally perform well are just two of many problems. Just what caused the failure isn't the immediate problem when an error occurs—fixing the problem is.

TIP   Fixing the problem often reveals the source of the failure. Rather than waste time in ritualistic finger pointing, fix the problem and don't worry about the cause immediately. After you fix the problem, you'll have a better idea of what caused it and can determine lessons learned (if any). In at least some cases, you'll be able to find the source of the problem right on Microsoft's Knowledge Base (http://support.microsoft.com/default.aspx?scid=fh;EN-US;KBHOWTO). The idea is to take care of the most important aspects of the failure and affix blame, if any, later.

Performing a Diagnostic

System hardware can fail, but it seldom does so instantly. Diagnostics provide an optimal approach to discovering failures before they become a problem. Most diagnostic aids help with hardware problems, but a few also help with software problems. For example, the "Discovering Nasty Intruders" section of Chapter 10 discusses how to locate spyware and adware on your system, which, in reality, is a form of failure that you can locate with a diagnostic.

TIP   It's easy for daily chores to sidetrack you so that you forget to take every possible precaution before you begin a task. In some cases, vendors make the problem worse by not providing robust products (or products that are overly complex). For example, many trade press magazines report that Microsoft finally admitted that the presence of any form of spyware on system could cause problems with the Windows XP SP2 installation. Check the articles at http://www.w2knews.com/index.cfm?id=491 and http://www.eweek.com/article2/0,1759,1642448,00.asp?kc=ewnws090304dtx1k0600599 to learn more about this issue. When it comes to discovering issues like this with Windows, check out the Sunbelt Web site at http://www.sunbelt-software.com/index.cfm. The W2Knews and WinXPnews newsletters (http://www.w2knews.com/subscribe.cfm?id=ssd) put out by this organization are unbiased and extremely helpful (they actually include problem solutions).

Hardware failures are important to the optimization of your system. For example, bad memory and damaged hard drive sections can cause application errors that wreck your attempts to optimize the system. Optimization tends to reveal errors that might have gone unnoticed because you're moving things around and using system resources more fully during the optimization process. Consequently, running a diagnostic on your system before beginning optimization can help prevent potential problems and alert you to a system resource degradation. Although this isn't a book about diagnosing hardware problems, it's important to know about the hardware connection in your optimization efforts.

Many commercial applications exist for diagnosing potential hardware failures. For example, Touch-Stone has produced CheckIt (`http://www.touchstonesoftware.com/products/products.htm`) for many years. One of the better failure options is to get CheckIt 7.0 Portable Edition because you can use this product even when Windows won't boot. (CheckIt 7.0 Portable Edition is one of the better tools to put in your toolkit when you have a lot of machines to manage.) The idea is to diagnose your system hardware problem so you can get Windows up and running and locate any additional problems. Other good options include #1-TuffTEST-Pro (`http://www.tufftest.com/ttp01.htm`) and PC-Technician (`http://www.windsortech.com/pctech.html`). All of these products also include diagnostics that you can run as a preventative measure. For example, you could use a diagnostic to monitor your hard drive and detect any media degradation that would lead to an eventual hard drive crash.

TIP The #1-TuffTEST-Pro diagnostic is one of the few try-before-you-buy diagnostics available today. In fact, #1-TuffTEST-Lite is free and you can download it at `http://www.tufftest.com/tt01-lite-dwnld.htm`. In short, this basic diagnostics program doesn't even cost you anything. Of course, the full-fledged product is better able to help you with significant hardware problems and you should consider getting a full-fledged diagnostic whenever possible.

Most of these utilities share several features. You normally won't need to provide special operating system support because they either run as part of an older Disk Operating System (DOS) setup, Windows, or provide a custom operating system of their own. Make sure you check the product documentation before you buy to ensure you get the operating system support you want. The diagnostics can run in an automatic mode, which is perfect for testing the entire system, or individual hardware element mode, which is perfect for verifying the functionality of a single hardware item such as the hard drive. The diagnostic provides some type of stress test to ensure the hardware runs under stressful conditions and you can sometimes simulate specific hardware failure scenarios to see how the hardware reacts.

Diagnostics are such an important part of optimizing your system and maintaining its reliability that there's no shortage of tools for the task. Many developers offer these tools as freeware or shareware, so you can find them listed on Web sites that specialize in this type of product. Here are a few places you can check for freeware and shareware diagnostics.

MajorGeeks.com `http://www.majorgeeks.com/downloads7.html`

Tucows `http://www.tucows.com/top_section_1571.html`

Winfiles.com `http://www.winfiles.com/utilities/?tag=wf.2018.txt`

Winternals `http://www.winternals.com/index2.asp`

Relying on Backups

Operating system and disk failures take many forms. Your best defense against errors is a good backup. The "Performing Backups" section of Chapter 8 helps you perform this task. However, once you have the backup, you need to consider how best to use it to repair your system, especially when you want to determine the cause of the failure. Fortunately, there's an optimal way to proceed in checking your system. Although the process in this section isn't as fast as immediately assuming that the first problem you see is the one you should correct, it does have the advantage of being very thorough—you know your system works once you accomplish it.

1. Test your hardware to ensure there aren't any hardware glitches. The "Performing a Diagnostic" section describes this process in detail. Replace any damaged hardware before you begin the recovery process.

2. Verify that Windows will start completely. If not, repair Windows first by placing the installation disk into your CD drive and following the recovery options when presented.

3. Check the event log for important clues using the information found in the "Using and Cleaning the Event Log" section of Chapter 8.

4. When Windows will boot, determine precisely which Windows feature or application doesn't work. Restore only the files you need to a temporary folder (rather than the original folder) to test the integrity of the backup.

5. Use the FC command described in the "Using Comp and FC" section of Chapter 3 to determine whether the backup matches the files on your hard drive (when they do match, you haven't found the problem and need to repeat step 4). Remember that data files also get corrupted, so you need to check data files as well as application files when a failure occurs.

6. Copy the restored files to the damaged directory and test the application or operating system feature. Once you verify the application or operating system feature works, you can delete the temporary files.

The idea behind this procedure is to start at the lowest possible source of failure and work your way up. By working this way, you can eliminate more potential sources of failure and make your backup work toward creating a stable and reliable system, as well as correcting the problem you're currently experiencing.

This process also reduces the chance that future problem resolution attempts will fail. For example, you might find that the backup fails to restore your system completely and might have to rely on restore points instead. The time used to correct the problem using this technique isn't wasted—you still get the benefits of ensuring all of the lower level features of your system are working as anticipated.

Relying on Restore Points

Always rely on restore points as your last option for fixing optimization errors on your machine. Restore points work well, but they're also extremely harsh. A restore point returns your system to a previous state regardless of whether that previous state is actually better than the current one.

Restore points won't help you uncover other problems with your system. For example, using a restore point won't fix a media error on your hard drive or even tell you that one exists. That's why you want to use other methods of restoring your system first. Until you uncover other potential sources of errors, you can't be sure a restore point will even work. Even so, restore points do provide one more way of getting your system back to a working configuration when an optimization goes bad. You can learn more about working with restore points in the "Rolling Back Bad Installations" section of Chapter 8.

Always record the set of problems that you noticed after your recent optimization and use this list as a checklist for resolving the errors. You need a baseline of comparison to know when you have gone far enough in the restoration process. When the problems you note on your list go away, you have fixed the problems that a restore point can fix.

The best way to work with restore points is to begin by attempting to fix the problem with your backup as described in the "Relying on Backups" section of the chapter. Assuming for a moment that the backup method doesn't work, then you can move on to restoring the first (newest) restore point on your machine—the one you created immediately before your current optimization. The reason that you don't want to go back several restore points immediately is that you want to use the newest restore point that fixes the problem. A newer restore point will cause fewer problems and it ensures that older changes you made stay intact.

Move to progressively older restore points when you find that a particular restore point doesn't fix the problem. Test all of the problems you noted when you started the restoration process, but don't complicate matters by attempting to fix problems you didn't note. People tend to become extra observant as they wrestle with problems on their system—errors you didn't notice before suddenly become quite visible. Adding additional faults to your list could make the task of restoring your system impossible because those errors could have existed since you installed Windows.

A terrible event can occur—you could run out of restore points, which is why you want to use restore points carefully. Like many of the optimization techniques discussed in this book, restore points might not always work. Reversing an optimization process doesn't always remove the effects of the optimization—restore points don't always work because they don't modify the data on your system and the data could be the source of the problem. Eventually, you could get to a point where you need to reinstall Windows. Although this event should be extremely rare, it can happen, so be prepared for it. Always assume in your preparations for fixing a problem caused by optimization (or anything else for that matter) that a point of no return can occur and the only fix that will work is installing a fresh copy of Windows.

Repairing Application Settings

Many of the tips and techniques you see on the Internet and in newsgroups define applications settings designed to make the user more efficient. Depending on the application type, the optimization that often results in the biggest performance gain is helping the user work faster while maintaining a specific quality level. Unfortunately, with such large potential gains in productivity come equally large risks in making the application unusable for the user. The problem isn't always that the application fails to work, but simply fails to work as expected. Unlike the operating system, you usually can't completely optimize an application because the user requires certain inefficiencies to work well. For example, a spelling checker that runs in the background might waste processing cycles, but the user requires it to maintain writing quality. With this issue in mind, here's a list of common user optimization problems that you might find yourself repairing.

One Size Fits All   Many optimizations that you read about treat users as if they are a commodity where one size fits all. The fact is that users are individuals with unique tastes, talents, and characteristics. Consequently, an optimization that works wonderfully for one user can fail for another user, even when the two users have similar experience and training levels. The optimizations that most often fail in this area are cosmetic. For example, a user might use what appears to be a cluttered desktop, but cleaning the desktop up actually reduces productivity.

User Skill Level   Some people discuss user skill levels as a static indication of a specific level of training. Unfortunately, you can't describe varying skill levels quite so easily. Two users might have five years of experience working with Word, but if one worked on Word XP for a law firm and another used different versions of Word for a construction company, their experiences are different and you can't directly compare their skill levels. Each user will have specific skills that make different optimizations useful.

Working Environment   Focusing on the application and the user alone is a mistake. The working environment also affects which optimizations work well and which don't. An optimization that works well in an office environment might not work well on a manufacturing floor. Even if you eliminate all other considerations, the working environment affects how the user works with the computer and therefore affects how the user perceives the optimizations. Consequently, you need to perform temporary optimizations in each working environment and commit only to those that users receive well. (See the "Undoing Temporary Changes" section of the chapter for details on this concept.)

Whether an optimization results in an application that won't run, documents that won't load, or users who can't work the need is the same—you have to reverse the optimization to get the application back into a working state. However, sometimes it's not a matter of simply reversing the settings. More than anything else, applications tend to store optimizations you make as part of document files, which means you also have to change the documents. In addition, an optimization might work, but not in the way that you made it, so you not only need to reverse the current optimization implementation, but redo it in a way that meets user needs. The following sections discuss these issues and more.

Restoring Settings Files

Settings files can include a wide variety of file types. However, you can follow general rules when working with most of them. Some settings files also offer special features that make them easier to work with or easier to manage. The following sections discuss various aspects of restoring settings files.

WORKING WITH INI FILES

The most common form of settings file for applications today is the INI (initialization) file. An INI file uses a straightforward structure that consists of three elements:

◆ Sections or Headings

◆ Entries

◆ Comments

Figure 12.1 shows a typical example of an INI file. In this case, you're looking at the WIN.INI file used to configure some Windows options.

The top line shows a comment. Most applications, including Windows, precede a comment with a semicolon (;) as shown in the figure, but some applications use the pound sign (#) instead. Comments document the INI file—the application skips them when it encounters them in the file. The next several lines contain section entries. Some people call them headings. No matter what you call them, a section entry doesn't contain any data, it's used to organize the content of the INI file. Section entries always appear within square brackets ([]). Finally, Figure 12.1 shows some entries. An entry normally consists of a name and value pair that is separated by an equals (=) sign. For example, the aif=MPEGVideo line shown in Figure 12.1 is an entry. The entries contain the data the application uses to configure itself.

FIGURE 12.1
INI files are one of
the most common
configuration options
in use today.

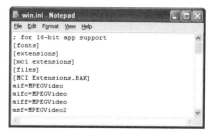

TIP   Sometimes you can save INI files settings by commenting out the old entry and creating another entry with the same name that has the new value you want to use. This technique requires an in-depth knowledge of the INI file, but can save you significant effort reversing unwanted changes. To reverse the change, simply remove the comment from the old entry and remove the new one. When you do change the INI file manually, make sure you use comments to document your changes as well so that the reason for a change is clear.

The best policy is to save a copy of all the INI files for an application after you first install it so you always have a baseline configuration to use for reversing changes or returning the application to the default state if necessary. In addition to the original INI, make sure you maintain a copy of the most recent INI file that provides usable results (as a minimum). Saving this file ensures you can restore the application state the user likes most when an optimization goes wrong. Keeping older INI files can prove useful so long as you document the age of each file carefully.

WORKING WITH XML FILES

Another common form of settings file is the eXtensible Markup Language (XML) file. This form of settings file relies on tags similar to those found in HyperText Markup Language (HTML) files such as those on Web sites, but the rules for using XML are much stricter than HTML. Most XML files have an XML file extension, but you'll find them with other extensions as well. For example, Figure 12.2 shows a FrontPage 2003 configuration (CONFIG) file.

You can recognize an XML file, no matter what file extension it uses, by the `<?xml version="1.0"?>` tag at the top. Some tags include additional information, but they all start out with the XML processing instruction. Generally, you won't want to modify XML files by hand unless you truly understand how XML works. In many cases, XML files are no more difficult to work with than INI files, but you always want to exercise care so that the XML file remains valid (doesn't break any of the rules). However, when you see XML files in the application directory, you'll want to save copies for later.

Some XML files are nearly impossible to read. The vendor might remove all of the extra spaces to make the file smaller and easier to manage. When this situation occurs, you can always open the XML file in Internet Explorer, as shown in Figure 12.3. Not only will Internet Explorer display the file in a nice format, but also it adds color coding to make the entries clearer and easier to read. Unfortunately, you can't use Internet Explorer to edit an XML file.

FIGURE 12.2
Some applications use
forms of the XML file to
provide configuration.

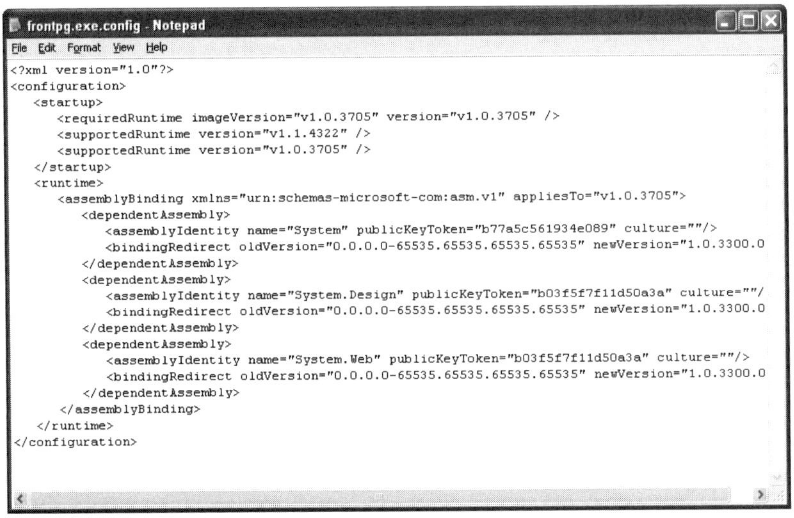

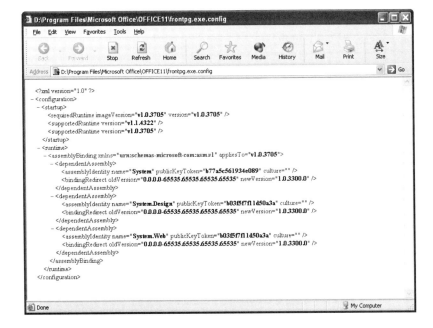

FIGURE 12.3
Use Internet Explorer
to view unformatted
XML files.

UNDERSTANDING RESTORATION DETAILS

No matter what type of settings file your application uses, it's important to back up these files regularly as part of your hard drive maintenance. Keeping copies of the files around reduces the time required to reinstall the application should it become unusable. Of course, you can run into issues when using older settings files. Here are some issues to consider.

Updates and Patches   Some vendors change applications significantly when you apply a patch or update. In some cases, the application gains one or more new features that require new settings. Consequently, the old settings file you have might work well with the original version of the application, but not with the updated or patched version on your system. Whenever you install a significant patch or update, check the application settings file for changes and delete any old settings files if you notice changes. Treat the updated or patched file as the first of a new version of the application.

Different User   It's essential to keep settings and configuration files with the machine on which you originally installed them. However, users tend to inherit machines from someone else. The original machine user might have a different skill level or tastes than the current user. Consequently, even when a settings file restores the application to working order after a failed optimization, the settings might not match those that the user expects. Make sure you update the settings file whenever a machine changes hands to ensure you have access to that user's preferences.

Machine Configuration   Many applications are completely unaffected by your machine configuration, but others are. A change in device driver or hardware such as a display adapter can have a big effect on some applications. It's important to create a new copy of the settings file whenever your machine configuration changes so that the new file reflects the current hardware and drivers.

TIP   It's possible that you will lose a driver and not have a good place to get another copy. Perhaps the vendor is no longer in business or you can't find the version you need. One place to look for drivers is WinDrivers (http://www.windrivers.com/). Although this site isn't free, the cost for downloading a driver you need is minimal and this is a reliable (virus free) place to look for drivers you need in a pinch.

Always restore the settings files starting from the newest usable file to the oldest file. Use the original settings files—the ones you saved from the installation—as a last resort for restoring the application. Using the original settings file means you lose any optimization and customization you performed, but you do save time in not having to reinstall the application from scratch.

WARNING   Never use settings files created for one machine on another machine because the settings files alone won't provide the information needed for a setup. Applications generally rely on a combination of registry settings, settings files, and special documents to provide a workable environment. In addition, differences in machine configuration and hardware can cause significant problems. Microsoft is currently pressing vendors to provide what they call an XCopy application setup (one where you can literally copy an application from one machine to another), but Microsoft doesn't follow its own advice. For example, Office applications are the worst offenders when it comes to putting settings in so many places that you can't copy an application from one system to another—you must install the application separately on each machine to get a good installation.

Using Registry Settings Exports

The registry provides a labyrinth of settings for many applications. It stores everything from file associations to application settings and much more. For example, many applications use special Dynamic Link Libraries (DLLs) and these DLLs can require entries in the registry (see the "Restoring DLLs and Executables" section for details). The "Working with Application Entries' section of Chapter 6 describes how to work with registry entries. However, the "Following the Flow of Registry Entries" section of Chapter 6 tells you how difficult it can be to follow even a simple file association through the registry—much less restore it to a usable condition. The following sections describe techniques you can use to work with registry settings and restore them after an optimization fails.

RESTORING VARIOUS REGISTRY SETTING TYPES

Working with the registry can be difficult. Fortunately, the situation isn't as bleak as it might appear. You can use the following techniques to save an application using registry settings.

User Settings   Most application settings—those that directly affect the user—appear in the HKEY_CURRENT_USER hive. You can export these settings regularly, load them into an archive, and use them as needed to restore an application. Save applications individually so that you don't restore more than one application by importing the REG file. In addition, you don't want to save old REG files because they might cause more harm than good.

Machine Settings   All application settings that affect everyone who uses the machine, whether they affect the machine or not, appear in the HKEY_LOCAL_MACHINE hive. Some applications have settings that affect both the user and the machine, so you need to save two REG files for that application. Make sure you save precisely the same level of application information, in both cases, so the machine and user settings match from a level perspective.

DLL Entries   Never attempt to save DLL entries because you'll generally miss a few. Instead of saving the registry settings, let the DLL make them for you. You can use the RegSvr32 utility to restore these settings as needed. The "Restoring DLLs and Executables" section tells you how to perform this task.

File Association Configuration   Many applications automatically restore their file associations when you start them. In some cases, the application will notice that the file associations are no longer intact and will display a message asking whether you want to reinstate them. A few applications provide an option to make the registry settings for you as part of the application setup. When you don't have any of these options available, you can always use Windows Explorer to associate an application with a file. Double-clicking the file normally displays a dialog box asking how you want to open the file, but you can also use the options on the File Types tab of the Folder Options dialog box accessible through the Tools ➢ Folder Options command of Windows Explorer.

Other Entries   An application can make other kinds of entries that you won't find easily and will have an even harder time restoring. For example, many applications hide their activation information deep in the registry. Fortunately, you can restore an activation entry by registering the application again. However, some entries are so obscure and difficult to find that you might have to resort to reinstalling the application to restore them. When this situation occurs, determine whether the application has a repair option available as part of the setup. Using the repair option can save considerable time because the application will only restore missing files and settings.

TIP   You can find some very good tips online for fixing other entry problems. For example, once you install certain Internet Explorer updates, you're out of luck if you want to reinstall an update to fix the application. However, by changing a certain registry entry, you can fool the update program into thinking that you haven't installed the update yet and it will reinstall itself—fixing whatever problem you have encountered. You can learn more about this particular fix on the PC Magazine site at http://www.pcmag.com/article2/0,1759,1561703,00.asp.

RESTORING REGISTRY SETTINGS USING COMPARISON

Sometimes you can make use of a special technique to load the user settings from another machine or even another location on the same machine into the registry editor. It's possible to use the loaded hive to perform a number of repair tasks. For example, you can compare the loaded hive to the current user's hive. In many cases, you can find a missing or damaged registry value using comparison. The process of loading a hive to use for comparison purposes is relatively safe (as long as you don't make any changes in the loaded hive) and simple. Begin by opening the HKEY_USERS hive shown in Figure 12.4.

The strange looking numbers in this figure, such as HKEY_USERS\S-1-5-18, are unique identifiers for the system and the users that work with it. Unfortunately, only the system really knows what the numbers mean, so you should avoid working with these entries. Choose the File ➤ Load Hive command to display the Load Hive dialog box shown in Figure 12.5. Notice that this file points to a user folder within the \Documents and Settings folder. The target file is NTUser.DAT—the file that stores the user registry settings. Remember that each user has an individual NTUser.DAT file, so you need to load the NTUser.DAT file of the user that you want to work with.

Click Open and you'll see another Load Hive dialog box. This dialog box asks you to provide a key name. To make it easy to tell which hive belongs to the user you want to work with, type the user's name and optionally, the user's domain. Don't use any special characters other than the underline for the key name because the Registry Editor can become confused otherwise. Click OK and the Registry Editor will load the user hive for you, as shown in Figure 12.6. This hive contains all of the unique user settings—it doesn't contain any other data.

FIGURE 12.4
The HKEY_USERS hive contains all of the user hives for the current machine.

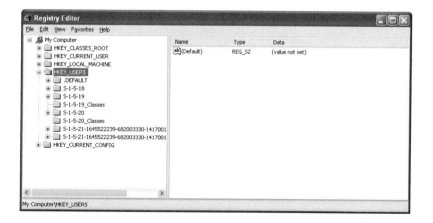

FIGURE 12.5
Load the registry settings
for the user you want to
work with.

FIGURE 12.6
The new hive contains all
of the unique user set-
tings for the selected user.

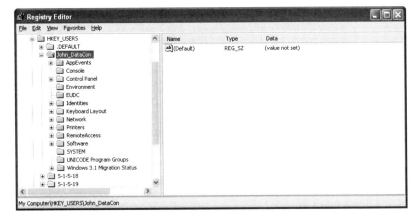

At some point, you'll want to unload the registry hive. To perform this task, highlight the hive and select the File ➢ Unload Hive command. The Registry Editor will ask if you're sure that you want to unload the hive. Click Yes and the Registry Editor will remove the hive.

When you want to work with other hives in the registry, such as HKEY_LOCAL_MACHINE, you'll need to load the remote registry. This feature only works when the remote machine is running the Remote Registry service. Because the Remote Registry service is dangerous to leave on all the time (someone could gain access to your registry over the Internet), you'll want to start it only when the Internet connection isn't in use. Make the remote access time as short as possible and stop the Remote Registry service as soon as possible.

To gain access to a remote registry, select the File ➢ Connect Network Registry command. You'll see a Select Computer dialog box where you can enter the name of the remote computer, as shown in Figure 12.7. Click Advanced when you want to use Windows to search for the computer and enter the name for you.

FIGURE 12.7
Connect to a remote machine running the Remote Registry service.

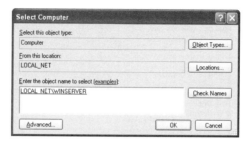

After you enter the name of the computer that you want to work with, click OK. The Registry Editor will try to make the connection for you. When the connection fails, you'll receive an error message. Otherwise, you'll see the HKEY_LOCAL_MACHINE and HKEY_USERS hives, as shown in Figure 12.8.

Obtaining access to HKEY_USERS also provides access to HKEY_CURRENT_USER in a way because the current user will appear in HKEY_USERS. Unfortunately, the HKEY_USERS hive contains the stored configuration—it won't reflect any configuration changes the current user makes to the registry. Notice also that the remote connection relies on a different icon than the local connection and includes the name of the remote computer.

To remove a remote registry connection from the Registry Editor, select the File ➤ Disconnect Network Registry command. You'll see the Disconnect Network Registry dialog box. Highlight the computer you want to disconnect from and click OK. The Registry Editor will clear the connection.

FIGURE 12.8
Remote connections provide access to the two most important keys for restoring registry settings.

RESTORING REGISTRY SETTINGS USING EDITED REG FILES

In some cases, you can do more than simply look at registry keys found on other machines—you can export the branch from a working registry setup and import it into the registry for an application that isn't working. However, you have to use this technique with care because you have to edit the REG files manually. The REG file will contain information for the other user or the other machine—not the current user or current machine.

Start this process by exporting the registry key that you want to use (see the "Saving Application Settings for Later" section of Chapter 6 for details). Open the file using Notepad or another text editor. You'll see a series of entries like the ones shown in Figure 12.9.

Notice that these keys use a path of HKEY_USERS\John_DataCon, which is fine for working with the exported user. However, you need the path to point to HKEY_CURRENT_USER so the exported settings end up in the current user's registry entries. Consequently, you need to perform a search and replace on this file to make the change from HKEY_USERS\John_DataCon to HKEY_CURRENT_USER. Now when you import the registry file using the technique in the "Restoring Application Settings" section of Chapter 6, the entries will end up in the right place.

FIGURE 12.9
Exported entries might be useful, but only if they contain the right key path.

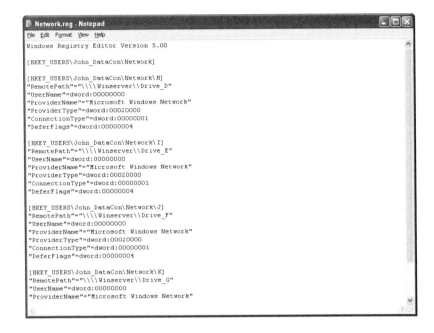

Manually Changing Settings

Manual changes are always risky because you can never be quite sure how they'll turn out. Something as simple as a typographical error could make a manual change appear not to work when it really should. Whenever possible, you should rely on automatic entry changes, but sometimes you must make manual changes to restore your system to good health. Here are some situations to consider where you might need to make a change manually, rather than use automation.

◆ The system doesn't provide any means of automatic entry for the required existing setting.

◆ You're creating a new setting and no automation exists to define it.

◆ The system provides automatic entry, but keeps using incorrect values based on incomplete or damaged information.

◆ A technical support representative or vendor knowledge base article directs you to make the change manually.

Generally, you'll find that manual settings are unnecessary—Windows and most applications provide good ways to make the change without manually entering it. In some cases, you can also use utilities, such as TweakUI (see the "Using TweakUI" section of Chapter 8 for details) to perform the task. Using automation helps you avoid common causes of problems such as adding values in the wrong location. Unfortunately, even the best utility doesn't help you adjust every possible setting. When you do need to make a setting change manually, make sure you follow these steps.

1. Attempt to find uninterrupted time to make the change. Make sure you have all of the materials you need to make the change to avoid interrupting the procedure to locate something.

2. Verify that you have the latest written instructions. When the instructions appear in electronic form, print them out because you don't know whether the changes will cause your system to freeze or otherwise become inaccessible.

3. Read the instructions and make sure you understand them before you touch your machine.

4. Perform each step precisely as written—don't read anything into the process. Even if you think you know how to perform the task better, follow the written instructions to ensure success.

5. Check each step off after you perform it to ensure you don't repeat a step.

6. Complete the procedure before you do anything else to ensure that you perform all of the steps.

7. Test the machine thoroughly to ensure the manual change works as anticipated.

8. Document the change in your machine log to ensure you remember you did it later.

Well-written manual procedures usually work well. Testing the system after you make the change will reduce any problems. You shouldn't approach manual procedures as something doomed to failure. Following the procedure carefully makes a manual change time consuming, but you'll find that the resulting change does everything automation could do. When you understand the change well enough, you might consider automating it to reduce errors in the future using the techniques discussed in Chapter 11.

Undoing Temporary Changes

Sometimes you want to try an optimization to see if it will work as you anticipate it will. The optimization might be fully tested and work on any number of other machines, but you just aren't sure in this case. Temporarily optimizing a machine is perfectly legitimate and you should experiment to see what works and what doesn't. A lack of experimentation often leads to suboptimal machines because the changes you aren't sure about often lead to surprising results. Of course, some of those results won't turn out as anticipated, so you'll want to ensure you can undo these temporary changes as fast (or perhaps faster) than you made them.

The most important step in undoing a temporary change is to document everything you do as you do it. Before you perform an optimization step, record it so that you remember precisely what you did when it comes time to undo the temporary change. Be very precise in recording what you do. Don't simply say that you made a registry change—record the actual registry change. Record these changes even though you back up every registry key before you modify it. The reason for being so precise is that you want to reverse your steps exactly, not just in a general way, when undoing a temporary change to ensure you get the best results.

TIP   It might sound odd, but capturing screenshots of system updates, message boxes, and status information is helpful. Save the screenshots to disk so you can view them later. Even simple screenshots are important. For example, Windows includes many DLLs with very similar names—some of them differ by a single letter. A message box that shows the DLL you actually registered during an optimization step can save a lot of grief later—errors are easier to reverse when you know precisely what you did, rather than what you think you did.

Even if you exercise extreme care when undoing a temporary change, some changes won't reverse completely or at least in the way you expected. Whenever you change settings on your system, the entire operating system has the potential to change. Not only the setting changes, but also system data files and status information can change. Reversing the process won't reverse these unintended changes, in many cases, so you need to recover from the temporary change using a backup or a restore point. However, a good written procedure and backup files can reverse many changes and the greater the care you exercise, the greater your chance of being successful.

Restoring DLLs and Other Executables

Windows and the applications it supports won't work well without the required executables. Beside the main executable (EXE) file, you also have to consider the DLLs the application requires. Without these executable files, you can't work with the application. The only problem is that a variety of events can corrupt these files or erase them completely, including errant optimization. DLLs are especially prone to damage when more than one application uses them. For example, an application might erase a DLL needed by another application when you uninstall it. In some cases, this event occurs after you tell the uninstall program to erase the file because you didn't know another application needs the DLL (the message is worded such that it appears the DLL is unused).

Now that you understand the problem, it's time to discover some solutions. The following sections discuss two important issues: getting the executable back once it's gone and registering DLLs that need it to ensure their registry entries are intact.

Getting Copies of Files

In most cases, you'll find copies of the files you need as part of the installation package provided by the vendor. However, before you can get copies of the file, you need to consider two problems. First, you need to know the filename. Second, you need to know where the file is located.

In many cases, you can solve the first problem by watching the application carefully. The error messages you receive will often tell you which of the files is missing, but sometimes it's buried in all of the extraneous garbage that some applications wrap around the error message. Make sure you look through all of the information the application provides. Another way to solve the first problem is to look through the vendor documentation. Sometimes the vendor provides a list of files that you need to run the application (don't expect such a list with large applications such as Microsoft Office). Look in the event log as well—many applications record missing elements there instead of displaying the information on screen. Finally, you can always look for the error message online. For example, you can go to the Google Advanced Search site (`http://www.google.com/advanced_search`) and type the precise error message in double quotes. Using double quotes forces Google to look for a particular phrase. Finally, as a last resort, get onto one of the newsgroups online and try to get an answer. Vendor-specific newsgroups are best, but choosing a newsgroup carefully is always helpful.

The second problem can be very easy to solve when working with smaller applications. These applications normally have just one CD or might even reside in a ZIP file, so all you need to do is look through the archive. However, when you start working with large applications, the file might appear on any of a number of CDs, all of which rely on compressed files. Sometimes it can take hours to search through the files individually. This is one time when the Windows XP ability to search through compressed files comes in very handy because you can use the Windows search feature to locate it. As mentioned in the "Windows Explorer Lies to You" section of Chapter 3, this technique doesn't always work, so you might end up using a manual search after all. As an alternative, you can sometimes find the file you need online. Simply search for the filename and see what comes up. However, use this technique with care because someone could provide you with a virus-laden file. Download files from sites that you trust to reduce the risk of getting a corrupted file.

UNDERSTANDING DLL HELL

DLLs also cause a problem known as DLL hell. You can run into this problem when you work with a system in any way, but it's especially prevalent when you install a new application or remove an old one as part of the optimization process. The problem occurs when two applications need the same DLL, but different versions of it. Application A only works with one version of the DLL and Application B only works with another version. When you need both applications, you can find it difficult to create a workaround.

Here's a typical scenario. Microsoft issues a DLL for displaying common dialog boxes, but it has a bug in it. Vendor A creates an application using the DLL with the bug and designs a clever workaround that makes the bug disappear (or, at least, become less noticeable). In the meantime, Microsoft releases a new version of the DLL and Vendor B uses it to create an application. Because the bug is gone, Vendor B doesn't have to create a workaround. You install both applications and find that the program from Vendor B doesn't work—it doesn't have the required workaround. Therefore, you also update your system with the new DLL. Unfortunately, because Vendor A does have a workaround in the application, it won't work with the new DLL. Welcome to DLL hell.

The best way to overcome DLL hell is to get versions of both applications that use the same DLL version. Vendors usually provide an update when enough users scream about the problem, so get started now. In the meantime, you might find that you have to choose between the two applications and potentially restore the older DLL to make the application from Vendor A work again. Here are some additional resources you can use to understand DLL hell better.

A Quick Overview `http://www.ssw.com.au/SSW/Database/DLLHell.aspx`

Microsoft's Somewhat Forgotten Promise `http://zdnet.com.com/2100-1104-991369.html`

A Developer View of DLL Hell `http://msdn.microsoft.com/msdnmag/issues/02/06/debug/default.aspx`

A Potential Solution Developers Should Consider `http://msdn.microsoft.com/msdnmag/issues/1000/metadata/`

DLL Hell Article `http://encyclopedia.thefreedictionary.com/DLL%20hell`

Restoring DLL Registration

Some DLLs require registration. The registration process loads the DLL, asks it to make any required registry entries, and then unloads the DLL. The reason for going through this process is to ensure the DLL works as required—that it has the required connectivity. The only problem is that you don't really know which DLLs require registration. For one thing, some DLLs have an EXE extension, while others have another extension such as OLE Custom eXtension (OCX) where OLE stands for Object Linking and Embedding. The best option is to try registering the suspected DLL. If the DLL doesn't provide any functionality that requires registry entries, the registration simply fails—you won't do any harm to the machine.

To register a DLL, type `RegSvr32 NameOfDll` at the command prompt and press Enter. You'll see a success message like the one shown in Figure 12.10 when the registration succeeds. Don't worry about registrations that fail—some DLLs don't require registration.

TIP Opening a command prompt to register a DLL might not be your idea of fun. The Graphical Interface to RegSvr32 1.0 tool at `http://www.majorgeeks.com/download3907.html` doesn't just have a long name; it provides a level of convenience when you need to register a number of DLLs. Best of all, this tool is free and easy-to-use.

FIGURE 12.10
Register the application DLLs to ensure the DLL has the required connectivity.

Restoring One Too Many Service Changes

One of the biggest problems that you can face is losing the benefits of a particular service and not knowing what to do about it. Consider the following scenario. You optimize your machine using the best possible information. Because you're so diligent about system maintenance, you decide to perform a backup immediately after the changes in addition to the backup you made before the changes. Unfortunately, the client refuses to give the server access. After several hours of scratching your head, you throw up your hands—all of the security settings are correct, but the client still doesn't want to talk to the server. You're using Windows XP SP2, so your first assumption is that the new service pack is living up to its reputation. Be prepared for the big surprise, the problem has nothing to do with the service pack.

This problem can occur when you have turned off too many services. When you don't see the client icon in the Network Neighborhood, the likely cause is that you have stopped the Server service. From a security perspective, this step is actually very good because normally, no one has the right to know your machine even exists unless you're providing a service (which most clients don't). However, setting the Server service to manual means that you must manually start the Server service when you need to perform a backup. Granting the server access to the client in order to perform a full backup is a server service.

However, your problem is that the icon appears in Network Neighborhood, but the client still won't allow access. The problem could be that the Windows Firewall/Internet Connection Sharing service (formerly the Internet Connection Firewall (ICF)/Internet Connection Sharing (ICS) service) is stopped. When using Windows XP SP2, this service relies on the Network Connections and Windows Management Instrumentation services, which in turn rely on the Remote Procedure Call (RPC) and Event Log services. In short, to gain access to a drive to back it up in Windows XP SP2, the client machine must run a minimum of six interrelated services.

Here's the catch to fixing this problem. Once you stop the service and its related services, you can't discover a list of dependencies for that service by right-clicking the service and choosing Properties. The Dependencies tab (shown in Figure 12.11 for the Internet Connection Firewall (ICF)/Internet Connection Sharing (ICS) service on a machine with a dial-up connection) tells you what the service requires to execute, but you can't access that tab any longer.

FIGURE 12.11

The Dependencies tab becomes unavailable when the dependent services are stopped.

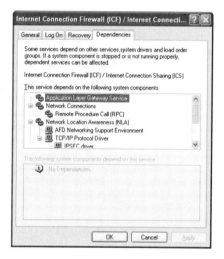

The easiest way to avoid this problem is to keep track of the dependencies for services that you stop. Write them down in a log or take several screenshots and save them. Whatever it takes, record the information before you stop the service.

Unfortunately, the easiest method of avoiding service problems might not be available. When this problem occurs, a careful comparison of the services on a machine that does work with the machine experiencing errors can help. You can simply start the services that aren't running on the errant machine. Of course, the two machines must run the same version of Windows with the same service packs installed. Microsoft often changes the names of services. For example, the change in the name of the Internet Connection Firewall (ICF)/Internet Connection Sharing (ICS) service from Windows XP SP1 to SP2 could pose a problem. In addition, this approach could mean spending hours figuring out precisely what went wrong so you can optimize the machine without losing access to required services.

Let's Start Fixing

This chapter has described some of the problems that can occur when an optimization goes wrong. Some problems result in disasters that you can't fix at all, so you start from scratch. The sun still rises in the morning and, hopefully, you still have your job. Fortunately, most errors aren't so severe that you can't fix them. The best piece of information you can take from this chapter is that you must think before you act. Think first about what will happen when you perform a particular optimization. Once a mistake occurs, think about it before you try to fix it. If necessary, own up to the mistake so you can get help.

It's time to create your own learning experience or mistake log. Don't create this log on your machine because you never know when you'll need it when your machine won't start. Nothing is worse than realizing you need the notes on the machine that won't start. After you create your log, start filling it out. Always add entries immediately after you make the mistake so all of the details are fresh in your mind. After a few years of making mistakes, you'll find that your log becomes an invaluable resource that optimizes the repair process. Your mistakes become a source of information that actually makes it faster to repair problems in the future.

Congratulations! You've reached the last chapter of the book. However, your journey should also include the appendices for this book. Appendix A helps you locate useful third party cleaning utilities. All of these utilities are quite helpful, most of them didn't appear anywhere in the book, so you won't have the complete story until you visit the appendix. Appendix B provides 52 helpful tips you can use to optimize Windows better and faster. Try reading one at the start of every week and you'll find that you have a wealth of new ideas by the end of the year. Make sure you contact me at `JMueller@mwt.net` if you have any questions about this book. I'd also love to hear about your experiences in optimizing your system. Also, look on my Web site at `http://www.mwt.net/~jmueller/` for updates and additional information.

Appendix A

Additional Cleaning Tools

The Internet contains so many cleaning tools of various types that it's difficult to choose which cleaning tools to recommend without extensive testing. In some cases, a perfectly good tool just didn't make it into one of the chapters because either it didn't present the required concepts or it was just a little too far off topic. This appendix contains additional cleaning tools that you'll want to consider adding to your toolbox. Most of them are free downloads. When you do download a shareware product that you like and plan to use, make sure you support the shareware author by sending in the usually modest registration fee. I'd also love to hear about your favorite cleaning aids. Send me email at JMueller@mwt.net to tell me about your cleaning utility and describe why you think it's such a good product.

Playing with Faber Toys

Sometimes a utility is part tool and part toy—Faber Toys (http://www.faberbox.com/) falls into this category. It lets you view the processes on your system from a new perspective. Instead of simply looking at the process, the tool helps you delve into how the process loads and what it uses to execute, as shown in Figure A.1. The upper list tells you which applications are executing on the machine, while the middle list tells you which modules (DLLs or other executables) the application loaded. The bottom window contains a list of modules that Windows wouldn't load—that Windows excluded—for some reason. Rarely will you see any entries in this window for a working application, but the list can provide hints about why a loaded application isn't operating correctly.

Each of the entries tells you the location of the executable, the amount of memory it uses, its execution priority, and the executable version. The version information is especially helpful when you're experiencing DLL hell problems because you can determine which version of a particular DLL causes problems for an application and which one it uses well. The screen also provides a description of the executable (which is somewhat terse in many cases) and the entity that executed the application.

Another useful feature is the autorun list. You access this feature using the Tools ➤ AutoRun command. Figure A.2 shows a typical list of entries. Notice that the list tells you the application name, location of autorun entry, application path, the application description, the application run state, and the date that you last modified the application. The description is the usual short bit of text that provides you with just enough information to figure the application out in most cases. All of this information gives you a good picture of what you have running on the system.

FIGURE A.1
Use Faber Toys to study the processes on your system in depth.

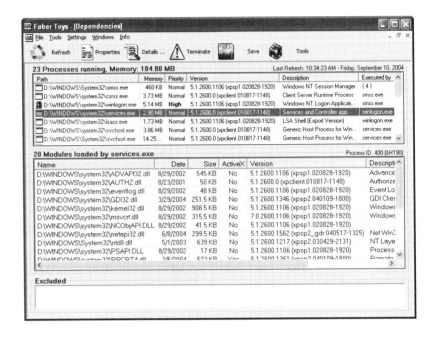

FIGURE A.2
Determine which applications run automatically using the autorun list.

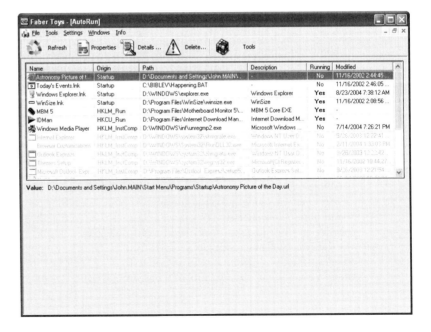

You can adjust the autorun entries. Right-click any entry and you'll find a number of selections. For example, when the process is running, you can click Select Process in Dependencies to see where the application appears in the process list. Use the Go To option to go directly to the application's entry in the registry or Startup folder. The Delete option removes the entry from the registry or Startup folder. You can also view the application properties or obtain a detailed view that isn't all that useful for optimization tasks, but is fun to look at.

The toy part of the application—at least from an optimization perspective—are the Properties and Details views. The Properties view is the same as the dialog that you obtain when you right-click the entry in Windows Explorer and choose Properties from the context menu. You can perform the same tasks—it's just easier to access that dialog from within this utility while you perform an optimization. The Details view is special. It provides specific information about the construction of the application file. Unless you're a developer, you won't need most of this information. However, it's interesting to review the list of imported and exported functions—sometimes developers use odd names for them.

Modifying the Windows Boot Cycle with Startup Mechanic

Getting Windows to startup correctly can be a painful experience. Startup Mechanic (`http://www.download.com/Startup-Mechanic/3000-2086-10316039.html?tag=lst-2-5`) makes the task of optimizing this process a lot easier. When you start the application, you see the Status Report tab where you click Scan. After the application scans your system, you see a list of startup items like the one shown in Figure A.3.

Startup Mechanic provides you with a relatively complete description of the application based on its filename. It also provides a full path and filename in most cases—in others, it only provides a filename. The other tabs on the System Scan tab sort the applications by type—the sorting mechanism relies on what Startup Mechanic knows about the executable, which might be nothing at all.

FIGURE A.3

Startup Mechanic provides an extremely simple interface that makes it easy to optimize your system.

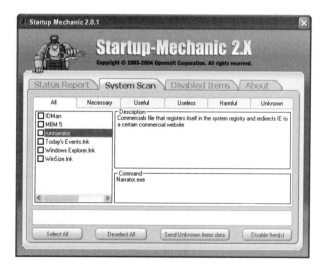

Look at the Harmful tab and you'll see all of the harmful applications on your system (which, interestingly, includes Internet Explorer). To disable a potentially harmful application without removing it from the system, check the application name and click Disable Item(s). Startup Mechanic will quarantine the application so that you can verify whether it is, indeed, harmful. All quarantined applications appear on the Disabled Items tab where you can restore them to use when desired.

Some of your applications are bound to have unique names. You can help the creator of Startup Mechanic identify these items by clicking Send Unknown Items Data. This act opens an email message that includes a list of the startup application in the list. Simply type a description for the application in question, along with any other identifying information you want to provide, and send the email. Because this is an email, you can provide as much or little information as you want.

This utility is very easy to use and it normally provides a good description of utilities, but you have to double-check its findings. For example, Figure A.3 shows a potentially dangerous application on the test machine. However, opening a command prompt and locating the file (because Startup Mechanic didn't provide a path) shows that this file is in the \Windows\System32 folder. Further investigation shows that this file is actually part of the Windows Accessibility feature—it's a screen reader for those who have trouble seeing the display. Disabling this application would cause harm because someone with special vision needs wouldn't have access to the required application.

Tracking System Activity with Process Explorer

Several sections of the book discuss the importance of knowing what processes are actually running on your machine. Unfortunately, it's difficult to obtain a true assessment of system activity in many cases. Process Explorer (http://www.sysinternals.com/) can make the task easier. Process Explorer provides exceptionally detailed information about the applications running on your system, as shown in Figure A.4.

FIGURE A.4

Use Process Explorer to track applications and to discover their performance characteristics.

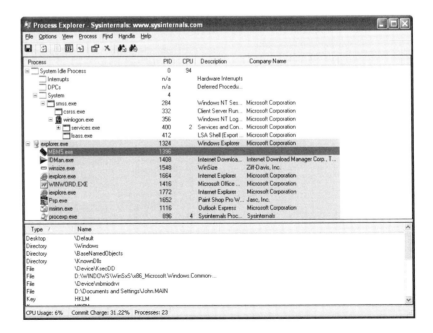

The upper window shows which applications are currently running on your system. This part of the application works much like Task Manager, but with a little more detail. In fact, Process Explorer includes an option to replace Task Manager. Like Task Manager, you can kill the process or give it a higher priority. However, you can't use Process Explorer to set the application affinity (determine which processor the application uses to execute) and this can be a problem on dual-processors (or higher) systems. Some applications require that you set the affinity so that it only runs on one processor. The usual result of failing to set the affinity is that the application freezes or simply quits.

TIP The creator of Process Explorer has a number of other useful utilities that you should consider adding to your toolbox. You can obtain all of these tools on the creator's Web site at `http://www.sysinternals.com/`. There are actually too many tools to describe here, but utilities such as Regjump can make life a lot easier. Regjump accepts a specific registry path as input and opens the Registry Editor to that point. You can use a batch file to create a list of places you commonly visit.

The lower window tells you about resources the application uses. For example, you can determine which registry keys that application has opened and which files it's accessing. Process Explorer also tells you which system events the vendor designed the application to handle. For example, an application might want to know when the user is about to log off so it can save its settings. All of this information can help you repair the application when you've run out of other ideas. For example, the list of registry keys can help you determine where else to look when you think the application makes nonstandard entries.

When you right-click one of the entries and choose Properties from the context menu, you don't see a standard Properties dialog box. Process Explorer provides a unique Properties dialog that includes tabs for exploring the application's performance and security. In fact, the security information is extremely detailed and tells you about specific rights that the application has. For example, you can determine whether the application has the right to load drivers. The Thread tab tells you about the threads that the application creates. This information gets very detailed, but can be helpful for optimization. For example, you can learn more about specific modules and discover what the thread has been doing by looking at the call stack. The Performance tab provides a standard graph showing performance, but instead of concentrating on system performance as a whole—you see the performance of the individual application.

Using the Microsoft Baseline Security Analyzer

Security is one of the optimizations discussed in the book, but maintaining a clean system is extremely difficult when you leave all of the security holes in place. The Microsoft Baseline Security Analyzer (MBSA) helps you locate, categorize, and track security problems on your system. Although it sounds as if Microsoft designed this tool for large corporations with multiple servers, it works well on many versions of Windows, including Windows 2000 and Windows XP. (It unfortunately won't work on Windows 9x.) MBSA can scan one or more machines during a single session so long as you connect those machines across a network. Microsoft has mixed new functionality with existing tools with this product and performed the task well. You can download MBSA at `http://www.microsoft.com/technet/security/tools/mbsahome.mspx#XSLTsection129121120120`.

NOTE The MBSA utility is a very good starting point for any organization. It provides you with a great idea of what is wrong on your system and can help you tighten security to reduce the potential for intrusions. However, it's not a perfect tool and some companies will require a more robust security aid. Tools such as Foundstone 4.0 (http://www.foundstone.com/) provide robust functionality for intense security scanning. You can find a review of this product at http://www.eweek.com/article2/0,1759,1641654,00.asp. You should also consider alternatives such as the TechRepublic Gap Analysis Tool (http://ct.com/click?q=f0-nv_DQWg9OnOpqu9vm5WFOMiim6lR) and Windows XP Security Assessment Tool (http://ct.com/click?q=7a-EE_AIPBNUlSH1YvVpaFffzxJpTuR). As with Foundstone and MBSA, these tools help you locate and fix problems in your Windows security shield.

When you start MBSA, the tool will ask whether you want to scan a single or multiple machines. Figure A.5 shows a typical example of the single machine scanning setup. If you scan a single machine, you can choose a specific machine name or enter an IP address. It's also important to check the scanning options. It's usually best to scan for all vulnerabilities because the check on a single machine doesn't take very long.

Scanning multiple machines means telling MBSA specifically what you want to scan. For example, you can type a domain name or a range of IP addresses. Typing a domain name means that MBSA will scan every machine in the domain, which can require a substantial amount of time. Selecting an IP address range is reasonable only if you know the current addresses of the machine—depending on how you set up your server, these addresses could change. If you're only concerned about the two machines on a home network, it's normally better to perform two single scans. Once you choose the identity of the machines that you want to check, you can select from the same options shown in Figure A.5. It's often more efficient to select specific options when scanning multiple machines, rather than performing the entire test.

FIGURE A.5
Select the identity and scanning options for the test system.

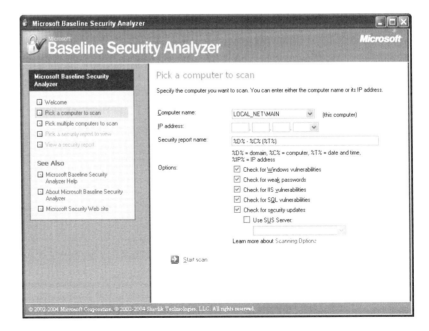

TIP The IIS Lockdown Tool described in the "Using the IIS Lockdown Tool" section of the chapter is one of the tools that you'll see mentioned as part of your MBSA scan. Generally, you want to install this tool on any system that could have any public access either now or in the future because the default IIS settings aren't secure.

After you select the machine identity and options you want, click Start Scan to begin the scanning process. Figure A.6 shows typical output from this program. You might be surprised at the number of security problems your machines have.

Notice that this machine is lacking service packs (I did the scan immediately before performing the required updates). If nothing else, running MBSA will ensure that you know service packs are missing, which lets you search for information about the service pack and determine whether you want to install it. MBSA also checks for other violations, such as the presence of more than two administrators on a machine or the use of a guest login. You'll also learn more about the macro status of your Office products and discover whether you have unnecessary services installed. In short, MBSA is a good tool for anyone to use, not just those in corporate settings.

NOTE MBSA tries to download a copy of the MSSecure.XML every time you start the program. If MBSA can't find an Internet connection or it can't contact the Microsoft Web site for some reason, the program will still work, but the results could be outdated. The best policy is to run the scans from a machine with an active Internet connection so MBSA can provide the latest results.

FIGURE A.6
Typical output
from MBSA after
a security scan.

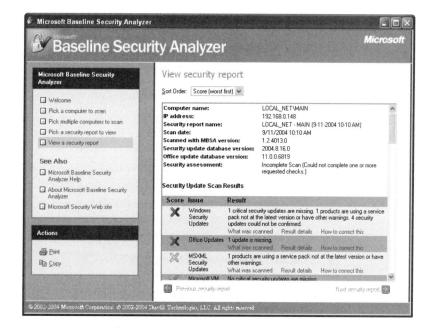

MBSA also includes a command line interface through MBSACli.EXE so you can use it within scripts. The default setup uses command line features that emulate the standard MBSA interface. If you don't select a particular feature, then MBSA will choose defaults. For example, if you type **MBSACli** alone, the program will perform a complete check of the local system. Here's a list of common MBSACli command line switches.

/C *Domain\Computer* Defines the name of the computer to check. When working in a workgroup, instead of a domain, replace the Domain entry with the name of the workgroup.

/I *IP Address* Tells MBSA to scan a particular IP address—you can use it in place of the /C switch.

/R *IP-IP* Tells MBSA to scan an IP address range, which includes the beginning and ending address that you supply. Separate the two addresses with a dash.

/D *Domain* Tells MBSA to scan an entire domain. Using this switch will greatly increase the scan time and you should only use it when you have a number of machines to work with. Supply a workgroup name when you work on a workgroup instead of a domain.

/N *Option* Determines which scans MBSA won't perform. The default setting performs all scans. The valid values are OS (operating system), SQL (SQL Server), IIS (Internet Information System), Updates (both Office and Windows patches and updates), and Password (verifying no passwords are simple or missing). You add multiple options using the plus (+) sign without any spaces. For example, adding the /N OS+SQL switch would tell MBSA not to perform operating system or SQL Server checks.

/O *Filename* Defines an XML output filename template. The arguments include %D% (domain or workgroup name), %C% (computer name), %T% (time and date you ran the scan), and %IP% (IP address of the computer). The filename template can also include path and standard text. By default, MBSA places the output in the \Documents and Settings*UserName*\SecurityScans folder of the system, where *UserName* is the logon name of the user performing the scan.

/F *Filename* Defines a text output filename template. You have the same options as when you use the /O option—only the output differs. Instead of an XML file, you receive a formatted text file that you can import into a word processor or simply send to the printer.

/QP Tells MBSA not to display the scan progress. Use this option when you want to continue working in the foreground while MBSA performs the check or to speed up the check slightly.

/QE Tells MBSA not to display the error list on completion of the scan. Use this option when you plan to use an automated method of analyzing the output information.

/QR Tells MBSA not to display the report list on completion of the scan.

/Q Tells MBSA not to display the scan progress, the error list, or the report list (a combination of /QP, /QE, and /QR). Use this switch when you want to perform uninterrupted background scans.

/S *Suppression Level* Defines what level of output information to suppress from the report. A value of 1 suppresses the security update check notes, level 2 suppresses both security update check notes and warnings, and level 3 suppresses all warning except for service packs. Use the suppression levels with extreme care because they can hide important update information from you. Because the purpose of using MBSA is to determine how secure your system is, purposely suppressing warnings is counterproductive.

/NVC   Tells MBSA not to check for a new version. Using this command line switch can reduce scanning time. However, you also can't be sure the scan is completely up-to-date. You could miss some service packs, patches, or updates that will help keep your system virus free.

/NOSUM   Tells MBSA not to perform a file checksum as part of the security update check. Using this command line switch can save considerable scan time. However, you also won't know whether someone has tampered with the files on your system. Because many viruses, adware, and spyware work by replacing genuine files with tampered versions, you shouldn't skip this check when you want to ensure your system is secure.

/SUS *[SUS Server URL | SUS Filename]*   Specifies the location of the Software Update Services (SUS) server or the path to an `ApprovedItems.TXT` file containing a list of approved software for the current system. When you don't provide either an URL or a filename, MBSA searches the registry for an appropriate value. SUS is a Microsoft product that you use to help maintain a large number of systems. You can learn more about this product at `http://www.microsoft.com/windowsserversystem/sus/default.mspx`.

/E   Tells MBSA to list the errors from the latest scan. This switch doesn't always work as expected—sometimes it doesn't produce any output at all. Use the /LR or /LD switches for better results.

/L   Lists all of the reports available for the current user on the current machine. You can't use the /C option to view reports on a different machine. MBSA makes a distinction between report and scan options and you can't combine the two.

/LS   Lists all of the reports from the latest scan. When you perform a scan on just one machine, there's just one report to view. However, when you scan a range of machines, then you have multiple reports from which to choose.

/LR *Filename*   Displays an overview report using the information found in the supplied filename. This report only displays a list of potential problems on the target system without explaining how to fix them. Use the /L or /LS option to obtain a list of valid filenames.

/LD *Filename*   Displays a detailed report using the information found in the supplied filename. The /LD command line switch provides recommended repair information, in addition to the list of issues that MBSA finds on the target system. Use the /L or /LS option to obtain a list of valid filenames.

/V   Tells MBSA to display the security update reason codes. You can sometimes use these codes to obtain additional information about a particular issue online.

/Unicode   Tells MBSA to use Unicode, rather than ASCII, as the output character scheme. Use Unicode on systems that rely on special symbols for machine, other device, or filenames. Always use this option when working with machines set up for non-English language use.

TIP   In many respects, MBSA overlaps the functionality provided by another tool, HFNetChk (see `http://www.microsoft.com/technet/security/tools/hfnetchk.mspx` for details). Don't worry about knowing anything about HFNetChk if you don't already—MBSA is far superior. If you want to emulate the behavior of the older HFNetChk tool, you can type **MBSACli /hf** in the script file. MBSA can use any HFNetChk command line option, which means MBSA is extremely flexible.

Using the IIS Lockdown Tool

No matter how you use your system, you should always perform certain kinds of security optimizations. Otherwise, you'll face problems that go well beyond ensuring your system runs reliably, provides a good user experience, or performs tasks fast. The IIS Lockdown Tool (`http://www.microsoft.com/downloads/details.aspx?FamilyID=dde9efc0-bb30-47eb-9a61-fd755d23cdec&displaylang=en`) helps you reconfigure the Internet Information Server (IIS) setup on your system for maximum security. It uses a number of templates to automate the task, or you can choose to perform the process by answering questions.

TIP   To test for the presence of IIS or any other Web server on your machine, open your browser. In the Address field, type **http://localhost** and press Enter. If you see a Page Not Found error, then you don't have IIS (or any other Web server) installed and running on your machine. If you see a page that you don't expect to see because you didn't explicitly install a Web server on your machine and there isn't any entry to remove the server in the Add or Remove Programs applet in the Control Panel, make sure you scan your system for potential viruses. If IIS doesn't appear in the standard application listing, you must open the list of Windows options to uninstall it.

When you start the IIS Lockdown Tool, it asks you to agree to the usual licensing statement and then displays a list of templates similar to the ones shown in Figure A.7 if it detects a copy of IIS on the local machine. Unlike MBSA, you must run the IIS Lockdown Tool on the host machine. It also doesn't pay to look for any command line options with this tool because running it from a script won't work very well.

FIGURE A.7
The IIS Lockdown Tool uses templates to make the configuration process easier.

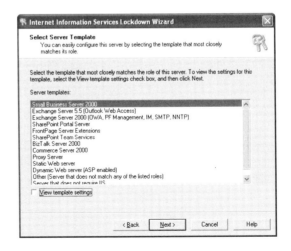

Notice the View Template Settings option at the bottom of the dialog box in Figure A.7. It usually pays to check this option so you can validate that the template settings are going to work for your system. When you select this option, you see a series of screens such as the one shown in Figure A.8. The screens take a while to read and verify, but you'll receive better results from the configuration if you take the required time.

The IIS Lockdown Tool also offers to install URLScan (see `http://www.microsoft.com/technet/security/tools/urlscan.mspx` for details). Essentially, this tool uses a rule base to block harmful requests from reaching the server. Even if you're running IIS on a home system, you should install URLScan to ensure your system remains safe.

NOTE   Any developer optimizing their machine should pay special attention to their URLScan setup. In general, if you install URLScan on your production systems, you should also include it on your development machine. The fact that this tool blocks certain requests means that you could run into situations where an application works fine on a development machine, but doesn't work at all on the production system. An URLScan problem can prove difficult to find because the tool blocks the request before it reaches the Web server. Consequently, many of the troubleshooting techniques you normally use won't work (including remote debugging).

Once you decide on the various settings (including the URLScan installation), the IIS Lockdown Tool displays a summary of the tasks that it will perform on your system. Use the Back button to change any settings that don't appear to fit within the security guidelines for your company. Click Next to begin the lockdown process. The IIS Lockdown Tool displays status information as it completes the task. At some point, the process will complete—simply follow the prompts to finish the process.

FIGURE A.8

Use the supplied template screens to customize the template configuration.

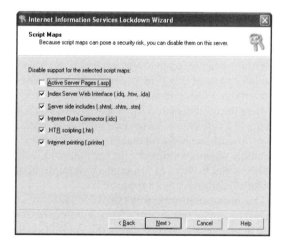

Examining Applications with Dependency Walker

The Dependency Walker (also called Depends for the name of the executable file) enables you to view the dependencies between various DLLs. For example, you might know that MyApp.EXE is the application you want to remove, but may not realize that MyApp.EXE also relies on DLLs to perform its work. The interdependencies between DLLs are the cause of a number of problems with older, unmanaged applications, which is why Microsoft is now promoting the .NET Framework. However, most (perhaps all) of the applications on your system still rely on these interconnections, so understanding which DLLs your application uses is important when you need to remove it manually.

NOTE   Normally, you can't get Depends without getting a Microsoft language product or at least performing an extraordinarily long download. The Depends utility is so useful, however, that you can find the latest version on a Web site devoted to the purpose at http://www.dependencywalker.com/. The Web site owner has a number of interesting notes about the Depends utility as well.

Determining Which DLLs Your Application Uses

Dependency Walker (or Depends, as it's listed on the Microsoft Visual Studio 6.0 Tools menu) helps you prevent the problem of the missing file. It lists every file that an application, DLL, or other executable files depend on to execute. You can use the output of this application to create a list of required files for your application or to discover the inner workings of DLLs. Generally, you'll use the required file feature for optimizing or repairing your system. Unlike a lot of other applications on the market, Depends continues to work even when the files you need aren't available on the system.

Loading a file for examination is as easy as using the File ➢ Open command to open the executable file that you want to examine. Figure A.9 shows an example of the output generated for the Notepad.EXE file. For such a small program, Notepad uses a ton of external DLLs. However, it doesn't stop there. For example, it noticed that Notepad calls COMDLG32.DLL, which calls many other DLLs including SHLWAPI.DLL. The point is that you can build a list of DLLs for your application and determine what to remove (and what to keep) based on your knowledge of the system. Depends will also tell you what DLLs are missing, which provides you with an easy way to fix applications should you remove a file accidentally.

Near the bottom of the Depends window, you'll see an alphabetical list of all of the files along with pertinent information like the executable file's version number and whether the DLL or other files relies on a debug version of that file. This list comes in handy when working with an application that's causing problems because the list can help you understand which features the application loads. The list helps you to check for problems that might occur when using an older version of DLL or detect potential corruption in a support file.

One of the interesting ways to use the file list is to check your application for potential problems caused by debug information. Some vendors have mistakenly sent debug versions of the DLLs for their application, which can cause the application to execute slowly or behave in an odd manner. By knowing how to find this information, you can locate subtle problems with your application and report them to the vendor. In many cases, the vendor will issue a patch or provide you with the file you need.

FIGURE A.9

Dependency Walker can help you determine what external files your component needs to operate.

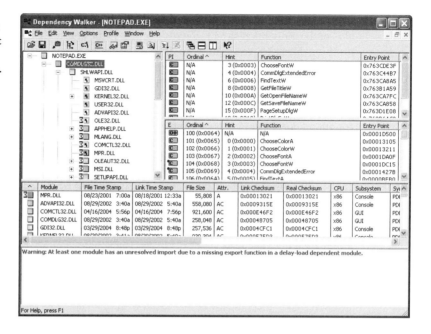

DISSECTING AN APPLICATION OR DLL

Depends really is a developer tool, but you can use it to explore your system at a level of detail that most people don't think is possible. To the right of the hierarchical view in the Depends window are two lists. The upper list tells you the functions the parent executable imports from the current file. The lower list tells you the functions the highlighted executable exports for other executables to use. You'll typically see a blank export list for applications. Most DLLs export functions, but some don't import anything. The presentation will vary depending on the type of file you view.

DLLs created with Visual C++ often have what's termed decoration in the function names. The decoration makes the function names almost unreadable to the average human. To undecorate the function names, right-click within the appropriate function-listing pane, and then choose Undecorate C++ Functions from the context menu.

It's interesting to note that Dependency Walker doesn't include any kind of print functionality. Fortunately, you can highlight a list of items you want to print, click Copy (or press Ctrl+C) to copy them to the clipboard. Use the Paste function in your favorite word processor to create a document you can print for future reference.

Newer versions of the Dependency Walker (including the version that ships with Visual Studio .NET) have a final window shown at the bottom. This window contains any messages that affect the display of the opened file. For example, User32.DLL or one of the imported DLLs in the hierarchy relies on a delay-loaded module (some executable file). The Dependency Walker might not be able to display this module if the associated executable doesn't document it properly.

Profiling an Application

One of the more interesting Depends features is the ability to profile your application. In this case, profiling doesn't have anything to do with performance; we're talking about tracing every call that your application makes. This might sound like overkill for optimizing a system and, generally, it is. You'd use this feature to fix a custom application or figure out why it performs poorly on a particular system. It's also a good way to learn how the application works so you can ask the right questions when talking with the developer. To start the profiling process, choose the Profile ➢ Start Profiling command. You'll see a Profile Module dialog box like the one shown in Figure A.10.

There are actually two sections to this dialog box. The first section provides a command line argument for the application and changes the application's starting path. The values you provide depend on the application—many don't provide command line arguments. In this case, Notepad lets you supply the name of a file to open. You can also choose whether Depends clears the Log window before it begins the profiling process.

The Simulate ShellExecute option determines how Depends starts the application. Normally, you'll keep this checked to ensure that Depends provides the application path information to the application when it starts. The only exception is when you're troubleshooting problems related to the application path. If you clear this option, then Dependency Walker will start the application using a technique that doesn't pass some of the environmental variables.

The second section contains a list of items that you want to monitor. For example, you might only be interested in profiling the libraries that your application loads and when it loads them. In this case, you'd select the Log LoadLibrary function calls option. The number of entries in the Log window can build very quickly, so it helps to decide what you really need to monitor at the outset, rather than wading through a lot of useless information that you don't really want. Figure A.10 shows the default information that Depends will collect about your application. This setup is useful in determining how an application uses the various libraries that it requires to operate.

Once you've decided how to start the application and what you want to monitor, click OK. Depends will load the application and start displaying profile information. In many cases, you'll need to clear the log entries shown in the bottom pane of the window before you profile your application; otherwise, there's simply too much material to check. Figure A.11 shows the Log window entries for Notepad.EXE.

FIGURE A.10

The Profile Module dialog box configures the profiling feature of the Dependency Walker.

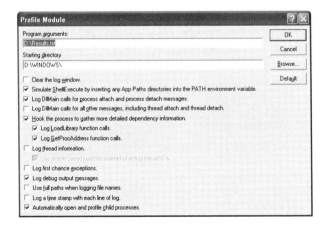

Depends returns control of the application to you as soon as the application finishes loading. You can work with the application just as you normally would and monitor the results in the Log window. When you finish working with an application, you can stop the logging process using the Depends Profile ➤ Stop Profiling command.

FIGURE A.11

Depends will help you monitor the startup activity for any application you start.

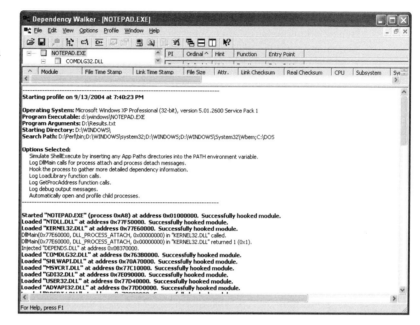

Appendix B

52 Quick Tips for Cleaning Windows

This appendix contains 52 helpful hints that you can use to keep Windows clean throughout the year. There's one tip for each week of the year. As you build new cleaning skills and optimize your system to match your needs, you'll find new ways to use your system. Because optimization isn't a one-time process or a static event that never changes, these tips provide a means for you to move beyond simple optimization into areas that truly make a difference in the way you work. Now that I've shared my tips with you, I'd love to hear about any tips you might have. Write me at JMueller@mwt.net to share them with me.

1. Sometimes it's inefficient or at least annoying to move your hand from the keyboard to the mouse. Unfortunately, it's hard to memorize all those shortcut keys that Microsoft provides for its applications. You can find a complete list of shortcuts for Microsoft applications at http://www.microsoft.com/enable/products/keyboard.aspx. Print out these shortcuts and keep them pasted near your workplace so all you need to do is glance at the sheet to remain productive.

2. Always create a complete backup of your system before performing an optimization. Remember that tape backups tend to provide lots of reliable data storage, but recordable DVDs and CDs are much faster. The fastest backups are made to hard drives, but hard drives are also the least reliable method available.

3. Managing your system manually is a good way to start. You should always know what is happening on your system at a low level. However, once you understand a process, automating it can save you time and ensure the system performs the task the same way each time. Consistency and efficiency are both parts of optimization, so automation is something to consider once you know that a particular optimization is safe.

4. Decide before you optimize how you want to optimize your system. Any optimization includes trade-offs. For example, optimizing for reliability and stability might mean reducing performance or making the environment less appealing for the end user. You might even have to make a few security trade-offs to achieve both reliability and stability. All of the other optimization combinations require trade-offs as well. Consequently, there's no perfect optimization—just the optimization that works best for you.

5. It's helpful to have a quick guide to fixing something on your system. TechRepublic makes a number of quick guides touching on subjects ranging from TCP/IP to spyware detection and removal available for a nominal fee at http://store6.esellerate.net/store/catalog.aspx?s=STR0618954706.

6. The problem you're experiencing with your browser might not have anything to do with your system configuration or the way you optimized it. Different browsers have differing capabilities—your browser might not include a required feature. The webmonkey chart at `http://webmonkey.wired.com/webmonkey/reference/browser_chart/index.html` provides a feature comparison of various browsers.

7. Should you decide to optimize for the user experience and want to make the Windows environment friendlier, you can use themes and other add-ons to do so at a smaller performance cost than other kinds of environment modifications such as specialty application skins or other gizmos. Although Web sites such as TGT Soft (`http://www.tgtsoft.com/`) and ThemeXP (`http://www.themexp.org/`) cater to Windows XP, you can also find generic themes at sites such as `http://www.tucows.com/top_program_7.html`. Don't forget that screen savers are also a relatively free user optimization from a performance perspective. You can find a wealth of safe screen savers at Screen Savers A2Z (`http://www.ratloaf.com`).

8. DOS might be dead (actually, it's quite alive), but the applications aren't gone. Some of the better applications can help you manage and optimize your system with greater efficiency than Windows alternatives. You can find a good selection of these applications at Interesting DOS Programs (`http://www.opus.co.tt/dave/`).

9. Before you optimize your system for security or performance, make sure your applications will actually run in the new environment. In many cases, you must check application requirements as well as test the application in the new environment on a test machine (when possible).

10. Always assume that if a problem can occur, it will. This pessimistic view of system failure is helpful because you can always celebrate computer uptime without additional preparation, but downtime usually catches people unprepared. Optimize your ability to both anticipate and react to system problems whenever possible.

11. Microsoft is constantly adding new tools to their arsenal of security aids. When you need to optimize your system for security, these tools can make a significant difference and the price is right—they're free. Check out the list of security tools at `http://www.microsoft.com/technet/security/tools/default.mspx`.

12. The more you can learn about the registry before you edit it, the better. The registry is one part of Windows that you want to treat with care. Knowledge helps you understand how the registry works, reduces the potential for error, and gives you the confidence to perform necessary registry editing. Even though this book contains a number of registry tricks, you can find out more at the Windows Registry Guide at `http://www.winguides.com/registry/`. Many of these tweaks work for more than one version of Windows.

13. Google can be a best friend in helping you find reliable DLLs on Microsoft's Web site. All you need to know is the DLL name and learn how to enter the information on the Advanced Search form at `http://www.google.com/advanced_search`. In the Domain field, type **www.microsoft.com**, **support.microsoft.com**, **download.microsoft.com**, or **msdn.microsoft.com** (try all four domains in succession). Never type the protocol in the Domain field (such as http). In the Find Results with All the Words field, type the name of the DLL (such as **CommDlg.DLL**) and the word **download**. Click Google Search to locate the file.

14. Not every application on your system is easy to find or figure out once you do find it. The Task List Programs page on the Answers that Work site at `http://www.answersthatwork.com/Tasklist_pages/tasklist.htm` can help you identify a program in the task list. Not all of these programs are evil spyware or adware—Microsoft simply uses odd names sometimes and you need to know what the name means to understand the application. The best part about this list is that it contains information about what you should do about the application in question.

15. Accidentally removing a DLL that you really needed is a problem that many people have faced. You can usually locate a copy of the DLL you need on the vendor-supplied CD or download. However, sometimes you can't find the DLL you need—all you know is that you need it because some program won't start without it. Fortunately, you can locate DLLs online from sources such as Analog's DLL Archive (`http://www.analogx.com/contents/download/system/dllarch.htm`) and www.dll-files.com (`http://www.dll-files.com/`). The important thing to remember is to download your DLLs from a reliable site and make sure you get the correct DLL version.

16. If you're a Windows XP user and have had the courage to install Service Pack 2 (SP2), you'll undoubtedly notice the Internet Explorer Information Bar located under the Address Bar. This new feature tells you how Internet Explorer reacts to various Web sites, such as when it blocks a pop-up on that site. Paying attention to this new information can help you optimize your Internet Explorer usage experience. Learn more about this feature at `http://www.microsoft.com/windowsxp/using/web/sp2_infobar.mspx`.

17. Removing temporary files is one of the best ways to optimize your system without causing any other problems. This optimization technique works no matter how you plan to focus your optimization efforts. Temporary files reduce performance, increase security risks, cause system reliability and stability problems, and diminish the user experience.

18. Before you attempt a new optimization task, check online sources for potential problems with that technique. Make sure you check the vendor site, as well as newsgroups and list servers. Check third party Web sites as well. In many cases, you'll gain a better understanding of the task as you research it, which reduces the potential for failure.

19. Using the Find and FindStr utilities can save you an enormous amount of time searching for data on your hard drive. These two utilities provide better results than Windows Explorer does, but they're also harder to use because you have to remember all of those command line switches. Because many people use the same switches all the time, it's possible to combine these utilities with a batch file. All you have to remember then is to type the name of the batch file, followed by the string you want to search for, and the search file match (wildcard or single file).

20. Knowledge is king—at least that's the common wisdom. However, it's often better to let someone else gather the knowledge and know where to find it when you need it. The Microsoft Knowledge Base is a vast source of knowledge that you can tap for a number of optimization tasks. Check it out at `http://support.microsoft.com/default.aspx?scid=fh;EN-US;KBHOWTO`.

21. Applications create LOG files to help you keep track of specific system events such as an application installation, update, or patch. Some applications also use LOG files to track operational events such as starting up, committing data transactions, or performing specific tasks. When a LOG file falls into the second category, you might find it locked. As the LOG file ages, the application will likely replace it with a new one, at which time you should erase the old LOG file from the drive after reviewing it.

22. Many Web sites provide helpful charts, graphs, and other information regarding viruses. When the information comes from a reliable site, you can use it as a means to increase your virus knowledge and check your system for flaws. TechRepublic provides several useful aids in detecting three common viruses: Bagel (`http://ct.com.com/click?q=91-EZnpQAzsNQBB40cBMGAUVoFynsiR`), MyDoom (`http://ct.com.com/click?q=a0-11h8QQBbN3jywblzZn201PK5gvlR`), and Lovegate (`http://ct.com.com/click?q=ec-MHyXQVy3Fg6GhPLGVI5AY23uGbPR`). You must register to use the resources on this site.

23. When compressing files, you can rely on the CAB or ZIP file format for compatibility purposes. The CAB file format provides the best compatibility because it works with every version of Windows. The ZIP file format provides the best functionality—you can use alternate compression types and protect the file with a password. Use alternative formats such as TAR and RAR when you require special functionality or need to move the file to another platform such as UNIX or Linux.

24. One form of decoration (user optimization) that Windows 9x users enjoy that Windows XP users can't is the startup logo. The best part is that this particular user optimization is free because it occurs during startup, rather than when the computer is performing a task for the user—it's a one-time charge. You can find startup logos, utilities for making your own startup logos, and other software such as screen savers on the XrX site at `http://www.nucleus.com/~kmcmurdo/logos/`.

25. Use the MSCONFIG utility for quick configuration tasks. You can use this utility to test whether removing an application or service from the startup list actually provides a performance boost or improves system reliability. In fact, you can use this technique to locate viruses, adware, and spyware on your system (within limits). However, MSCONFIG is generally better used as a temporary solution and you should use an uninstall application or a registry edit to make the change permanent.

26. Many people are unaware of how they use system resources. Even though you usually consider audits and quotas monitoring aids for other users, it's also possible to use them as self-monitoring aids to improve your own usage habits. In many cases, you can obtain a significant productivity and performance boost from changing bad usage habits without any loss of system functionality. In addition, many people find that the Windows usage experience is much better.

27. Everyone can use a utility program to accomplish tasks faster. The NONAGS Web site at `http://www.tusafe.com/nonags/index.html` contains links to a wealth of interesting utilities you can use to optimize your system. The best part of this Web site is the overview it provides and the way it organizes the entries. However, you do have to drill down to locate utilities in some cases.

28. Browse the \Windows\System32 folder as you have time to discover new executable files. Spend time learning what tasks these files perform and then begin using them (if possible) to help you maintain your system. In some cases, you'll find that you can't use the file, but in many others, you'll find a new tool that you can use to improve your system in some way. The best place to start your utility information search is the Microsoft reference at http:// www.microsoft.com/resources/documentation/windows/xp/all/proddocs/en-us/ ntcmds.mspx.

29. Protect your system investment and optimize your system at the same time by performing regular maintenance. It might not seem like a very big issue to clean up temporary files, back up your system, defragment your hard drive, and then run diagnostics, but this small investment can pay big dividends. All of these steps help you focus on the health of your system and can reduce the chance that you'll miss an important sign that something is failing.

30. Always create automation in at least three stages. First, perform the task manually until you understand it fully. Second, write batch or script files as needed to automate the task. Test the automation fully before you trust it. Third, schedule the automate task to run at specific times to ensure the task is performed regularly. Optimization only works well when you perform it regularly and consistently.

31. Microsoft provides an interesting article that presents several short and quick ways to improve Windows XP performance at http://www.microsoft.com/windowsxp/using/setup/ expert/northrup_restoreperf.mspx. Interestingly enough, many of these tips are also useful with other versions of Windows. Longer (more detailed) versions of all these tips appear in this book.

32. This book contains a wealth of information on command line utilities. Always make sure you use such utilities with extreme care because most of them are unforgiving. Verify that you're using the correct command line switches and have provided all of the input information the utility requires before you execute it. As with all optimization, your best defense against a utility gone wrong is a great backup.

33. Gamers have good news and bad news when it comes to Windows XP SP2. The good news is that you get an updated version of DirectX that appears to make many games look nicer and perform better. The bad news is that your Internet games, such as Massively Multiplayer Online Role Playing Games (MMORPG), will require help to get through the firewall. You can learn more about this issue at http://www.microsoft.com/windowsxp/using/games/ expert/durham_gamesp2.mspx.

34. A good optimization rule to follow is to think before you act. Consider the results of an act before you perform it. Although you'll take safeguards to make recovering from an errant optimization step possible, preventing the step in the first place is better.

35. Removing unneeded services from your system isn't just a matter of optimizing it for performance—unneeded services also pose security risks. In some cases, removing an unneeded service can reduce user errors. However, removing services can also reduce system flexibility and diminish the user computing experience. For example, stopping the indexing service can save resources and improve system performance. Stopping the indexing service can also reduce user error by forcing Windows Explorer to read the drive every time the user makes a request.

However, because the indexing service reduces user search time, you're actually diminishing the user's ability to perform tasks quickly.

36. Always look for the easiest and simplest solution to a problem. In many cases, an optimization fails because the solution to a problem is too complex. For example, even though you can write a complex script to make using a command line utility easier, a simple batch file will often do the trick with a lot less effort.

37. You can use the MSCONFIG utility described in the "Using MSCONFIG" section of Chapter 7 to turn spyware off (or at least determine whether a particular application is spyware). Learn more about this technique at `http://www.pcmag.com/article2/0,1759,1644030,00.asp`.

38. Complete system optimization, even when you have a specific goal in mind, isn't always obtainable or even desirable. Optimization is often a balancing act where you must consider the complete picture. For example, optimizing your system so it provides the ultimate performance isn't a good idea when the optimization removes important security features or makes the system hard to use.

39. Always reduce the size of the paging file when defragmenting the hard drive on a machine with a single partition. Reducing the paging file size lets the defragmenter do a better job over a larger percentage of the hard drive. Switch the paging file to another partition when you have more than one partition to work with on the machine. Moving the paging file to another partition frees up the space that the paging file would use so the disk defragmenter can work faster.

40. Ridding your system of viruses, adware, and spyware is difficult—keeping them away can prove impossible without good information. TechRepublic provides a great guide entitled, "Windows XP Professional Security TechProGuide 1: Viruses, Worms, and Spyware" at `http://techrepublic.com.com/5138-22-5221091.html?tag=tr.e099.0902`. (You'll need to register with the magazine to download the guide.)

41. Remember to save all of your personal settings, including those found in the registry, before you perform a complex optimization task. You should also save these settings when you move to another machine or when you need to install new hardware such as a hard drive. Remember that your personal registry settings appear in the `NTUser.DAT` file located in your personal folder in the `\Documents and Settings` folder.

42. Use alternative browsers such as Firefox, Opera, and Mozilla whenever possible to optimize your system for security. These browsers probably have security holes too, but because they have a smaller percentage of the market, virus writers are less interested in them. Unfortunately, you can't use any of these alternatives with Windows Update and other Web sites will likely fail as well. See a list of alternative browsers on the Searchalot Directory at `http://www.searchalot.com/Top/Computers/Software/Freeware/Internet/Clients/WWW/Browsers/`.

43. Consider using online email when you use multiple computers or you spend a lot of time traveling. Online email provides an advantage in resource usage (no local storage) and accessibility from multiple machines. However, it's also important to remember that online email will slow your email access because you have to download more information. In addition, this email setup isn't under your control, so you might find that service interruptions reduce your ability to retrieve email precisely when you need it.

44. Sometimes, the best way to make registry entries is to let the computer do it for you. For example, many DLLs are self-registering with the RegSvr32 utility. In addition, many applications register themselves when you first start them. If the registry settings become damaged, the application often detects the problem and fixes the errors for you. Even when the fix isn't automatic, application configuration options can make the changes for you. Research these alternatives before you attempt to change the registry by hand.

45. Command line utilities are essential when you want to use batch files or scripts to perform tasks. However, because command line utilities are harder to use, you should look for a GUI alternative when you can to perform tasks manually. Every optimization has a trade-off. In this case, command line utilities are more flexible and offer possible automation, while GUI utilities offer ease of use. Make sure you look for the hybrid application as well. For example, the Microsoft Baseline Security Analyzer (MBSA) offers both a GUI and a command line interface so you get the best of both worlds.

46. Although Windows 9x is less capable than Windows NT-based systems such as Windows 2000 and Windows XP when it comes to optimizing your system, you can still rely on third party utilities to help you. In addition, some optimization features are simply different when using Windows 9x. For example, you access the Task Manager by pressing Ctrl+Alt+Del.

47. Always use the FAT file system when compatibility is the main issue on your system. Using FAT allows you to work with multiple versions of Windows on the same system or even install DOS and Windows XP on the same machine. Use NTFS when you want to obtain the best performance, along with all of the great features that NTFS provides including better security, file compression, and efficient data storage.

48. Installing Windows XP SP2 modifies the way Outlook Express works for the better. Instead of automatically displaying pictures provided with HTML email, SP2 sets Outlook Express to ignore the pictures. Because pictures can contain unwanted viruses, this feature can help protect your system and optimize it for security, rather than user needs. In addition, this feature provides you with a small performance boost. You can discover more about Outlook Express changes at http://email.about.com/b/a/104504.htm.

49. Use the four security zones that Internet Explorer provides to your advantage. Remember that each security level equates to the amount of trust you place in a Web site. Place each Web site in a zone that reflects how you view it from a security perspective and you'll find that your system is less likely to pick up adware and spyware.

50. It pays to spend time online keeping up-to-date with the latest technology because these technologies can help you avoid optimization problems. For example, spam is a major optimization problem—it fills your hard drive with all kinds of entries that you don't need or want. Unfortunately, the spam artists are particularly good at creating spam and the tools we have aren't particularly successful at blocking it. This issue could change with new technologies that detect spam by tracking the sender's patterns (see the eWeek article at http://www.eweek.com/article2/0,1759,1645021,00.asp?kc=ewnws091304dtx1k0000599 for details).

51. Test your backup system regularly. Perform a test backup on a number of areas on your hard drive. Make sure you include network drives as needed—test at least one area on each network drive you can access. After you perform the backup, restore the files to a different location of your local drive. Use the FC utility to compare the restored file to the original. If the two files don't match, you have a backup problem and need to fix it—your current backups are untrustworthy.

52. Do you need a list of spyware that might be infesting your system? You can find such a list on the Sysinfo.org site at `http://www.sysinfo.org/startuplist.php`. In many cases, knowing the name of a bad application is the first step in removing it from your system.

Glossary

This book includes a glossary so that you can find terms and acronyms easily. It has several important features you need to know about. Every acronym in the entire book appears here (except common acronyms such as units of measure).

These definitions are specific to the book. In other words, when you look through this glossary, you're seeing the words defined in the context in which they're used in this the book. This might or might not always coincide with current industry usage since the computer industry changes the meaning of words so often.

I've used a conversational tone for the definitions in most cases. This means that the definitions might sacrifice a bit of accuracy for the sake of better understanding. The purpose of this glossary is to define the terms to reduce misunderstanding the intent of the book as a whole.

While this glossary is as complete as I can make it, you'll run into situations when you need to know more. In addition to the technical information found in the book, I've directed your attention to numerous online sources of information throughout the book; and few of the terms the Web site owners use will appear here unless I also chose to use them in the book. Fortunately, many sites on the Internet provide partial or complete glossaries to fill in the gaps:

Acronym Finder `http://www.acronymfinder.com/`

Free Online Dictionary Of Computing (FOLDOC) `http://nightflight.com/foldoc/`

Microsoft Business Users Glossary `http://www.microsoft.com/atwork/glossary.mspx`

Microsoft Encarta `http://encarta.msn.com/`

Microsoft Management Console (MMC) Glossary `http://msdn.microsoft.com/library/en-us/mmc/mmc/mmc_glossary_gly.asp`

Microsoft Media Glossary (Audio and Video) `http://msdn.microsoft.com/library/en-us/wmcodecs/htm/glossary.asp`

Microsoft Security Glossary `http://msdn.microsoft.com/library/en-us/dnanchor/html/securityanchor.asp`

Microsoft Task Scheduler Glossary `http://msdn.microsoft.com/library/en-us/taskschd/taskschd/task_scheduler_glossary.asp`

Webopedia `http://webopedia.internet.com/`

yourDictionary.com `http://www.yourdictionary.com/`

Some entries in this list are quite specialized. For example, the Microsoft Management Console (MMC) Glossary provides definitions for terms that you'll encounter when using one of the Consoles found in the Administrative Tools folder of the Control Panel. You can find other Microsoft Glossaries listed at `http://www.microsoft.com/resources/glossary/default.mspx`. If you still don't find what you need, try the Microsoft Search page at `http://search.microsoft.com/`, type the word *glossary*, add a specific area such as network, and click Go.

A

Access Control Entry (ACE)

Defines the object rights for a single user or group. Every ACE has a header that defines the type, size and flags for the ACE. Next comes an access mask that defines the rights a user or group has to the object. Finally, there's an entry for the user's or group's Security IDentifier (SID).

Access Control List (ACL)

Part of the Windows NT-based operating system security Application Programming Interface (API) used to determine both access and monitoring properties for an object. Each ACL contains one or more Access Control Entries (ACEs) that define the security properties for an individual or group. There are two major ACL groups: Security Access Control List (SACL) and Discretionary Access Control List (DACL). The SACL controls Windows auditing feature. The DACL controls access to the object.

ACE

See Access Control Entry

ACL

See Access Control List

Adware

A type of application that monitors a user's activity on the Internet. Adware products always install after asking the user's permission, so the user knows about the presence of adware on their machine. (Some industry observers say that adware information purposely leaves out information the user needs to make a good decision.) In addition, the user normally receives adware in exchange for a service or other feature of a Web site. Because adware's purported reason to exist is to sell the user products, the user will receive constant reminders about the adware installation on their machine through the advertisements it displays. Finally, adware is normally easy to uninstall using standard application uninstall techniques. When the user uninstalls the adware, the user also loses access to any Web site functionality that the adware supports.

American Standard Code for Information Interchange (ASCII)

A standard method of equating the numeric representations available in a computer to human-readable form. For example, the number 32 represents a space. The standard ASCII code contains 128 characters (7 bits). The extended ASCII code uses 8 bits for 256 characters. Display adapters from the same machine type usually use the same upper 128 characters. Printers, however, might reserve these upper 128 characters for nonstandard characters. For example, many older Epson printers use them for the italic representations of the lower 128 characters. This is the standard character set used by all Windows 9x implementations.

Applet

A helper or utility application that normally performs a task within a specialized environment such as a browser or as part of an operating system. Java is one of the most commonly used languages for creating applets for browser applications. Another example is the Control Panel applications used to configure Windows. In both cases, the applications perform a limited task within a specialized environment.

Application

One or more executable files that include machine-readable code and specialized data. The complete program or group of programs. An application is a complete environment for performing one or more related tasks. Applications perform tasks for the user or system based on a specific need.

ALG

Application Layer Gateway

ASCII

See American Standard Code for Information Interchange

Attribute

An attribute expresses some feature peculiar to an object. When referring to a database, each field has an attribute that expresses what type of information it contains, the length of the field, the field name, and the number of decimals. When referring to a display, the attribute expresses pixel color, intensity, and position. In programming, an attribute can also specify some type of object functionality, such as the method used to implement security.

B

Bandwidth

A measure of the amount of data a device can transfer in a given time. For example, the amount of data a processor can send to memory every second. In many cases, bandwidth also considers software limitations, such as the estimated bandwidth of an Internet connection.

Basic Input/Output System (BIOS)

A set of low-level computer interface functions stored in a chip on a computer's motherboard. The BIOS performs basic tasks like booting the computer during startup and performing the power-on startup tests (POST). Older operating systems, such as DOS, rely heavily on the BIOS to perform all types of low-level device interface tasks.

Binary

1. A numbering system that only uses two digits: 0 and 1. 2. A method used to store worksheets, graphic files, and other nontext information. The data store can appear in memory, but most often appears in a file on disk. While you can use the DOS TYPE command to send these files to the display, the contents of the file remain unreadable. Other binary files include programs with extensions of EXE, DLL, or COM.

BIOS

See Basic Input/Output System

Browser

A special application, such as Internet Explorer, Opera, or Netscape, normally used to display data downloaded from the Internet. The most common form of Internet data is the HTML (HyperText Markup Language) page. However, modern browsers can also display various types of graphics and even standard desktop application files such as Word for Windows documents directly. The actual capabilities provided by a browser vary widely depending on the software vendor and platform.

C

CAB

See Cabinet File

Cabinet File (CAB)

1. A compressed-format file similar to the ZIP files used to transfer code and data from one location to another. Only developers who work with Microsoft language products normally use the CAB format, but anyone working in the Windows environment could use them by creating the file with the Compress utility. You can also decompress the file using the Expand utility. 2. A single file created to hold a number of compressed files. A related set of cabinet files can be contained in a folder. During installation of a program, the compressed files in a cabinet are decompressed and copied to an appropriate directory for the user.

Cache

A storage area for data, code, or other resources normally associated with memory or a special file on a hard drive. Both hardware and applications rely on the cache to improve performance.

CD

Compact Disc

CIAC

See Computer Incident Advisory Capability

Class Identifier (CLSID)

A method of assigning a unique number to each object used by Windows. These numbers normally appear in the registry and Windows uses them for reference purposes. The number normally appears in the form {00000000-0000-0000-0000-000000000000}, but can take on other forms as well. This term also refers to various high-level language constructs used by programming languages.

Client

The requestor and recipient of data, services, or other resources from a file or other server type. This term can refer to a workstation or an application. Often used in conjunction with the term *server*, this is usually another PC or an application.

Client Server Runtime Service Shell (CSRSS)

This application handles all of the graphics and windows on the host system, along with some other low-level process management.

CLSID

See Class Identifier

COM

See Component Object Model

Comma Separated Value (CSV)

A type of text database file where the data fields are separated from one another using commas. Each carriage return/line feed combination (new line) creates a new record. Many applications can retrieve CSV files and convert them to other database representations.

Component Object Model (COM)

A Microsoft specification for a binary-based, object-oriented code and data encapsulation method and transference technique. It's the basis for technologies such as OLE (Object Linking and Embedding) and ActiveX (components and controls). COM is limited to local connections.

Computer Incident Advisory Capability (CIAC)

An office of the United States Department of Energy (DOE) tasked with tracking viruses, Trojan Horses, worms, system vulnerabilities, common patches, and other security related information.

Connectivity

A measure of the interactions between clients and servers. In many cases, connectivity begins with the local machine and the interactions between applications and components. Local Area Networks (LANs) introduce another level of connectivity with machine-to-machine communications. Finally, Wide Area Networks (WANs), Metro Area Networks (MANs), intranets, and the Internet all introduce further levels of connectivity concerns.

Console

1. A type of character-mode application that normally runs at the DOS (command) prompt. A console application normally performs a simple or utilitarian task that doesn't require the Graphical User Interface (GUI) associated with most application development today. 2. The generic term for a workstation used to monitor server status information. In most cases, the workstation and server are the same device. Most people associate consoles with a character mode interface, but this isn't a requirement. 3. A short version of the longer term Microsoft Management Console (MMC). (See Microsoft Management Console for details.)

Control Panel Library (CPL)

The file extension used for configuration applications that appear within the Windows Control Panel. Some references also call this file type a Control Panel Extension. The configuration application provides access to a service or specialized application. You change the settings to ensure the service or specialized application reacts as intended. In many cases, the Control Panel Extension also modifies Windows settings within the registry. Double-clicking a file with the CPL extension opens the configuration application directly, without having to use the Control Panel.

Cookie

A value stored in one or more special files managed by a Web browser. The cookie can hold site-specific settings or other information specific to Web pages. In addition, the cookie can last just for the current session or the browser can hold it until some future expiration date. A developer always saves and restores the cookie as part of a Web page programming task using a programming language such as ASP, ASP.NET, JavaScript, Java, VBScript, or CGI. In most cases, this is the only file that a developer can access on the client site's hard drive. The cookie could appear in one or more files anywhere on the hard drive, depending on the browser currently in use.

Microsoft Internet Explorer uses one file for each site storing a cookie. Netscape Navigator uses a single file named COOKIE.TXT to store all of the cookies from all sites.

Counter

1. An application designed to measure performance on a Windows system. The counter is part of a performance object. It's normally stored with other counters associated with the same performance object within a Dynamic Link Library (DLL) on the host machine. A counter may allow monitoring of one or more instances of the same type of device or other object as individual performance statistics. 2. A specialized programming structure used to track application data. In some cases, the counter is a specialized object the developer adds to the application for the purpose for statistical data collection.

CPL

See Control Panel Library

CSRSS

See Client Server Runtime Service Shell

CSV

See Comma Separated Value

D

DACL

See Discretionary Access Control List

DAT

See Digital Audio Tape Drive

Database

A data collection that consists of one or more storage elements and any associated objects. The organization of the database depends on the features and functionality of the Database Management System (DBMS) used to maintain it. A database normally uses a hierarchical or tabular format. A hierarchical database relies on nodes connected in any of a number of ways, such as record pointers. The tabular format relies on rows (records) made up of columns (fields). A database can appear as a single file, as part of a collection with the DBMS, as part of a worksheet for a spreadsheet, or any other organized disk format.

Database Management System (DBMS)

A method for storing and retrieving data based on tables, forms, queries, reports, fields, and other data elements. Each field represents a specific piece of data, such as an employee's last name. Records are made up of one or more fields. Each record is one complete entry in a table. A table contains one type of data, such as the names and addresses of all the employees in a company. It's composed of records (rows) and fields (columns), just like the tables you see in books. A database may contain one or more related tables. It may include a list of employees in one table, for example, and the pay records for each of those employees in a second table. Sometimes also referred to as a Relational Database Management System (RDBMS) that includes products such as SQL Server and Oracle.

DBMS

See Database Management System

DDF

See Diamond Directive File

Delimiter

1. A special symbol or symbols used to separate text. For example, many programming languages use the single (') or double (") quote to separate text elements. 2. A boundary between two different objects. The boundary normally consists of a special symbol or group of symbols. A delimited file contains variable length records. Each field normally uses a comma as a delimiter. Each record normally uses a carriage return as a delimiter.

Denial of Service (DoS)

A type of Web-based attack that crackers perpetrate against larger organizations such as companies and standards groups. The cracker attempts to flood organization routers with useless requests in order to cause the router to crash or make it unavailable for legitimate requests. The attack often depends on servers from other organizations and individuals (known as zombies) that the cracker has infected and taken over. These other servers all generate random messages with improper content in an attempt to overload the target systems. DoS attacks also rely on viruses created by the cracker that install the zombie program on the host computer. For example, the Code Red virus uses this technique in order to commit a DoS attack.

Device Driver

A special program used to extend the functionality of an operating system. Device drivers normally contain specific code used to control a hardware or software device. Hardware devices include tape drives and high-resolution monitors, and software devices include data streams (such as those used to download pictures from a remote location) and memory managers.

Diamond Directive File (DDF)

Similar to an INF (information) or BAT (batch) file, the DDF provides instructions to a CAB (cabinet) creation utility such as DIANTZ for compressing one or more files into a single storage file. CAB files are normally used to distribute data locally, using a CD or other similar type of media, or remotely, through an Internet or other server connection. The DDF can also list files needed for a complete installation, but stored in other locations. Normally, these missing files will already appear on the user's computer, so downloading them again would waste time. The DDF makes it possible to download them only as needed.

Digital Audio Tape (DAT) Drive

A tape drive that uses a cassette to store data. The cassette and drive use the same technology as the audio version of the DAT drive. The internal circuitry of the drive formats the tape for use with a computer system, however. The vendor must also design the interface circuitry with computer needs in mind. DAT allows you to store large amounts of information in a relatively small amount of space. Typical drive capacities range from 1.2GB to 24GB (and higher).

Digital Video Disk (DVD)

A high capacity optical storage media with capacities of 4.7GB to 17GB and data transfer rates of 600KBps to 1.3GBps. A single DVD can hold the contents of an entire movie or approximate 7.4 CD-ROMs. DVDs come in several formats including DVD-R, DVD-RW, DVD+R, DVD+RW and DVD-RAM that allow read-only or read-write access. Newer dual-layer DVDs promise even greater storage capacities. All DVD drives include a second laser assembly used to read existing CD-ROMs. Some magazines will also use the term *digital versatile disk* for this storage media.

Directory

A storage unit description used with DOS, many character mode applications, and the Windows command prompt. Directories provide a means of separating files into different locations based on type or use. Using directories makes it easier to locate data and use applications.

Discretionary Access Control List (DACL)

A Windows security component. The DACL controls access to an object. You can assign both groups and individual users to a specific object.

Disk Operating System (DOS)

The underlying management software used by older PCs to provide basic system services and to allow the user to run application software. The operating system performs many low-level tasks through the basic input/output system (BIOS). The revision number determines the specifics of the services that DOS offers; check your user manual for details.

Disk Quota

A limit placed on the amount of hard drive space that a user can rely on to hold data. Many administrators use disk quotas to keep hard disk resource usage under control. In a shared environment, disk quotas ensure that each user receives a fair share of the available disk space.

DLL

See Dynamic Link Library

DoS

See Denial of Service

DOS

See Disk Operating System

Double Word (DWORD)

A special data type designation used in many places including the Windows registry and low-level application source code. The DWORD is a 32-bit value that can range from 0 to 4,294,967,295 in decimal or 0 to FFFFFFFF in hexadecimal.

DVD

See Digital Video Disk

DWORD

See Double Word

Dynamic Link Library (DLL)

A specific form of application code loaded into memory by request. It's not executable by itself like an EXE is. A DLL does contain one or more discrete routines that an application may use to provide specific features. For example, a DLL could provide a common set of file dialogs used to access information on the hard drive. More than one application can use the functions provided by a DLL, reducing overall memory requirements when more than one application is running. DLLs have a number of purposes. For example, they can contain device-specific code in the form of a device driver. Some types of COM objects also rely on DLLs.

E

ECMA

See European Computer Manufacturer's Association

Encryption

The act of making data unreadable using a mathematical conversion. The data remains unreadable unless the reader provides a password or other key value. Encryption makes data safe for transport in unsecured environments like the Internet.

Error Trapping

The additional code required to detect, analyze, repair, report, and overcome errors in an application. An error trapping routine normally locates the precise origin of the error, determines the error type, and defines a course of action for repairing the error when possible. If the application can't recover, the error trapping routine helps the application fail gracefully after reporting the source and cause of the error to the application user.

European Computer Manufacturer's Association (ECMA)

A standards committee originally founded in 1961. ECMA is dedicated to standardizing information and communication systems. For example, it created the ECMAScript standard used for many Web page designs today. You can also find ECMA standards for product safety, security, networks, and storage media.

Event Log File (EVT)

1. A file used to hold the event log entries for a particular aspect of system performance. For example, there are separate files for application, security, and system entries. Each log file can hold several different event types including audit, informational, warning, and error events. 2. An application event destination. The application never interacts with the EVT file itself since more than one application requires access to the EVT file at one time. A well-designed application will always use the Windows API to perform this task.

EVT

See Event Log File

EXE

See Executable File

Executable File (EXE)

1. A binary file that contains machine code (procedural steps the machine can understand), instructions, and data that an operating system can read to perform tasks. An executable file normally contains an application, but it can contain any form of code and resources. 2. A file containing tokenized data

where a token relates to a specific instruction. A special runtime application reads the tokens, interprets them, and sends the results binary machine code to the operating system for execution. The use of tokens lets a single executable work on more that one operating system or machine type, but slows application execution.

Expandable String

A type of Windows registry data value. This data type is a string that includes a special expansion element. For example, the special text %WinDir% defines the location of the Windows folder on the host machine. When a string contains this value, it can point to locations without having to know where these locations actually are on the machine. Windows automatically expands the special text when it reads the string from the registry. For example, %WinDir%\MyFlower.BMP might actually point to C:\Windows\MyFlower.BMP on the host system. Although the registry normally uses expandable strings for data paths, they can expand to any environmental value. For example, the %OS% expandable string refers to the operating system installed on the machine.

eXtensible Markup Language (XML)

1. A method used to store information in an organized manner. The storage technique relies on hierarchical organization and uses special statements called tags to separate each storage element. Each tag defines a data attribute and can contain properties that further define each data element. 2. A standardized Web page design language used to incorporate data structuring within standard HTML documents. For example, you could use XML to display database information using something other than forms or tables. It's actually a lightweight version of Standard Generalized Markup language (SGML) and is supported by the SGML community. XML also supports tag extensions that allow various parts of a Web-based application to exchange information. For example, once a user makes a choice within a catalog, that information could be added to an order entry form with a minimum of effort on the part of the developer. Since XML is easy to extend, some developers look at it as more of a base specification for other languages, rather than a complete language.

F

FAT

See File Allocation Table

FAT32

See File Allocation Table 32-bit

File Allocation Table (FAT)

The method of formatting a hard disk drive used by DOS and other operating systems. This technique is one of the oldest formatting methods available. There have been several different versions of FAT based on the number of bits used to store disk locations. The original form was 12 bits, which was quickly followed by the 16-bit version used by many computers today. A 32-bit version of FAT, also called FAT32, was introduced with the OSR2 version of Windows 98. This new version of FAT stores data more efficiently on the large hard drives available on today's computers.

File Allocation Table 32-bit (FAT32)

See the definition for File Allocation Table (FAT).

File Extension

The characters used to define the kind of data the file contains. For example, the TXT extension identifies files with text (string) data in them; usually in human-readable form. The file extension appears after a final period in the filename such as MyFile.TXT. Windows relies mainly on three letter file extensions, but file extensions with four or more letters are becoming more common.

Firewall

Hardware or software (or a combination of both) used to prevent unauthorized access to a private network. The firewall can use any of a number of techniques to detect unauthorized packets and deny access to them. Some firewalls not only check incoming packets, but outgoing packets as well.

There are many types of firewalls including packet filter, application gateway, proxy server, and circuit-level gateway. For maximum protection, the proxy server normally works best in a hardware configuration.

FIRST

See Forum of Incident Response and Security Teams

Folder

A specialized area for storing files on the hard drive. Folders help you manage both data and applications by breaking them up into smaller and easier to recognize groups. The folder acts as a storage receptacle. The DOS and command prompt equivalent term for folders is directories; the same term used by many other operating systems.

Forum of Incident Response and Security Teams (FIRST)

An organization devoted to tracking and providing support for security events that affect large numbers of organizations.

G

Globally Unique Identifier (GUID)

A 128-bit number used to identify a Component Object Model (COM) object within the Windows registry. The GUID is used to find the object definition and allow applications to create instances of that object. GUIDs can include any kind of object, even nonvisual elements. In addition, some types of complex objects are actually aggregates of simple objects. For example, an object that implements a property page will normally have a minimum of two GUIDs: one for the property page and another for the object itself.

Graphical User Interface (GUI)

1. A method of displaying information that depends on both hardware capabilities and software instructions. A GUI uses the graphics capability of a display adapter to improve communication between the computer and its user. Using a GUI involves a large investment in both programming and hardware resources. 2. A system of icons and graphic images that replaces the character-mode menu system used by many older machines including "green screen" terminals that are connected to mainframes and sometimes to cash registers. The GUI can ride on top of another operating system (such as DOS, Linux, and UNIX) or reside as part of the operating system itself (such as the Macintosh and Windows). Advantages of a GUI are ease of use and high-resolution graphics. Disadvantages include cost, higher workstation hardware requirements, and lower performance over a similar system using a character mode interface.

GUI

See Graphical User Interface

GUID

See Globally Unique Identifier

H

HTML

See HyperText Markup Language

HTTP

See HyperText Transfer Protocol

HTTPS

See HyperText Transfer Protocol Secure sockets

HyperText Markup Language (HTML)

1. A data presentation and description (markup) language for the Internet that depends on the use of tags (keywords within angle brackets <>) to display formatted information on screen in a non-platform-specific manner. The non-platform-specific nature of this markup language makes it difficult to perform some basic tasks such as placement of a screen element at a specific location. However, the language does provide for the use of fonts, color, and various other enhancements on screen. There are also tags for displaying graphic images. Scripting tags for using scripting languages such as VBScript and JavaScript are available, although not all browsers support this

addition. The <OBJECT> tag addition allows the use of ActiveX controls. 2. One method of displaying text, graphics, and sound on the Internet. HTML provides an ASCII-formatted page of information read by a special application called a browser. Depending on the browser's capabilities, some key words are translated into graphics elements, sounds, or text with special characteristics, such as color, font, or other attributes. Most browsers discard any keywords they don't understand, allowing browsers of various capabilities to explore the same page without problem. Obviously, there's a loss of capability if a browser doesn't support a specific keyword.

HyperText Transfer Protocol (HTTP)

One of several common data transfer protocols for the Internet. HTTP normally transfers textual data of some type. For example, the HyperText Markup Language (HTML) relies on HTTP to transfer the Web pages it defines from the server to the client. The eXtensible Markup Language and Simple Object Access Protocol (SOAP) also commonly rely on HTTP to transfer data between client and server. It's important to note that HTTP is separate from the data it transfers. For example, it's possible for SOAP to use the Simple Mail Transfer Protocol (SMTP) to perform data transfers between client and server.

HyperText Transfer Protocol Secure sockets (HTTPS)

A secure form of HTTP that relies on the secure sockets encryption technology to transfer data.

I

ICF

See Internet Connection Firewall

ICS

See Internet Connection Sharing

Infrastructure

The underlying base of an organization or system. One way to view infrastructure is a foundation on which all other elements of a system or organization are attached. Many vendors use this term to indicate the compatibility of their product with existing installations.

Internet Connection Firewall (ICF)

A special service that monitors the flow of data to and from the Internet for a specific machine. A firewall disallows unwanted requests and helps keep a system free from viruses, adware, and spyware. The value of this service depends on the version of Windows running; newer versions provide better protection. On Windows XP systems, this service combines with Internet Connection Sharing to create the Internet Connection Firewall (ICF)/Internet Connection Sharing (ICS) service.

Internet Connection Sharing (ICS)

A special type of proxy server (service) that allows more than one workstation on a peer-to-peer network to share a single Internet connection. The host machine makes the connection and the client machines log into it to make requests. The feature is available on newer versions of Windows starting with Windows 2000. You must configure the host machine to allow Internet connection sharing; this feature is stopped by default to reduce the security risks associated with connection sharing.

Internet Protocol (IP)

The information exchange portion of the TCP/IP protocol used by the Internet. IP is an actual data transfer protocol that defines how the sender places information into packets and transmits from one place to another. TCP (Transmission Control Protocol) is the protocol that defines how the actual data transfer takes place.

Internet Service Provider (ISP)

A vendor that provides one or more Internet-related services through a dial-up, Digital Subscriber Line (DSL), Integrated Services Digital Network (ISDN), or other outside connection. Normal services include email, newsgroup access, full Internet Web site access, and personal Web page hosting.

IP

See Internet Protocol

ISP

See Internet Service Provider

J

JAR

See Java Archive File

Java Archive File (JAR)

A form of data storage that includes compression capability and provides an easy method of distributing all of the components for Java applets. To execute a Java applet, the host machine must have the Java Virtual Machine (JVM) installed.

Java Virtual Machine (JVM)

The application used to interpret the Java language originally developed by Sun Microsystems. This includes both text and byte code .CLASS files containing common routines. Java is similar to C++, but eliminates many of the complex programming constructs and uses a more restrictive security scheme. Many operating systems have a Java Virtual Machine including most versions of Windows, Mac OS, and Unix. The use of text files means that Java applets can run on any number of operating system platforms without modifications, but the use of an interpreter implies slower execution speed.

JavaScript (JS)

A file containing a program written in JavaScript; a language with a C-like syntax. Don't confuse Java and JavaScript; the two languages are not the same. Most browsers support JavaScript and developers like to use it for local and remote applications alike. There are many versions of JavaScript, including Microsoft's JScript and the European Computer Manufacturer's Association (ECMA) ECMAScript.

JS

See JavaScript

JVM

See Java Virtual Machine

L

LAN

See Local Area Network

Lempel-Ziv-Welch (LZW)

A form of data compression originally created in 1977 by J. Ziv and A. Lempel. Terry Welch later refined the compression technique that appears in many applications today. Many file formats rely on LZW compression, including both Graphics Interchange Format (GIF) and Tagged Image File Format (TIFF). The LZW compression algorithm also appears within the Windows operating system and many other commercial applications.

Local Area Network (LAN)

Two or more devices located in a relatively small physical area connected together using a combination of hardware and software. The devices, normally computers and peripheral equipment such as printers, are called nodes. An NIC (network interface card) provides the hardware communication between nodes through an appropriate medium (cable or microwave transmission). The actual connection is provided through cables, in many cases, but can also rely on radio waves, infrared, and other technologies. There are two common types of LANs (also called networks). Peer-to-peer networks allow each node to connect to any other node on the network with shareable resources. This is a distributed method of files and peripheral devices. A client-server network uses one or more servers to share resources. This is a centralized method of sharing files and peripheral devices. A server provides resources to clients (usually workstations).

Local Security Authority (LSA)

The portion of Windows that monitors local security activities.

Local Security Authority Service Shell (LSASS)

An application that authenticates a user and provides a token specifying the user's privileges. Windows uses the security token to initialize the session and launch applications on the user's behalf.

LSA

See Local Security Authority

LSASS

See Local Security Authority Service Shell

LZW

See Lempel-Ziv-Welch

M

MBSA

Microsoft Baseline Security Analyzer

Microsoft Management Console (MMC)

A special application that displays special programs called snap-ins that help the user manage Windows, a device, or an application. MMC acts as an object container for Windows management objects like Component Services and Computer Management. The management objects are actually special components that provide interfaces that allow the user to access them within MMC to maintain and control the operation of Windows. A developer can create special versions of these objects for application management or other tasks. Using a single application like MMC helps maintain the same user interface across all management applications.

MIME

See Multipurpose Internet Mail Extensions

MMC

See Microsoft Management Console

MSCONFIG

Microsoft Configuration Utility for Windows

Multipurpose Internet Mail Extensions (MIME)

The standard method for defining the content of Internet messages. This standard allows computers to exchange objects, character sets, and multimedia using email without regard to the computer's underlying operating system. MIME is defined in the Internet Engineering Task Force (IETF) Request for Comment (RFC) 1521 standard.

N

NTFS

See Windows New Technology File System

O

Object Linking and Embedding (OLE)

The process of packaging a filename or data, server name (generally an application), and any required parameters into an object, and then placing this object into the file created by another application. For example, a user could place a graphic object within a word processing document or spreadsheet. OLE supports both linking (placing a pointer to the source data in permanent storage in the target file) and embedding (placing the actual data into the target file). When you look at the object it appears as if you simply pasted the data from the originating application into the current application, which is similar to Dynamic Data Exchange (DDE). However, the data object created by OLE automatically changes as you change the data in the original object (provided you use the linking portion of the technology). It also contains the intelligence to know which application created the data. Generally, you can start the originating application and automatically load the required data by double clicking on the object.

OCX

See OLE Custom eXtension

ODBC

See Open Database Connectivity

OLE

See Object Linking and Embedding

OLE Custom eXtension (OCX)

A component or control designed to make adding various capabilities to an application easier for the programmer. Essentially, an OCX is a DLL with added programmer and Component Object Model (COM) interfaces. Component technology has evolved to include a wide variety of uses including both client-side and server-side application elements. A component differs from a control in that a component is usually used for a processing task and lacks a user interface. Controls include application elements such as push buttons and text boxes.

Open Database Connectivity (ODBC)

One of several methods for exchanging data between DBMSs. In most cases, this involves three steps: installing an appropriate driver, adding a source to the Data Sources (ODBC) applet in the Control Panel, and using specialized statements, such as Structured Query Language (SQL), to access the database.

Optimization

The configuration and organization of an operating system such that it provides specific functionality and performance in any of several areas including speed, reliability, usability, stability, security, and resource usage. Improving one area generally degrades one or more other areas so that the act of optimization also requires balancing the goals so that the optimization meets specific needs. For example, optimizing a system to provide better security generally reduces usability and speed, and increases resource usage. In some cases, a security update could even affect system reliability and stability.

P

P3P

See Platform for Privacy Preferences

Parameter

A value received by a function or procedure from another function or procedure, the command line, or some other source.

Patch

When applied to software, a term that normally defines a small piece of code designed to provide an upgrade. (Some vendors are stretching the size of some patches so they're almost as large as the actual application.) In most cases, a patch will repair a programming error of some type. It could also improve security or add application features. The methods of creating a patch include complete executable replacement or executable modification using an external application. Patches can also affect application data and support files.

Peer-to-Peer Network

A group of connected computers where every computer can act as a server and a client. Selected computers normally provide services to others, but unlike a client/server network, the network administrator can distribute the processing load over several machines. In addition, all nodes of a peer-to-peer network also act as workstations.

PERL

See Practical Extraction and Report Language

PID

See Process Identifier

Platform

A description of the combination of software and hardware used to create a computing system. For example, many users use a combination of the Windows operating system and an Intel processor. The combination often appears as the Wintel platform. In some cases, a discussion will only use the operating system as the basis for a platform. A developer might create applications only for the Windows platform. The use of the term *platform* is often ambiguous and requires the actual platform type to make the meaning clear.

Platform for Privacy Preferences (P3P)

A Worldwide Web Consortium (W3C) sponsored technique for ensuring privacy through specialized programming techniques. The specification defines methods of communicating information requests, use, storage technique, and requirements to the requestor. The requestor then decides whether the requirements are acceptable and optionally transfers the necessary information.

Plug and Play

The combination of Basic Input/Output System (BIOS), operating system, and peripheral device components that provides a self-configuring environment. This self-configuring feature allows the operating system to avoid potential hardware conflicts by polling the peripheral devices, assessing their requirements, and determining and implementing optimal settings for each device.

Practical Extraction and Report Language (PERL)

Originally designed as a report generation language for the Internet, PERL has found other uses, as well, for more general Internet programming needs. PERL is normally an interpreted scripting language.

Process Identifier (PID)

A numeric value associated with a process running on a specific machine. Every process has a unique PID, making it possible to locate a specific process, even if there are multiple copies of a single application running on the machine. The PID is used by a wide variety of monitoring applications. It's also used to access an application or as a means of identification when terminating an errant application.

Q

Query

A request or question made by a user of an application program using an interface. The query can appear as part of a form or other type of input, or the user can make the query as part of a script when using automation. Common queries include search requests for documents or a request to perform a task such as checking the status of the computer hardware.

R

RAID

See Redundant Array of Independent (or Inexpensive) Disks

RAM

See Random Access Memory

Random Access Memory (RAM)

The basic term used to describe volatile data storage within a computer system. RAM comes in a variety of types such as Direct Rambus Dynamic Random Access Memory (DRDRAM), Double Data Rate Synchronous Dynamic Random Access Memory (DDR SDRAM), Dual-Ported Video RAM (VRAM), Extended Data Out Dynamic Random Access Memory (EDO DRAM), and Static Random Access Memory (SRAM). Each of these RAM types has specialized features. These special features make some kinds of RAM more acceptable for some storage tasks than others.

Redundant Array of Independent (or Inexpensive) Disks (RAID)

A set of interconnected drives that reside outside the server, in many cases, but are connected to the server through cabling. Workstation RAID setups tend to reside in the workstation cabinet. There are several levels of RAID. Each level defines precisely how the data is placed on each of the drives. In all cases, all the drives in a group share responsibility for storing the data. They act in parallel to both read and write the data. In addition, there's a special drive in most of these systems devoted to helping the network recover when one drive fails. In most cases, the user never even knows that anything happened, the "spare drive" takes over for the failed drive without any noticeable degradation in network operation. RAID systems increase network reliability and throughput.

Registry

A specialized hierarchical database used to hold settings, configuration, file associations, and other information for Windows. The registry is a hierarchy or tree consisting of keys and associated values. The operating system searches the registry tree for keys that it requires, then requests values for those keys in order to perform tasks such as configure an application. The registry is organized into hives. Each hive contains settings for a particular operating system element such as user information and hardware configuration. Users share common hives such as those used for hardware, but have separate hives for their information as long as Windows is configured to provide separate desktops for each user.

Registry Key

A registry entry; a method of organizing registry data. It provides the structure required to hold configuration values and other information required by both Windows and the applications it runs. Each registry key resides within a hive and can contain zero or more values. Children of registry keys are called subkeys.

Registry Setting

The combination of a registry key and one or more registry values that describe an option such as an application configuration value. A registry setting could describe where to find additional values for an executable file. The setting provides a complete description of a single data element.

Registry Value

An individual piece of data within the Windows registry database. Each value provides some type of information associated with a registry key, such as configuration information, a globally unique identifier (GUID), human readable value, numeric value, binary sequence, or other appropriate data. The common registry data types include string, DWORD, binary, multi-string, and expandable string. Of these values, the string data types are easiest to read and understand.

Remote Procedure Call (RPC)

One of several methods for accessing data within another application. RPC is designed to look for the application first on the local workstation, and then across the network at the applications stored on other workstations.

Remote Registry

A term that describes access to the registry on another Windows machine from a local Windows machine. This feature only works when the remote machine is running the Remote Registry service. Because the Remote Registry service is dangerous to leave on all the time (someone could gain access to the remote registry over the Internet), it's important to start it only when the Internet connection isn't in use. Make the remote access time as short as possible and stop the Remote Registry service as soon as possible.

RPC

See Remote Procedure Call

S

SACL

See Security Access Control List

SANS

See SysAdmin, Audit, Network, Security Institute

Script

Usually associated with an interpreted macro language used to create simple applications, productivity enhancers, or automated data manipulators. Most operating systems support at least one scripting language. You'll also find scripting capability in many higher end applications such as Web browsers and word processors. Scripts are normally used to write small utility-type applications rather than large-scale applications that require the use of a compiled language. In addition, many scripting languages are limited in their access of the full set of operating system features.

Secure Socket Layer (SSL)

A digital signature technology used for exchanging information between a client and a server. Essentially an SSL-compliant server will request a digital certificate from the client machine. The client can likewise request a digital certificate from the server. Companies or individuals obtain these digital certificates from a third party vendor like VeriSign or other trusted source that can vouch for the identity of both parties.

Security Access Control List (SACL)

One of several specialized Access Control Lists (ACL) used to maintain object integrity. This list controls Windows' auditing feature. Every time a user or group accesses an object and the auditing feature for that object is turned on, Windows makes an entry in the audit log.

Security Identifier (SID)

The part of an access token that identifies the object throughout the network; it's like having an account number. The access token that the SID identifies tells what groups the object belongs to and what privileges the object has.

Self-Monitoring and Reporting Technology (SMART)

A specialized disk drive monitoring capability that reports on issues such as drive health and performance. The essential goal of this technology is to provide a warning of impending drive failure.

Server

1. A specialized computer designed to answer client requests for services such as printing and centralized file storage. 2. An application or workstation that provides services, resources, or data to a client application or workstation. The client usually makes requests in the form of Object Linking and Embedding (OLE), Dynamic Data Exchange (DDE), Distributed Component Object Model (DCOM), Component Object Model Plus (COM+), HyperText Markup Language (HTML), or other command formats. The server response to a request is service, resource, data, error message, or an access denied message.

Session Manager Service Shell (SMSS)

This application starts, manages, and deletes user sessions in Windows. In addition, Terminal Services uses this application to work with client sessions.

SID

See Security Identifier

SMART

See Self-Monitoring and Reporting Technology

SMSS

See Session Manager Service Shell

Software Update Services (SUS)

A Microsoft server technology designed to ease the deployment of patches and updates.

SP2

Service Pack 2

Spyware

A covert application designed to track user input and actions. The makers of this kind of application hope the slip in unnoticed to observe the user quietly. The spyware developer hopes the user won't notice the intrusion and usually has something more personal than the user's buying habits in mind (see adware for comparison). For example, spyware is one technique people use to steal the user's identity. They gain information about the user as they type passwords, account numbers, and other valuable information. Spyware usually makes it quite hard for the user to remove the software and often stores multiple copies of itself on the host machine.

SQL

See Structured Query Language

SSL

See Secure Socket Layer

String

Two or more characters connected to form a word or other character-based information. Strings normally provide human-readable data, but you can find non-human readable forms. For example, even though a path and filename normally appear in a string, you have to know how to read the string to interpret it correctly.

Structured Query Language (SQL)

Most Database Management Systems (DBMSs) use this language to exchange information; many also use it as their native language. SQL provides a method for manipulating data controlled by the DBMS. It defines which table or tables to use, determines what information to get from the table, and resolves how to sort the information. A typical request will include the name of the database, table, and columns needed for display or editing purposes. SQL can filter a request and limit the number of rows using special features. Developers also use SQL to manipulate database information by adding, deleting, modifying, or searching records. IBM research center designed SQL between 1974 and 1975. Oracle introduced the first product to use SQL in 1979. SQL originally appeared on mainframe and minicomputers. Today it's a favorite language for most PC DBMS as well. There are many versions of SQL.

SUS

See Software Update Services

SysAdmin, Audit, Network, Security (SANS) Institute

An organization primarily concerned with computer security, training, certification, and research. One of the most well known outputs of this organization is the SANS Top 20 Internet Security Vulnerabilities, which is updated annually to reflect changes in the computer environment.

System Restore Point

A specialized data file used to store precise system configuration information. The system restore point is part of a Windows operating system feature that helps the system recover from catastrophic failure. Using a system restore point lets you return the system to a configuration prior to the failure. However, to use this feature successfully, Windows must work well enough to boot fully (at least in safe mode).

T

Tab Separated Value (TSV)

A type of text database file where the data fields are separated from one another using tabs. Each carriage return/line feed combination (new line) creates a new record. Many applications can retrieve TSV files and convert them to other database representations.

Tagged Image File Format (TIFF)

A bit-mapped (raster) graphics file format used on the PC and Macintosh. The TIFF file format offers a broad range of color formats including black and white, gray scale, and color. One of the advantages of using TIFF is that it provides a variety of compression methods and offers smaller storage form factor. Files on the PC often use a TIF extension.

Tape Backup

A combination of hardware and software that relies on tape as a storage media. Tape backups provide a lot of data storage in a very small space. Generally, tape systems provide very reliable backup, but you should test them regularly. Typical examples of tape drives include the Quarter Inch Cassette (QIC) and Digital Audio Tape (DAT).

TCP/IP

See Transmission Control Protocol/Internet Protocol

Thread Identifier (TID)

A numeric value associated with a thread running on a specific machine. Threads are always associated with a process; the process starts one or more threads during execution. Every process has a unique PID, making it possible to locate a specific process, even if there are multiple copies of a single application running on the machine.

TID

See Thread Identifier

TIFF

See Tagged Image File Format

Transmission Control Protocol/Internet Protocol (TCP/IP)

A standard communication line protocol (set of rules) developed by the U.S. Department of Defense. The protocol defines how two devices talk to each other. TCP defines a communication methodology where it guarantees packet delivery and also ensures the packets appear at the recipient in the same order they were sent. IP defines the packet characteristics.

Trojan Horse

An application or data file that disguises a virus, monitoring application, or other harmful content as something useful or worthwhile. As the user interacts with the useful content, the application or data file (normally using macros) installs the harmful content on the host machine. Unlike viruses, Trojan Horse applications generally remain hidden so they can perform their assigned task in the background without the user's knowledge. In addition, a Trojan Horse application generally doesn't replicate itself.

TSV

See Tab Separated Value

U

UI

See User Interface

Unicode Character

A double byte (16-bit) character used to represent more than the character set used by the English language. Unicode character sets are standardized by

international convention. Advanced operating systems normally rely on Unicode for enhanced language support and consistent data handling. This is the standard character set used by newer versions of Windows; although, all versions of Windows can still use ASCII characters when needed for compatibility purposes.

Uniform Resource Locator (URL)

A text representation of a specific location on the Internet. URLs normally include the protocol (`http://` for example), the target location (World Wide Web or `www`), the domain or server name (`mycompany`), and a domain type (`com` for commercial). It can also include a hierarchical location within that Web site. The URL usually specifies a particular file on the Web server, although there are some situations when a Web server will use a default filename. For example, asking the browser to find `http://www.mycompany.com`, would probably display the `DEFAULT.HTM` or `INDEX.HTM` file at that location. The actual default filename depends on the Web server used. In some cases, the default filename is configurable and could be any of a number of files. For example, Internet Information Server (IIS) offers this feature, so the developer can use anything from an HTM, to an ASP, to an XML file as the default.

Uninterruptible Power Source (UPS)

Usually a combination of an inverter (a DC to AC power converter) and a battery used to provide power to one or more electrical devices during a power outage. A UPS normally contains power-sensing circuitry and surge-suppression modules. Some UPSs provide standby power and a direct connection between the power source and the protected equipment. Other UPSs use the power source to charge the battery constantly. The protected equipment always derives its power from the inverter, effectively isolating the equipment from the power source.

Universal Serial Bus (USB)

A form of serial bus that allows multiple external devices to share a single port. This technique reduces the number of interrupts and port addresses required to service the needs of devices such as mice and modems. Most USB connections also provide enhanced performance and management capability over the serial and parallel port connections that they replace. The advantages are so great that many computers no longer support either serial or parallel connections.

UPS

See Uninterruptible Power Source

URL

See Uniform Resource Locator

USB

See Universal Serial Bus

User Interface (UI)

The portion of an application that contains user accessible controls and data manipulation elements. The user interface for a Windows application is commonly comprised of buttons, text boxes, static text, graphics, and other design elements.

V

VBE

See Visual Basic Editor

VBS

See Visual Basic Script

Visual Basic Editor (VBE)

A development environment normally used to create and edit Visual Basic Script (VBS) or Visual Basic for Applications (VBA) code. VBE is also the extension used for many modern script files. The VBE extension replaces the Visual Basic Script (VBS) extension used in the past.

Visual Basic Script (VBS)

A file containing a program that relies on a subset of the full Visual Basic language. Users normally rely on VBS to create small applications and macros. Visual

Basic Script or VBScript works well as a stand-alone language. Many developers also use it within Web pages and as part of Internet Information Server (IIS) Active Server Pages (ASP).

W

Windows New Technology File System (NTFS)

The method of formatting a hard disk drive used by Windows NT/2000/XP/2003. While it provides significant speed advantages over other formatting techniques, only these newer versions of the Windows operating system and applications designed to work with that operating system can access a drive formatted using this technique. Windows 2000 uses NTFS5, a version of this file system designed to provide additional features, like enhanced security. Windows XP uses a newer version of NTFS than Windows 2000 that provides other improvements such as encrypted file sharing.

Windows Script Host (WSH)

The Windows capability to write and execute scripts at the system level. This service allows the user to reduce the number of repetitive tasks required to get applications to work together. A user can use a script, for example, that scans their hard drive for errors, backs it up, then optimizes it—all without any work on the user's part except for the initial script execution. The user may have to perform additional work if the script encounters an error, but nothing more than the user would normally do. Scripts can employ one of two default languages, JavaScript or VBScript. The user can also create scripts via languages such as REXX and Perl when working with a third party add-in product.

Worm

A special kind of virus that focuses on replicating, rather than infecting a system, using a special application. In many cases, a worm increases its use of resources, such as memory or network bandwidth, until the host system crashes or experiences some other fatal result, such as the loss of data. Worms travel through files, but they don't need a specific file.

For example, some worms travel through Excel documents; it doesn't matter which Excel document. Most worms will try to infect as many files as possible, so getting rid of one damaged file isn't enough; the user must get rid of all of the worm infected files to assure a complete cleanup. In addition, worms travel between machines using any conduit available, including the Internet and Local Area Networks (LANs). Generally, worms become very visible, quite quickly, but their behavior makes cleanup especially difficult.

WSH

See Windows Script Host

X

XML

See eXtensible Markup Language

Z

Zip

A file that acts as a container for other files. The Zip normally provides some level of data compression to make the resulting package smaller than the individual files. Some operating systems such as Windows XP provide built-in support for the Zip file. However, in many cases, you need to buy or download an application that provides the Zip file functionality.

Index

Note to the Reader: Throughout this index page numbers in bold indicate primary discussions of a topic. Italicized page numbers indicate illustrations.

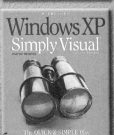

TELL US WHAT YOU THINK!

Your feedback is critical to our efforts to provide you with the best books and software on the market. Tell us what you think about the products you've purchased. It's simple:

1. Go to the Sybex website.
2. Find your book by typing the ISBN or title into the Search field.
3. Click on the book title when it appears.
4. Click **Submit a Review.**
5. Fill out the questionnaire and comments.
6. Click **Submit.**

With your feedback, we can continue to publish the highest quality computer books and software products that today's busy IT professionals deserve.

www.sybex.com

SYBEX Inc. • 1151 Marina Village Parkway, Alameda, CA 94501 • 510-523-8233